The Origin of Organized Crime in America

Routledge Advances in American History

**1. The Origin of Organized Crime
in America**
The New York City Mafia, 1891–1931
David Critchley

The Origin of Organized Crime in America

The New York City Mafia, 1891–1931

David Critchley

Routledge
Taylor & Francis Group
New York   London

First published 2009
by Routledge
270 Madison Ave, New York, NY 10016

Simultaneously published in the UK
by Routledge
2 Park Square, Milton Park, Abingdon, Oxon OX14 4RN

Routledge is an imprint of the Taylor & Francis Group, an informa business

© 2009 Taylor & Francis

Typeset in Sabon by IBT Global.

Library of Congress Cataloging in Publication Data
Critchley, David.
  The origin of organized crime in America : the New York City Mafia, 1891–1931 / by David Critchley.
    p. cm. — (Routledge advances in American history)
  Includes bibliographical references and index.
  ISBN 978-0-415-99030-1
  1. Mafia—New York (State)—New York—History. 2. Organized crime—New York (State)—New York—History. I. Title.
  HV6452.N7C75 2009
  364.1'06097471—dc22   2008017733

ISBN10: 0-415-99030-0 (hbk)
ISBN10: 0-203-88907-X (ebk)

ISBN13: 978-0-415-99030-1 (hbk)
ISBN13: 978-0-203-88907-7 (ebk)

Contents

List of Photographs   vii
List of Charts   xi
Acknowledgments   xiii

1   Introduction   1

2   Black Hand, Calabrians, and the Mafia   14

3   "First Family" of the New York Mafia   36

4   The Mafia and the Baff Murder   72

5   The Neapolitan Challenge   105

6   New York City in the 1920s   138

7   Castellammare War and "La Cosa Nostra"   165

8   Americanization and the Families   198

9   Localism, Tradition, and Innovation   234

Notes   241
Selected Bibliography   319
About the Author   323
Index   325

Photographs

CHAPTER 2

2.1. Immigrants in New York harbor. 15

2.2. Mulberry Street's "Little Italy." 16

2.3. Joseph Pinzolo, 1908. 28

2.4. Joseph Morello, 1900. 30

CHAPTER 3

3.1. Corleone. 37

3.2. Salvatore Clemente. 40

3.3. Vito Cascioferro. 41

3.4. Vito LaDuca. 44

3.5. Giovanni Zarcone. 45

3.6. Ignazio Lupo, 1910. 47

3.7. Joseph Morello, 1910. 49

3.8. Santo "Joseph" Calamia. 57

3.9. Joseph Petrosino. 65

3.10. Joseph Fontana. 67

3.11. Giovanni Pecoraro. 68

CHAPTER 4

4.1.	John Tartamella.	78
4.2.	Giuseppe Arichiello.	80
4.3.	Barnet Baff/Giuseppe Arichiello.	81
4.4.	Jack Dragna, 1915.	87
4.5.	Gagliano-Greco saloon.	88
4.6.	Sebastiano "Buster" Domingo, 1933.	98
4.7.	Fortunato Lomonte grave.	100
4.8.	*New York Herald*, February 13, 1916.	102

CHAPTER 5

5.1.	Ralph Daniello.	107
5.2.	Giosue Gallucci.	110
5.3.	Navy Street congregation.	114
5.4.	Generoso Nazzaro.	115
5.5.	Ciro Terranova.	128
5.6.	Alessandro Vollero.	129
5.7.	Stefano LaSalle.	131
5.8.	Vito Genovese naturalization record.	133

CHAPTER 6

6.1.	Maranzano Distillery, Dutchess County, 1930.	145
6.2.	Tommaso Gagliano.	149
6.3.	Participants at Cleveland assembly, December 5, 1928.	159

CHAPTER 7

7.1.   Joseph Valachi.   167

7.2.   Nicolo Gentile.   170

7.3.   Gaetano Reina family.   174

7.4.   Stefano Ferrigno and Manfredi Mineo, November 5, 1930.   183

7.5.   Gaspare Messina.   184

7.6.   Dutch Schultz.   192

7.7.   Salvatore Maranzano's body, September 10, 1931.   194

CHAPTER 8

8.1   Salvatore Lucania.   201

8.2.   Saverio Pollaccia.   212

8.3.   Nicolo Schiro.   214

8.4.   Stefano Magaddino.   217

8.5.   Pietro Magaddino grave.   218

8.6.   Vito Bonventre.   220

8.7.   "Good Killers."   221

8.8.   Giovanni Torres.   227

Charts

CHAPTER 2

2.1. Birthplaces of selected Sicilian-born American Mafiosi.   17

2.2. East 107th Street.   18

CHAPTER 3

3.1. Morello-Terranova family tree.   53

CHAPTER 4

4.1. Gagliano-Rao family tree.   90

CHAPTER 6

6.1. Gagliano related businesses.   150

CHAPTER 7

7.1. Masseria-Maranzano war and evolution of gang control, 1930 to present.   169

CHAPTER 8

8.1. Castellammaresi kinship connections.   215

Acknowledgments

For the second printing of this book, corrections and additional information has been added. Indispensable to the production of this book over the many years it took to research and to write were three individuals who in particular gave much of their time, offering a sympathetic ear, excellent advice and in some cases, finance: Steve Turner (London), Bill Feather (Wales) and Lennert van't Riet (Netherlands).

Archivists and librarians to whom this book owes a debt of gratitude are Martha Murphy, Ed Barnes, William H. Davis, David Pfeiffer, Suzanne Harris and Fred Romanski at the U.S. National Archives, Kenneth Cobb and the Staff of the New York Municipal Archives, the Old Records division at 31 Chambers Street under Joseph VanNostrand, New York Public Library's microform and genealogy departments, Elizabeth Harvey at the Brooklyn Public Library, Brooklyn Collection, the Brooklyn county clerk's office, Mark Nusenbaum (Bronx County Clerk's office), Wayne Everard (New Orleans Public Library), and Elaine Massena (Westchester County Archives).

Others who gave advice and material were author and researcher Mike Dash, Jon Black, Michael Tona, Chris Geels, Tom Hunt, Richard Warner, and Michael Ravnitzky. For their help in translating Sicilian documents, I am obliged to Alison Newman, Mariella Mangiarotti and Luisa Carella, formerly of Salford University. Help with securing photographs came from Rob Jenson, Joe McCary, and John Hyslop in the Queens Library

Several individuals gave generously of their time to search for information in New York City. This dedicated band included David Priever, Joel Singer, Diane Jacobs and Diana Stark. Other American states' libraries were covered by James Schaefer (New York State Library, Albany), Walt Fontane (St. Louis), Patricia LaCroix (New Orleans), Gail Moreau-Desharnais (Detroit), Peter McGivney (Howland Public Library, Dutchess County), Rafael Joseph and Mike Tona (Buffalo) Rosalyn Gibbs (Tampa), and Jill Rauh (Benton Harbor).

Family trees could not have been created without the help of several descendents of deceased Mafia figures, namely Enid Ruzicka, Kenneth T. Calamia, M.D., Frances E. Messina and Marina Riggio. Others chose to remain anonymous. Rosanna Rizzo of Corleone helped to compile the Morello-Terranova line.

Peter Gill and Michael Woodiwiss gave invaluable suggestions after reading an early draft of chapter one. Thanks also go to the peer reviewers. Benjamin Holtzman at Routledge showed great patience in accommodating my requests and answering questions. Scott Deitche, Frank Bojczuk, and Francis Valentino, S.J., furnished other support.

1   Introduction

This is far from the first book covering organized crime and the Italian-American Mafia[1] in New York City before the 1940s. Journalists writing long after the events depicted have had a free hand to write stories that inflate the Mafia peril. Under the headline "The Conglomerate of Crime," for example, *Time* magazine in 1969 declared, "The biggest and most important truth is that La Cosa Nostra and the many satellite elements that constitute organized crime are big and powerful enough to affect the quality of American life."[2]

Forbes alerted its readers, "Organized crime's profits—some $50 billion a year—are in a class by themselves."[3] Such sources have, in the absence of critical historical research, formed the empirical foundation of much of the current historiography.

Off-the-shelf narratives of colorful New York crime figures of the stripe of Arnold Rothstein, Frank Costello and Lucky Luciano are much the most popular form of propagation of this history. They frequently trade mass-market sales for lack of context, repetition, and a cavalier attitude towards precision and verification. But with few exceptions, social scientists and researchers have avoided the field of empirical research into American Mafia organizational structure and composition. Left unanswered are a number of important questions.

New York City's organized crime "Families" that America's governments, since the 1950s, have spent so much time and manpower fighting are the direct successors to the Mafia constructions attended to in this book. But what has been strikingly absent is a fresh look at this history, systematically marshalling the full range of resources presently available in order to interrogate benchmark accounts.

Because "real life" cases have informed the theoretical proposals and are frequently used for illustrative purposes by scholars, they are included here where appropriate. Easily overlooked, in addition, is the inescapable fact that journalists have been by far the most active in attempting to chronicle this history. Texts "of varying quality," Jacobs revealed, are "typically the only readily available account of various events and personalities."[4]

The book charts the growth of New York City Italian-American Mafias between 1891 and 1931 within the framework of a dispersed, and in large measure restrictive Italian-American criminal underworld. Reports that a far more dangerous creature emerged in 1931, La Cosa Nostra (LCN), are explored and counterposed against earlier forms of Mafia organization, principally those centered on New York City.

A misleading historiography of the formative organization of New York City Mafia crime has arguably distorted governmental priorities, diverting scarce resources to fight a largely mythical foe utilizing tools that threaten civil liberties and democratic accountability, but which have had a wide appeal in Western Europe. According to Alexander and Caiden, "Laws continue to be framed with the Mafia mystique in mind."[5] Fijnaut and Paoli among others argue that European governments have blithely accepted an alarmist history of the U.S. experience of Mafias in order to frame domestic legislation "towards the suppression of this particular type of crime."[6] Block and Chambliss referred to "the Al Capone or gangster imagery" as having "a rather perverse effect on European scholarship."[6] "This conception of organized crime," Paoli contended, "has been imported into Europe, with particular success in those countries with little or no direct experience of the mafia phenomenon."[7] The strategic danger from contemporary organized crime has also been contrasted against a history of the U.S. Mafia's evolution that embodies caricatures and exaggerations.

Material collected for this book suggests that New York City's Mafias were localized and diffuse in their procesess and structure, and that ties to other U.S. Mafia groups were loosely defined and operationally devolved. No single line of development uniting Mafia groups was discernible beyond the need at the enterprise level to respond in comparable ways to market conditions.

Nonetheless, in major East Coast cities such as Buffalo, Philadelphia, and New York City, similar organizational forms, means of adjusting disputes and admission rituals were noticeable, suggesting a common historical root in Sicily. In other U.S. locales, the "Sicilian" effect was weaker.

One type of Mafia historiography proven especially influential detects U.S. organized crime history as moving through successive evolutionary stages towards a single destination. The credibility of the approach depended on the writer in question lumping together disparate time frames, cities and organizations in order to fit a preconceived pattern at the cost of denying the reality of innumerable variations that spoiled the resulting explanatory norm.[8]

PERSPECTIVES ON MAFIA ORGANIZATIONS

Cressey's concern in 1969 was that organized criminals were "gradually but inexorably stealing our nation."[9] Underpinning his hypothesis was the supposition that American Mafias were enough alike in their goals, lines of authority and communication systems to permit a unity of purpose and action. Within this scenario, the LCN became part of a single nationwide conspiracy, a view that continues to carry considerable weight outside of academia.[10] But concrete evidence for the thesis remains elusive.

The previous view (more evident in Italy than in America) of the Mafia as a "state of mind" rather than as a structured set of organizations[11] was shattered by *pentito* Tommaso Buscetta with respect to Sicily in 1984, when he detailed a set of powerful "*Cosa Nostra*" ("Our Thing") criminal syndicates that he and others belonged to. Subsequent Sicilian cooperating witnesses[12] have confirmed Buscetta's seminal description, which matched the data released in America years earlier.

In the United States, statements casting the Mafia as a menace to national security were a recurrent theme but lacked factual support. They were nonetheless given official sanction by the Kefauver Committee in 1951 and through periodical pronouncements made by the Federal Bureau of Narcotics (FBN), which had chased Italian narcotics traffickers since the 1930s.[13]

The discovery of several dozen Italians at the Apalachin, upstate New York, estate of Joseph Barbara Sr., in November 1957, ignited a national debate. Through its post-Apalachin "strategic intelligence" gathering operations, the Federal Bureau of Investigation (FBI) uncovered the specifics of several of the larger Mafia formations, and learned of the existence of the "Commission" which is addressed in Chapter 8.[14]

During the latter part of 1962, a federal inmate convicted of heroin trafficking, Joseph Valachi, began to talk to the FBN and later to the FBI about the inner workings of the New York City Mafia as he knew it as a Genovese organized crime Family "soldier." Valachi's 1963 recollections before the Senate Permanent Subcommittee on Investigations, as they were construed, formed the empirical basis for subsequently devised models.

Valachi was judged by the Subcommittee in its 1965 report to have exposed "the reality of organized crime."[15] The "alien conspiracy" case that emerged from this interpretation reflected central assumptions made in the 1950s, tracing the evolution of American *Cosa Nostra* organizations from Mafia infested towns and villages of rural Sicily where it functioned as a "terrorist society."[16]

An unambiguous thread of understanding led from the discovery of the Apalachin meeting, to Valachi's recollections, to the passage of contentious anti-racketeering laws after 1970. A version of Valachi's testimony as specifying a centralized, rigidly hierarchical, and monolithic criminal empire run by Italians, stood as the framework used to explain the former, and gave a reason why the latter measures were justified.

But intelligence data publicly surfacing from 1969 cast doubt upon the perspective. Primarily the result of prolonged FBI surveillance work, a reasonably consistent picture emerged which was at odds with the interpretation favored in political and media circles after Valachi's testimony. The released information made no mention of a nationwide conspiracy. Instead, it indicated a fragmentation of structure with no overarching control system apparent. Businesses connected to Mafia members tended towards a modesty of scale, whether operating in the licit or illicit spheres.[17]

Notwithstanding signs of a shift in the historiography attempting to take into account the revelations, no study has yet related the discourse to the history of Mafia organization in that most influential site of activities, in the five boroughs of New York City. Perhaps because of a misguided perception of the difficulty of the task, the formative years of Mafia evolution in New York have failed to elicit sufficient attention, in spite of their importance.

TIME FRAME CHOSEN

The selection of 1931 as the end point for the volume reflected suppositions about the manner in which Mafia groups emerged into a dominating force by means of the La Cosa Nostra, instituted according to legend in 1931. Anchored to the LCN agenda was the "Americanization" proposal that referred to the same events and that remains a principal explanation of change at the leadership level. But neither the LCN approach, nor the Americanization proposal, is empirically sustainable.

Subtopics influenced by the LCN and "Americanization" hypotheses include relations between the U.S. Mafia and the Black Hand (Chapter 2), interactions with Sicilian Mafias (Chapter 3), U.S. recruitment practices (Chapter 4), and the admission of non-Sicilian Italians into the New York City Families (Chapters 5 and 8). The implications for existing theory are summarized and assessed within each chapter.

NEW YORK CITY

New York was, over the period 1890 to 1931, the biggest American city with the greatest number of Italian immigrant residents. Between 1901 and 1913, "a little less than a quarter" of Sicily's population departed for America, most living in New York for a time if not setting up permanent residence there.[18] Nelli calculated that "In the years before World War I, New York housed more Italians than Florence, Venice and Genoa combined."[19]

How the American Mafia phenomenon has been depicted is heavily attuned to the professed experience of Mafia groups in New York City. "Out of town" police witnesses before the 1963 "Valachi Hearings" for example felt a continuous need to refer to their "own" crime syndicates in ways that matched in their form New York City's Mafias as they were believed to function and to organize.[20]

The application to other cities of "titles" and of an organizational structure mainly found within the New York Mafia, together with the LCN approach—

based on a New York City Mafia history—have slanted the record. New York City has housed the largest number of American men of honor,[21] who have functioned as a reference point for lesser Mafia organizations.

A comprehensive and accurate exposition of the city's history is therefore essential if the U.S. Mafia phenomenon is to be better understood. And conclusions made about New York City's first Mafias have a wider resonance than for any other site of American Mafia operations.

DATA SOURCES

Unlike researchers in Sicily, American historians have fought shy of devoting the required time and resources to systematically exploring this topic using archival assets. According to Reuter, "It would be difficult to identify as many as half a dozen books that report major research findings, or even that many articles."[22] Potter complained, "Researchers initiating a project soon find that they are immersed in tainted data of questionable validity and almost no reliability."[23]

Margaret Beare spoke for many, when she contended, "All too much of what passes for information consists of oft-repeated anecdote combined with "moral panic" generalizations."[24] For Albini, "the literature reveals a multitude of contradictions that reduce the lay reader, as well as the researcher of organized crime, to a state of almost complete confusion." Lupsha argued the case for "data, testable conceptualization, and analytical rigor," while Albanese called for "objective and detailed information that meets a high standard of proof."[25]

"So many writers have accepted and repeated myths and distortions of fact so many times," Nelli commented, "that inaccuracies have become accepted as truths."[26] "As far as New York is concerned," according to Block, "it is dismally clear that historical studies of organized crime outside the popular genre are virtually absent and sorely needed."[27]

Due to the lack of alternatives, respondents in the sample of researchers noted by Gallagher and Cain found themselves stuck to studying familiar informational pathways.[28] The demand for more systematically accurate and precise data harnessed to the explanatory level is plain and pressing.

Firestone wrongly attributed the difficulties identified to "the lack of primary source material."[29] Three principal types of data are used in this study: newspaper articles, the statements of cooperating witnesses and informers, and other official records.

Press stories supplied indispensable information, but concentrated on the more "newsworthy" items, usually involving momentary cases of public disorder or violence. Long range historical analysis was not their forte. Their accuracy was also sometimes questionable.

Trial transcripts, police reports and evidence before government committees were only partly satisfactory for this project, since they doggedly pursued a particular reading of the materials. Sundry official documents such as naturalization papers and census returns were required for checking basic facts and for generating leads.

Allegations made by Mafiosi facing prosecution must be viewed with skepticism, since "true repentance in a man of honour is comparatively rare."[30] Many defectors "are opportunists who attempt to give the kind of information they believe their interrogators wish to hear."[31] They may also repeat gossip that made for good headlines—but not for good history.[32]

Mistaken beliefs were sometimes the result of the way in which information in the mob was passed along. The FBI was thus given information from a member source that many first-generation Mafia leaders came to America to escape "the purges directed at them" by Fascists, then in power in Sicily.[33] Yet as Chapter 8 explains, virtually none came from Sicily in the time frame.

Even the experienced Nicolo Gentile was taken in by the great Purge myth of 1931 when stating, "60 fellows destined to die. My name also appeared on this list."[34] At other times events were inflated in significance by publications to increase sales, or to support a preset thesis. Nevertheless, such sources supply essential material.

A reliance on documentary materials has limitations. We cannot question them, and they sometimes address themes of little interest. Most were created with scant regard to the requirements of historical research. Similarly to other sources, they may create errors or compound ones already made.

Information can be categorized according to the degree of corroboration attached to it. Particularly where single items are deployed, the origin and type of data is considered before an assessment is made as to its value and validity.

When material from a large variety of resources was collected and sifted, biases became transparent, to act as a means for understanding the sources of divisions and conflicts. Factual discrepancies also emerge. Through the mechanism of multiple sourcing, the problem of over dependence on solitary pieces of untested data is directly and comprehensively addressed.

PREVIOUS WRITINGS

Within the sphere of published works, few have emerged since the 1970s that cover in a substantial manner the formative years of Italian-American organized crime. With a handful of exceptions, efforts to address the early Mafia issue have been poorly formulated, sketchily drawn, and empirically weak. Conjecture has for too long replaced substantiated information.

The otherwise valuable Jacobs et al. volumes on the New York *Cosa Nostra* do not add to a debate on the early years.[35] In an otherwise important study, Block in 1980 did not attempt to connect his evidence of the 1930s to the issue of Mafia organizations, and his conclusion that "The most efficient 'organized criminals' were the most individualistic; the least committed to particular structures" was atypical within the Mafia segment of organized crime.[36]

Albini in 1971 put forward propositions about the characteristics of criminal syndicates as generic forms. But he barely mentioned New York, aside from an extended debunking of Joseph Valachi's evidence on *La Cosa Nostra*.[37]

The Iannis' fieldwork was important but, for the historian, extremely frustrating. In order to preserve the anonymity of their subjects, they used pseudonyms throughout, disallowing followup researchers from independently evaluating the usefulness or validity of their findings.[38]

Petersen's "The Mob" attempted to trace "200 years of organized crime in New York." Petersen's uncritical use of often-cited sources however gave the book a familiar feel that opened up no new possibilities.[39] Reuter's otherwise perceptive study of gambling in 1960s New York City barely touched on the Mafia issue, while Haller's contributions were limited, on the Mafia specifically, to a few pages of observations.[40]

Within the popular literary genre, "Gang Rule in New York" by Thompson and Raymond (1940), reflected the somewhat sensationalistic treatment afforded to gangsters of its era.[41] "Murder Inc." by Burton B. Turkus and Sid Feder (1952), can be read similarly.[42]

In 2004, Patrick Downey's "Gangster City" covered some of the same terrain as the present work, but with an over reliance on the agendas set by mass-market pubications. While well written, "Gangster City" suffered from a lack of originality or ambition, the general absence of information beyond accounts of violence, and a repetition of errors first made elsewhere.[43]

As Block argued, "In a subject plagued by unreliable works, based on unsubstantiated sources, one must go as often as possible to the actual record."[44] A sufficient quantity exists to make robust and defendable conclusions.

Not unexpectedly given the subject area, a number of gaps in the record were encountered. But they did not interfere with the task of assessing the current historiography on the topic, and of presenting alternatives to prevailing beliefs and frameworks.

SOCIETAL CONTEXT

A work like this, seeking to isolate the history of Mafia organizations from background factors, is by definition narrower in its focus and scope than an alternative that includes broader political, economic and social variables in the analysis. "None of these organized activities," Beare argued for the latter school, "can be understood without understanding the social, economic, and political context."[45]

Because of their preoccupation with contextual factors related to organized criminality, researchers adopting the perspective have little incentive to explore the history of a city's Mafia organization. Indeed, attempts to resurrect talk of the Mafia and nationwide conspiracies featuring Italian mobsters only serves "to confuse and distract attention away from failed policies, institutional corruption, and much systematic criminal activity that was more costly, damaging, and destructive than 'Mafia' crimes."[46] Emphasizing the Italian-Americans in organized crime diverts awareness from exploring societal causes of deviance.

The "enterprise" explanatory model, recognizing the economic activities of organized criminals as no different in principle from those in the legitimate sphere, partly shares this standpoint. Both seek to explore the wider landscape and the social construction of concepts of organized crime; but with a major drawback that the specific features of Mafias are submerged.

At its extreme, the contextual perspective may deny the very existence of the U.S. Mafia as an important form of criminal organization, despite the wealth of evidence to the contrary that has emerged from both sides of the Atlantic.[47] Such a position refers to a time before the 1970s in America (the 1980s in Sicily) when the misrepresenting of basic facts by writers was commonplace, caused by the lack of high-grade source information.[48]

After stating that, for example, "the nature of organized crime in North America has been based largely on unprovable assertions," Jay Albanese asks why *La Cosa Nostra* was not heard of before Valachi's appearance before the American public. In fact, FBI surveillance picked up the term from at least 1961.

Albanese also questions why "historical inquiries (have) been unable to corroborate Valachi's account of a national 'Castellammare War'."[49] But Valachi was not the only witness to the War, and the expositions of two other participants do not significantly conflict with Valachi's.

Within this setting, Potter and Jenkins' book *The City and the Syndicate* (Lexington, Mass.: Ginn Press, 1985), is notable for missing the large quantity of records later unearthed by Celeste A. Morello in three books on the Philadelphia Mafia.[50] Such skeptics, while making excellent points on other aspects of organized crime, have apparently not delved beyond predominantly English-language and published items. Although one can argue about the place of the Mafia in organized crime, neither its existence, nor its presence in America since the late 19th century, is any longer in doubt.

The agenda ignored or debased the special strengths of Mafias. Many recommend decriminalization and regulation of "victimless crimes" as a solution to removing gangster types from whole sectors of the economy.[51] However, the decriminalization case assumes a high degree of Mafia involvement in the activity in question to be effective.

This belief may be only partly true, an argument pursued in Chapter 9.[52] Decriminalization in New York and adjoining states of forms of gambling previously prohibited had, for instance, a modest impact at most on Mafia influence in the aggregate.[53]

Furthermore, Mafia members have exploited opportunities to make money within licitly regulated industries. The New York City's Mafia's increasingly powerful "predatory" (non-market driven) enterprises have no relevance to the decriminalization discourse and legalization campaigns.[54] Once present, Mafia power in segments of the licit economy is highly resistant to removal.[55]

"The Mafia provides," Reuter stressed, "the most enduring and significant form of organized crime."[56] Kelly indeed found that there would still be a "racketeering" problem without the Mafia.[57] But Italian-Americans in organized crime maximized the openings created by faultily designed regulatory regimes, frequently deploying the economic leverage their control over corrupt labor unions permitted.

The approach this book adopts understands the exceptionality of Mafia organizations and their resilience in the face of changing marketplace and state conditions. The limiting of political, economic and social variables from the analysis also permits a clearer comparison to be made against other writings on the topic. It, lastly, acknowledges that this history is where the most empirical research needs to be conducted.

HISTORICAL DEVELOPMENT

For New York City, two long-range historical trends were identified. The ability of Mafia syndicates to create and to defend a territorial domain indicated the limits of Mafia political and economic influence at any juncture. "Cosa Nostra is like a state," Dickie maintained, "because it aims to control territory."[58] "Any cosca," Paoli wrote of Calabria and Sicily, "associated with either Cosa Nostra or the 'Ndragheta claims sovereignty over a well-defined territory, usually corresponding to a town or a village."[59]

Each ethnic group involved in organized crime in New York City had its own distinctive territorial boundaries.[60] Territorial control had an economic component as the best means to exercise a high level of control over the types of crimes that Mafia Family members operated. Bonanno, the former head of one, stated, "in the economic sphere one of the objectives of a Family was to set up monopolies as far as it was possible."[61] Politically, power over a large territory was a road to heightened status in the Mafia fraternity.

Contrary to the Sicilian experience, where labor unions proved unable to embed themselves into the economic fabric,[62] they were powerful in New York City. A second dimension to territoriality therefore emerged in New York, in which Mafiosi attached themselves to union locals chiefly representing Italian-American workers in blue-collar occupations. *Cosa Nostra* bosses regarded such locals as "property" to be utilized and defended as a base by Family members, alike to geographical hegemony. Following the movement of their *paesani* into organized labor was the major method, outside of the trade in narcotics, by which men of honor broadened their influence across the city.

Compared to their Sicilian counterparts, New York Family members could move across geographical divisions with ease in pursuit of opportunities. In other contexts, territorial boundaries could be a bone of contention. However, a mechanism for resolving inter-Family problems ensured that the Mafia element of the New York underworld did not suffer warfare over disputed terrain. Family members were instructed to "clear" their illicit activities with superiors in the organization, for instance, and the information was passed to other Families affected.[63]

Equally important was residential movement. Upcoming Mafia leaders such as Salvatore D'Aquila, for example, lived for years in East Harlem before moving elsewhere in the city to form their own Mafia organizations. But they retained fraternal connections to Harlem men of honor that could smooth over difficulties as required.

U.S. Mafias were mostly found where a substantial and densely populated southern Italian immigrant community existed. When Mafia men ventured far from familiar streets, they were usually less sure-footed. "Once they move abroad," Behan observed, "major criminals do not wield the same influence they previously did at home."[64]

A further feature was that of a steadily rising complexity of Mafia organization. The earliest known New York City Mafia formation (dealt with in this book) had few "ranks," with direct communication between leaders and followers the norm. Few barriers existed between the bosses and underlings. An influx of new members after the 1940s apparently altered this relationship, making face-to-face contact less feasible.[65]

By the 1960s, a several-layered organizational structure had solidified. Through the means of passing down instructions via a few trusted confidants, "top-ranking members" avoided "all obvious links to criminal operations."[66] The "insulating" mechanism that developed made prosecution of Mafia's bosses "usually extremely difficult and sometimes impossible." Its significance was underscored by the Senate for helping to preserve "30 years of silence, broken publicly only by Joseph Valachi."[67]

Typical positions in a 1960s New York City Family ranged from the "boss," (*capo, representando officiale* or simply "Father") through to "underboss" (*sottocapo*), *consiglieri* (advisor) and "acting boss." Beneath were "crews" or "*regimes*" led by group leaders or "*caporegimes*"(Americanized as "captains," "skippers" or "lieutenants").

The lowest level in the typical Mafia hierarchy, and by far the most numerous, was rank and file members. They were colloquially known as "button men," "good fellows," or "soldiers" (*soldato*).[68]

The noun "Family"[69] (*Famiglia*) is here deployed to indicate individual groups or units in the Mafia (*Cosa Nostra,* honored society or *Onorata Societa*) community. Less employed terms to designate an Mafia organization included "*borgata,*" "*brugad,*" and "administration." In western Sicily, individual Mafia groups were also known as *cosca,* in the plural as *cosche.*

American Mafiosi were, of any status, referred to as *"amici nostri"* ("friends of ours"), "men of respect," "wiseguys," "button men," or "men of honour." Initiated members were said to be "made" or "straightened out."

A degree of variation given to the "name" of exclusively Italian American criminal organizations by their own members existed. According to an informer, for instance, the Milwaukee "outfit" met in August 1963 to discuss reports on Joseph Valachi's information. Of the approximately 15 people there, only 2 had heard the name *"Cosa Nostra."* "The consensus of opinion of those present was that *Cosa Nostra* was just another name for the Mafia."[70]

Albini emphasized the point that such "positions" are better understood as denoting differences of power, as opposed to being analogous to the "fixed" patterns characterizing a bureaucratic structure of authority.[71] Consequently, "In an enterprise where nothing was ever written down, lines of authority might cross, be cut, or become entangled."[72]

The Pittsburgh *capo,* for example, "had the office," but the lowly member Nicolo Gentile "had the power."[73] It followed that "not all members of the same ranks are necessarily equal."[74]

CHAPTERS

To avoid drowning the analyses in a mountain of specifics, a decision was taken to insert the secondary material with the endnotes, where it can be consulted alongside the sources. Factual mistakes made in other works are by and large also noted in the endnotes.

Within each chronologically ordered chapter is an examination of the key issues thrown up by the information presented. In keeping with the objective of deploying fresh materials wherever possible, original records are stressed in the main text.

Chapter 2 outlines the immigration backdrop and the first sizeable Italian toeholds in New York City's organized crime. Prior to the mass arrival of Sicilians to New York, a thriving "Italian" underworld existed. The chapter progresses to the infamous "Black Hand," that criminal phenomenon that had a distant relationship to the American Mafia. Data is presented suggesting that Mafia organizations rarely became involved in this form of extortion. Long neglected, the Calabrians were an important Black Hand element.

Questions are asked in Chapter 3 as to whether New York Mafias were exact replicas of organizations in Sicily. One influential paradigm for instance posited that the American Mafia phenomenon was wholly the outcome of American conditions. Excellently situated to examine the matter was the counterfeiting combine led by Giuseppe Morello, head of the first of New York's five Families. Empirical findings identify striking similarities with Sicilian practices, and routinized links are revealed between America and Sicily.

The Morellos' staple illicit enterprise required, though, a readiness to adapt to local circumstances. Connections to other American cities are noted, but they do not suggest the existence of a vast criminal network with Morello at its core. Nor did the Morello hierarchy resemble that described in the 1960s.

The Morellos were but one of two factions emerging from the Sicilian Mafia base of Corleone. Exhaustively covered in Chapter 4, the Barnet Baff murder investigation exposed a cadre of Corleonesi with links to both Sicilian and American men of respect, yet acting in an industry where Jewish organized crime was of primary importance.

Three issues unfolding from the Baff case are pursued. First is the influence of locality and kinship in structuring Mafia relationships. Second, the opportunity is afforded to revise theory on recruitment routes into Mafia organized crime. Third, the effect of ethnicity in the context of industrial racketeering comes under scrutiny.

Sicilians were not alone in Italian-American crime. From their headquarters in Brooklyn, Chapter 5 portrays how a formidable Neapolitan crime organization with substantial resources, connections in the municipal government, and a fearsome fighting ability mounted a temporarily effective assault on the Morellos' Manhattan strongholds. Organizational differences with the Morellos are explained, as is the role of the wider Mafia constellation in the conflict.

Selectively admitting mainland Italians into the American honored society, to the chagrin of traditionalists, averted another interracial conflict. Non-Sicilians formed the nucleus of the "Americanized" leadership cadre that came to dominate popular depictions of the "Mafia" faction of U.S. organized crime.

The 18th Amendment to the Constitution embargo over the domestic manufacture and sale of alcoholic beverages, in January 1920, was a gift not only to upcoming crime figures but also to established *amici nostri*, who easily realized the potential for profit. Yet bootlegging encompassed a vast array of interests and ethnicities, in which the Italians were but a minority. Licit enterprises like those analyzed in Chapter 6 are frequently overlooked. The racketeering issue is reintroduced. Furthermore, while Chicago's experience over the course of National Prohibition was "the one that everyone associates with the regime of the gangsters,"[75] it failed to capture the variations and fissures in New York City.

By the end of the 1920s, the Mafia structure in New York City was stronger than before. New Families were formed, triggering tensions that formed a backcloth to the celebrated "Castellammare War." Because of its role in creating a series of powerful myths about the course of historical development in the American Mafia, issues surrounding the War occupy the whole of Chapters 7 and 8.[76]

Among others, Lupsha identified the Castellammare War as indicating "a turning point in Italian-American groups and in the further Americanization of organized crime in the United States."[77] But the War's actual impact was limited even within New York City, where a traditionalistic power structure remained.

The evidence presented is summarized and extended in Chapter 9. Questions are asked as to the American Mafia's control over gambling, where Mafia power was assumed to be at its most potent. Allegations made of the profitability of Mafia run organized crime are also queried. Ethnic factors have limited Mafia influence. Given the rewards to be gained by Mafia membership or affiliation as denoted by Haller and others,[78] Mafiosi have tended to shun extensively working with non-Italian operators, limiting their overall influence in organized crime.

2 Black Hand, Calabrians, and the Mafia

INTRODUCTION

As economic and political conditions worsened or refused to improve, emigration from Italy to the new world rose. Immigration to New York from Italy jumped from 74,687 in 1890, to 145,429 by 1900.[1] Between 1900 and 1910, 2.1 million Italians came to the United States, over 80 percent from the south where secret criminal societies were active.[2] Newly accommodated Italian immigrants tended to huddle into subgroups. "A spirit of regionalism, or *campanilismo*, prevailed," that could erupt into hostilities with outsiders but which could also lead to cooperation.[3]

Selvaggi noted, "Once settled in their new homeland, the Italian immigrants faced a grim reality: crowded, noisy, filthy slums, endemic unemployment and ugly prejudice."[4] Problems facing the southern Italian and Sicilian masses after their arrival in the Promised Land promoted the re-emergence of ethnically based organized crime.

Joseph "Joe Cago" Valachi, born to immigrant Neapolitan parents in East Harlem, explained, "I came from the poorest family on earth—at least that was the way I felt when I was a little boy."[5] Valachi used to bring home wood from work and coal from dumps to keep warm; his mother made bedroom sheets from old cement bags sewn together.[6] Stealing to help pay the rent, Valachi walked with bandages around his feet for shoes.[7]

Although a large concentration of Italian immigrants was a precondition for the emergent of a Family in America, many came from the centre and north of Italy, where Mafia-type societies were absent. As a result, U.S. Mafia penetration, even in Italian communities, was uneven. Networks of immigrants from particular localities in Sicily would commonly reside in the same American area or town, following work opportunities and the availability of support services. Chart 2.1 indicates a selection of localities in Sicily from which American *Mafiosi* traveled.

Some returned to Italy, a feature that encouraged the movement of Mafiosi between American and Sicily.[8] The shape and composition of Italian immigration also supplied the territorial outlines that Mafia groups would eventually inhabit. Sections of Manhattan, Brooklyn and the Bronx became notorious for harboring Mafia elements. "Such neighborhoods," remarked

Figure 2.1 Immigrants in New York harbor. (Courtesy of the Library of Congress)

Abadinsky, "have traditionally provided the recruiting grounds that ensure the continuity of traditional organized crime."[9]

Oldest of the New York City "Little Italies" was that which centered around Mulberry Street in lower Manhattan, where "green" immigrants got their first taste of the downside of living in America. "Mulberry Bend," including Mulberry, Mott, Hester, Prince and Elizabeth Streets, was notorious for an unsavory, decrepit appearance.[10] In "The Bend," individuals and families "lived in damp basements, leaky garrets, clammy cellars and outhouses and stables converted into dwellings."[11]

Overcrowding, the search for work, and congestion led to the development of Manhattan's second Italian settlement based around East 108th Street, and was made up predominantly of southern Italians. "At its peak, Italian

Figure 2.2   Mulberry Street's "Little Italy." (Courtesy of the Library of Congress)

Harlem extended to about 104th Street on the south, Third Avenue on the west, north to about 120th Street, and east to the river," Orsi remarked.[12]

Chart 2.2 indicates the degree of Sicilian and Neapolitan criminal involvement on East 107th Street. The chart also denotes businesses mentioned in Chapter 4.

Several of the conspirators in the Baff murder of 1914 had addresses in close proximity to each other in East Harlem. Antonio Ferrara was born on East 108th Street and lived on 107th St. for some 20 years, where the Zaffaranos (Antonio and Joseph), had a feed or feather store. Giuseppe Arichiello resided on 107th Street across the way from Tony Ferrara. Tony Cardinale had a chicken market on 108th Street, near First Avenue. At the time of his death, furthermore, Ippolito Greco was accommodated at 230 East 107th Street.

Partly in reaction to the underdeveloped welfare infrastructure, but also to preserve cherished cultural values and institutions, Italians in New York City "lived together as far as possible, intermarrying and celebrating the traditional fests."[13] "Among ourselves," observed Joseph Bonanno, "we spoke Sicilian. English was hardly necessary to our lives."[14]

Wherever Italians settled in larger numbers, they gained a reputation for "banditry and general turbulence."[15] Sporadic outbursts of bloodletting appeared to vindicate the stereotype. In 1922, for example, Giovanni Magliocco was arrested for the shooting of Frank D'Agati. Evidence

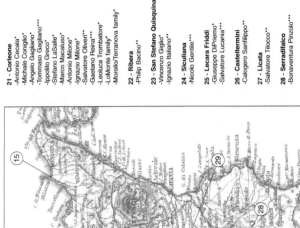

20 - Sambuca
-Calogero Gulotta*

21 - Corleone
-Antonio Cecala*
-Michele Coniglio*
-Angelo Gagliano**
-Tommaso Gagliano***
-Ippolito Greco*
-Stefano LaSalle*
-Marco Macaluso*
-Antonio Milone*
-Ignazio Milone*
-Salvatore Oliveri**
-Gaetano Reina*
-Leoluca Trombatore*
-LoMonte family*
-Morello/Terranova family*

22 - Ribera
-Philip Bacino**

23 - San Stefano Quisquina
-Vincenzo Giglio*
-Ignazio Italiano**

24 - Siculiana
-Nicolo Gentile***

25 - Lecara Friddi
-Giuseppe DiPriemo*
-Salvatore Lucania***

26 - Casteltermini
-Calogero Sanfilippo**

27 - Licata
-Salvatore Tilocco**

28 - Serradifalco
-Bonaventura Pinzolo***

29 - Vallelunga
-Cassandro Bonasera
-Samuel* and Joseph DiCarlo†

**1900s Morello member or associate.
**Attendee at 1928 Cleveland meeting.
***1930/1931 Castellammarese War figure.
†Other prominent Mafia figure

13 - Termini Imerese
Vincenzo Moreci*

14 - Cerda
-Michael Russo**

15 - Barcellona
-Joseph Biondo***
-Umberto Valenti†

16 - Salemi
-Frank Cucchiara†
-Gaspare Messina***
-Joseph Lombardo†

17 - Partanna
-Giuseppe Palermo*

18 - Gibellina
-Salvatore Lombardino**
-Santo Calarnia*

19 - San Giuseppe Iato
-Vincenzo Troia***
-Francesco Longo†
-Zito family

1 - Marsala
Giuseppe Masseria***

2 - Castellammare del Golfo
-Salvatore Maranzano***
-Gaspare Milazzo***
-Bonanno family**
-Bonventre family***
-Buccellato family
-DiGregorio family***
-Magaddino family***
-Sabella family***

3 - Camporeale
-Joseph Scaccio**

4 - Partinico
-Carlo Costantino*
-Antonio Passanante*

5 - Cinisi
-Paolo Palazzolo*

6 - Carini
-Giuseppe Fanaro*
-Vito LaDuca*
-Tomasso Petto*

7 - Belmonte Mazzango
-Giuseppe Traina**/***

8 - Monreale
-Joseph Vaglica**

9 - Palermo
-Vito Cascioferro*
-Salvatore Cina*
-Salvatore D'Aquila†
-Pasquale Enea*
-Salvatore LoVerde***
-Gaetano Lucchese***
-Ignazio Lupo*
-Vincenzo**/*** and Filippo Mangano
-Stefano Rannelli***
-Gambino family***

10 - Piana Dei Greci
-Giovanni Pecoraro*

11 - Villabate
-Emanuel Cammarata**
-Giuseppe Fontana*
-Giuseppe Magliocco**
-Joseph Profaci**

12 - Bagheria
-Giuseppe Aiello***
-Giovanni Zarcone*

Chart 2.1 Birthplaces of selected Sicilian-born American Mafiosi.

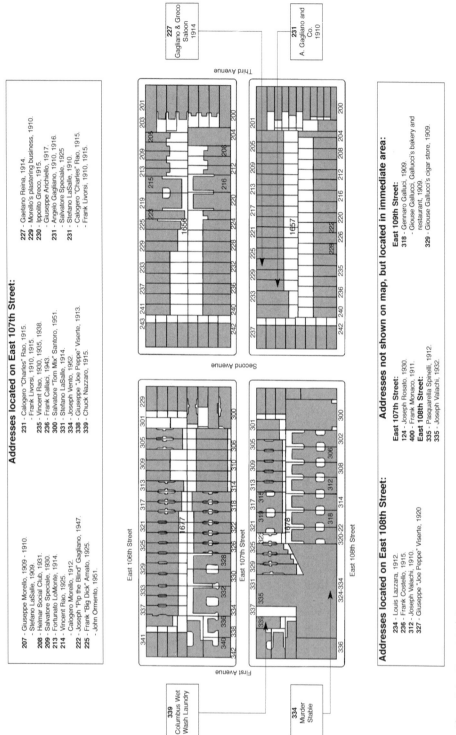

Addresses located on East 107th Street:

207 - Giuseppe Morello, 1909 - 1910.
    - Stefano LaSalle, 1909.
208 - Helmar Social Club, 1931.
209 - Salvatore Speciale, 1930.
213 - Fortunato LoMonte, 1914.
214 - Vincent Rao, 1925.
    - Calogero Morello, 1912.
222 - Joseph "Pip the Blind" Gagliano, 1947.
225 - Frank "Big Dick" Amato, 1925.
    - John Ormento, 1951.

231 - Calogero "Charles" Rao, 1915.
    - Frank Livorsi, 1910, 1915.
235 - Vincent Rao, 1930, 1935, 1938.
236 - Frank Callaci, 1943.
300 - Salvatore "Tom Mix" Santoro, 1951.
331 - Stefano LaSalle, 1914.
334 - Joseph Vento, 1952.
338 - Giuseppe "Joe Peppe" Viserte, 1913.
339 - Chuck Nazzaro, 1915.

227 - Gaetano Reina, 1914.
229 - Morello's plastering business, 1910.
230 - Ippolito Greco, 1915.
    - Giuseppe Archiello, 1917.
231 - Angelo Gagliano, 1910, 1916.
    - Salvatore Speciale, 1925
231 - Stefano LaSalle, 1910.
    - Calogero "Charles" Rao, 1915.
    - Frank Livorsi, 1910, 1915.

227 Gagliano & Greco Saloon 1914

231 A. Gagliano and Co. 1910

339 Columbus Wet Wash Laundry

334 Murder Stable

Addresses located on East 108th Street:

234 - Louis Lazzara, 1912.
236 - Frank Costello, 1915.
312 - Joseph Valachi, 1910.
327 - Giuseppe "Joe Peppe" Viserte, 1920

Addresses not shown on map, but located in immediate area:

East 107th Street:
124 - Joseph Rosato, 1930.
400 - Frank Monaco, 1911.

East 108th Street:
335 - Pasquarella Spinelli, 1912.
335 - Joseph Valachi, 1932.

East 109th Street:
318 - Gennaro Gallucci, 1909.
    - Giouse Gallucci, Gallucci's bakery and restaurant, 1909.
329 - Giouse Gallucci's cigar store, 1909.

Chart 2.2 East 107th Street.

adduced that D'Agati in a drunken stupor had shot and killed his wife Antonia Magliocco.

Her father Giovanni Magliocco, who lived in the same building on Union Street, turned a revolver on D'Agati. His plea of self-defense was accepted and Giovanni Magliocco was freed.[16] Magliocco was the father of three brothers who went on the either run or to participate in the Profaci organized crime Family in Brooklyn (Chapter 6).

A few Sicilians chose to pursue a double life, on the one hand engaged in organized crime, on the other achieving acceptance as generous benefactors. The descendant of one, Gaetano "Tommy" Reina, remembered him best as a "hard working immigrant that made a life for his family with a legitimate business venture . . . at a time when many families could not feed themselves." Reina should "be remembered as an American success story."[17] The offspring of another, Vincent Mangano, explained, "Joining a 'family' comprised of their fellow countrymen gave the Italians a certain power over their own survival and a fighting chance in the 'food chain.'"[18]

PAOLO ANTONIO "PAUL KELLY" VACCARELLI

Even before Sicilians made a mark, Italians were powerful in New York City. In this era, former professional flyweight boxer Paolo "Paul Kelly" Vaccarelli was "perhaps the most successful and the most influential gangster in New York history,"[19] as the leader of the Five Points gang, active in the area between Broadway and the Bowery, 14th Street and City Hall Park. Kelly's gang was predominantly Italian, while his chief rival, Monk Eastman, (real name Edward Osterman), was Jewish.[20]

Both Eastman and Kelly had connections to the New York County Democratic political organization, colloquially known as "Tammany Hall."[21] "There was always some unseen but powerful influence," said the *New York Times,* "that reached out and saved Kelly from more serious charges."[22] The two gangs furnished "repeat" voters to favored district politicians, in exchange for virtual immunity from arrest or prosecution. Always a worry for their political patrons though were cases where gunfights forced them to intercede, and the police to launch "crackdowns."

Kelly, born in 1876 in New York City to parents from Potenza, Italy,[23] was later depicted as "a perfect example" of the "dapper, soft-spoken chap who seldom engaged in rough-and-tumble fighting . . ."[24] Kelly's commercial interests included the New Brighton Dance Hall on Great Jones Street (his headquarters), the Noonday Social Club, a "disorderly house," the Stag Auto Garage, and the Independent Inglander Dramatic and Pleasure Club, a "high class gambling joint."[25]

In the wake of Monk Eastman's jailing for ten years in April 1904,[26] Vaccarelli's stock briefly rose. But action against his saloon and the Paul Kelly Association in 1905 soured the triumph, as did reform group campaigning;[27] he moved uptown for good.[28] Kelly went on to pursue a successful career in organized labor, and was among the first of the Brooklyn "waterfront czars."

Intimations emerged of Vaccarelli's ties to the rising New York Mafia. He lived for a time on East 116th Street with the Terranovas, according to Thompson and Raymond.[29] Valachi also mentioned "Paul Vaccarelli" as having a partnership in a Bronx numbers bank in the early 1930s with Valachi's chum Girolamo "Bobby Doyle" Santuccio, and other upcoming Family members.[30]

THE "BLACK HAND"

Black Hand crimes defined the southern Italian immigrant experience so far as the public was concerned.[31] The stigma of the Black Hand was applied "to the Italian community's criminal problem and sometimes to Italians in general."[32]

Such was the political impact of the Black Hand issue that it influenced the debate on immigration, with a rise in Black Hand atrocities correlating to the laxity of controls at ports that permitted criminals from Italy to enter apparently unhindered.[33] Presuming that the problem lay in the Italian badlands from whence the perpetrators came, it was argued that the Black Hand would also be eradicated by the better use of police resources, and through better intelligence given to the police by the Italian-American community.[34]

It was pointed out that the overwhelming number of victims of the Black Hand was also from Italian stock. Nelli's research indicated, moreover, that Black Hand activity was exclusive to those districts where "compliant, hard-working" victims were concentrated.[35] While there were non-Italians who indulged in blackmailing, their use of the technique was far less systematic.[36]

HISTORIOGRAPHY AND DEFINITION

Because it was content to replicate the contents of articles on the Black Hand's rise and decline, Pitkin's book, the sole one devoted to this phenomenon, was of limited value. The key question of whether or how the Black Hand related to the Mafia was sidelined, and arising theoretical issues were left in abeyance. Like the Fried,[37] Rockaway[38] and Joselit works,[39] Pitkin dealt with published reactions to minority claims from within the agenda of crime scares.

Confusion surrounds the correct categorization, and the parameters, of the "Black Hand." Downey and Messick believed that Mafia families were once called Black Hand gangs.[40] Flynn called the early Mafia "the Black-Hand Society,"[41] whereas Joseph Petrosino, the great New York

City detective, thought the Black Hand was "practically identical" to the Camorra, a criminal society active in Naples and surrounding provinces.[42]

The Black Hand label was applied to most unsolved "Italian-on-Italian" crimes. As Lombardo argued, "Because of newspaper publicity, vendetta killings and almost every other crime in the Italian community was soon attributed to the Black Hand."[43] It echoed Landesco's comment; "The police call every mystery murder in the Italian community (murders in which no information is forthcoming) a 'black hand' murder."[44]

Assuming that unsolved homicides involving Italians were automatically the work of the Black Hand could obscure the real reasons for fatalities. Pellegrino Scaglia (alias Antonio Viola) was arrested in St. Louis in August 1911 for the slaying of Bartholdi Cardinali, assassinated as he sat at the window of his 21st Street home.[45] Scaglia had previously been seriously wounded in a "stiletto" attack; raising the spectre of a feud slaying or of the dreaded Black Hand.[46]

One of Batholdi's brothers, Giuseppe, had been assassinated in 1908, his body found in Coffey Park, Brooklyn. A friend had gone to Giuseppe for help once he received a Black Hand letter. Giuseppe also received a death threat, and Scaglia was the last person known to have seen him alive. Scaglia disappeared until he was reported as residing in St. Louis.[47]

An investigation revealed that the Scaglia and Cardinali families had been warring in their native town of Burgio, Sicily, and that the American deaths were probably tied to that cause, accounting for another Cardinali murder in New York.[48] Bartholdi's uncle perished in the conflict, and a sniper resembling Scaglia mortally wounded Bartholdi in 1911. Scaglia became affiliated with the Pueblo *Famiglia* and was mowed down in Pueblo, Colorado, in May 1922.[49]

In December 1910, fruit dealer Damien Capuano was killed in "Dago Hill," St. Louis. Joe and Tommaso Viviano, brothers or cousins, were held for the crime. Capuano was a friend of Tommaso's, who was arrested nearby the Capuano body with a discharged pistol in his hand, which Tommaso said was only used to attract the police to the crime scene.

It was reported as another "Black Hand" case. But there was no attempt at robbery; it was an act of revenge.[50] Capuano's daughter later married Pasquale Santino, a high-ranking St. Louis organized crime figure assassinated in 1927.

The Black Hand, in its letter writing form, was simply one method of parting a susceptible Italian immigrant from his money. Yet though usually defined by the sending of correspondence signed with the "Black Hand" or "*La Mano Nera*" emblem utilized to frighten victims,[51] many of the larger "Black Hand societies" employed neither letters, nor the Black Hand logo.

Pennsylvania "Black Hand" societies for example, were equally in the blackmail game, but did so by pressuring victims into paying a "membership fee," the chief source of their income, for which little was received in return.[52]

NEW YORK CITY BLACK HAND

The constant factor throughout was the extortion of the Italian-born via threats of harm to persons and/or property if their demands were unmet. Within the letter-writing wing, a Black Hand episode began with the sending of several letters. If these failed to have the desired effect, a "friend" of the victim may have conveniently appeared on the scene, in the role of a conciliator anxious to settle the matter to the satisfaction of everyone by arriving at a compromise figure. Once it was paid, however, the extortionists might return for more. Bomb attacks were a trademark of the letter sending variant of the Black Hand (guns and knives were rarely used).

The Cappiello case of September 1903 was the first reported use of the term "Black Hand."[53] Nicolo Cappiello, a wealthy contractor of 2nd Place, Brooklyn, received a letter signed by the "Mano Nera," demanding $1,000 with the warning that his house would be otherwise dynamited. When the money was duly supplied, another $3,000 was asked for. At this point, Cappiello went to the police and Biaggio Giordano of Sackett Street was arrested.[54]

The Black Hand was prevalent in every American city with a sizeable Italian community, with New York City being the largest single site of activity. Recorded bombings rose there from 44 in 1908, to 70 in 1911. One estimate claimed that for every incidence of blackmail reported, 250 went unrecorded.

In response to the upsurge of Italian crime, Police Commissioner William McAdoo in September 1904 announced the creation of an "Italian Squad"[55] under Detective Sergeant Joseph Petrosino, which soon increased in size to 30 men with a branch in Brooklyn under Lt. Antonio Vachris. But convictions remained rare. (In 1908, for instance, only 36 were noted in "Black Hand cases."[56])

MOTIVES

In opposition to the popular perception of the Black Hand victim and his tormentor invariably being strangers,[57] Petrosino suggested that Black Hand criminals often had a prior relationship with their targets.[58] Cases were by no means unknown of less prosperous Italians helping Black Handers to select their more successful victims.[59] Failing merchants, in addition, might work hand in glove with arsonists assuming the guise of the Black Hand to burn down their premises for insurance money.[60]

Business rivalry furnished another rationale for a Black Hand scare. A case in point was the bombing in 1908 of the home of Joseph DiGiorgio, a fruit importer of Baltimore, who received intimidating letters from his chief commercial rival Antonio Lanasa. "The obvious objective of the operation," Nelli observed, "was to eliminate Lanasa's rival, using the Black Hand as cover."[61]

Another instance concerned a dispute between two saloonkeepers on East 151st Street. After the rent was raised, causing his competitor to promptly take over his business, the ousted businessman ended up throwing a bomb into a crowd. A suspect was arrested.[62] A defector from a "Black Hand" gang similarly explained how jealousy between grocers on East 108th Street was the cause of a bombing being contracted.[63]

Black Hand practices could be founded on feelings of injustice. Antonio Fazia was arraigned in September 1905 for threatening his former employer, Serrino Nizzarri, and demanding $300. Nizzarri, a "prosperous Italian baker," had sacked Fazia while owing him money. Fazia made up the story that he was a member of a secret society in order to frighten Nizzarri.[64]

BLACK HAND ORGANIZATION

In the letter-writing branch of the Black Hand, there was no "regular organization, outside the columns of the yellow press."[65] Whether in Italy or the United States, no Black Hand Society coordinated and centralized the acts of extortion; Black Handers were either individuals working alone, or in small-scale partnerships and with, at most, the loosest of links to similar groups.

Woods contended, "Given a number of Italians with money, and two or three ex-convicts, you have all the elements necessary for a first-rate Black Hand campaign."[66] The views of Petrosino on the Black Hand were equally emphatic, "there is no big central organization of criminals called the 'Black Hand'."[67] According to *Cosmopolitan*, "A sheet of paper, pen and ink, and enough knowledge of Italian to scrawl a few lines of demand and the accompanying threat are all that is necessary."[68] The Assistant District Attorney and William J. Flynn of the New York Secret Service agreed, though conceding that gangs worked together "now and then."[69]

LARGER ENTERPRISES

Isolated extortionists had a strong incentive in portraying themselves as part of a wider ring. However, a few operations were indeed larger than the norm. In 1913, the New York police dismantled a gang that not only wrote letters and planted bombs, but also engaged in a panoply of other crimes, ranging from horse-theft, robbery and burglary, and becoming involved in labour strikes, where they were hired by strike organizers in the garment industry. "As high as $300 was paid by the strikers for one of the explosions," taking place in the factories of recalcitrant employers.

A rudimentary division of labor developed, in which one crew in the gang was tasked with finding explosives, another with letter-writing while a third selected victims to send the correspondence to. According to the *New York Times*, "They found the work fairly safe, and were seldom in any danger of arrest."[70] The organization was held responsible for an estimated 30 burglaries, 40 bombings and 30 horse and wagon thefts.[71]

Black Hand organizations of the admission fee-paying variety operated on a bigger scale. A relatively structured Black Hand outfit was bared in White Plains, New York. Its members named it *"Societa Camorra de Lucre."*

One witness to the group, Salvatore Mara, whose son and nephew were killed by the society, related how he was forced to join in 1909, paying $50 when the gang "placed a revolver at my ear." According to a statement he made in 1913, the big men were Edwardo Bueta and Rafael Bova. Ciccio Filastro in New York was their patron.

An initiation ceremony was observed, in which "They prick themselves on the wrist and suck their blood and swear on that blood." Bizarre sounding phrases were used as passwords to identify other members.

A connection was noted with the infamous Calabrian bandit Giuseppe Musolino, the two brothers Filastro being his reputed cousins.[72] Musolino, the "Calabrian brigand," was imprisoned for 20 years on disputed evidence in 1897 but broke out of jail, whereupon he "began a vendetta that would become a centerpiece of Calabrian criminal mythology."[73] Musolino evaded capture until 1901, when he tried to make his way northwards.[74]

In White Plains, younger recruits (*Desgaros*) did the dirty work and had their own section. Older members, "*Camorrista*," held regular and structured meetings, attended by those holding positions such as those of Master (Bueta), Secretary (Bova)[75] and Assistant (Rocco Pellegrino).

In October 1913, Bova was jailed for 20 years to life for shooting Filipo Carido to death.[76] But the group lived on in attenuated form through "The Old Man" Pellegrino, a future *caporegime* in the Genovese Family and "Head of underworld in Westchester County."[77]

Another cousin of Musolino was reported as active in Toronto, Canada. Giuseppe Musolino "held court" in a restaurant boarding house, and led a gang coercing similar "initiation fees" from Calabrian newcomers. This Musolino, according to Edwards and Nicaso, was initiated into the *Picciotteria* (Camorra) in 1896, but had fled Italy when a warrant was issued for him along with ones for other Musolino members.[78]

A third alleged Musolino connection was discovered in Mahoning Valley, straddling Ohio and Pennsylvania, in 1907–8.[79] Similarly to the White Plains organization, the New Castle, Ohio, Calabrian group was composed of "ranks" from *capo* to ordinary members.[80] In Hillsville, Joe Bagnano was the headman, succeeding Rocco Racco and Ferdinando Surace. It was called "the family," but there was no formal initiation ritual.[81]

Admission money of up to $400 was demanded, depending on the assets of the victim, though the gains to be had from membership were more theoretical than real.[82] "Individual enterprise" involving members was frowned upon and punished by a fine, a beating, "or both."[83]

John Jatti, who ran a "School for Assassins," was understood to be a "pupil" of Musolino, coming from the same village of Santo Stefano d'Aspromonte.[84] Jatti, in legend, escaped the roundup of Musolino's followers and went to America, ending up in the Mahoning Valley.[85]

But its means of ensuring organizational survival was as poorly formulated as that which characterized its White Plains counterpart. The Mahoning Valley organization was talked about freely and proved vulnerable to penetration by undercover agents.[86] Stiff jail sentences of up to five years were meted out in June 1907 to the membership in New Castle, after which it disintegrated.[87]

Akin to the "Camorra" syndicates addressed in Chapter 5, the White Hand and New Castle groups succumbed chiefly because of casually devised security practices within the organizations. Added to that were salutory sentences handed out to those convicted.

Nicolo Ciurleo, a witness at a hearing in July 1907, for instance, told how when he refused to hand over $100 as an "initiation fee," he was slapped hard by the society members present and covered with filth from a broom. They then let him go. "After that," Ciurleo stated, "I was almost ignored by the men who had been in the room," and several even apologized for his mistreatment later.[88]

Alike to the White Plains enterprise, traces of the Ohio-Pennsylvania organization may have lasted. According to FBI sources in Youngstown, during the 1960s, Paul Romeo[89] and afterwards Dominico S. Mallamo[90] led a "Calabrese" group in the city that had started out, like the 1900s New Castle entity, "shaking down" Italian immigrants working in mills.[91]Mallamo was recorded as presiding over an admission ceremony unlike that recognized in the Sicilian-American underworld.[92] The group demanded an entry fee ($100), and levied a monthly assessment from its members ($10).

"BLACK HAND" RITUALS

An initiation ritual sometimes characterized bigger Black Hand societies. During raids against Joseph Morello's counterfeiters in 1909, a "small black book" was reputedly discovered on a forgery colleague, Joseph Palermo, containing the "codified rules of the Black Hand."[93]

This so-called "bible of the Black-Handers" included strictures against informing, "offending a companion," and "refusal to serve the society." Decision-making was based on the principle of unanimity through a voting procedure.[94]

A proposed member, one who had learned the society's "by-laws," would be taken into a meeting blindfolded. When it was removed, he saw those assembled there, who remained masked. The leader, who wore a handkerchief, spoke to those present. After a verbal exchange, the masks were whipped from the members' faces.[95]

The *New York Sun* in December 1910 revealed the contents of "an authentic statute of the Black Hand consisting of thirty-nine articles." "Written in very bad Italian with many grammatical errors and replete with words in the Calabrian and Sicilian dialects and in slang and jargon," articles ranged from codes against informing, "offending a comrade," deceiving a comrade, showing weakness or abandoning a comrade, and keeping money without authorization.

This Black Hand treasurer reported daily to the boss, and held the "social money" divided among the gang membership. The head received a fixed share of the proceeds and there was an entrance fee, "but the family may make reductions." Elections were held for the treasurer and the chief. "The family meets regularly twice a week," and extraordinary meetings were called. The chief "has the right to replace senior and junior members three times every year at his pleasure." There were senior members (*camuffo*) and *sgarritto* (junior members).[96]

A Black Hand "rule book" was seized in McKean County, Pennsylvania. It was said to belong to John Rotundo, a Calabrian sought for the homicide of John Caputo in Cattasaugus County in 1928. This organization was known as the "Society of Humility" in its original incarnation.

Of most interest was a book, written in Italian but printed in Spain, found in the belongings of Rotundo. It consisted of the "by-laws" of the society, describing the ranking structure from new recruit to *capo*.[97]

A ritual in which the initiate's forearm was cut typified a final "Black Hand" formation, this one based in Paterson, New Jersey and headed by Gaetano Pettenelli, probably from Naples.[98] Drops of blood drawn from the incision were mixed with that of a member. The initiate then took an oath of silence, and an instruction against divulging the secrets of the society was given to him, while a dagger was pressed to his chest. As a "guarantee of good faith," new members were required to name a wealthy Italian who could afford to "contribute" to the gang's coffers.[99]

Seized "Black Hand" notebooks were likely to have belonged to groups with mainland Italian backgrounds, who were not subject to the absolute prohibition in Sicily of Mafia members recording their activities and practices. No single initiation model characterized Black Hand groups, partially reflecting the diverse origins of their members in Italy. So-called Black Hand rulebooks may have been collected for any number of reasons, most of which did not approximate real-life processes and structures. Some ceremonies may have been created for the occasion; others were perhaps based on practices performed in their birthplaces. Their existence demonstrated the fact of blackmailing societies with a rudimentary hierarchy and a crudely defined division of labor, consisting of several members and performing entry rituals possibly referring to Old World practices.

MAFIA AND BLACK HAND

Standard works shy clear of discussing the relationship between the Black Hand and Mafiosi. Petacco, one of the few who ventured an opinion, subscribed to the theory that Mafia organizations preyed "upon their own compatriots."[100]

But case studies show a weak association between Mafia membership and Black Hand racketeering. Sicilians did mount Black Hand forays, but almost always acted on an individual basis and did so before joining an organized crime Family, where the activity was considered as disrespectful of the ideals of the *Onorata Societa*[101] as they were transmitted from Sicily.

In Sicily, "In the beginning racketeering was undertaken with a degree of wariness, almost as if they were looking for justification."[102] The Catania, Sicily, *cosca* never thought of "wholesale extortion," or of demanding "a cut" from shopkeepers. "If we had to think about extortion," Catania member Antonino Calderone stated, "we'd think about the big landowners, about the rich and not the small."[103] Celeste Morello contended that U.S. Mafiosi acted as protectors of the community from attack; "The Mafiosi held themselves out respectfully as law-abiding and their neighbors knew to go to these men if any extortionists harassed them."[104]

No case emerged of U.S. Mafia organizations involving themselves in the Black Hand. Furthermore, the potentially risky shakedown racket went against the instinct of first generation U.S. Mafia leaders to favor caution in their ventures.[105] Original American Mafia chieftains were frequently pillars of the Italian community, involving themselves in politics, and earning a living from self-employment.

Vito Guardalabene, the 1910s Milwaukee boss, and his underboss Joseph Vallone, were typical.[106] Guardalabene, until his 1921 death, was as active as Vallone in legitimate ventures, and "His approval was necessary to any political aspirant in the Third Ward" of the city.[107] His neighbors knew Philadelphia Family head Salvatore Sabella as a "respected storekeeper."[108] Buffalo's Joseph Peter DiCarlo was equally recognized, as one of the "better" class of Italians in the city.

However, several instances were identified of men who would later join and even lead Families being involved in the Black Hand prior to their Mafia membership. Joseph DiGiovanni, subsequently of the Kansas City "outfit's" elite, was arrested in July 1915, with several associates, for sending a Black Hand letter.[109] Jack Dragna, 1940s boss of the Los Angeles *brugad*, was accused of sending Dominick Lauricella threatening letters, also in July 1915, when handwriting experts linked him to the notes.

Chicago's Bruno Roti could be included in this bunch, operating as a "big shot" in the Black Hand at the turn of the century."[110] Sam Zito, a brother of Springfield Mafia boss Frank Zito, was seized in 1914 "using the United States mails for blackmailing purposes" in Benld, Illinois. A "prominent Italian merchant" in the town had been threatened unless he handed over $1,000. The letter "was signed with a dagger and cross."[111] Zito was believed to be a member of a gang "active throughout the state of late."[112]

Frank Corbi, afterwards a Gambino Family crew leader in Baltimore, was a brother of Pasquale "Patsy" Corbi. A reported attempt was made to kidnap the child of a wealthy merchant for ransom in 1923 Clarksburg, West Virginia: a bomb had also wrecked his store a year earlier. Nine men were arrested, including Patsy Corbi.[113]

Gang leaders were Calabrian, apparently with their own initiation rituals. The same crowd also gunned down Angelo Cambria in Uniontown, after he left the restaurant owned by Gaetano "Guy" Volpe, one of six Volpes of the Pittsburgh Mafia (also Calabrians).

Stefano "Steve" Zoccoli and Stanislao "Charles" Carbone, later to become members of the San Jose (California) *Famiglia*, were suspected Black Handers in their younger days. Both born in the same town in Calabria, Pennsylvania, Zoccoli was said to have engaged in the Black Hand in the 1920s. Carbone was an alleged member of a Johnsonburg (Pennsylvania) ring, and was acquitted of the 1927 murder of Bruno Valva, another member who challenged him for the gang's leadership. Also in the category of future Mafiosi who practiced the Black Hand were the Pittston identities

Figure 2.3   Joseph Pinzolo, 1908. (Courtesy of the *New York Times*)

Steve LaTorre and Charles Bufalino. In May 1907, they were among 11 men convicted in Wilkes-Barre, Pennsylvania, of conspiracy to terrorize mine workers into paying protection monies.

A similar case was encountered in New York City. In 1930, Bonaventura "Joseph" Pinzolo[114] would come to lead the Reina *borgata*. But in July 1908, Pinzolo was arrested for trying to dynamite a tenement building at 314 East 11th Street, part of an orchestrated campaign to force the owner, Francisco Spinelli, to concede to Black Hand demands.[115] Two members of the Italian Squad lying in wait caught Pinzolo red-handed with a stick of dynamite he was about to light. In Pinzolo's pocket was found a letter threatening Spinelli if he did not "come to terms."[116]

Pinzolo gave detectives "the name of the man higher up," Giuseppe Costabile.[117] Costabile was a native of Calabria, hung out at the Three Deuces where Pinzolo lived,[118] and had given Pinzolo the bomb with which to blow up the tenement house.[119] But Pinzolo, jailed for 2 years 8 months to 5 years, would only give information on Costabile in confidence.[120]

Pinzolo's perilous choice of criminal activity was reflective of his newly arrived status[121] and lack of experience in the New York City *milieu*. Train portrayed Costabile as a New York "Camorra" leader who "held undisputed sway of the territory south of Houston Street as far as Canal Street from Broadway to the East River."[122] In 1911, Costabile was charged with possession of a "large yellow bomb concealed under his coat," and was put away for from 3½–7 years in the New York State prison. (Costabile accused the arresting officers of planting the explosive device on his person after they warned him what might happen.[123])

Of particular interest was the situation of Giuseppe "Joseph" Morello, whose ventures are covered in Chapter 3. Reports vastly inflated his role in the Black Hand; Secret Service chief John Wilkie, for instance, equated the Mafia with the Black Hand by implying that Morello was a Black Hand boss.

Wilkie furthermore asserted that the Morello band were "responsible for 60 per cent of the Black Hand extortion that has gone on in the United States in the last ten years."[124] An official history of the Secret Service stressed the Morellos' alleged role in demanding money with menaces.[125] Flynn's book underscored this analysis.[126]

Morello was linked to extortionate enterprises by a number of books and by letters seized in 1903 in rooms he occupied in Chrystie Street, and those of his associates. According to reports, the materials indicated "a blackmailing scheme which the men are believed to have worked for many months, perhaps years."[127] But charges were not brought.

Because Morello was the assumed head of the Black Hand, his incarceration in early 1910 was predicted to have dramatic effects on the level of Black Hand shakedowns in the city. The Secret Service, sure enough, recorded that Black Hand type crimes decreased "more than 75 per cent . . . among the Italians in New York," once the Morello ringleaders were incarcerated.[128] But in 1911, there were 70 Black Hand bomb explosions in the city compared to 35 in 1910.[129]

Figure 2.4   Joseph Morello, 1900. (Courtesy of the U.S. National Archives)

In truth, the Morello combine concentrated primarily on counterfeiting; "Black Hand" ventures were marginal. Vito LaDuca, involved with Morello in the "Barrel" affair (Chapter 3) had indistinct links to Baltimore businessman Antonio Lanasa, general manager of the Lanasa-Goffe Steamship Importing Company, who stood trial for the dynamiting of the Joseph DiGiorgio home. Three letters were dispatched to DiGiorgio demanding $10,000, before DiGiorgio's suburban residence was dynamited.

During Lanasa's trial, he admitted that his "best friend" LaDuca had christened his child, and that LaDuca was Lanasa's collaborator in a lemon importing concern. On April 22, 1908, Lanasa was convicted of plotting to destroy the DiGiorgio house.[130]

LaDuca's name also emerged during the probe of the kidnapping for ransom of Anthony Mannino in August 1904. Mannino had been lured to Manhattan to act as an "interpreter," before going off to 39th Street with two strangers.[131]Angelo Buccoza on his arrest told detectives that "a man known to him as Ladua" had proposed that he join the conspirators in order to have enough funds be able to return to Italy.[132] Mannino was returned unharmed on August 19, in circumstances as mysterious as those around his abduction.

The victim's father, John Mannino, had a prior history with the Morellos, either having bailed them out after their arrest in the "Barrel" murder, or having contributed to their defense fund.[133] Because of his obvious affluence, Morello members may have viewed Mannino as a soft touch, and the events supported a theory that $500 had been paid for the return of Anthony by his father. LaDuca was arrested for the kidnapping, but subsequently freed.

John Bozzuffi, a First Avenue Italian banker, suffered his 14 year-old son Antonio being kidnapped in March 1906. After being missing for 3 days and a demand for $20,000 being posted, Antonio was freed to tell his story.[134] His kidnappers, "apparently becoming frightened," had left the boy in rooms they had rented. It was reported that his father had refused to give a penny to the captors and that he had immediately notified the police of the abduction. Morello's lieutenant Ignazio Lupo was questioned.[135]

Like John Mannino, the educated and relatively affluent Bozzuffi had an earlier acquaintance with the Morellos, having "filed and recorded" the Certificate of Incorporation of the Ignatz Florio Co-operative Association Among Corleonesi in 1902 (Chapter 3). In May 1908, a bomb exploded in the hallway of a First Avenue building owned by Bozzuffi, who "had suffered before at the hands of the Black Hand."[136]

Ignazio Lupo figured in a final Morello related "Black Hand" episode, when Salvatore Manzella, a wine and Italian produce importer on Elizabeth Street, filed for bankruptcy. During insolvency proceedings, he testified that Lupo had financially drained him using Black Hand methods. In fear of his life, so he said, Manzella gave Lupo nearly $10,000 in cash and checks. According to Manzella, Lupo had victimized others.[137] On November 17, 1909, Lupo was held for the shakedown of Manzella to the value of $4,000. But when Manzella failed to appear at a hearing, Lupo was discharged.[138]

There was no suggestion that the Morellos were collectively involved in extortion. Upon his arrest for counterfeiting in 1909, letters were seized in Joseph Morello's apartment indicating a role as an intermediary between the victims of blackmailers and their tormentors.[139] Morello would use his influence to settle the matter for a lower sum than the blackmailers wanted—and by so doing placing the man or woman in his debt.[140]

Aside from the practical advantage of distancing him from any direct involvement in a serious crime, such a mediating function was an extension of a traditional role performed by men of honour, in assisting *paesani* in difficulty.[141] The reward for Morello was in the form of favors, not cash.

Within the Sicilian cultural context, this type of arbitration role was often judged as a legitimate exercise of Mafia power where Mafiosi "represented the victim and negotiated the sums demanded" by bandits and highwaymen. Bill Bonanno noted how in Brooklyn the Bonannos helped "men and women who did not have enough to eat or to pay their rent or to find good doctors for their children."[142] Joseph Bonanno observed,

"By performing such favors, large and small, the "man of honor" made himself indispensable."[143]

Specifics of the quid pro quo for Morello's help came to light. The mother of Dr. Salvatore Romano, who like Morello came from Corleone, received menacing letters. Once Morello intervened, those preying off Romano were willing to settle for $1,000. In the end, Salvatore only paid $100, with Morello paying (so he said) the balance.

The matter placed the Romanos under Morello's thumb. Whenever a member of the gang or one of Morello's relatives took sick, Romano treated him free of charge.[144] Worse, Romano was pressured to commit perjury during Morello's trial in 1910, by falsely stating that Morello was in bed with rheumatism when his crimes were committed.[145]

No doubt Morello's reputation as a Mafioso was the back of the minds of those who turned to him for relief.[146] In 1913, "the Terranova boys" were reported as strong-arming "store keepers and others." The Iannis similarly reported that "Giuseppe Lupollo," the anonymous head of a New York City Mafia syndicate, "offered his services as a negotiator for a victim in dire straights with the Black Hand group involved." If the victim had to borrow money to pay them off from Lupollo at an exorbitant interest rate, he "reaped double profits from the operation."[147]

Gambetta contended that the Black Hand was unknown in Italy. But letter senders in New York may have drawn inspiration from the analogous Sicilian practice of sending out *"lettere di scrocco,"* so-called "scrounging" letters excluding the Black Hand symbol.[148] Illustrative of that was the case of the Pecoraro brothers (Chapter 3).

BLACK HAND AND TERRITORIAL ISSUES

Despite Lombardo's assertion that they were politically shielded, public outrage at dynamiting outrages guaranteed that the type of tacit official protection offered to gambling entrepreneurs was not extended to Black Hand operators. Black Hand merchants consequently took every measure to ensure that the terror their letters inspired in victims, together with the ineffectiveness of the police, would be sufficient to being victims to heel.

Although blackmailers had no territorial ambitions, their threat or use of violence across neighborhoods with scant regard for the toes they stepped on caused difficulties for the emergent Families, by severely curtailing their attempts to achieve a measure of local control. This feature was evident in the territorial bailiwicks of East Harlem (the province of the Morellos), Williamsburg (Schiro group) and the lower east side of Manhattan (base for the D'Aquila and Morello syndicates).

In July 1904, the doorway of a grocery store at 252 Elizabeth Street (lower east side) was blown up, "wrecking the store." The owner and his wife were thrown out of their beds. He had received demands for $2,000 by letter. The police had started work on the case once the first was received, but there were no clues as to the writer's identity.[149]

When the Roebling Street (Williamsburg) grocery store of Anton Galinto was bombed in March 1908, "the entire neighborhood" was shaken. The Black Hand had been flourishing among the area's Italians. Galinto had ignored earlier mail demanding "various sums of money." The *Tribune* took the occasion to comment, "The dread of Il Mano Negro (sic) has spread among the Italians in Williamsburg, and has caused many of them to move away."[150]

In East Harlem, an explosion rocked the tenement building at 231 East 107th Street in March 1909 that would house important Mafiosi. The *New York Times* chronicled the event: "The interior of the small inclosure was wrecked and the door blown from its hinges. That was all the damage done."[151]

The residence of Morello kinsman Vincent Terranova on East 109th Street was damaged in January 1913, when a bomb "wrecked the front door and shattered the show window" of a grocery store housed in the tenement building. Twenty-four Italian families lived there.[152]

Reflective of the high level of disorder that the freewheeling Black Hand encouraged, was the shooting down of police officers assigned to "Italian" quarters. Kansas City patrolman Joseph Raimo was shot dead in March 1911, while working the Italian section of the city. In Boston, three police officers, a lieutenant and two patrolmen, who "had "been unremitting in their efforts to stamp out crime in the Italian quarter" in the North End around Prince Street were marked for assassination by "La Camora."[153]

A "gang of Sicilian outlaws" assassinated patrolman Wilson in 1908 in the midst of an upsurge of Black Hand activity taking place in Detroit.[154] Detective Emmanuel Roggers, charged with investigating the same Sicilian district, was cut down in July 1917 after threats had been made against his life.[155] During 1918, Detroit patrolman William Struchfield was "shot by a unidentified man in a motor car."[156] Almost a year later, Detroit plainclothesman Harold Roughley became another fatality.[157]

Organized crime figures were not immune. Black Hand entrepreneurs persecuted Chicago's James Colosimo, notwithstanding his exalted underworld status. Colosimo lacked an effective means to counter their deprivations, despite the redoubtable Johnny Torrio joining his organization.[158] Colosimo's refusal to bow to Black Hand demands was one theory advanced to account for his murder in 1920.[159]

If his story is to be believed, Ignazio Lupo was still another Black Hand sufferer. He owned a wholesale grocery on Mott Street until it failed in November 1908 owing $100,000. Lupo vanished when a petition for bankruptcy was filed against him. Re-emerging in November 1909 to face his creditors, he told a tale of being extorted for $10,000, handing over the cash on Brooklyn Bridge, leaving him virtually penniless.[160]

LEGACY

Black Hand activities slowly but erratically receded after 1915, lasting into the 1920s in areas of Pennsylvania. Part of the improvement was caused by effective enforcement of federal laws related to the contents of mail crossing state lines. Sentences meted out by federal judges proved uncompromising in sending out a message of deterrence. Declining Black Hand activity was also related to tighter immigration controls in the years following 1914.

The belief that former Black Handers transferred into the bootlegging racket after 1920 has a flimsy factual basis. Nelli called attention to the role of the Black Hand in laying part of the "groundwork" for developments that saw the Italians emerging as top dogs in the underworld. "During prohibition, professional criminals" he wrote, "abandoned their former practices in the Italian community and joined the growing ranks of bootleggers."[161] Pitkin and Lombardo also argued that a portion of the Black Hand fraternity "turned eagerly to bootlegging" in the 1920s.[162]

A few did make the move into the 1920s contraband alcohol field, but beer and liquor trafficking seem to have been performed by others. Nelli illustrated his thesis by citing Frankie Yale, the Gennas, Joseph DiGiovanni and Vincenzo "Cosmanno" (sic). Yet of these, only Kansas City's DiGiovanni was known to practice the Black Hand, and Cosmano, who was indeed a pre-Prohibition bomb thrower, quickly faded into obscurity.

CONCLUSION

Territorially strong forms of Italian-American organized crime existed before Mafias emerged as a force in New York City's organized crime, exemplified by the saga of the Paul Kelly (Paolo Vaccarelli) criminal combine. It proved ephemeral however. Since the activities run by the Kellys were "victimless," they were easy to overlook. In having this advantage, they were the polar opposite of Black Hand extortionists, or of the counterfeiters of the next chapter, whose enterprises generated complaints and attracted (in the case of counterfeiters) a plethora of law enforcement interest.

Dickie was wrong to place the Mafia in relation to American "protection rackets."[163] Gambetta's similar presumption, that American Mafias were engaged in "protection markets," was equally uncorroborated.[164] Black Handers and Mafiosi apparently lived in the same sections, but the former undermined the authority of the latter.[165]

Schiavo asserted that conditions exclusive to America were responsible for the Black Hand.[166] Lombardo similarly argued that the Black Hand was "the outcome of conditions existing within American society," specified in terms of native prejudice, poverty, the isolation of the immigrant community, and their distrust of formal machineries.[167]

The association between "imported" and "domestic" influences was, in fact, reciprocal. The letter-writing practice was probably inspired by a modus operandi first utilized in Sicily, but in order to flourish as powerfully as it did in America, it required a particular set of circumstances that was found in the local environment.

The relationship of Mafia Families to the Black Hand was at most circuitous. The Iannis correctly noted, with reference to the Black Hand, "there is no evidence which suggests that there was any higher level of organization or any tie with the Mafia in Sicily or the Camorra in Naples."[168]

Over the 1920s, a "Green Ones" faction of the Italian underworld reportedly extracted "tribute money" from St. Louis shopkeepers and butchers.[169] That instance aside, the Black Hand could not be viewed as representing a "stage" in the evolution of U.S. organized crime, or a "training ground" for prohibition era Mafiosi. Black Handers hardly ever progressed into other forms of organized crime that yielded larger profits with less risk.

Chapter 3 furthers our analysis of the Morellos. Many aspects of the Morello's organization; its hierarchy, means of recruitment, activities, scale and connections to other American cities have been obscured or left unexplored. The thorny question of whether the Morello setup was modeled on Sicilian *cosche* and drew strength from Sicilian resources is discussed.

3 "First Family" of the New York Mafia

INTRODUCTION

Few other American Mafias have commanded the same level of interest as that headed by Giuseppe "Joseph" Morello. Chandler correctly argued that the Morello-Terranova family "would provide a continuous link in New York's organized crime history." Although it was an exaggeration to contend that the Morellos were "perhaps the deadliest kinship group ever to enter the county,"[1] their influence extended to Chicago and Louisiana, and the American Mafia community held Morello in esteem.

Bill Bonanno stated that three, not five, Italian-American organized crime Families existed in Metropolitan New York by the turn of the 20th century.[2] Independently of the Morellos, a second Family was ensconced in Brooklyn under the patronage of Nicolo Schiro. A third Mafia organization, led by Salvatore D'Aquila, was an outgrowth of the Morellos.

(Manfredi Mineo, setting foot in New York in 1911 and allegedly commanding a third faction, was identified by Nicolo Gentile as later part of the D'Aquila borgata.)[3] A final Mafia, based in Harlem, was run by the remnants of the Morello outfit.[4]

While incorrectly assumed to be heavily involved in the Black Hand, the Morello network nonetheless engaged in a variety of other types of organized crime. One of the key questions pursued is whether the Morello group was a de facto "branch" of the Sicilian Mafia. Or did localized—"American"—influences condition the organizational form that emerged in New York City?

U.S. *borgata* were never "offshoots" of a command structure with headquarters in Palermo, as Reid claimed.[5] But American Mafias such as those led by Morello did maintain fraternal connections to the old country, albeit on the individual scale, and operated forms of organizational governance in New York City that would be familiar to Sicilian *cosche*.

Secret Service operatives were among the first and most formidable foes of the American Families. Virtually corruption-free, they recruited informers who could damage Mafia activities.The counterfeiting activity in which the Morellos were primarily engaged, being risky and attracting stiff penalties after capture, engendered a high level of violence. For their part, the

Secret Service kept a close surveillance eye on the Morellos, effectively deploying a network of spies, and looking for weaknesses. Acting under that pressure, Morello and his cohorts became accustomed to attempting to stop leaks through the murder of suspected traitors.

GIUSEPPE MORELLO

Giuseppe Morello was born May 2, 1867 in Corleone, the son of Calogero "Carlo" Morello and Angelina Piazza.[6] Until he was 12, Chandler claimed, Morello attended school. He then worked on his father's farm.[7] Morello was admitted into the Corleone Mafia *cosca*, his passage into it perhaps facilitated by the fact that Giuseppe Battaglia, a leader, was one of Morello's uncles.[8]

Giovanni Vella was gunned down on December 29, 1889, near his home while standing for election as "Chief of the Sylvan Guards," who protected landed estates, in Corleone. Vella had discovered Morello's ties

Figure 3.1   Corleone. (Drawn from Studio Fotografico Oliveri-Corleone)

to the Corleone *cosca* headed by Paolino Streva, who had "a baneful influence over the community the same as his uncle had done before him."[9]

A female witness to the Vella killing, Anna DiPuma (or DiPrima), witnessed Morello with another man lurking in the shadows from where a shot was fired at Vella. When she told neighbors and threatened to go to the local magistrate, DiPuma was herself murdered, a misdeed for which Morello was questioned.[10]

Francesco Ortoleva, who had stood against Vella in the election, identified Vella's slayers as including Morello, an "agricultural laborer, from Corleone, married and currently in America." With Morello in the Vella conspiracy were Michele Coniglio "agricultural laborer, from Corleone, currently in America as well," Giovanni Scaligi, Streva, "25 year old land owner, from Corleone," and "other accomplices."[11]

With DiPuma silenced, Ortoleva was jailed for life for Vella's murder largely on circumstantial evidence. Biaggia Milone who, it was rumored, could also link Morello to the case, made her way to her cousin Domenico Milone in New York. Milone ran a grocery store at East 97th Street that was the distributing station for counterfeit currency manufactured by the Morello syndicate later. Streva disappeared from Corleone, "and his whereabouts are not known."[12]

On September 14, 1894, Morello was sentenced (possibly *in absentia*) to 6 years and 45 days plus fine for counterfeiting, and "perpetually deprived of the right to hold any public office of trust."[13] He appears to have left Sicily for New York at about this time.[14]

Morello's half-brother Ciro Terranova gave an account of what happened next. Finding himself unemployed in New York, Morello moved to Louisiana in the mid 1890s. The rest of the Morello-Terranova family joined. The following year, they planted and picked cotton in Texas.[15] Contracting malaria, they returned to New York about 1897. Morello lost money on a Stanton Street, lower Manhattan, saloon and on a date factory, before investing in a saloon at 8 Prince Street in around 1902, which was to become a hangout for his gang members.

COUNTERFEITING 1895–1902

From the late 1880's, Italians dominated the counterfeit note business in New York City. Primarily active within the Italian-American population and working with Italian (mostly Sicilian) immigrants, counterfeiting projects conducted by Morello in New York were not a radical departure from those conducted in Sicily. Morello's was one of several Mafia linked counterfeiting rings dismantled in Sicily in the late 19th century. Giuseppe Fontana was implicated in another. Counterfeiting was also a cause of violence between *cosche* in Sicily.[16]

Sicilians had been active in New York City counterfeiting as early as the 1860s. In 1865, a body was found in woods near Greenwood Cemetery,

Brooklyn, with pistol shot wounds to the head. Follow-up police action led to the seizure of "plates, paper, a printing press, and $19,000 in counterfeit notes, plus five trunks of stolen goods."[17]

The victim, a recent addition from Messina, was identified as Antonio Deodati. He was mixed up with a counterfeiting gang, almost all of the participants also from Messina, and was reportedly killed as a traitor.[18] Deodati's death was among those listed in 1875 by the Prefect of Messina as part of fighting between two "Mafia" factions that had resulted in other murders.

According to the Prefect, Deodati had fled Sicily, but was tracked down by assassins who "overtook" him in New York. A letter sent to the Brooklyn police in 1866 alleged that the Deodati executioners were indeed hired in Sicily, and intended to go to Mexico or Canada immediately after committing the deed.[19]

William J. Flynn, chief of the New York office of the Secret Service, was convinced that the Mafia played a role in the execution of Antonino Flaccomio.[20] Flaccomio was slain in October 1888 in front of the Cooper Institute. New York's Inspector Thomas Byrnes was also quoted as stating that it was a product of a "Mafia" *vendetta*. A coroner's jury decided otherwise, however, and others suggested that Flaccomio's involvement in counterfeiting was the cause of his undoing.[21]

Morello (nicknamed "One Finger Jack" by the Secret Service), and Calogero Maggiore were among those picked up in June 1900 for selling a poor quality forged $5 bill.[22] The accused subsequently escaped trial except for Maggiore, who was given 6 years in New York State prison and a $1 fine.

Diverging from Sicilian practice, an alliance was formed with a counterfeiting syndicate of which the formidable and experienced female Stella Frauto was head. It was considered to be "the most ingenious and persistent" of its type "for a decade."[23] Because of her reputation in the field, Morello may have discarded any misgivings he would have otherwise had about working with a woman.

THE HACKENSACK PLANT

In May 1902, New York Detective Sergeant Joseph Petrosino received an anonymous letter alleging that Frauto and her possible husband, Salvatore "The Dude" Clemente, ran a counterfeiting plant in Hackensack, New Jersey. The group also involved Frauto operatives Giuseppe Romano (a First Avenue barber), and Andrea Romano.[24] Clemente had been jailed for 8 years in 1895 in Erie County for counterfeiting when, with Frauto and her companions, he was found with bogus coins at an address on East 70th Street.[25] Clemente was also an acquaintance of Nicholas Terranova, a half brother to Joseph Morello.

Secret Service agents pounced on Dyatt Street, Hackensack, in time to seize a large amount of forged currency and equipment.[26] Visitors to the Clemente house were observed carrying parcels under their arms, and Clemente was

Figure 3.2   Salvatore Clemente. (Courtesy of the U.S. National Archives)

often seen catching the train carrying a bundle of clothing.[27] The counterfeits were carried to Romano's barber's shop, from where they were distributed.

A roundup on May 22, 1902, snared Stella Frauto, Antonio Frauto, Giuseppe Romano, Giuseppe Clemente—and Vito Cascioferro.[28] Cascioferro, giving his address as 361 First Avenue, was seized in Romano's premises on First Avenue with a loaded revolver.[29]

The Secret Service had just captured probably the most powerful Sicilian *cosca* leader of the age. Vito Cascioferro was born in Palermo, but at an early age his family moved to Sambuca Zabat, where he lived for approximately 24 years before relocating to Bisacquino, his acknowledged power base in the Mafia. Sentenced for the imprisoning of the Baroness of Valpetrosa in 1898, Cascioferro was released in 1900 and thereupon sailed to America, arriving in New York at the end of September 1901. Apparently acting as an importer of fruits and foods, Cascioferro lived for about 2½ years in New York, spending a further 6 months in New Orleans.[30]

The arrests signified the end for Frauto's band. Stella Frauto was sentenced on June 27, 1902 to over 3 years imprisonment with hard labor at Auburn Prison. Giuseppe Romano was jailed for 2 years and fined $200 in the U.S. District Court in Newark.[31] *Nolle prosequi* was entered as to Antonio Frauto and Salvatore Clemente on May 9, 1906, but Salvatore was jailed in Toronto for selling imitation Canadian currency. Cascioferro's alibi that he worked in a paper mill in Hackensack could not be shaken and he was released, returning to Sicily in September 1904.

Andrea Romano, the last of the Frauto ring then at large, was arrested at Niagara Falls while negotiating the sale of the 8 Prince Street saloon, perhaps to Morello. Romano was freed at trial after the only witness against him, Antonio D'Andrea, described as a "well known leader in Chicago Italian affairs," refused to testify.

D'Andrea contended, in a statement made to the Secret Service, that he had bought the counterfeit coins from Romano "at an elevated railroad station in New York." But "on the stand D'Andrea said he did not know Romano and had never seen him." D'Andrea told the Secret Service, "his life would be taken, if he dared to testify against the other Italian."[32]

Mafia troubleshooter Gentile knew D'Andrea as the Chicago Mafia *capo* before his murder in May 1921, a by-product of "political warfare"

Figure 3.3 Vito Cascioferro. (Courtesy of the U.S. National Archives)

in the 19th Ward.[33] For his counterfeiting activities, D'Andrea was jailed for 13 months on April 24, 1903, in the Illinois State Penitentiary.

MURDER AND THE MORELLOS

Morello's proclivity towards the use of violence directed against those in his group with loose tongues, or their nearest available kin, was first displayed in 1902. The grizzly details splashed across newspapers brought them to a wider public attention, with ultimately ruinous results. Other Mafias operated enterprises that could be managed without attracting the same exemplary punishments for failure that was a feature of the counterfeiting business.

The body of 30-year-old Giuseppe Catania, beaten savagely and with his throat slit, was found on July 23, 1902, jammed inside a pair of potato sacks on the shore at Bay Ridge. It was believed that he was lured to his place of death "for revenge."[34] Catania's alleged status as a "capo in charge of the southern Brooklyn docks area," is, however, fanciful a claim. Neither was Catania the father of Giuseppe "Joe the Baker" Catania (see below).[35] Catania was poor, and the small amount of money Vincenzo Troyia, or Trica, the original suspect in his murder, owed him ($14) was needed to pay his broker.[36]

From a jail cell in Ontario, Salvatore Clemente in January 1903 disclosed to the Secret Service that Morello and "Dominico Pecorara" were behind the Bay Ridge slaying of "Giuseppe Ditrapani" (Catania), who had been careless with his talk when drunk. Clemente's own source, Antonio Casano, portrayed to him a Manhattan based gang that dealt in counterfeit $5 notes, and that included Pecoraro, Ignazio Lupo, Isadore Crocervera and Paolo Marchese, who figures later.[37]

Lupo was supposed to have been the last person seen with Catania on the day before Catania's body was found.[38] No charges were brought. Benedetto Madonia's fate further underlined Morello's unsubtle approach towards those considered unreliable. In another trademark of killings linked to the Morello organization, police enquires into Madonia's death led nowhere.

The body of a man with his throat cut was found stuffed in a barrel in front of 743 East 11th Street on April 14, 1903. His head was almost severed from the body. He had been stabbed 18 times and his watch was missing, though the watch chain survived.[39]

Salvatore Romano of the Frauto group had been arrested in January 1903 with Giuseppe DePriema and Isadoro Crocervera in Yonkers for passing forged $5 notes, as part of the Morello operation.[40] DePriema, Madonia's brother in law, was imprisoned for 4 years, and identified Madonia as the murder victim, as did Madonia's wife.[41]

The Secret Service was already hot on the trail of Morello's men. Surveilling a butcher's shop at 16 Stanton Street owned by Giovanni Zarcone and frequented by Morello, Lupo and Tommaso Petto, "The Newcomer" (later identified as Madonia) was last seen alive on April 13, walking away from it with Morello and Pecoraro. It was theorized that the execution of Madonia occurred in the 226 Elizabeth Street pastry shop belonging to Pietro Inzerillo in which the gang met daily. Further, it was considered that Petto had knifed Madonia to death in Inzerillo's establishment.[42]

Madonia was eliminated, it was supposed, for being either a squealer or for threatening to leave the gang.[43] The last supposition saw DePriema as bitter at how the gang apparently failed to help him when he got into trouble, sending Madonia to confront Morello and his pals in New York City over misused defense money. When the gang prevaricated, Madonia made the fatal mistake of threatening to talk.[44]

Flynn subsequently disclosed that when Crocervera et al. were seized in early 1903, he "hit upon the idea" of giving Crocervera the impression that DePriema had talked. That tactic, which did not have the desired effect in making Crocervera open up, appears to have prompted Morello into sentencing Madonia to death. Though the Morellos could not get at DePriema, they could execute his "nearest male relative," the hapless Madonia.[45]

Arrested as material witnesses were:
Giuseppe Fanaro
Antonio "Messina" Genova
Pietro Inzerillo
Vito LaDuca (employed as a butcher by Giovanni Zarcone)
Giuseppe Lalamia
Lorenzo and Vito Lobido (brothers or nephews)
Ignazio Lupo
Giuseppe Morello
Domenico Pecoraro
Tommaso Petto
Nicolo Testa

In Morello's Chrystie Street apartment was material suggesting, it was asserted, that he was head of the Mafia society in Palermo operating in America, and having influence in other U.S. cities.[46] Reflecting the fear engendered by Morello in Italian neighborhoods, a collection was organized for those accused in the "Barrel" case extending to the Bronx.[47] Complaints were received of threats being made if money was not forthcoming. (In Newark, Italians armed themselves after refusing to contribute to the fund.[48])

The coroner's inquest into the Madonia death opened on May 1, 1903. But "the Italians called as witnesses showed utter lack of knowledge of things they were known to have seen, and even denied being acquainted with friends."[49] DePriema was now unclear about what he had said to Petrosino, Madonia's wife and son were confused and Morello denied almost everything. On May 8, the Coroner's jury returned the verdict that Madonia was slain by persons unknown.[50]

Figure 3.4　Vito LaDuca. (Courtesy of the U.S. National Archives)

Individuals identified with the case became marked men and were either arrested for other offences or slain. Inzerillo was harassed by regulatory agencies.[51] In February 1908, Vito LaDuca was "shot and killed as he was leaving the theatre" in Carini, near to Palermo.[52] DePriema and Giuseppe Fanaro were murdered, as was Fanaro in November 1913 "by the Lamonti (Lomonte) and Manfredi (Mineo) gangs."[53]

Giovanni Zarcone was mortally wounded in July 1909 in a hospital in Danbury, Connecticut, "his head riddled with shot."[54] Zarcone had moved from Brooklyn after the Madonia furor and in Danbury, was known as a man of means, his fruit farm on Hospital Avenue being the most extensive of its kind in the area.[55]

One line of enquiry that was pursued was whether his death was in revenge for Madonia's.[56] Another supposed that Giovanni's pregnant girl-friend (who he had visited in hospital just before his death) had been poisoned by one of the Zarcones, after she tried to poison them. In retaliation, her brothers supposedly slew Giovanni.[57]

Figure 3.5 Giovanni Zarcone. (Courtesy of Marina Riggio)

Tommaso Petto was formally charged with Madonia's death, but released in 1904.[58] Traveling as Luciano Perrino, "an Italian business man of Pittston," on October 21, 1905, Petto was "found in a dying condition and covered with blood" by his wife outside their Browntown, Pennsylvania, home. As he stepped into the backyard, he was shot-gunned to death.[59] Petto's fearsome reputation in New York had preceded him within the local Italian population.[60]

DOWNFALL OF THE MORELLOS

Incorporated in December 1902, the Ignatz Florio Co-Operative Association of Corleonesi[61] had offices at 630 East 138th Street, where Morello for a time lived. Among the first directors of the Co-Operative was Morello (later president) and Marco Macaluso.[62] (Macaluso, born 1875 in Corleone, was the father of Mariano Macaluso, 1960s Lucchese Family *consiglieri*) Another Ignazio Co-Operative director and owner of the largest bloc of shares, Antonio B. Milone, was involved in the Morello counterfeiting operation of 1908–9.

Its business was to buy and sell tenement houses to Italian immigrants, and to accumulate sufficient funds to erect tenements in the Bronx using the sale of stocks. Functioning apparently legally for several years while Morello's counterfeiting activities were in abeyance, commercial difficulties affecting the Co-Operative altered its purpose. The Morellos resumed counterfeiting operations in December 1908, passing on some of the fake currency as Co-Operative dividends.[63]

Fresh people, ones unfamiliar to Morello or his associates, were brought in. This elementary mistake, belying Morello's reputation as a savvy operator, cost the Morellos their freedom.

Counterfeit $2 and $5 notes reappeared in May 1909 in several American cities, causing uproar from banks and merchants.[64] An "ex-Black Hander" told Flynn about the manufacturing plant run by Morello and Lupo.[65] The focus moved to a wholesale store owned by Domenico Milone that was described as the "clearing house" for counterfeits manufactured by the gang in Highland, New York.

It was learned that each man had his own role in the enterprise. Giuseppe Calicchio was the lithograph engraver, who learned his trade in Italy. Salvatore Cina was his godfather.[66] The Corleonesi Antonio Cecala was most trusted, acting as Morello's main distributor of counterfeit currency. Giuseppe Calicchio, like Antonio Comito a printer by profession, was assigned to help. Vincenzo Giglio was the owner, with Cina, of the farm.[67]

Giuseppe "Uncle Salvatore" Palermo's function was that of a "financier" and "overseer." Palermo also supplied food and beverages to those doing the work in the stone house. Nicholas Sylvester brought paper and plates and helped Comito with the printing.[68] Ignazio Lupo arrived at Highland in February 1909, "a well dressed man in fur coat and overcoat of about thirty years of age,"[69] as they were ready to distribute the notes. This aside, Lupo "did nothing" except to pass the time of day.[70]

Hunt has difficulty in deciding whom of Morello and Lupo was the "boss."[71] But Gentile—a man in an excellent position to know the truth—recorded that Morello was the *capo di capi* (boss of bosses) of the entire American Mafia.

According to Comito, Morello was also "a leader and the deference shown to him at all times was convincing of his high standing among these men."[72] Chief Wilkie of the Secret Service knew of Morello's dominancy despite the publicity given Lupo. Lupo "was in reality but a tool" of Morello's.[73]

"The career of Lupo," the *New York Times* commented, "is as strange a mixture of hard luck and good fortune as ever cropped out of the picturesque section of the city in which he operated."[74]But Lupo never "perfected and fostered the Black Hand extortion technique in America."[75] Nor was he "one of the most desperate and blood-thirsty criminals this country has

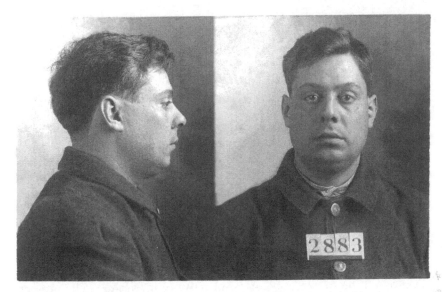

Figure 3.6 Ignazio Lupo, 1910. (Courtesy of the U.S. National Archives)

ever seen."[76] Like the circumstances around Morello's departure, Ignazio Lupo's exit from Sicily was a reaction to police interest.

Lupo, born March 1877 in Palermo, was the son of Rocco Lupo and Onofria Saietta.[77] Connected to the Palermo Mafia, when explaining the difficulties that led to his hasty removal from Sicily, Lupo recounted that he became embroiled in a dispute in his store in Palermo during October 1898, ending with Salvatore Morello[78] attacking Lupo with a dagger. In self-defense, Lupo killed Morello. Lupo "went into hiding" and on the advice of his parents fled Italy, reaching New York by way of Liverpool, Montreal and Buffalo.[79]

In early December 1908, the Morello syndicate began making Canadian $5 bills.[80] They printed $2 notes in another farm in the area.[81] Using better chemicals and ink, work was continued in March 1909. In total, Comito helped to forge over $46,000. In May 1909, the work ended and the press was dismantled. There were calls in June for more $2 notes, and Calicchio was arranging this when the ring was broken up.[82]

The big roundup took place on November 15, 1909, capturing "the last of one of the biggest hands of counterfeiters that has ever operated in this country." When Morello's house at 207 East 107th Street was searched, they found his son Calogero in one bed and Morello in another. Six letters were taken.[83]

As the police were searching Milone's store on East 97th Street, Nicholas Terranova rushed in and was seized. He lived in the same apartment house as Morello, Ciro Terranova, and the Morello-allied Stefano LaSalle, of whom more in Chapters 4 and 5.[84] Joseph Palermo owned a Poughkeepsie macaroni factory where Cina and Giglio were arrested on January 5, 1910, and on which street Cina lived.[85] Lupo and Palermo were picked up 3 days later in Lupo's Bath Beach house.[86]

When the ringleaders appeared at trial, the Secret Service had Antonio Comito's confession to hand. Comito was apprehended in early January 1910 and almost immediately made a statement that turned into the centerpiece of the case against his former co-workers. "Without his confession and testimony," said the U.S. Attorney for the Southern District of New York, "the Government could not have obtained a conviction."[87]

Comito recalled before the jury how he had come from Cananzero, Calabria, in June 1907, as a printer in search of work. A chance meeting of the Order of the Sons of Italy led to a job working for Cecala, described to Comito as the owner of a printing shop in Philadelphia. Comito said that he initially thought they were going there.[88] But with his partner Katrina Pascuzzo, Comito ended up in Highland, where the counterfeiting equipment arrived in December 1908.[89]

Due to his centrality to the government's case, it was opportune for the prosecution to portray Comito as naive, not criminal. The prosecution depicted Comito as an innocent dupe who had unwittingly become entangled in the gang's machinations. He "was not at heart a criminal, or had he profited at all by the counterfeiting scheme" argued Flynn,[90] but was "afraid to denounce them," because he "was constantly in danger of losing his life."[91]

In the U.S. Circuit Court, the accused were convicted on February 19, 1910. Before their sentencing, Judge Ray remarked, "There has never been such a round-up and such a line of convictions before."[92] The defendants and the punishments meted out were:

Lupo–30 years and fine
Morello–25 years and fine
Palermo–18 years and fine
Calicchio–17 years and fine
Sylvester–15 years and fine
Cecala–15 years and fine
Giglio–15 years and fine
Cina–15 years and fine

When Morello heard this, "The once-powerful Mafioso stared open-mouthed at the judge, then suddenly wavered and collapsed in a dead faint. He was promptly carried from the courtroom."[93] The notoriety of the accused, as Black Hand kings, may have played a part in the severity of their sentences.[94] Giuseppe Boscarino, another member of the Morello organization, was incarcerated for 15 years in December 1910 for putting the counterfeits into circulation. Comito was a witness at his trial too.

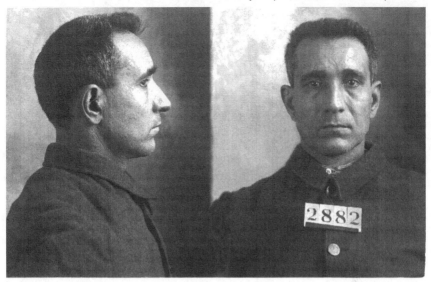

Figure 3.7   Joseph Morello, 1910. (Courtesy of the U.S. National Archives)

FALLOUT

Under Nick Morello, the syndicate retreated to an East 107th Street saloon headquarters. The Morello organization was never successful in this activity again. Nor was it authorized in Mafia councils; a ban on taking part in counterfeiting became part of the initiation ritual, in one version.[95] It was a wise move, since the federal government "was traditionally (and not unreasonably) obsessed with cases involving the counterfeiting of its money, there was little likelihood of getting any kind of break."[96]

Although the Morello name lived on in U.S. organized crime annals, the power of the Corleonesi faction of which they were a key part was weakened by Joseph Morello's removal to the penitentiary. Salvatore D'Aquila was the chief beneficiary, stepping into Morello's shoes as the replacement "boss of bosses."

Several of Morello's counterfeiters traded information for their liberty, detailing the operation and suggesting where the plates might be found. The majority of the Morellos dispatched to Atlanta federal penitentiary in 1910 faded into obscurity following their release. Joseph Palermo, after suffering a stroke, was paroled in 1920 and lived quietly on Elizabeth Street until his death in 1924.[97] Cina's sentence was commuted to 10 years, expiring in November 1916 when he was freed. Sylvester was eligible for parole in February 1915; Calicchio was paroled in 1920. Giglio died in May 1914 of a heart attack while serving his sentence. Cecala was paroled in 1915,[98] later on exhibiting prudence in his choice of business ventures (Chapter 6).

Morello's term was commuted in 1918 to 15 years, and he was released in March 1920. At some juncture, Morello joined the Mafia coalition headed by Giuseppe "Joe the Boss" Masseria (Chapter 6).

Lupo was given a conditional commutation by President Warren G. Harding in June 1920.[99] Lupo and his wife Salvatrice lived with the Terranovas at 338 East 116th Street until 1927, when they moved to Brooklyn courtesy of Ciro and Tessie Terranova who in May 1926 conveyed a lot to the Lupos to build an "elaborate house" on.[100]

After Italian bakers in Brooklyn made complaints to the State Governor, Lupo's commutation was revoked in July 1936 on a warrant signed by President Roosevelt.[101]Lupo thereafter became "the oldest living public enemy in the United States." The bakers had complained that that they were "being bombed, beaten and driven out of business."[102] Various other episodes raised doubts that Lupo had given up the rackets.[103]

ORGANIZATIONAL SECURITY

As the original "boss of bosses," the question of Morello's influence in the American Mafia is of special interest. After removing his ephemeral, task-oriented counterfeiting contacts, the number and type of Morello's contacts in the Mafia society indicated that he was no titan in organized crime. Because the Morello syndicate lacked depth and strength in numbers, it was eventually forced to recruit outsiders to the Sicilian tradition, with disastrous effects.

Exaggerated notions of the Morellos' collective power and ability to maintain secrecy were suggested by references to the number of individuals purportedly dying at their hands.[104] Although the Morellos were certainly not averse to the use of murder, several homicides identified in Sicilian police reports remain unsubstantiated. They were of Corleonesi living in New York, reported as seen before their deaths in the company of Morello and his associates Giuseppe Fontana and Ignazio Milone:[105]

Giuseppe Canale[106]
Andrea Fendi (June 1906)
Salvatore Sperizza, "Forsyth Street saloon keeper" (1906)[107]
An unidentified man who perished in July 1906

Outside of his violence-prone reputation—less deserved in some cases than in others—Dickie reflects a strand of opinion in perceiving the success of Morello partly in terms of his ability to obtain the prerequisite police and political cover.[108] Cecala likewise thought that Morello was "tipped off" by police officers when he was "in danger of arrest."[109] Yet Morello's chief activity, counterfeiting, was outside the corrupt crime-police nexus. Furthermore, none of the surveillance reports on the Morellos disclosed even a hint of official corruption.

Cook perceived the Morellos as "so well-protected, so isolated behind the screen of their principal lieutenants" that detectives "could not pin directly upon them any of the heinous crimes" for which they were responsible.[110] The assumption was made that Morello had enough men in his organization to remove him from the nitty gritty work that could lead him into trouble. Yet gatherings of the Morellos in Manhattan could comfortably be called in one location.

Small-scale meetings occurred in Sicily "on a restricted basis" as well, in order to discipline members, to share out loot, and to organize crimes.[111] Commensurately to the Morellos in New York, the number of men in a Sicilian *cosca* was "never very large," allowing direct contact between members at every rank. Bosses were not insulated from the consequences of their actions. A typical Sicilian group would usually number up to 10 men in the 19th century.[112]

Following Cascioferro's discharge in the Hackensack affair, he was found at both the 8 Prince Street restaurant which Morello and Lupo visited, and at 226 Elizabeth Street (Inzerillo's establishment). A particular meeting was observed by the Secret Service, held at the rear of Prince Street in March 1903, attended by Cascioferro and "practically all of the Morello gang"[113] of "not less than ten men." About 25 Morellos and Terranovas also attended a meeting in early 1912 on Lewis Street "in regard to separating from the Brooklyn gang, which latter is controlled by Sebastiano diGitano."[114]

In large part because his organization was no giant in local organized crime, and security was lax, "boss of bosses" Morello was only one step removed from his rank and file, creating an obvious risk of exposure of the leadership to prosecution, if the organization began to collapse. Antonio Comito, at the trial of the counterfeiters, related how in February 1909, he met Morello at the offices of the Ignatz Florio Co-Operative to get the correct shade of ink to make $2 bills. Morello criticized Cecala for bringing them there, since "there is a lot of detectives (sic) after him." Two of Morello's men had been arrested two nights previously.

Morello arranged for the matter to be corrected through Antonio Milone, who made the plates.[115] Comito, with whom the Morellos had not worked before, also witnessed the entire group together in New York in early March 1909. This was the venue used by Lupo to criticize Comito for the poor quality of his workmanship.[116] Drawing upon a memory of these events, Comito was able to give devastating eyewitness testimony against the Morello bosses.

MORELLO-TERRANOVA ORGANIZATION

Those related to Morello by biology or marriage were the driving force in the group. A number of incorrect beliefs surround the early lives of the Morello and Terranova males. As Hunt observed, Peter and Giuseppe Morello were one and the same.[117] Assertions made by Pasley, Selvaggi and Chandler about the Morello-Terranova clan also failed to withstand scrutiny.[118]

Chart 3.1 shows selective relationships within the Morello, Terranova and Catania families. Only males linked to organized crime are included; daughters "played no significant role in the family's criminal life."[119]

The major members of the Morello and Terranova families, without Joseph Morello, arrived on March 8, 1893 on the steamship Alsatia. Among them was Bernardo Terranova, his wife Angela Piazza, Maria Rosa Marvalesi, wife of Morello, Maria Morello (Morello's sister), and the 4 children of the Terranovas: Ciro, Vincent, Nicolo and Rosalia.[120] Bernardo Terranova was a member of the Corleone *cosca*, known as the "Fratuzzi" ("Brothers"), and had attended a meeting of the group at which peasant movement leader Bernard Verro was initiated in 1893.[121]

Terranova had married Angelina Piazza, the mother of Joseph Morello and the Terranova boys. Calogero "Carlo" Morello married Piazza on February 11, 1866. When Calogero died in 1872, Piazza married Bernardo Terranova in Corleone a year later.[122] Calogero "Charles" Morello, probably born November 1892 in Corleone, was the offspring of the short union of Joseph Morello to Rosa Marvalisi.[123]

Marvalisi died in 1898. Joseph Morello re-married in the early 1900s to Nicolina "Lena" Morello (1884–1967), who stuck by him until the end.[124] She initially stayed in New York City with Gioacchino Lima, husband of Marie Morello. Born 1870 in Corleone, Gioacchino lived with his wife for a time next to the offices of the Ignatz Florio Co-Operative in the Bronx.[125]

Ciro Terranova was born July 1888 in Corleone, Vincenzo Terranova in May 1886.[126] The daughter of Giacomo Reina, Bernarda "Biaggia" Reina, married Vincenzo in July of 1913. Giacomo, as did Angelo Gagliano (Chapter 4), testified for Morello at his 1910 trial, Reina stating that he had known Morello in Corleone and in New York.[127]

The Lupos became related to the Terranovas, therefore to the Morellos, when Ignazio Lupo married Salvatrice Terranova on December 23, 1903, at St. Lucy's Catholic church in Manhattan. Giuseppe Morello and Nicolina Salemi witnessed the ceremony.[128]

The Terranovas were connected by marriage to Bronx racketeer Giuseppe "Joe the Baker" Catania, a prominent Mafia identity in the late 1920s. It came about when Ciro Terranova married Teresina "Tessie" Catania in April 1909 in New York City.[129] Catania's brother Antonio, a baker, was born 1873 in Palermo. He originally lived in East Harlem with Frances LaScala, and with their sons Giuseppe (born 1902), and James "Jimmy the Baker" Catania.[130]

The Morello-Terranova family was linked to Louisiana Mafia identity Santo "Joseph" Calamia. Calamia was born 1875 in Gibellina, Sicily. In

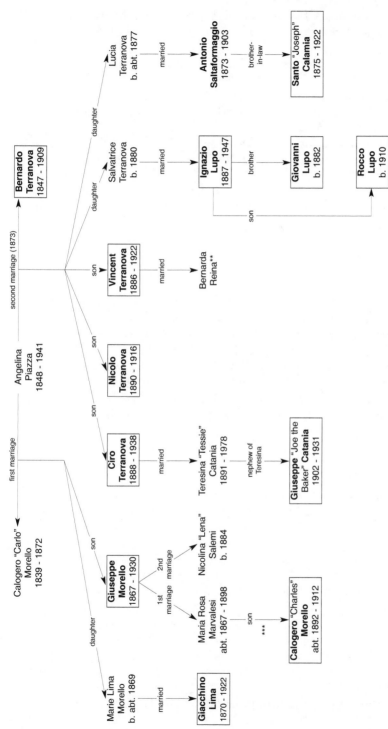

Chart 3.1 Morello-Terranova family tree.

* Only major relationships shown

** Father Giacomo Reina testified for the defence in the Morello counterfeiting case in 1910.

*** May be second son

Crime figures boxed

1901, Calamia married Teresina "Tessie" Saltamaggio, the sister of Antonio Saltamaggio[131] who had wed Lucia Terranova, a sister of the Terranova brothers, in 1894.[132]

Saltamaggio was found murdered in 1903 (below). In December 1904, Lena Morello's brother, Vincenzo Salemi, married Saltamaggio's widow. Vincenzo was shot to death on June 19, 1923 on Third Avenue, New York, by "two gangsters, who escaped before the passing crowd saw them plainly enough to give the police descriptions."[133]

Ciro Terranova testified in 1910 that when he and his family decamped to Louisiana in the mid 1890s to join Joseph Morello, they knew a "cousin" who got Morello and Ciro's father Bernardo work planting sugar cane.[134] The cousin was likely as not Saltamaggio, who indeed operated as a labor agent for Italians wanting work on cotton plantations.

OTHER RELATIONSHIPS

Complexity marked the relationship between members of the Family in New York City. Intersecting with a core group of kinsmen surrounding Morello, such as Lupo, was those from Corleone who were trusted by the bosses. "Italians from Corleone, Sicily," said Flynn, "were the only Italians who were trusted in these centers by the Morello-Lupo gang."[135]

A letter taken from Morello in 1909 named Ciro, Vincenzo and "Coco" Terranova, Gaetano Lomonte, Fortunato Lomonte, Stefano LaSala, Michele Coniglio (identified in the Vella conspiracy) and four others, who signed it "All of Corleone."[136] Gioacchino Lima also seems to have been included within the favored circle because of his close relationship to Morello and his former life in Corleone. Lima jointly ran with the Lomontes a saloon at 237 East 107th Street.[137]

A secondary category of membership was less connected to the Morello-Terranova leadership, consisting of individuals from other parts of Sicily and occasionally from southern Italy. In many cases, a "vouching" system was utilized on this type of member. Writing about Calogero Costantino living in Louisiana, for example, Morello was relieved to know that he came from a "good family." However, "We of Corleone have never had any dealings with them," so others must "assume the responsibility of said individual."[138]

A Secret Service source in 1912 likewise stated that within the New York City Mafia "when a new member is proposed for any one of the four gangs, it is always brought up before the four gangs."[139] The need for the leadership to be able to have confidence in those they worked with was a constant imperative.

Those identified with different phases of the Morello operations were:

Ignatz Florio Co-Operative of Corleone (1902)

Name	*Place of birth*
Marco Macaluso	Corleone
Antonio Milone	Corleone
Giuseppe Morello	Corleone

Morello counterfeiting combine/Barrel murder case (ca. 1903)

Vito Cascioferro	Bisaquino base
Joseph DePriema	Lercara
Pietro Inzerillo	Sperra Cavallo
Vito LaDuca	Carini
Giovanni Zarcone	Bagheria (parents)

Morello's New Orleans contacts (ca. 1909–1920)

Santo Calamia	Gibellina
Francesco Genova	"Palermo"
Calogero Gullotta	Sambuca
Vincenzo Moreci	Termini Imerese
Ben/John Piro	Monreale
Leoluca Trombatore	Corleone

Counterfeiting (1908–9)

Giuseppe Callichio	Poulia, Campagna
Antonio Cecala	Corleone
Salvatore Cina	"Palermo"
Antonio Comito	Catanzaro, Calabria
Vincenzo Giglio	Santo Stefano Quisquina
Ignazio Lupo	Palermo
"Michele the Calabrian"	Calabria
Giuseppe Palermo	Partanna
Nicolo Sylvester	Furmia

Petrosino homicide (1909)

Calogero Costantino	Partinico
Pasquale Enea	Palermo
Giuseppe Fontana	Villabate
Ignazio Milone	Corleone
Giovanni Pecoraro	Piana Dei Greci

In fact, the majority of those aligned with Morello in New York and Louisiana were not from Corleone, nor were they related to the New York leadership. These individuals would have probably have undergone the "vouching" system, if they did not have their own power base that made it irrelevant.

To be successful, counterfeiting required a high degree of expertise that implied a partial discarding of traditional distinctions separating Sicilians and mainland Italians since qualified men able and willing to fill the dangerous role of notes-maker were in short supply. Morello's New York organization held though to a convention of dealing when available with Sicilian born *paesani*. Only where the technical expertise of non-Sicilians was required, were they brought in.

THE WIDER MORELLO NETWORK

A total of 27 individuals were identified as components in the Morello sphere of influence. Excluding those Corleonesi who set up the Ignatz Florio Co-Operative focusing on immigrants from Corleone, only 4 others from this batch were from Corleone. This fell to 1 in New Orleans (Trombatore) and to none of the 4 associated with Morello in the 1903 "Barrel" case.

Disregarding a Chicago contact, Rosario Dispenza,[140] Morello's interstate network of Mafiosi was apparently limited to several figures living in Louisiana.

Morello's Louisiana contacts were revealed through two means. When Morello's house was searched during the 1909 raids, "Seven black hand (sic) letters" were seized, either "written by Morello to New Orleans merchants,"[141] or penned by blackmailers and passed to Morello for resolution.[142] Added to this material was a list of visitors to Morello, and persons to whom Morello wrote while he was serving time in Atlanta Penitentiary.

Morello's handful of New Orleans connections were prone to infighting and fragmentation. Neither did they seem to be significant players in local or regional organized crime. Those associated in New Orleans with Morello were:

SANTO "JOSEPH" CALAMIA

Morello received prison visits from Santo Calamia in 1917, 1918, 1919 and 1920. Calamia was married to Morello's half-sister Lucia Terranova. A settling of scores scarred Calamia's first years in New Orleans.

The turmoil initially involved the brothers Antonio and Salvatore Luciano, Francesco Genova (below) and Charles DiChristina.[143] Problems erupted in 1902, when DiChristina persuaded Antonio Luciano to invest in a Donaldsonville pasta factory.

The partners fell out over the profits, and the Lucianos came into conflict with the others over the supplying of pastas to stores, with Genova accused of taking trade from the Lucianos. The dispute ultimately caused the wounding, in May 1902, of Calamia, Joseph Geraci, DiChristina and Genova, and the shooting dead in June that year of Salvatore Luciano and two others, including Vincent Vutera, a cousin of the Lucianos.[144] Calamia and Genova were charged with the Luciano and Vutera murders but were acquitted.

Calamia died in 1922 in Sicily after returning to arrange a tomb for the burial of his father. It was not before the *vendetta* claimed the life of

Figure 3.8 Santo "Joseph" Calamia. (Courtesy of the U.S. National Archives)

his brother-in-law Antonio Saltamaggio, whose body was found knifed and strangled in April 1903 in a plantation canal near Whitecastle, Louisiana.[145]

VITO DIGIORGIO

Vito DiGiorgio, mentioned by Gentile as a *capo* in Los Angeles around 1920, had begun his American sojourn in New Orleans. In November 1909, Morello sent Vincenzo Moreci correspondence ending with his "cordial greetings" to "the friend Zito, Piro, Sunsseri, Benanti and their families as also Vito Di Giorgi."[146] While incarcerated in Atlanta, Morello wrote two letters to "Vito DiGiorgio" (June 24, 1917, January 25, 1920) described by Morello as a "friend" or as "a cousin."[147]

When and where DiGiorgio was born is something of a mystery.[148] But after setting foot in New York, he made his way to New Orleans. The story resumed when Joseph Serio's store was bombed in June 1908, causing $500 of damage. Serio had received several letters demanding $1,000 believed penned by Joseph Caronia, an alias used by DiGiorgio.[149] The case against DiGiorgio was dropped.

DiGiorgio and a companion, Jake Gilardo, were fired on in May 1916, supposedly by Angelo DePeche, in the yard of DiGiorgio's saloon and grocery store. The reason for the attack was not discerned, and DePeche's trial for Gilardo's murder was abandoned.[150]

DiGiorgio appears to have relocated to Los Angeles in 1920 or 1921, the family renting a house in the City of Angels. He was shot in 1921 as he was about to enter his East 21st Street home, sustaining three wounds. The attack may have been the continuation of a quarrel spilling over from New Orleans, cumulating in the finding of two bodies in front of the New Orleans home of Leonardo Cipolla.[151]

After the second attempt on his life, DiGiorgio returned to New Orleans but traveled to other cities on business. On May 13, 1922, DiGiorgio and a companion, James Cascio, were felled in a Chicago barbershop and pool-room.[152] The reason for the murders was as murky as DiGiorgio's life in the Mafia had been.

FRANCESCO GENOVA

Antonio Genova, arrested in the 1903 "Barrel" affair, was apparently a brother of Francesco Genova.[153] Like Paolo Marchese, Francesco Genova had a business relationship to Morello. "F. Genova" wrote to Morello from New Orleans, bringing up the subject of Marchese and the "house of Lupo."

Kendall writes that Francesco Genova, under his real name of Francesco Matesi, was born in Sicily in the 1860s. In Kendall's narrative, Matesi was a Mafia leader and municipal politician in Palermo before being charged for his Mafia activities and indicted for a killing in Trapani. Convicted in his absence in both jurisdictions, he made his way to New Orleans, where he assumed the Genova alias.

Matesi/Genova became the "Chief Mafioso" in New Orleans, where he hooked up with the Charles DiChristina figuring in the story of Paolo Marchese, and who built the macaroni factory in Donaldsonville with the Lucianos.[154] Genova operated an Italian paste shop, before coming under suspicion in the 1907 Lamana kidnapping case, causing the "better class" of Italians to "turn their backs on him." "The last ever heard of him," Kendall conveyed, "was about 1910, when he was in London."[155]

CALOGERO GULOTTA

When Morello was arrested in 1900, a letter was found on him from Calogero Gulotta.[156] Gulotta was also mentioned in the cited mail of November 1909, in which Gulotta and Morello made an unspecified "agreement."[157] Whilst in the penitentiary, Morello wrote to his "cousin" Gulotta once, in October 1919.

Upon arriving in New York in 1899, Gulotta went to New Orleans, where he died in 1932, aged 82.[158] Gulotta was the father of Pietro Gulotta who under the name of Pete Herman became bantamweight-boxing champion of the world. His other son, Gaspare, was a French Quarter Mafioso, involved with the Carlos Marcello syndicate.[159]

FRANCESCO PAOLO MARCHESE

In mid 1902, Marchese, then resident in New Orleans, testified for Cala-mia's defense when Calamia was charged with the deaths of Luciano and Vutera, stating that he had known Calamia since he was born.[160] Perhaps to escape the bloodshed in New Orleans, Marchese shortly moved to New York.

Letters found in Morello's rooms in 1903, during the "Barrel" searches, included one addressed to Morello from Francesco Genova, recommending Marchese, "a young man just come from Italy," who had fled from a 30 years jail sentence in Palermo and now needed help. Marchese had joined Lupo in New York.

Genova guaranteed his character: "I can tell you that he is a good young man, and on account of his youth is in need of help." At the Madonia inquest, Morello admitted that Marchese worked for him tending bar at 8 Prince Street, [161] confirming information held by the Secret Service.[162]

Leaving New York in 1903, Marchese returned to New Orleans to become Paolo DiChristina.[163] It was under the DiChristina name, and as the head of the local Mafia according to Kendall, that Marchese was shot to death on April 14, 1910, as he was entering the doorway of his grocery and saloon.

Pietro Pepitone confessed to committing the crime, claiming that DiChristina not only owed him rent, but had assaulted Pepitone when he went to collect it.[164] Mrs. Michael Pepitone stated that two days before the shooting, Marchese was in Pepitone's store and threatened Pepitone with the warning: "You took your house away, now I will take your life." Pepitone was found guilty of the manslaughter in the Criminal District Court.[165]

VINCENZO MORECI

Flynn referenced a letter addressed to Vincenzo Moreci from Morello, in which Morello refers to a reorganization of the Louisiana family, ending with "cordial greetings . . . to Vito DiGiorgi," and to others.[166] Moreci was a native of Termini, born around 1856.[167]

Moreci appears to have been in close contact with the Matrangas, prom-inent in the circumstances ending in mass lynchings in 1891.[168] According to Kendall, Moreci was later part of a "Mafia" faction in opposition to the Giaconas, the Pepitones and DiMartini.[169] Moreci was reputed to have fought the Black Hand, and was a member of several Italian societies while being a friend of the Giaconas,[170] identified in years to come as among the New Orleans Mafia elite.

Moreci was badly wounded in March 1910 "by an assassin who contrived to make his escape without being recognized." He professed ignorance of the identity of his assailant.[171] Moreci was arrested in 1910 for the killing of

George DiMartini, a follower of Genova and the deceased Paolo DiChristina[172] and perished by gunfire on November 19, 1915, on his way back home from the docks.

LEOLUCA TROMBATORE

Born March of 1888 in Corleone, Trombatore lived in New Orleans for 58 years, first arriving in New York in November 1907.[173] Morello wrote to his "nephew" Trombatore 4 times, in 1919 and 1920.[174]

An FBI report stated that Leoluca "Mr. Luke" Trombatore was the New Orleans Mafia boss during the 1940s until his death in 1963.[175] That belief connected to Chandler's that a "Leoluca T." was the "obscure" head of the local *Famiglia*.[176] Trombatore died in January 1963.

IN PERSPECTIVE

The New Orleans group tied to the Morellos in New York were conflict-ridden, loosely intertwined, and appeared to have little in common when assessed by their place of birth or the ventures they individually pursued in New Orleans. In 1909, matters came to a head. Morello advised Moreci that he supported a "reorganization" of "the family . . . because it seems it is not just to stay without a king nor country."[177] No doubt because of the chronic disunity evident in the faction and the attrition by murder of the local membership that went with it, the Corleonesi were a spent force in the New Orleans Mafia by the 1920s. Only Trombatore rose to a position of power that lasted more than a few years, and his alleged leadership role in New Orleans is unconfirmed.

By virtue of their small numbers and disintegrating tendencies, the city-wide impact of Morello's allies in New Orleans was negligible. The "big" names in New Orleans' crime subsequently included those from elsewhere in Italy. Among them was Carlos Marcello, who forged a partnership in the 1940s with New Yorker's Frank Costello, Philip Kastel and the Lanskys.[178] Haller's list of leading bootleggers in the 1920s also omitted Morello's confederates in New Orleans.[179]

Morello's prestige in the Mafia was insufficient to prevent the warfare in Louisiana, or the murder of Rosario Dispenza in Chicago. Morello's role as "boss of bosses" was that of arbitrator and advisor, the polar opposite of depictions of the man in question as having despotic powers who as a consequence could force a settlement on his affiliates who were in conflict.

THE IMPACT OF SICILY

The broader issue arising is to whether Mafias in New York were but subdivisions of a centralized command system based in Sicily. Two perspectives have developed, the conclusions drawn in part depending on how a Sicilian "effect" in New York City was measured. Kefauver[180] and the Federal Narcotics Bureau[181] referred for instance to organizational forms that Sicilian Mafiosi were reputed to have introduced to America, after Italian government crackdowns forced large numbers of Mafia members to migrate to the New World.[182]

Controversy rages around this subject because of the difficulty in accessing a sufficient amount of reliable data. Though current theory gives greater weight to "American" factors in determining U.S. Mafia structure and activities, Sicilian features were predominant in shaping forms of governance and internal practices in New York City's Families.

Echoing the majority opinion, Cressey argued, "Whatever was imported has been modified to fit the conditions of American life,"[183] matching Albini's view that Italian-American syndicates developed "within the American social structure," and adapted according to "the American model."[184] Since the Sicilian Mafia was "an outgrowth of the particular form that the process of state-formation took in Italy,"[185] it followed that it could not be transplanted onto U.S. soil. It was admitted that Sicilian newcomers could bring cultural attitudes with them, however, with "ethnic cohesion and group loyalty" being paramount, generating and maintaining organized crime.[186]

Facing this viewpoint was an older perspective. It argued that conditions exclusive to Sicily and southern Italy caused an upsurge of the Black Hand and other forms of immigrant crime in America. The solution through policymaking was the imposition of tougher immigration controls, and greater cooperation between the two governments to eradicate the difficulty at its source.[187]

Whether the socio-political differences between rural western Sicily and big-city East Coast America were as irreconcilable as was assumed has been questioned. Dickie persuasively argued that many Sicilians in New York "had no illusions about what it took to get on in politics and business." Furthermore, "Neither Sicilian politics, nor the island's sophisticated violence industry, had much antiquated about it."[188]

Features of the local political economy in New York created a role for Mafiosi reflective of that in Sicily, though not on anything like the same scale. Within Italian colonies, immigrants frequently "turned to fellow villagers already established in the ports for essential economic and social services, and for psychological support."[189] And when disputes arose, men of respect in New York City could be counted on to perform a comparable role to that seen in Sicily, as a mediator with "a thousand friendships."[190]

SICILIAN MAFIA STRUCTURE

The form of the Morello organization in New York City strongly resembled what is known about Sicilian *cosche*. The centrality of kin when structuring *borgata* in Sicily and the first Families in New York City[191] was a case in point. "Mafia adherence," it was reported, "was generally considered to be heredity. It was virtually a birthright of the sons of a Mafioso."[192]

According to Blok, a Sicilian *cosche* is best understood as a series of connections involving sets of brothers. They were the hub of networks that included "other mafiosi, kinsmen, friends, and many others."[193] "The core of the cosca," Hess repeated, "consists often of brothers, brothers-in-law, or a father and his sons,"[194] a characteristic mentioned by Fentress.[195]

They tended to set policy.[196] The institutions of *comparatico* and *compare* (godparenthood) augmented that of kin. Beyond kin and godparents, the *cosca* worked with a large number of "associates."[197]

NEW YORK CITY ORGANIZATION

Commenting on the American situation, Cressey asserted, "The early Sicilian Mafia groups were kin groups, with a hierarchy of authority relevant only to family affairs."[198] Angelo DeCarlo, a veteran New Jersey member, recalled, "Before it was all relationships–it was through relations–cousins. That's the way it started in Italy . . . You had it for your son to get in, brother, son-in-law. You had to be in the family to get into it." In order to ensure quality control, recruitment was extremely selective. DeCarlo thought they might "make five maybe in every five years."[199]

Organizational "titles" such as *caporegime* used in New York mirrored those found in western Sicily, denoting equivalent power differentials.[200] U.S. Mafias also shared the same "democratic" ideals and practices, expressed in existence of an election system to choose a new boss.[201] But the voting process afforded a cloak of legitimacy to a deeply flawed system, in which the incumbent leadership was routinely re-elected.[202]

Letters taken from Morello in the 1900s suggested a set of arrangements within his Family that was understood and recognized widely. One translated note cryptically mentioned a "Council," which was "separated from the Assembly;" "Councilmen" could not apparently speak or vote at the Assembly.

Dr. Melchiorre Allegra in Sicily explained that from the time he was "made" in 1916, the Sicilian system he learned of consisted of "families" led by a "chief." Larger groups had a section head. The association he joined had "powerful ramifications" in, among other places, America.[203] Gentile stressed, "in Sicily and anywhere the Mafia operates, the structure is the same."[204]

Dual membership of an American and Sicilian Mafia organization was a result. A telegram or "letter of consent" preceded or followed the Sicilian member traveling in the United States. The letter was sent after the Sicilian member transmitted to his *capo* in Sicily a telegram indicating which American Family he wished to belong to. The letter of consent, written by the boss of the Sicilian Family, was accepted as "proof" by the Americans that the man was trustworthy enough to be admitted into their Family.[205] This system was reminiscent of the contents of items seized from Morello.

INITIATION PRACTICES

Considerable likenesses developed between Mafia ceremonies in Sicily and the United States. Gambetta detailed 13 Mafia rituals, 2 in America, before concluding that their outlines were identical.[206]

Valachi gave what has become accepted as the "classic" initiation ritual, in his case performed during the Castellammare War.[207] Inside a room with a "long table," Valachi remembered, "I was directed to sit next to Mr. Maranzano, and on the table there was a gun and a knife." "I repeated some words they told me . . . in Italian," amounting to the protocols of *Cosa Nostra*. A piece of paper was burned in Valachi's hands and more words in Italian were spoken. Bonanno was allegedly chosen as Valachi's "godfather" (denied by Bonanno) in a finger throwing exercise, and Bonanno pricked Valachi's finger. The assembly shook hands at the end of the session.[208]

Initiation ceremonies that approximated that undergone by Valachi were uncovered in Youngstown, Los Angeles, Pittsburgh, Boston, and within the Bonanno, Lucchese and Genovese (New York) organizations.[209] In Los Angeles, those present were reported as first joining hands then releasing them, a process repeated at the end at the command of the leader.[210]

Allegra noted a near identical Sicilian practice to the majority American one when he was initiated into the Pagliarelli (Palermo) Family.[211] The ritual deployed by the *Stoppaglieri* clan precisely followed this pattern.[212] It was also displayed in 1870s Palermo, among the Favara sect known as the *Fratellanza* ("Brotherhood").[213]

Bernardo Verro gave a glimpse into the workings of the Corleone *cosca* of which Morello was once a member. Verro told how, in 1893, he was admitted into the "*Fratuzzi.*" Verro's right hand thumb was pricked and the blood smeared on the image of a skull that was burned. Dickie continued, "In the light of the flames, Verro exchanged a fraternal kiss with each of the mafiosi in turn."[214]

The Catania, Sicily, ritual was indistinguishable to the one portrayed by Valachi, according to Mafia *pentito* Antonino Calderone. Nonetheless, Calderone noted the existence of variations from this norm, "according to local custom."[215]

Gentile showed the Russian journalist Leonid Kolosov "two ancient documents on yellowing parchment" in 1964. One was the "oath of loyalty" of what was labeled by Gentile as the "Brotherhood," identical in its form to the ritual undergone by Valachi, except that an image of a saint was replaced by a paper with "a drawing of a crossbones on it," like that observed in Corleone.[216]

Chicago's multi-ethnic "outfit," where non-Italians occupied leadership roles, fit most uneasily with the paradigm. In Chicago, no formal ceremony reputedly took place. A banquet was arranged, attended by the Italian components after which the man was pronounced part of the group. "After reaching their decision concerning the candidate, if he is accepted for membership, his sponsor is advised and the sponsor, in turn, advises the candidate that he is "in" or "made."[217]

With a handful of exceptions, Chicago gangster figures were unrelated to each other, and the Chicago syndicate's origins were to be found in Calabria and Naples. Its members were chiefly linked by business and neighborhood ties, not via kinship.[218]

RECOGNITION PASSWORDS

Contrary to Nelli's assumption that they belonged to a bygone era,[219] highly formalized ceremonies continued to be an effective mechanism to bind Italian-American syndicates together as a distinct force in organized crime. Passwords were originally used to identify other Mafiosi, often deployed in a conversation structured on a fictional sore tooth. Reference to a toothache by the speaker triggered words from the listener that enabled members to identify one another.

"Recognition passwords in the form of a special dialogue" were noted within the Sicilian *Fratellanza*, *Stoppaglieri,* "and the other contemporary sects."[220] The use in western Sicily of "recognition code words" had faded by the 1920s,[221] to be replaced—in both Sicily and the United States—with a "third party" method of introduction.[222]

In 1962, Lou Larasso, a member of the Elizabeth (New Jersey) Family, was overheard in conversation. Someone recalled how "when two fellows would meet and they wanted to introduce themselves, one would say (there followed a phrase in Italian)." Verbal exchanges between members consisting of jargon were known as "pig language." Since then, things had changed: "with us you can't introduce yourself."[223]

THE PETROSINO ASSASSINATION AND THE MAFIA

The Morellos in New York City followed the practice replicated in Sicily of initially recruiting from those who were kin and/or those with the right qualities from the same town or region in Sicily. In order to further discern the extent of Sicilian Mafia influence in the Morello's regime, its connections to the Petrosino murder are explored.

In Antonio Comito's unpublished manuscript, the New York Morellos' responsibility in the execution of Joseph Petrosino is clearer than in either William J. Flynn's book, or in the 1910 trial transcript.[224] Comito indicated that there was foreknowledge of the Petrosino slaying inside the Morello counterfeiting organization to which he belonged, and that they celebrated his death.[225]

Figure 3.9 Joseph Petrosino. (Courtesy of the U.S. Library of Congress)

After the Morellos heard that Petrosino had perished, Ignazio Lupo was alleged to have said to Antonio Cecala, "The way it was planned, it never could have missed in Palermo." Petrosino's murder could not have happened in New York because his security was tight. Lupo continued, "the money who carried you know who there to do the 'job' was money from New York." "Some credit is due us though the Palermo gathering will get most."[226]

Detective Lieutenant Petrosino, head of the New York Police Department's "Italian Squad," left for Italy on February 9, 1909, arriving in Palermo almost three weeks later. The specifics of his journey were leaked to the press (the Italian-language media reported his trip and objectives on February 5) and Petrosino was felled by 4 shots into his back on March 12, at the base of the statue of Garibaldi in the Piazza Marina. Passers-by were attracted to the scene by the sound of the shots.[227]

Petrosino had carried a list of 300 Italian criminals in America. All had been convicted in Italy, but had broken their terms of parole by leaving the country. Petrosino was arranging their return to Italy for violation of parole and for entering American territory illegally.[228] Information passed to Petrosino in Italy could, in addition, be used to locate and remove Italians who had fled the jurisdiction of the Italian state before serving their correct terms of imprisonment.[229]

Petrosino's activities made life difficult for Italian criminals in New York. In addition, Petrosino uniquely symbolized the fight against the Mafia and Black Hand. Petacco observed, "he arrested them whenever possible, he harassed their friends and customers, until the criminals finally found themselves completely cut off and so shifted their operations to more tolerant regions."[230] These were reasons enough for the Morellos to want him dead, particularly given the kudos in Mafia circles everywhere that an involvement in Petrosino's murder would win for the perpetrators.

Because of the consequences of the Petrosino homicide for U.S.-Italian relations, the murder investigation launched by Palermo Police Commissioner Baldassare Ceola was closely followed in Rome; the Italian Prime Minister "personally interested himself" in the case.[231]

Sicilian police reports revealed the involvement in the execution of individuals having Sicilian and New York City Mafia credentials. The New Yorkers implicated were named as Morello, Lupo, the two Terranova brothers and Pietro Inzerillo.

Those initially named on the Sicilian side as suspects were:

Pasquale Enea
Giovanni Battista Finazzo[232]
Giuseppe Fontana
Gioacchino Lima
Ignazio Milone
Giovanni Pecoraro

Barring Finazzo, about whom little is known, each of these identified had strong ties to Sicilian Mafia groups as well as to the Morello network. Pasquale Enea, born 1869 at Palermo, first arrived in New York in 1901. Enea, who "must have known who killed Petrosino," was the one time owner of a grocery shop at 66 Oliver Street, New York, that "was a meeting place for Italian blackmailers and thieves." (G. Battista Ruisi, another linked to the Petrosino case, was headed there when he disembarked in New York in February 1906.) Enea's lover, Concetta Salomone, returned to Sicily amply provided for, "clearly the fruits of crimes committed by Enea and his accomplices."[233]

Alleged to be part of the Villabate Mafia, Giuseppe Fontana's activities were notorious. Born October 1852 in Villabate, from 1872 to 1897, Fontana was arrested six times for crimes ranging from homicide to Mafia association and counterfeiting. The city of Palermo's police chief considered Fontana "a dangerous criminal, a most suspicious character." "Many and grave are the offences alleged to have been committed by him, but of which the proofs were always lacking."[234] Fontana's most infamous deed was an unproven involvement in the knifing death of Emmanuele Notarbartolo in 1893.[235]

Fontana left for New York upon being freed in the case.[236] In New York, he ran a grocery store on East 106th Street,[237] and owned with

Figure 3.10   Joseph Fontana. (Courtesy of the Queens Borough Public Library)

Ignazio Milone a "beer-hall of the very worst type," frequented by the criminal class.[238] Fontana returned to Italy when Petrosino began delving into his American affairs, but it was in New York City where he was shot to death in 1913 (Chapter 4).

Portrayed by the Sicilian police as a "Black Hand leader and brother in law of Morello," Gioacchino Lima, married to Morello's wife's sister, had been a cart-driver in Corleone. Lima vanished from Corleone in 1892 when an arrest warrant was issued for him for the death of Antonino Dimiceli.[239]

Giovanni Pecoraro, born 1867 in Piana Dei Greci, was acquitted in 1898 of embezzlement while operating as a broker living in Sancipirrello. In April 1901, he was arrested and acquitted for the murder of Santo Calanna. The police superintendent of San Giuseppe Iato wrote that Pecoraro was a Mafioso sending "threatening letters to important people in the community and if they do not reply, they threaten reprisals."[240]

Pecoraro, like Lupo, went to America to escape an arrest warrant. Cascioferro met Pecoraro when they lived in New York,[241] and in 1903, Pecoraro was momentarily mistaken for Tommaso Petto as part of the "Barrel" investigation.[242] Along with several confederates, Pecoraro was arrested in February 1908 as a bomb-throwing suspect.[243] Comito and Cecala, the

Figure 3.11   Giovanni Pecoraro. (Courtesy of the U.S. National Archives)

Morello forgers, met Pecoraro as a wine merchant on East 39th Street in early 1909, Pecoraro seeming to know the background to the visit, and he saw them on the train back to Highlands.[244]

Pecoraro was mowed down in March 1923, the police assumed in a "bootleggers' feud." Philip Mangano, brother of Vincent Mangano (Chapter 7) was charged in the case.[245]

Commissioner Ceola narrowed down the list of suspects in the Petrosino matter to three, headed by Vito Cascioferro, the former Hackensack arrestee and Morello confidant in New York, Calogero Costantino and Antonino Passananti of Partinico.[246] Cascioferro had an alibi for the entire period from March 6–14 when Petrosino as assassinated, by occupying the Burgio house of his political patron, De Michele Ferrantelli.[247] New York related items were seized in his house, among them correspondence written while he was in Brooklyn inviting Morello, Costantino and two others to eat at the home of Salvatore Brancaccio.[248]

Costantino, born 1874 in Partinico, had voyaged to New York in June 1905.[249] Costantino and Passananti, "cautious in their journey" back to Italy, were observed together in Palermo's Martina Square and used assumed names.[250]

They had returned to Sicily on February 26, and Costantino gave contradictory accounts to the police. Their reason for returning to Sicily was considered flimsy, and an enigmatic telegram sent by Costantino to Morello cast more doubt on his story. Passananti also disappeared from Partinico on the day Petrosino perished.[251]

Unreported by the New York press, the case was effectively closed when the Sicilian Court of Appeals in July 1911 released Cascioferro, Costantino and Passananti, because of insufficient evidence to send them to trial.[252] Those linked to Petrosino's death indicated the reality of Sicilian Mafia involvement in New York City. The presence of individuals aligned with Sicily showed the ease with which the trans-Atlantic transfer process operated, and the compatibility of organizations in New York with those in Sicily.

1908–1909 NEW YORK COUNTERFEITERS

Less is known of the backgrounds of those involved in the Morello counterfeiting enterprises in New York, though the majority of those identified with the second Morello counterfeiting initiative (1908–9) were involved in criminal activity in Sicily (accounting for 6 from 7 in the sample). A similar number were also participants in crime in New York prior to their joining Morello and Lupo in the city.

In New York, Cecala was in the grocery business with Morello on Mott Street until it was made bankrupt. Cecala then opened gambling houses on Mott and Elizabeth Streets, which closed after he stopped "feeding" the police.[253] Cecala next led a band of arsonists who set fire to houses and stores with the connivance of the owners for insurance money.[254]

Salvatore Cina confided to Comito that he had been with "Vassolona," a bandit in Bivona, Sicily,[255] and was caught up in the death of a teacher in Bivona, compelling Cina to flee Sicily and to make his way to New York[256] His first years in America were spent in Tampa, Florida, with his brother-in-law Giglio, where they learned how to make cigars. They remained there until returning in about 1906 to New York because of Cina's health problems.[257] Cina was Calicchio's godfather.

Vincenzo Giglio was born in Santo Stefano Quisquina, Sicily, and arrived in New York in 1895, traveling to Tampa with Cina.[258] Giglio returned with Cina to New York, where they bought a farm in Highland, sold on to Joseph Palermo in 1909.[259] Giglio told Comito that he was never arrested, although he stole a horse and carriage in Newburg. "Shots were fired at him but they missed."[260]

Joseph Palermo went under the name of Salvatore Saracina.[261] Palermo, born in 1862 in Partanna, Sicily, was wanted in Italy as a fugitive from justice upon being sentenced to 31 years imprisonment for a double homicide and kidnapping. Operating as Saracina, Palermo shared a directorship in the Co-Operative Society of Sicily, established in Elizabeth Street, Manhattan, to promote and encourage co-operative business endeavors, and to "act as agent and broker of any person, company firm or corporation."[262] Palermo was said to have absconded in 1907 with funds deposited in his Upper East Side bank.[263] It was Palermo who was said to have owned the Black Hand rulebook referred to in Chapter 2.

Giuseppe Calicchio confessed to Comito that in Italy, he had printed forgeries for "aristocratic families there who were in 'Hard Luck.'"[264] Nicholas Sylvester was jailed as a minor for 5 years, for "striking people down in dark places and taking all they had." Sylvester was also convicted of carrying concealed weapons. He told Comito that he had first met one of the Terranovas while he was in jail, where they became friends. They drifted into the Black Hand, working with Morello's son "and his brother." It led to an arrest.[265]

In his hometown, the Sicilian "Uncle Vincent" (not further identified) had been accused of killing two men. He told Comito about a mysterious society be belonged to with global tentacles. It was not a mutual assistance organization and had no name but was present "in all parts of the world except Japan."

Perplexingly, given the "Sicilian" bias in the New York Mafia, he was open about its existence with the Calabrian Comito, and even offered Comito the prospect of joining if he proved himself by performing a "courageous deed." Then Comito would be "christened." Vincent claimed that all of Comito's counterfeiting cohorts were members.[266]

Rarely did the rank and file know the identity of the society leaders, according to Uncle Vincent, a strange observation given the Mafia's proclivity for recruiting from the nearest male kin. Vincent's description of a conspiracy, "stronger than countries and police," could have been invented to draw Comito closer into the group, since Comito later claimed that he was there under duress.

In reality, the Morello elite lived only one step from penury and Vincent Terranova was observed doing his rounds as an iceman. The likelihood exists that Vincent was attempting to impress Comito with fanciful but empty tales of the power he would gain once he was "baptized" into the worldwide society. The story was conveyed also to let Comito know of the grave danger he would be in if he betrayed his co-workers.

SUBSEQUENT RELATIONS WITH SICILY

As part of the post-Castellammare War settlement, around 1931, a "subsidiary agreement" mandated that "membership in the Sicilian Mafia was no longer a sufficient qualification for membership in the American organization."[267] The idea was to stop American Families growing uncontrollably in size. A second reason for stopping recruitment from Sicily was probable disquiet over the discord that Sicilian imports brought, especially ones with ambition like Joseph Masseria and Salvatore Maranzano.

"The significance of the year 1930, as the point at which self-governing rights were reportedly granted to the United States group," said the FBI, "could relate to the major internal warfare that prevailed within La Cosa Nostra, or the Mafia as it was then known, during that year."[268] This historical juncture represented the true "Americanization" of the New York City Mafia.[269] The ban extended to Canada,[270] and explained some of the complexities attending the 1980s "Pizza Connection" narcotics cases.[271]

CONCLU.3SION

The question as to whether American organizations were offshoots of a powerful Mafia command structure based in Palermo has taxed commentators. Ianni argued that the Mafia in Sicily "could not and did not originate as organizations to the United States."[272] He highlighted "cultural" attitudes brought over from Sicily to America in creating a Mafia supportive climate.[273] Yet the Black Hand, unconnected to U.S. Mafia organizations (Chapter 2), fitted the cultural model better, since it preyed on Italian immigrant's fears but typically had slight organizational backup.

Cultural and socio-economic factors could not clarify those organizational similarities identified between Mafia organizations in Sicily and America. Nor could those connections between New York and Sicilian Family heads denoted by Gentile and featured in the Morello correspondence be passed off as merely coincidental.

The mechanism that evolved to permit Sicilian members to access New York contacts accounted for the presence in New York of Sicilian figures of the standing of Vito CascioFerro, Nicolo Gentile, and Salvatore Maranzano. But transatlantic links were on a particularized basis; there was no evidence that the contacts between Sicily and America went further.[274] The one exception in this period seems to have been the joint planning that went into the Petrosino murder.

To be successfully implemented, it required an extraordinary unity of action by Mafias in Palermo and New York that was justified because of Petrosino's renown as the chief foe of the Italian underworld in New York. Hearing of Petrosino's demise, Uncle Vincent was supposed to have said, "No one will now dare to go to Palermo for in going they will find death."[275]

The next chapter follows chapter two in suggesting the limits of Mafia influence in a decade when territorial disorganization was rife. Several upcoming and established groups fought for dominance inside East Harlem. A sensational murder case from the period, furthermore, leads to a questioning of the received orthodoxy on the manner in which new blood was brought into the New York City Families. In addition, Chapter 4 highlights the significance of ethnicity as imposing a limit to the expansion of racketeering enterprises by men of honor in New York City.

4   The Mafia and the Baff Murder

INTRODUCTION

On the evening of November 24, 1914, West Washington Market live ("kosher") poultry dealer Barnet Baff answered a phone call at his place of business. Baff "was scarcely gone 75 feet when he was approached from behind by two men, each of whom fired a shot that pierced his back—one piercing his heart and he died almost instantly."[1] Having set up Baff, the assassins escaped in a waiting car.

What transpired from the official investigation of the Baff fatality was a glimpse into racketeering. Though missed in the literature on organized crime,[2] the case had implications for a history of the Mafia.

It seemed that the Baff assassination was meticulously planned. Occurring on the second day before Thanksgiving, the car carrying assassins in the Market would not attract suspicion, and the killers could run away through piles of crates. Baff was summoned from his stall by a telephone call related to thefts, which had concerned him. He perished on his way to meet the contact.[3] The murderers knew that the streets in the vicinity of the Market were quiet between 5pm and 6pm, when they struck.[4] Officials concluded, "It was the slickest get-a-way for as daring a piece of crime as New York has been treated in a lifetime."[5]

Mayor John Purroy Mitchel promised the citizens of New York that the Baff gunmen would be brought to justice. Since it was known that there were persistent problems of anti-competitive behavior in the poultry industry, Baff's fall was immediately blamed on business competitors. It demonstrated that "no merchant is safe who arouses the enmity of unscrupulous rivals."[6]

The *New York Times* similarly thundered: "The murder of Baff will not soon be forgotten, it is no ordinary case, and extraordinary efforts should be made to prevent such crimes in the future."[7] Police action was indeed vigorous and determined, eventually crossing over into claims of malpractice.

Baff's death took place when the Police Department was undergoing radical change following the election in 1914 of Mitchel on a reformist ticket. Mitchel "cut waste and introduced improved accounting practices designed to make it difficult for patronage and corruption to spread unchecked."[8] In

1915, 79 percent of those arrested were convicted, "the highest record of convictions ever obtained by the department."[9] After Arthur Woods was appointed as Police Commissioner, the detective branch was freed from political interference, reporting directly to Woods.[10]

Mitchel and Woods shared a belief in "professionalization" as the answer to issues of police conduct and effectiveness. Combined with this, however, was the continuation of a heavy-handed approach when dealing with less cooperative suspects. "Use of the nightstick and revolver," Johnson observed, "were encouraged, and brutality complaints by real or suspected criminals were ignored."[11]

NEW YORK CITY LIVE POULTRY MARKET

The first part of this chapter dwells on structural factors promoting corruption in industries such as poultry in which the Baff shooting occurred and that supplied the reason for the killing. Later explored are evolving recruitment patterns among New York City Mafia *borgata,* utilizing Baff case figures for illustrative purposes. The final part of this chapter is taken up with territorial questions affecting the ability of Families to stake a firm claim in the criminal underworld and to be able to recruit unhindered and without fear of betrayal.

The Baff case suggested that embedded malpractices caused by structural deficiencies in an industry could exist without any form of Italian-American racketeer participation. Despite its apparently favorable conditions for racketeers, Mafia involvement in the poultry market was puny. The predominant ethnic makeup of the industry in question was the key to understanding this apparent anomaly.

INDUSTRIAL CONTEXT

Lynch called the poultry racket one of the "oldest" in New York.[12] The New York Metropolitan area nationally consumed some 80 percent of the live poultry moved to market, 90 percent of it consumed by Jews, who also dominated the supply chain in the city.[13] During the 1930s, the live poultry trade in New York City was the largest in the world and those set in New York were the basis for national prices.[14]

Prosecutions alone could not remove abuses from the industry, when its very constitution furnished powerful and continuing incentives for participants to engage in illegal activities.[15] The sector was rife with unethical, when not illegal, practices that attracted "wily, scheming and in some cases dangerous" figures. Cutting corners was commonplace between poultry dealers, and joint agreements were abrogated if they proved inconvenient to one of the parties. The point was reached where it was difficult to make a profit without engaging in dishonesty.[16]

In April 1910, 87 kosher poultry dealers pleaded guilty to running a "Poultry Trust" or cartel. It was argued in mitigation that they were being persecuted for "practices that have been a customary part of their business."[17] The cartel cornered the market on the distribution of shipments of the live birds from the West, fixing the price so that its members could sell it at a guaranteed profit.

In 1911, thirteen poultry commission merchants doing business at the West Washington Market were convicted of plotting to restrain trade and establish a monopoly in the first case of its kind in New York County.[18] Baff had given important information and tip-offs to the District Attorney, drawing upon his experience as a former "insider" to the cartel's machinations.[19]

From about 1902, Barnet Baff entered the poultry business as a wholesaler. In 1910, he became a receiver but also operated slaughterhouses where the birds were ritually dispatched by "kosher killers" (*schochtim*). After Baff became one, "he stood in a different position" from other receivers, who sold live poultry to the slaughterhouses on commission as their sole means of livelihood. By means of the economies so achieved, Baff forced the key slaughterhouse men to "sue for terms of peace," by buying car lots of poultry from him at above quotation prices. Baff used identical economic leverage to force butchers to buy his surplus stock at a premium price. He also made his own deliveries, angering the trucking company and Teamsters Local 449 unionists.

Given that background, "Baff was cordially hated by everyone in the West Washington Market,"[20] a fact clear from the first to detectives investigating his demise,[21] and furnishing his competitors with a powerful reason to see Baff dead.[22] The timing of Baff's slaying was based on information that must have come from within the industry, for poultry merchants were about to lose large sums through his methods at Thanksgiving.[23]

Joseph "Big Joe" Cohen was the president or treasurer of the Live Poultry Dealers' Protective Association.[24] The aim was ostensibly the laudable one of eradicating an "overcropping" malpractice pursued by Baff, involving the starving of chickens for slaughter until they reached the city where they were fed a combination of sand and gravel that increased their weight but swindled unsuspecting customers.[25]

But Baff also stood in the way of a less publicized scheme to use the Association as a tool to create a monopoly.[26] During a 1913 strike or lockout involving slaughterhouse employers, for example, Baff pursued an independent line, making agreements with Teamsters local 449 and Live Poultry Workers' local 14542, guaranteeing that he alone would be spared industrial conflict.[27] A few weeks before Baff's murder, moreover, indictments were brought against 18 officers and members of Cohen's Association, for antitrust offences using threats of physical violence and refusing deliveries until retailers joined. "Any dealer who sought to buy from outside the trust could expect a beating or the wrecking of his shop."[28]

Although the Baff murder was an extreme case, corruption and the use of violence to achieve commercial objectives were thus no strangers to the industry, with Baff involved in misconduct almost as much as those who plotted his downfall. Demonstrating the apparent intractability of these problems was that even after Baff's perpetrators were jailed, malpractices remained endemic to the industry.

During May 1916, for instance, the State Commissioner of Foods and Markets heard complaints that the market was rigged. The firm of B. Baff and Sons was implicated in abuses including the "overcropping" racket. Witnesses also accused Harry Baff of manipulating the market.[29] In late 1916, the Harlem and Bronx Live Poultry Association was indicted for violations of anti-trust laws.[30] By 1917, Harry Baff was in dispute with some 6,000 independent poultry dealers over his defiance of a boycott on the West Washington Market, and by buying up almost all the available poultry in order to make exorbitant profits.[31]

Further charges of a cartel creation were made in 1920 before the Commissioner of Accounts; it "fixed prices and forced independent dealers to sell out under threats of assault and injury to credit."[32] Threats were made against smaller players if they refused to go along.[33] The live poultry business again came under the official spotlight in 1926, when the Attorney General began yet another inquiry into price fixing.[34]

Attempts to inject legally and ethically acceptable practices into the poultry business through self-regulation failed. In 1926, the Greater New York Live Poultry Chamber of Commerce was formed to improve working conditions. But in August 1928, a group of retailers applied for an injunction restraining the Chamber of Commerce and 2 Teamster unions from "continuing strong arm methods and restraining trade." Refusal to comply with the Chamber of Commerce and union demands resulted in attacks and damage.[35]

Seventy-one defendants were indicted for attempting to corner the market using boycotts, threats and violence.[36] Bombs, incendiary devices and gases were deployed against dealers, butchers and market men.[37] Sixty persons and the Chamber itself were convicted, and individuals sentenced for up to three months' imprisonment.[38]

POULTRY RACKETEERING

The fragmented and intensely competitive New York City live poultry sector stimulated the creation of cartels, for it could be extremely profitable if organized under monopoly conditions, arguably using a system enforced by gangsters. Racketeer prone fields tended to include those features, among others.[39]

Common denominators identified in industries that have historically attracted racketeering have included: the pre-existence of small business units serving local markets faced with intense competitive pressures squeezing profit margins, and negotiating with powerful (and occasionally corrupt) labor unions that could stymie their plans.[40]

According to Joselit, there were some "fifteen discrete steps in the preparation of poultry before it reached the consumer."[41] If any were blocked or disrupted, a chain-reaction would produce chaos and ultimate ruin for both producers and sellers. Racketeer leverage was greatest where professional criminals seized control over such bottlenecks to the production process, forcing those employers affected to concede to racketeering demands. Racketeers "exploited their strategic leverage to solicit bribes, extort pay-offs or obtain other criminal benefits."[42]

The poultry industry therefore appeared ripe for racketeer incursions. In addition, racketeers could positively contribute to employers' need for industrial peace, by injecting a greater measure of predictability (thus profitability) to the business, by moderating the demands made by unions under their influence and actively discouraging, largely by virtue of their intimidating reputation, competition from outsiders to the system. Crime syndicates "can use their network of relationships throughout the (affected) industry to reduce uncertainties and promote needed stability."[43]

A measure of organized crime involvement in the sector dated from the early 1910s. The inquiry into Baff's demise "revealed the extent to which businessmen . . . and gangsters conspired to control" the West Washington Market.[44] Friction between local 449 (West Side) and local 14542 (East Side) unfolded over their respective jurisdictions, the latter approaching Benjamin "Dopey" Fein to safeguard them against the Hudson Gophers gang backing the Teamsters local.[45] Jake Williams denied however that while chairman of local 14542, he offered $2,500 to Fein in order to get Fein's men to help it.[46] The overture made to Fein failed, allegedly because Fein was acquainted with the local 449-aligned Joseph Cohen, and Fein refused to harm Cohen's business.

Local 14542 had attempted to intimidate the slaughterhousemen to sign agreements with them, using the mob led by Jack "Big Jack" Sirocco,[47] a former Five Points gang member. But goons employed by local 449 repulsed Sirocco's men, and it was later decided that the Market 'belonged' to 449.[48]

Fein and Sirocco left the sector as quickly as they had arrived, for reasons that are unclear but that challenged the conventional view of gangster "infiltration" of an industry as often irreversible.

There was less need for professional racketeers to function as a stabilizing force in an industry characterized by overarching trade associations. Their discrete function, to steady or increase profit levels, made racketeering incursions less necessary or functional, though links to a pliable union were always desirable.

It was consequently not always the case that "it was easier to hire gangsters than it was to fire them."[49] The degree of organized crime "penetration" of an industry ranged from "ad hoc" or passing cooperation with a Dopey Fein and Jack Sirocco, through to the durability of later incursions.

ETHNICITY AND RACKETEERING

None of those identified as "poultry racketeers" either on the management or union sides were of Italian extraction or connected to Mafia

Families.[50]A reason lay in a feature that went beyond the mismatched industrial structure. In a perverse form of "ethnic succession," industrial racketeering largely fed off the movement of rank and file workers (and to a degree employers) of the same ethnicity as the racketeering perpetrators. This phenomenon in part explained the unpredictable level of Mafia infiltration into otherwise similarly susceptible markets.

Where an industry remained solidly "Jewish" in its workforce composition, the Mafia was generally absent. Aside from the appearance of Italian gunmen plotting the Baff murder in 1914, there were few recorded cases where Mafia figures became involved in the poultry market.[51] Industries like dock work (in Brooklyn),[52] garbage disposal,[53] and construction were obvious candidates for Mafia exploitation because of their use of large amounts of unskilled or semi-skilled Italian labor.

Under the rule of the Mangano Family, the casualized employment system in force on the Brooklyn waterfront proved to be an environment in which under-the-counter payoffs were customary.[54] Where Irish longshoremen were in the majority, on the West Side docks, racketeers were invariably Sons of Erin.

The Journeymen Barbers' International Union was a further case of this pattern. Overwhelmingly composed of southern Italians, Bonanno Family *consiglieri* Giovanni "John" Tartamella sat on the union's executive. Born 1892 in Castellammare del Golfo, Sicily, Tartamella devoted much of his time to the cause of the barbers. He was a prominent union organizer, first in Brooklyn and leading his local into the CIO following a breakdown of relations with the AFL.[55]

Praised at the 1943 national convention for his "persistence" and for his "dynamism," Tartamella espoused an articulate and informed view of the road the union might take.[56] Because of his radical views, in 1943 Tartamella was among a group expelled by the Italian-American Labor Council.[57] His obituary in 1966 made no mention of Mafia connections.[58] Tartamella's son Sereno was a guest at the wedding of Bonanno leader Gaspare DiGregorio's daughter in 1965, and Sereno was questioned over a shooting during the 1960s "Banana War."[59]

Tartamella also had garment interests, where reports of Mafia racketeering reflected the gradual movement of Italian workers into the business. Aside from the cloak, suit and skirt trades, by the 1930s the Italians outnumbered Jewish workers in the New York City garment industry, reversing the 1910s figures.[60] Garment district employers were increasingly of Italian heritage; in the suits and coats branch, 175 Italian contractors employed about 5,000 workers in the 1930s.[61]

First attempts by Italian-American racketeers to exploit the newfound strength of their *paesani* working in the garment business were based on "muscle."[62] James Plumeri, Johnny Dio (both later of the Lucchese Family) and (until he was killed) Dominick Didato ran the Five Boroughs Truckmen's Service Association. Danny Richter, a Louis "Lepke" Buchalter man, had formed the Association in 1929.[63] The threat of physical violence

Figure 4.1   John Tartamella. (Author's possession)

against truck owners and their vehicles if they refused to join the Association, or failed to follow Association rules, was enough to secure compliance until a few victims went to District Attorney Thomas E. Dewey for relief. Dewey claimed that Natale Evola, an upcoming Bonanno Family member who attended Salvatore Maranzano's feast (Chapter 7), was part of the Five Boroughs group "to help with the rough work."[64]

As more Italians were introduced to the garment sector through legitimate channels, Mafia power in the garment district enlarged. Gaetano Lucchese, the Gagliano Family underboss, entered the New York dress business in about 1945 eclipsing the once dominant Jewish clique around "Lepke" Buchalter.[65] By the early 1980s, Chinese mobsters were similarly using their "economic clout" in the garment district to demand a better say in its rackets, from the Italians.[66]

The key figures in the live poultry racket by the latter 1920s were Arthur "Tootsie" Herbert, local 167 delegate of the International Brotherhood of Chauffeurs, Teamsters, Stablemen, and Helpers of America, his pal Joey Weiner, and Sidney Rosenstein, head of the organization supplying the vast majority of the feed for the fowl.[67] "At the age of twenty-four," Thomas E. Dewey declared, "Tootsie Herbert bullied his way into a job as delegate for the chicken drivers' union," and "had himself elected head of the union for life, and he abolished elections altogether."[68]

Herbert arranged for his partner Joey Weiner to take over the chicken killers' union. In February 1937, Weiner was ordered to prison,[69] as was poultry industry "czar" Herbert in August.[70]

That year, the "excessive cost of handling the poultry on the New York end" was noted by a Senate Committee, explained as the result of "a monopoly maintained by a group of racketeers," using "violence, arson, and murder." Conditions were depicted as "no better" than in 1929. Indeed, the National Recovery Act (NRA) code pertaining to the industry "had served merely to legalize the racketeers' monopoly, since many provisions in the code were dictated by influential members associated with the poultry racketeers."[71]

The workplace context of the "Jewish" live poultry trade was one in which the ethnicity of Mafiosi was a decided disadvantage. In the case of international unions with a number of locals in one American city, it was likewise those composed of a primarily Italian membership that were "captured" by Mafiosi.

New York City politics and traditional industries within it were saturated by ethnic differentials. Reflecting the discordant makeup of the metropolitan economy, the nationality of Mafiosi was a barrier to the extension of Italian-American racketeering.

BAFF TRIALS

Like archetypal Mafia executions, Baff's was performed as part of a wider conspiracy. However, the extreme riskiness of the Baff affair for the conspirators, which was also casually and clumsily carried out, was a departure from the belief that potential Mafia recruits were chary about who they worked with, and who went about assignments "with quiet expertise."[72] Secrecy was missing, the men chosen to shoot Baff proved to be unreliable, and most of the perpetrators were prosecuted and convicted. Detectives quickly formulated the theory that would end with the paymasters and their co-conspirators standing trial.

Details that emerged from 3 trials demonstrated those flaws in planning that would expose the principals to prosecution. Three of those linked to the killing were affiliated with Harlem based Mafiosi, two of whom would become Mafia heads. The "Al Capone of Los Angeles,"[73] Jack Dragna's supposed involvement requires explanation, as does that of Gaetano "Tommy" Reina, who became "one of the biggest Mafia leaders in the Bronx."[74]

GIUSEPPE ARICHIELLO

To understand why these formidable characters may have decided to take the extremely hazardous Baff contract, we must first outline the events as they were described in court. Proceedings as they unraveled also revealed important connections in the Harlem crime setup. Carmine DiPaolo "broke" the case upon his arrest for assault in the Bronx and his decision, in January and February 1916, to cooperate.[75] But DiPaolo's allegations were uncorroborated until a confession also emerged from Giuseppe Arichiello.

DiPaolo recounted in the Criminal Branch of the Supreme Court that he and his pal Carmelo "Charlie Ross" Russo were given money for the murder job by Harlem saloonkeeper Ippolito Greco. Joseph Zaffarano and Greco persuaded DiPaolo and Russo to join the plot, but diPaolo stated that he withdrew when he doubted if it could succeed. Greco replaced diPaolo with Arichiello.

DiPaolo witnessed Greco give $100 to Arichiello after the murder of Baff, inside Greco's saloon at 227 East 107th Street.[76] Greco's crony Zaffarano supplied the guns and made the arrangements, but Frank Ferrara,

Figure 4.2   Giuseppe Arichiello. (Courtesy of the New York State Library)

Figure 4.3 Barnet Baff/Giuseppe Arichiello. (Courtesy of the Queens Borough Public Library)

Antonio Cardinale, Joseph Greco (Ippolito's brother) and Tony Zaffarano were in on the planning.[77]

Arichiello was expected to testify at his trial that Greco had coerced him into taking part, but that he and Gaetano Reina jointly shot to death the poultry entrepreneur. In a January 1916 statement, Arichiello had alleged that he had refused to participate until threatened by Greco. He admitted to firing at Baff with Reina, who received $700 alone. Ferrara got $150, Joe and Tony Zaffarano $300 each, Greco $900, his brother Joe Greco $600 and Arichiello $100.[78] Higher-ups that Arichiello knew of were Greco and Antonio Cardinale, a former East 108th Street chicken market owner who subsequently joined the Italian army.[79]

When he took the stand, though, Arichiello said that detectives beat the confession out of him, and that his only connections to the case were in frequenting Greco's saloon, and working in a laundry owned by Greco's business partner, Angelo Gagliano. When Reina was brought into the courtroom, Arichiello said he did not recognize him.[80]

But the interrogating detectives denied mistreating Arichiello and there were no marks on his body from a police beating.[81] On April 7, 1916,

Giuseppe Arichiello was convicted of the first-degree murder of Baff.[82] After the verdict was announced, the District Attorney was said to be hunting for the poultry rivals of Baff's that contributed to a $4,500 fund handled by Greco and Cardinale, and who supplied the reason for the slaying.

FRANK FERRARA

At Frank Ferrara's trial starting on April 12, 1916, diPaolo repeated a statement that Greco had told him that Baff was ruining business and had to be eliminated.[83] Cardinale was in charge of the money. Cardinale engaged Greco to select the men for the job, who turned to diPaolo and Russo and the two Zaffarano brothers.[84] But the difficulties in getting to Baff in the West Washington Market, where he had a stall, were such that after several failed attempts,[85] diPaolo and Russo left the conspiracy.[86] Ferrara stood accused of acting as the driver in the getaway car.

According to diPaolo, the first trip to the Market was on August 25, 1914, when a cop spotted them. Baff was missing when they returned on another day.[87] A third visit abruptly ended when Harry Baff was seen with his father. In total, six trips to the Market were mounted,[88] causing diPaolo and Russo to depart. They were also concerned by the small amount of money on offer for such a high-risk job. DiPaolo had been paid $50 on account.[89]

DiPaolo went on to say that Arichiello and Gaetano Reina, East 107th Street characters with connections to Greco's saloon, replaced diPaolo and Russo as the gunmen.[90] DiPaolo happened to be present in Greco's saloon four days after Baff was slain, in time to see the two Greco brothers, Ferrara, Arichiello and others at a table, with Greco paying Ferrara and "John," later identified as Reina. The cash came from Cardinale. DiPaolo had never seen Reina before, and had only heard of him from Ferrara.[91]

Ferrara made three conflicting statements when questioned in February 1916: to the detective bureau, at police headquarters, and in the District Attorney's office. In the first two, Ferrara indeed admitted that he drove the car used in the Baff slaying, for which he received $100 from Greco as a "present."[92] But he had assumed on the day of the murder that the job he was given was a legitimate one, after receiving a telephone call from Arichiello, driving customers to the West Washington Market.[93]

His passengers were gone 15–20 minutes; they then ran back to the car. Upon their getting out, Ferrara drove back to the 104th Street garage where he worked, none the wiser. After he realized that Baff had been assassinated, three days later, Greco ordered him to keep quiet.[94] That was the last time he saw any of them.[95]

Ferrara's statement to the District Attorney was very different. In this version, Ferrara was chosen as the wheelman fully knowing what was expected of him.[96] Greco told him that they were going to kill a man, and Ferrara was promised over $200 to drive. Those involved were the two Grecos, Giuseppe

Arichiello, Gaetano Reina, Joe and Tony Cardinale and Carmine DiPaolo.[97] Greco stated that Reina and Arichiello were to be the shooters.[98]

Three trips made to the Market to get Baff were unsuccessful,[99] and they agreed to kill the poultry man during Thanksgiving week.[100] Ferrara drove the Grecos, Cardinale, DiPaolo, Reina, the Zaffaranos, and Arichiello to the Market on November 24. Ferrara next heard two shots[101] and drove them away.[102] Reina, who he now claimed to have known for several years,[103] had shot Baff in the back.[104]

At his trial, Ferrara claimed that this statement was forced from him after he was assaulted,[105] and that Reina's name was given to him.[106] This police witnesses refuted.[107] Ferrara denied knowing DiPaolo, Zaffarano or Arichiello,[108] and so far as he knew, he was simply hired to fetch a man from hospital.[109] This evidence mirrored his two other statements. On the day of Baff's shooting, two strangers got in the car with Greco; the men left, he heard shots and the three men ran back to the car.[110] Greco gave him $6 and told him to keep his mouth shut.[111]

Yet the prosecution made the telling point that it was hardly credible that the gunmen would hire Ferrara if he were a complete innocent to gang affairs, and who would therefore be likely to squeal to authorities at the first opportunity. Indeed, Ferrara had kept quiet until his arrest. His self-incriminating statement was the true one, written by Ferrara in an attempt to save himself.[112]

On April 13, 1916, Ferrara, "the most intelligent of the four men arrested for the Baff killing," was convicted of first-degree homicide, and seven days later sentenced to death. Reflecting an identical comment made at the conclusion of the Arichiello trial, it was hoped by the District Attorney that Ferrara, with nothing now to lose, would name the masterminds of the conspiracy.[113]

JOSEPH COHEN, JACOB COHEN, DAVID JACOBS AND ABE GRAFF

On trial in June 1917 for having "counseled, aided, abetted and advised other persons" in the Barnet Baff murder, were Joseph Cohen, Jacob Cohen, David Jacobs (Joseph Cohen's brother in law) and Abe Graff. They were the organizers. Their counsel argued that the case was based on "the confessions of murder accomplices and scoundrels acting on the impulse of saving their own necks."[114]

A witness who had not appeared previously was Antonio Cardinale, the middleman between those standing trial and the assassins. Cardinale had protested his innocence until November 1916, when the lawyer for Ferrara and Arichiello saw him in order to get a new trial for his clients.[115] Cardinale was returned from Italy and given immunity in America in return for his testimony.[116] Like other poultry dealers, Cardinale had suffered from Baff's business methods, especially the overcropping scam.[117]

In order to scare Baff, Cardinale—backed by Cohen and, it was suspected, the New York Live Poultry Dealers' Association—got his employee Joseph Sorro and "Harlem gangsters" to plant a bomb outside Baff's home on Long Island in 1913.[118] Sorro, Frank Burke and one "Tony Nino" placed the device, supplied by Greco by way of Cardinale, but it exploded harmlessly.[119] Burke confessed his role in the bomb plot and was jailed.[120] Sorro admitted knowing Tony Nino and Burke and like Burke, acknowledged his part.[121]

A scheme was next hatched to set fire to the stall of Aaron Newmark, a friend of Baff.[122] Newmark's place was almost destroyed.[123] Greco later suggested that they poison Baff's milk on the doorstep of his home. Joseph Cohen vetoed this idea, as the whole Baff family might die.[124]

A proposal to get him with sniper fire from a loft in the Market[125] was discarded when they were discovered, and when Baff did not pass by.[126] Chicken handler Daniel Jones identified a photograph of Ben "Tita" Rizzotta as similar to a man he saw in the loft with a rifle. Cardinale was also up there.[127]

It was decided that Baff would have to be openly murdered in the Market. A couple of other alternatives failed to take off, including one to get Baff at the 109th Street market that Newmark used to own,[128] and to ambush Baff from a wagon with a hole in the back from which a gun would be fired.[129] With time running out, on Cohen's suggestion Baff was to be executed in the Market for $500, later increased to $700.[130] Cardinale saw Greco about the offer and Greco took the job.[131]

According to Cardinale, a few days before the actual murder, he met Graff and the gunmen, and they determined the date of the shooting.[132] During each of these attempts, Cardinale was in contact with Joe Cohen, Moe Rosenstein and Graff, who urged him on and directed proceedings.[133]

The night after Baff perished, Graff gave up $500 in Greco's saloon. Cohen ultimately came across with $1,000, but the assassins wanted more and threatened to shoot up the Market.[134]

Cardinale refused to say on the stand who the gunmen were, since it might "incriminate" him.[135] It would also cause "great annoyance and displeasure among their relatives and friends," and for fear of harm to Cardinale's family still living in Harlem.[136] Cardinale only wished to place the blame "where it belongs."[137]

Once his conviction was affirmed and he faced the death penalty, Ferrara in early July 1917 became a state's witness, and first revealed to the public the names of Dragna and Tita,[138] in the expectation that "by telling the truth" he would receive leniency.[139] Ferrara claimed that on the day before the Baff death, a certain Charles Dragna came to the shop where he worked and asked for a car to be ready for the next day.[140]

On the day of the deed, Ferrara met both Dragna and Tita.[141] They drove to the Market but there were too many witnesses around and a cop, so they waited for dark.[142] Rosenstein signaled when they should close in to slay Baff.[143] Ferrara drove in and Dragna and Tita alighted. Ferrara next heard two shots. Dragna and Tita ran back to the car and Ferrara drove it away.[144]

Ferrara said that his police interrogators in 1916 had given him the names of Arichiello and Reina to give the court at his own trial, even though he had never met either.[145] Dragna and Tita were the actual executioners of Baff,[146] as he had initially told them. The 2 men "I had in the car were arrested for blackmailing."(Dragna was convicted of extortion in 1915.) But Ferrara was ignored.[147] Di Paolo, Joe Zaffarano and Arichiello were not with him at any time, and he only picked out Ippolito Greco for culpability because Greco was dead.[148]

Ferrara kept the Dragnas out of his written confession because he was afraid of the detectives' reaction, so he went along with the false story they gave him.[149] Dragna was the "short" assassin of Baff he now identified.[150] Ferrara had known Dragna since 1913, when Ferrara did a job at the Columbus Wet Wash Laundry on East 107th Street where Dragna drove a wagon.[151] He had only known Dragna's partner Tita since October 1914.[152]

Ferrara went on to contend that in late October/early November, Charlie Dragna approached him.[153] He was promised $200 to "do a Jewish poultry dealer downtown." Dragna wanted Ferrara to drive the car.[154] Following Baff's slaying Dragna gave Ferrara various amounts of money.[155] Ferrara saw Tita for the last time on the night of the assassination.[156]

On August 17, 1917, Joseph Cohen was sentenced to the death penalty for planning and procuring Baff's homicide. Abraham Graff was sentenced to a term of imprisonment of from 10 to 20 years for first-degree manslaughter.[157]

Yet because of inconsistencies in the evidence given at the trials, and new information that came to light, most of those convicted were eventually released. Cohen was freed in 1922 when Joseph Sorro's perjured evidence was exposed.[158] A new trial was initially planned but the case was eventually dropped. Three "unidentified gunmen" shot Cohen dead in April 1932 as he opened the door at his Prospect Park South, Brooklyn, home. Nine shots were heard.[159]

Graff was released in 1923 when his sentence was commuted. Moe Rosenstein was allowed to plead to manslaughter; he became a witness for the state in June, 1917 and was pardoned.[160] Ferrara's sentence was commuted to life imprisonment, and he was pardoned in 1928. A motion for a new trial was granted to Arichiello in September 1917. He was released on a suspended sentence after pleading guilty to manslaughter.

DISCUSSION

Baff's death was the outcome of a series of fragile and disjointed conspiracies held together by a commercial motive shared by those directing matters. Concealment, the supposed centerpiece of murders involving Mafia aspirants like

Reina and Dragna, was absent. New people were introduced to the scheming with backgrounds unknown to most of the others, and decisions were arrived at with little thought for their practicality. Indecision, squabbling, and a general lack of forethought among the participants were vital to cracking the case from the inside.

Gaetano Reina, Angelo Gagliano and Jack Dragna were associated in the episode. Reina apparently knew both Ippolito Greco and Gagliano, men with potent contacts in the Italian Harlem underworld. There was no hint that Reina or Dragna were then Mafiosi. On the other hand, they were born in Corleone, they knew Greco and Gagliano, and in Dragna's case, had recognized Sicilian Mafia links.

Given their connections to Mafiosi in Corleone and New York, why Dragna and Reina ended up partaking in such a casually approached and sloppily implemented scheme, despite the gravity of the consequences, was an apparent puzzle. It posed the obvious question of why their influential contacts in the New York Mafia were not used by Reina and Dragna to offer a safer way of making money through crime. To attempt to answer this, we need to explore the paths that existed into U.S. Mafia membership before the 1930s.

GAETANO AND ANTONIO REINA

Gaetano Reina lived at the time of the Baff slaying above the Greco saloon.[161] He was never tried, the only evidence against him being "the false information given to us by Arichiello and by Ferrara for the purpose of protecting the real men."[162]

Reina was born September of 1889 in Corleone, the son of Giacomo Reina and Carmela Rumore. Like many immigrants from Corleone, Reina lived for years on East 107th Street, where he met his future wife Angelina and where they raised a family.[163]

Gaetano's brother, Antonio ("Tony" or "Nino") Reina, was born about 1893 in Corleone, arriving in New York in October 1909 and later working like Gaetano in the Gagliano run Columbus Wet Wash Laundry.[164] Tony Reina participated in the bombing of Baff's house in 1913.[165]

IGNAZIO I. DRAGNA

Ignazio Jack Dragna left New York in December 1914, and did not return until his May 1917 arrest. The indictment against Dragna was dismissed in 1919.[166] Dragna was referred to during the trials as Charles Dragnia and Jack Rizzotta.[167] His partner in the crime, "Tita," was also known as Ben Rizzotta and Giovanni Batista De Sota.[168]

Jack Dragna was born April 18, 1891 in Corleone, the son of Francesco and Anna Dragna. With his parents and brother, Gaetano "Tom" Dragna,

Jack made the journey to New York in November 1898. He went back in 1908 to Sicily with his family, but returned to New York in March 1914 to live with his brother at 337 East 106th Street. Within three months, Dragna filed his first naturalization papers (as "Charles" Dragna) using that address, and recording his occupation as the Wet Wash laundry driver.[169]

The Dragnas' alignment with the Morello Family in Harlem is indicated from the apartment building they both shared. Morello's wife Lena Salemi stayed in 1903 with Lima, husband of Morello's sister, at 337 East 106th Street. It was also the house in which Francesca Rizzotta (Jack Dragna's future wife) was born.[170]

During Dragna's trial in 1915 for sending "Black Hand" letters in California, it was disclosed that Dragna was "the principal friend," while serving in the Italian army camp between 1911 and 1913 stationed in Corleone, of "Mr. Streva, an alleged member of the Mafia."[171] The reference was likely as not to Paolino Streva, head of the Corleone Mafia and Joseph Morello's former *cosca* patron.[172]

Figure 4.4 Jack Dragna, 1915. (Courtesy of the California State Archives)

ANGELO GAGLIANO[173]

The third figure of interest in the Baff chapter is Angelo Gagliano. According to Carmine diPaolo, Gagliano knew about the conspiracy against Baff: Gagliano was in the saloon at the planning stage, had once asked if they were going to the Market, and Greco assured him that he hoped matters would be resolved.[174] Gagliano was in the Greco-Gagliano saloon when the payment for the murder was divided. In May 1916, Gagliano was charged with the murder.[175]

While perhaps not a "made" Mafiosi, Gagliano had friends among the Morellos, and functioned as the employer of Reina and Dragna in the Columbus Wet Wash Laundry at 339 East 107th Street. Nicholas Morello ran a devolved system of relationships, which was encapsulated in Gagliano's eclectic ties to individuals associated with the Morello crowd, and concurrently to fellow Corleonesi Ippolito[176] Greco, linked to the 1914 conspiracies and to feuds in Harlem (below).

Marco Macaluso was witness to Gagliano's naturalization. Gioacchino Lima, Morello's brother in law, lived part of the early 1910s at the Gagliano

Figure 4.5 Gagliano-Greco saloon. (Courtesy of the New York State Library)

and Greco saloon. Salvatore Clemente, one of the Secret Service's best informers, advised in March 1912 that Morello's relatives, the Lomonte brothers, had taken a saloon on East 107th Street with "Gagliana."[177]

Other links to the Morellos were exposed through research. For in 1912, Gagliano lived at the 231 East 107th Street residence used by Stefano LaSalle and Vincent Rao.[178] In 1910, doing business from there as a plasterer, Gagliano testified for Morello in Morello's counterfeiting trial.[179] (Morello counterfeiter Nicholas Sylvester had been Gagliano's plastering apprentice before his arrest.[180])

The future Tommaso Gagliano *borgata* was also represented among Angelo Gagliano's contacts. Mariano Marsalisi witnessed Tommaso Gagliano's citizenship papers in addition to those of Lucchese member Nunzio Pomilla (Angelo Gagliano's lathing partner) and Vincenzo Gagliano (Angelo Gagliano's brother). (Marsalisi appeared on the Federal Narcotics Bureau's "International List" of major narcotics violators.[181]) A familial relationship existed between Angelo Gagliano and the Rao brothers, who were to become Tommaso Gagliano Family members.

Dragna had worked in the Angelo Gagliano run laundry for months on a regular basis before November 1914.[182] Arichiello was also employed there as an "extra man."[183] Reina was the third Gagliano laundry employee who was implicated in the Baff homicide. And the "Murder Stable," dealt with below, was that out of which Gagliano drove his laundry wagons.[184] Gagliano was lastly related to Antonio Cardinale, the intermediary in the case.[185]

Chart 4.1 denotes major relationships involving Angelo Gagliano and Harlem Mafiosi.[186] Some like Vincent and Charles Rao, later went into real estate. Others, for instance Salvatore Speciale and Joseph Gagliano, were renowned narcotics traffickers.[187]

MODES OF RECRUITMENT INTO THE U.S. MAFIA

A variety of pathways into the U.S. Mafia developed after 1900. The clearest and largest dichotomy emerged between recruitment sources commonly used by first and second-generation Family bosses, but other divisions existed. Across the epochs, enrolment into American Mafias came from three distinct pools:

- Previous membership in a Sicilian Mafia organization,
- Birth in a Sicilian locale that was known to be under the sway of the Mafia, and thus where Sicilian Mafiosi could "vouch" for a prospective American member,
- Growing in significance after 1920 was prior membership of a street gang in America, if it was active in the same territory as a U.S. Family.

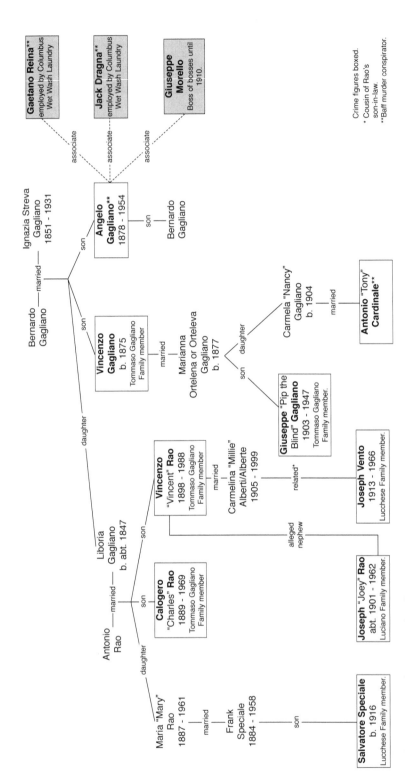

Chart 4.1 Gagliano-Rao family tree.

The third means of entry into a U.S. *borgata* was best known, and correlated to the notion of the U.S. Mafia membership as "Americanized."[188] The Americanization formulation said little though about what went on before the 1940s. Though a variation of this method had existed for suitably qualified immigrants from Sicily, the fully developed "vouching" mode of recruitment was of particular relevance to mainland Italians, unable to be "made" under the first two arrangements.

Within the last phase, neglected "Italian" enclaves in New York, Chicago, Boston, Buffalo and other U.S. cities were believed to be the primary recruiting bases for organized criminals. Local Mafiosi acted as role models for disaffected youths. "From each generation," according to Tyler, "issue new gangs, supplying fresh recruits to the underworld."[189] Salerno espoused an identical view: "The recruiting grounds for organized crime are clearly identified" in those areas of inner-city America "where existing antisocial feelings can be exploited."[190]

U.S. Mafiosi defectors from the 1960s onwards were revealed as growing to adulthood in precisely those neighborhoods where gangsters were perceived as local celebrities.[191] George Barone of the Genovese Family grew up in Hell's Kitchen on the West Side of Manhattan. Barone at first ran with the Jets, running gambling, loan sharking and heists, reporting to Vito Genovese on Thompson Street.

Salvatore "Sammy Bull" Gravano came to maturity in Bensonhurst, a mainly Italian area of Brooklyn and "a prime spawning ground for Cosa Nostra." A former member of the Rampers, Gravano hooked up with Shorty Spero of the Colombo Family, who became his mob mentor.[192]

Nicholas Caramandi and Thomas DelGiorno of the Philadelphia Mafia matured in an area where the local *borgata* was strong. From an early age, they strove to emulate neighborhood "wiseguys."[193]

A fortuitous set of circumstances leading to membership was also sometimes required, even for those raised in a Mafia influenced area. Through mixing with Cleveland members and associates on his travels, Aladena "Jimmy" Fratianno for instance encountered Lucky Luciano, James Licavoli and other important "made" men. In prison, he met Thomas Licavoli, who was impressed enough to recommend Fratianno to the Los Angeles group. Before his induction into their ranks, he came to know the Los Angeles members socially.

FBI reports are replete with descriptions of the American Mafia recruitment process from within that context. Local Family members discretely observed prospective members for their conduct in the field. If deemed sufficiently trustworthy and competent, they were "schooled" in the ways of the *Cosa Nostra* group in question after the man's history was checked for potential problems. FBI undercover agent Joseph Pistone's Mafia mentor, Lefty Ruggerio, summed up the system: "You handle yourself right, keep your nose clean, keep on the good side of people, I'll propose you for membership."[194] As a test of his loyalty and toughness, a prospective member might be asked to commit a murder.[195] Upon meeting the admission criteria, a budding Mafiosi had to wait (perhaps for years) until the "books opened," and recruitment resumed.

When this practice was observed by social scientists, more former street gang members had made the transition into membership of a *Famiglia*.[196] However, the primary sources of recruitment before the 1930s were from:

RELATIVES

In 1965, the U.S. Senate claimed that American Mafia membership until the 1920s was "limited to Sicilians."[197] The Iannis, in their study of the "Lupollos," concurred, "Relatives were always more dependable than others; and, failing kinship, cultural affinity and the network of friendship were almost as secure."[198] For relatives of the bosses, membership in a *cosca* was "virtually a birthright."[199]

The kin centered system offered a tried and tested assurance that other *amici nostri* could be trusted without undergoing the kind of lengthy probationary period believed as necessary when considering American source candidates. Because of their perceived trustworthiness, blood relations were perceived as indispensable to running a *Famiglia*.

Entry into a Family for individuals in this bracket was comparatively effortless. There were, moreover, few other obvious manpower sources in the early years of New York City Mafia development. Sicilian born and socialized relatives supplied the bulk of the membership in groups like the Morellos and the Williamsburg, Brooklyn, organization. By and large, the U.S. born (so-called "Americanized") offspring of these first generation Sicilian-American immigrants would only become old enough to themselves join Families from the late 1920s.

Speaking of Family founder Giuseppe Lupollo's business, "The cohesiveness of the business was rooted in Giuseppe's firm resolve to keep all the activities within his own family and, moreover, to employ relatives—of whom there were many—at every level of every enterprise."[200]

With a sound background in Sicilian organized crime, his parents took young Joseph Bonanno (born January 1905) to Brooklyn in about 1908, where the family settled among *paesani*. His Sicilian experiences, Bonanno wrote, "greatly facilitated my passage into this immigrant society."[201] Philadelphia's Harry Riccobene made the transition to becoming a U.S. Mafioso at a young age, "not yet seventeen." There again, Riccobene "was from a long line of Mafiosi in Enna, Sicily, and his father Mario had been in the Philadelphia Family longer than (Salvatore) Sabella had been a member."[202]

Angelo Lonardo, the 1980s Cleveland boss, was the son of Joseph Lonardo, leader of the Cleveland Mafia organization until his 1927 assassination. And Michael "Mikey Scars" DiLeonardo's grandfather was a Salvatore D'Aquila syndicate member. DiLeonardo grew to manhood surrounded with some of the "big" names in organized crime, including Carlo

Gambino. DiLeonardo's grandfather, Jimmy DiLeonardo, "was much older than him, and he was like, almost like a protégé of the old timers at that time, Carlo, and he would come by the house for advice at times."[203]

But since few aspirants to U.S. Mafia membership had this edge, it was "very hard for a member to qualify." Potential members otherwise "had to be extremely well known to their sponsors."[204]

OTHERS

Without a familial relationship to an existing member, birth in the same town as the leadership of the American Family that an individual aspired to join might be beneficial. Previous Sicilian Mafia membership would open many doors before 1931, as noted in Chapter 3. "Because of his position in Sicily," thus, Salvatore "Maranzano was accepted into the Castellammarese Family in Brooklyn when he immigrated."[205]

Nicolo Gentile was as favorably positioned, by being a member in the Porto Empedocle (Sicily) *cosca*, but confusion surrounds when he was "made" in Sicily, and therefore when he first benefitted from this fact.[206] After leaving Sicily, Gentile labored on the railroad tracks in Kansas until he learned how to sell fake linen for six years. In 1915, Gentile met Gregorio Conti, his first mention of an encounter with American Mafiosi. Questioned as to this, Gentile replied "The heads gladly keep themselves in contact with young people that are making a name."[207]

A further variable in influencing the possibility and timing of entry of a man was the stage of development of a Mafia organization in a U.S. locality. Where, for example, only a feeble Mafia organization existed at most, even those with good Sicilian credentials might find themselves adrift. In many areas of the United States, no Mafia group existed for aspirants to join. The Morello-Terranova family of the 1890s was a case in point, drifting to Louisiana in search of employment evidently without outside assistance before coalescing into a force back in New York.

Jack Dragna's ties to the Corleone *cosca* were similarily of no value on the West Coast, to where he moved. Bereft of useful contacts, Dragna and Ben Rizzotto were arrested for the Baff murder in May 1917 while working as car washers on 7th and Alameda Streets in Los Angeles. Dragna was detained without difficulty, but Rizzotto "dashed into the darkness" and escaped.[208]

ALTERNATIVE MECHANISMS

We do not know the circumstances that prompted Families to expand their membership rolls to embrace those from non-traditional sources. One was the imminence of armed conflict. Without the mobilization of the Castellammare War, for instance, it was unlikely that Joseph Valachi and his Neapolitan associates would have been initiated.[209]

Since those groups preparing for conflict could identify some of those recruited by their opponents through the orthodox means, it made sense to import fresh manpower from other sources. Chapter 5 denotes other reasons for the change of emphasis within previously Sicilian member organizations.

Because operating gambling and loan-sharking enterprises inside a safe territorial environment rarely attracted official complaints or action, the arrest sheets of Mafiosi coming up the first 2 ways tended to be short and rarely showed jail time. By contrast, the rap sheets of unconnected individuals who made it to Mafia membership the "hard way," lacking an inside edge to membership such as a family connection, involved their participation in dangerous escapades of the sort that often attracted a spell of imprisonment. But only then would they be judged by recruiters to have proved themselves fit for membership.[210]

CASTELLAMMARE WAR RECRUITMENT

Biographies of shooters participating in the 1930–1931 Castellammare War revealed the two types that came to become Mafiosi in New York City. Some were recruited the traditional (first and second) ways, through kin and Sicilian links (mainly those named in the Maranzano Family). Others (in the Tommaso Gagliano organization) represented the third mechanism, having been engaged from outside of the conventional system by dint of their singular reputations for toughness, discretion when discussing mob business, following orders and a willingness to commit murder.

Individuals responsible for committing Castellammare War murders were identified by cooperating witness Joseph "Joe Cago" Valachi as:

Killer(s)	Victim(s)
Sebastiano "Buster from Chicago" Domingo	Joseph Morello, Manfredi Mineo Stefano Ferrigno, Joseph Catania.
Girolomo "Bobby Doyle" Santuccio	Joseph Pinzolo, Mineo, Ferrigno
Nick Capuzzi	Mineo, Ferrigno, Catania
Salvatore "Sally Shields" Shillitani	Catania

Excepting Domingo, they were Gagliano faction members. Attempts to learn more about Nick Capuzzi were unavailing, given insufficient detail in published descriptions of Capuzzi.

All had known (and frequently worked with) Valachi, who signified the third means of recruitment.[211] "During his eight years of criminal apprenticeship on the streets of New York," the committee which took Valachi's testimony concluded, "Joseph Valachi associated with so many men who later joined the Mafia that his own gravitation toward the secret society of criminals was inevitable."[212]

GAGLIANO FAMILY

Indicating the deprivation that spurred individuals from non-traditional backgrounds into the Mafia, Valachi began stealing to make ends meet. Valachi was New York born in September 1903.

Some of Valachi's early memories were as a truant from school, until he hit a teacher in her eye with a stone, for which he "went away for 2 years."[213] Up to 1930, he had been arrested 11 times, on charges ranging from burglary to grand larceny and assault.[214]

From 1921, Valachi ran with a burglary gang. The hazards were forcibly brought home when Valachi was shot in the back of the head during a heist. He was at first left for dead by his pals, but they returned and took Valachi to a doctor. "They gave me a whole bottle of Scotch for anaesthetic and the doctor took the bullet out."[215]

Valachi's reasons for joining the Gaglianos in 1930 were pragmatic. Burglary was getting trickier to pull off, and his friend Dominick "The Gap" Petrelli assured Valachi that differences between Sicilians and Neapolitans in the mob were a thing of the past.[216] "They were talking about radio cars," Valachi explained, "With that I had in mind and the proposition I got, I accepted."[217]

Unlike those Mafia traditionalists aligned with Maranzano who were motivated to fight "Joe the Boss" Masseria for abstract reasons around ideas of justice Mafia-style, there was no suggestion that idealism played any part in Valachi's reasoning. His counterpart Joseph Bonanno referred to Masseria's "tyranny" in "forcing his way to the top by enslaving others," as justifying an assault on him.[218]

But Valachi only found out about the wider aspects to the Castellammare War in the fall of 1930, after Joseph Profaci related the story.[219] Until then, Valachi was prepared to kill Masseria and his men without knowing why.

Like many who surrounded Valachi, Salvatore "Sally Shields" Shillitani was removed from the streets not long after the Castellammare War's end. As the FBI noted in 1963, Shillitani was confined to prison "for all but approximately five years since 1925."[220] He was born in 1906 as Salvatore Scillitano in New York City, one of three sons of Michale Scillitano and Gaetana Giorga. As a member of Valachi's burglary crew,[221] he served 5–10 years for attempted robbery in 1925.[222]

Girolomo "Bobby Doyle" Santuccio was responsible for three deaths in the War. Santuccio was born in January 1900 in Floridia, Sicily, to Joseph Santuccio and Amalia "Josephine" Quartararo. He was arrested 6 times between 1916 and 1926,[223] including once for felonious assault and burglary. Santuccio's only incarceration was in August 1926, serving 20 months for carrying a concealed weapon.

In September 1921, the body of Joseph Santuccio, Girolomo's brother, was found in front of 175 Thompson Street.[224] It signaled the start of a feud with Louis Lamole, who was shot four times in March 1924 in a hallway on Wooster Street. "A minute later" Santuccio "ran into the arms" of three policemen and was temporarily locked up.[225]

In what was reported as a continuation of a quarrel, in August 1924, Santuccio was ambushed and shot at "for the second time in three months," from a car.[226] Events came to a climax on June 30, 1932, when Lamole was gunned down.[227] Santuccio was charged with the homicide, but the case was dismissed several weeks later.[228]

MARANZANO FAMILY

Counterposed against the Gaglianos were four individuals recruited into the Maranzano wing of the New York City Mafia, who would fight in the War alongside Valachi and his group. These Maranzanos' experiences before their initiation into the New York City Mafia markedly diverged from that the Gaglianos described had to undergo as a test of their suitability.

Joseph Bonanno's youth in Castellammare del Golfo was without nearly the same level of privation suffered by Valachi, or his companions. His horizons were also much wider. "Most of all," he said, "I wanted to command men."[229] Bonanno was accepted in the Nautical Institute in Palermo, but for his refusal to tow the Fascist line was expelled. He decided to "start anew in another land" in 1924.[230] Within a year of settling within the protective embrace of Brooklyn's Castellammare population, Bonanno was confidant of the powerful Sicilian Mafia transplant Salvatore Maranzano, an avowed ally of the Magaddinos, related to the Bonannos, from his years in Castellammare. Bonanno fell foul of the police only once before 1930, for an immigration violation. Bonanno's subsequent arrests attracted no jail time.[231]

Maranzano member Gaspare DiGregorio's first booking was in 1934, but DiGregorio was never convicted over a long career in Mafia crime, including a stint as leader. DiGregorio was a witness to the November 1931 marriage of Joe Bonanno to Filippa Labruzzo in Brooklyn,[232] and was Stefano Magaddino's brother-in-law (marrying Marie Magaddino until her death in 1927). DiGregorio died of lung cancer in 1970.[233]

Bonanno depicted Calogero "Charlie Buffalo" DiBenedetto as "the best English-speaker" among those who followed Maranzano's cause. "Like the rest of us, Charlie could handle a gun without embarrassing himself."[234] Allegedly born in New York in about 1906, DiBenedetto had equally accommodating interlocking kinship connections in the Brooklyn and Buffalo Mafias of the 1910s and 1920s.[235]

SEBASTIANO "BUSTER" DOMINGO

Our final Castellammare War case history is that of Sebastiano "Buster from Chicago" Domingo.[236] The true identity of Buster has "perplexed organized crime fans" since his existence was placed in the public record in 1963 by Valachi.[237] As much as his life, researchers have disagreed on the time and place of Buster's murder.

Domingo was one of Maranzano's "secret weapons," functioning, akin to Valachi with the Gaglianos, as a stranger to Masseria who could move about unnoticed. During the War, "The lead scout car would usually contain Gaspar DiGregorio, Bastiano Domingo and Vincent Danna." Bonanno thought highly of Domingo's abilities; "He could shoot from any angle and from any direction."[238]

Domingo's circumstances were unusual. Although he was connected, in the traditional manner, by place of birth (and possibly by marriage) to the upper reaches of the Maranzano Family, and was the son of parents from Mafia infested Castellammare, most of his years were lived away from Mafia influences. Domingo's life reflected these contradictory currents.

Domingo was born in Castellammare del Golfo in 1910, the son of a Giuseppe Domingo and Mattia, or Matilda, Farina.[239] Leaving Castellammare with his mother and siblings in 1913, after stopping in a poverty-stricken and seedy district of Chicago,[240][1] they moved to Benton Harbor, Michigan, joining kinfolk in the "Brooklyn" neighborhood.[241]

Over the 1920s, Benton Harbor became important as a leisure center for Capone gangsters, with regular passenger links between the two. The *News-Palladium* complained, "Capone's presence has become so matter-of-fact here that the local citizenry, refusing to get excited about the proximity of one more headliner, has ceased to pay much attention to the comings and goings of Capone's fleet of 16-cylinder sedans."[242]

The body of an Italian shot to death was found September 1928, in Hagar Township near Benton Harbor. Detectives believed that it was of Chicago *capo* Tony Lombardo's killer, who was tracked there after fleeing Chicago.[243]

Inside its Italian community, a self-contained alcohol manufacturing and selling fraternity thrived, operated by the Domingos and their relatives originating in Castellammare.[244] In April 1927, the Sheriff's department seized an 80 gallon still, liquor and mash from Sebastiano's brother Tony Domingo's farm.[245]

On the last day of 1925, Matilda Domingo, daughter of Tony (Sebastiano's older brother) and his wife Mary Domingo, was accidentally shot in the home of Tony's parents in law by her playmate, who discharged a gun left behind by a visitor from Chicago.[246] Driving back from Benton Harbor to their farm, Mary was blown apart on October 22, 1927 when a bomb planted in the Ford Coupe car she was driving belonging to Tony exploded. The detonation "rocked houses a quarter of a mile away from the blast."[247] Mary's body was thrown 15 feet away from the wreckage of the car and was "mutilated almost beyond recognition."[248]

Newspaper accounts described the equally dramatic aftermath. Tony and Sebastiano Domingo opened fire in the Republican Club where Mary's alleged assassin, Louie Vieglo, was hiding. But Vieglo escaped. Shooting carried on in nearby streets. The pair was finally arrested while vainly looking for Vieglo at his store.[249]

Tony and Sebastiano were held at the county jail for questioning. Sebastiano accused Vieglo, a local grocer, of planting the explosive. According to Vieglo's wife, Tony Domingo blamed her for his estrangement from his wife, and the families had not spoken for a year.[250] The police however believed that the liquor traffic underlay the murder.[251]

Regardless of these catastrophes befalling the family, the male line of the Domingos remained stubbornly attached to the profits from moonshining. It was shown later in 1927, when Frank Domingo (Sebastiano's younger brother) was charged with selling liquor in his grocery store, and was jailed as a second offender.[252]

Tony Domingo sold up to return to Chicago where, in a North Side café on August 29, 1929, he was murdered; his back was to the door when nine shots were fired into him.[253] Sebastiano Domingo was mentioned during the inquest as meeting Tony in front of a West Erie Street candy store "for the past several weeks."[254] Upon hearing of his undoing, the *News-Palladium* commented that Tony's "vow to avenge the dynamite death of his wife . . . must remain forever unfulfilled." [255]

At the time of census taking in April 1930, Sebastiano had moved to rented accommodation in New Castle Township, Westchester County.[256]

Figure 4.6   Sebastiano "Buster" Domingo, 1933. (John Binder Collection)

Nearer to New York City, he was poised to join the Castellammare War alongside Maranzano.

The bloodshed that surrounded him attuned Domingo into settling quarrels through violence, and he met a fitting end. Domingo's fall came on May 30, 1933. Four gunmen burst into the Castle Café on East First Street, Manhattan, lined up the card-players inside and riddled Domingo with bullets.[257] Five others were wounded in the attack, one dying, for which there were no arrests and no identified motive.[258]

Similarly to the experience undergone by other bootlegging Maranzanos, the Domingos were by and large left to ply the trade without police interference. There is evidence that the Domingos were linked to the Maranzano *caporegime* Vito Bonventre through marriage. Maranzano may thus have been informed of Domingo's prowess in Michigan through Bonventre, and their joint Castellammare heritage overcame any qualms that Maranzano may have had about his group not being able to observe Domingo in action prior to his recruitment for the War.

Not to be disregarded was the excitement that came with participating in a Mafia war, no matter which recruitment process the contestants emerged from. Gentile had a burning desire in his Sicilian hometown to "affirm" himself.[259] Bonanno wanted more than a career as a "breadmaker."[260] "The structure of the underworld," Haller noted, "gives free rein to personalities that take pleasure in deals, hustling, and risk-taking."[261] It was an attitude that united members, no matter how they became Mafiosi.

TERRITORIAL QUESTIONS

Territorial fragility was associated with East Harlem's organized crime structure in the 1910s. No overall control was achieved, and networks formed and reformed. With the incarceration of Joseph Morello, his group splintered while maintaining loose links to characters such as Angelo Gagliano.

The chaos was partly explicable in terms of the manner in which immigrants from across southern Italy lived together around 107th and 109th Streets. The "Sicilian" Morellos were strong on 107th Street, whereas Neapolitans were dominant on 109th Street. Much of the fighting involved those subgroups in competition.

Lines of authority could crosscut. Angelo Gagliano for example was allied with the Morellos, therefore with the Lomonte brothers who were Morello's cousins.[262] Yet Charles and Tommaso Lomonte, with a hay and feed business a few doors from the "Murder Stable" (see below), were also friendly with Giosue Gallucci[263] whose rackets the Morellos coveted.

By 1913, tensions had unfolded between established Sicilian organizations in Harlem and that of Salvatore D'Aquila, who was seeking to widen his reach as the relatively newly installed "boss of bosses." Joseph Fontana—a suspect in the Petrosino murder of 1909—perished on November 4, 1913 by shots fired from "an alley-way on 105th Street between 1st and

2nd Avenues." The Mineo and Harlem Mafia factions were held responsible by a Secret Service source who believed it was an outgrowth of warfare involving the D'Aquila organization to which Fontana belonged.[264]

D'Aquila took revenge. A gunman stepped up behind and shot to death Fortunato Lomonte, depicted as the owner of a saloon between Second and Third Avenues "where the Terranova boys hung out,"[265] on May 23, 1914 as he was walking to his grain business. The culprit escaped through a hallway.[266] Two D'Aquila men from the Lower East Side Italian community, Umberto Valenti and Accursio Dimino,[267] were used. Thereafter, according to Nicolo Gentile, D'Aquila "controlled the quarter."[268]

After Fortunato Lomonte's demise, his brother Tommaso played a dangerous game. Captain William Jones, in charge of the squad investigating the Baff case, recorded how Tommaso gave his squad vital information at the expense of Ippolito Greco. Lomonte "used to be Greco's most intimate friend before they became rivals for leadership in that quarter."[269]

Six days after the slaying of Greco himself on October 7, 1915, Lomonte was mortally wounded as he was escorting his cousin Rosalie along 116th Street and First Avenue.[270] The killer threw away a pistol and ran into a house on 115th Street, where he was arrested.

Figure 4.7　Fortunato Lomonte grave. (Author's possession)

The detained man, Antonio Impoluzzo from Castrofilippo, Sicily, stood trial and was convicted in January 1916 for first-degree murder. Impoluzzo, a saloon owner on 38th Street, had rented a First Avenue apartment ten days before Lomonte's death, along with two other Italians. It gave an excellent view of Lomonte's movements as he visited a 115th Street saloon he frequented.[271]

In February 1916, detectives working on the Baff case interviewed Impoluzzo in the New York State prison death house. They believed that Impoluzzo was given the task of preventing Lomonte from squealing about those involved.[272] But Impoluzzo chose to remain silent and was electrocuted on March 9, 1917.[273]

HARLEM'S "MURDER STABLE"

Horse rustling was big business. In 1908, a band of Italian horse thieves were collared after over 100 complaints from victims of the crime, the activity causing insurance rates to rise.[274] A year later, another network was discovered, "working on a scale unknown even in the days of 'horse lifting' in the West." Up to 800 animals were stolen and taken to the stable of a confederate, "ostensibly kept for hiring and boarding horses, but in reality for receiving stolen horses."[275] No other enterprise better demonstrated the perilous characteristics of relationships in East Harlem.

The Terranovas were caught up in it. Counterfeiter Nicholas Sylvester met one of the Terranova brothers while they were together in jail. "They stole horses in New York and sold them in other cities at reduced prices; or they would bring the horses to friends in the country (Highland) and receive payment."[276]

The police believed that a 334–337 East 108th Street stable—referred to in the press as the "Murder Stable"—was the hub around which the section's horse stealing business revolved. According to Selvaggi, it was a meeting place "for all sorts of persons of ill fame" and a training ground for criminals of every stripe.[277] The premises took on mythical proportions as the source of most of the assassinations in the neighborhood.[278] But "Though it makes for good reading," Downey warned his readers, "the Murder Stable slayings are more legend than fact."[279]

A series of murders linked to the stable began on October 29, 1911, when Nicolina "Nellie" Lenere stabbed Frank "Chick" Monaco, part of a local gang, to death at her home on East 109th Street.[280] The dead man, she informed police, was slain upon trying to rob her mother's safe, and then for beating her when she refused to help. It was subsequently learned that Lenere had taken up with Monaco, but became upset when he told her that she would have to earn a living.

Lenere returned to her mother Pasquarella Spinelli.[281] Spinelli, probably from Marcianise near Naples,[282] was the next to go, fatally wounded on March 20, 1912.[283] Two gunmen did the job near to the stable door, possibly in retaliation for Monaco's slaying.[284] Her business partner, Luigi Lazzara, suspected of helping the murderers, was slain in a knife attack in February 1914.[285] Arrested in 1912 for rustling,[286] Lazzara was a friend to the slain Monaco.

Other information received by the police suggested that Aniello Prisco had shot Spinella on the orders of Giosue Gallucci, because she gave them tip offs as to the identity of her son-in-law's assassin.[287] Ippolito Greco, a third stable owner, was shot from behind as he walked from the doorway of the place.[288]

Joseph "Diamond Joe" Viserti was at the periphery of the stable slayings. Viserti was linked to the deaths of Jerry Maida, a police informer, in 1913,[289] Amadeo Buonomo that year, and to Ippolito Greco's demise,[290] though only the Maida charge stuck. Like most of those connected to the stable's history, Viserti was Neapolitan.[291]

The number of murders declined towards the end of the 1910s, perhaps in part because of the removal of the "Camorra" organizations in Brooklyn that had added to the slaughter (Chapter 5). As automobile usage climbed,

"Murder Stable" Around Which Baff Case Centres Is Scene or Cause of 14 Deaths

Figure 4.8 *New York Herald*, February 13, 1916. (Courtesy of the Queens Borough Public Library)

the demand for the services of horse thieves declined. The 108th Street stable property was acquired in 1924 by a partnership including Angelo Gagliano and Philip Picataggi,[292] a "minor racketeer of Coney Island" gunned down in 1931.[293]

CONCLUSION

The conflicts characterizing Italian Harlem's gangland sharply contrasted to conditions applying on the lower east side under the stewardship of the Jewish Benjamin "Dopey" Fein. Fein was "the organizer of the gangster business who placed it on an economical basis."[294]

"Benny's specific genius," Fried stated, "lay in rationalizing the Lower East Side labor protecting market," and in "working out an elaborate system of territorial jurisdictions."[295] Arrangements were hammered out with other mobs for the agreeing of territorial rights, and they cooperated where necessary.[296] In keeping with the strongly functioning ethnic ingredient to industrial racketeering noted, Fein worked for Jewish unions in dispute with Jewish garment manufacturers.[297]

Was Reina or Dragna the Baff killer? The evidence points to Dragna as being the most likely candidate. He was missing from the Columbus Wet Wash laundry on the day of the homicide. The day after the murder, Dragna did not turn up for work, and was next sighted in California. Neither did Dragna return to New York of his own volition to face his accusers, even though the papers in 1917 were "full" of the case.[298]

Dragna became renowned for his occasionally similarly audacious capers, including an interest in two gaming vessels anchored offshore at Long Beach, California, in 1930–1.[299] Named as the leading Mafioso in California by the Kefauver Committee, and by the Governor's Commission on Organized Crime, Dragna died in 1956 in a Hollywood hotel room.

Reina quietly rose to a position of power in the New York likely as not leading the former Morello syndicate. *Onorata Societa*, until he was shot down in 1930. Reina was only known at the time of his death as a "wealthy wholesale ice dealer."[300]

Perhaps because of their mutual connections in East Harlem, the Lucchese Family, a successor organization to Reina's, became the principal contact on the *Cosa Nostra* Commission for the Los Angeles Mafia under Dragna.[301] His brother Gaetano, with whom he had stayed in Harlem, became Jack's *consiglieri*. "Tommy" Lucchese knew Dragna from the time when Dragna's family "lived across the street from where I lived" in Harlem.[302]

This exploration of the background and roles of Reina and Dragna in the Baff slaying displayed an important but overlooked aspect of recruitment into *borgata*. Usually disregarded were "traditional" manpower sources deployed by New York City *borgata* for 30 years and more. The classic

American gangster figure as portrayed in fiction and cinema was rarely if ever an original Family member.

Several means existed to access the New York Mafia system, ranging from a kinship contact inside a Family to a lengthy "apprenticeship" as an associate, in the hope of being given a break. As kinship links became, in some crime organizations, a less potent force, recruitment increasingly came from "American" sources, now drawn from disaffected youths active in neighborhoods where the Mafia was almost an institution.

Distinctions made between Sicilian and other members eroded over time. For a time, Neapolitans in New York City's organized crime *milieu* exceeded the Morello Sicilians in their ability to mount territorial incursions. Yet the Morellos, the target of their attacks, received no support from nearby Mafia groups. Other issues emerging from the Sicilian-Neapolitan conflict, addressed next, include the structure and conventions of non-Sicilian crime syndicates. Following on, the later role of mainland Italians in the New York organizations is examined and analysed. They introduced a greater level of innovation into those Families where they were members, a few becoming household names.

5 The Neapolitan Challenge

INTRODUCTION

Neapolitan immigration to New York City was tiny compared to that from the rest of southern Italy and Sicily. This fact belied their disproportionate effect on 1910s New York organized crime.[1] Since Neapolitan groups have been poorly covered elsewhere, and ramifications from cases involving them have not been previously explored, they are dealt with in detail.

For convenience, the Neapolitan gangs in the chapter are referred to as "Camorra" organizations; but although they had a membership ritual and came from Campagna, their recorded links to secret societies in Italy were weak to non-existent. Because they were Brooklyn based, they are referred to in this chapter as "Brooklyn Camorra" groups.

Italians settled in Brooklyn in order to escape overcrowding in the Lower East Side of Manhattan, living in Williamsburg and along Union and President Streets, in the Navy Yard district, and in East New York.[2] Yet "living conditions in these communities were generally deplorable,"[3] and criminality was a feature of the landscape.

At the heart of this chapter, furnishing the majority of the original material used, is the record of a series of stunning trials that took place in Manhattan, Brooklyn and White Plains between 1918 and 1926, offering a unique insight into the mechanisms inside Neapolitan organized crime of the era.[4] Judged by any standard, the Brooklyn Neapolitans were an impressive force.

HISTORIOGRAPHY

In spite of its significance to the history, the Brooklyn Camorra has received perfunctory attention. Peterson's only reference to it was through the mortal wounding of Joseph DeMarco, which he erroneously asserted was a response to the challenge that the victim posed to Ciro Terranova.[5] Pitkin restricted his account to uncritically summarizing the contents of newspaper articles, commenting that the Camorra was "as vicious a group of assorted criminals as had often had their affairs aired in American courts."[6] Reid's exposition has Morello members embedded in their Harlem stronghold planning to take over Brooklyn, including the absorbtion of Pellegrino Morano's "narcotics racket."[7] Reid's focus was on secrecy, criminal conspiracy (over 3 pages were devoted to the initiation ritual alone) and acts of violence. Chandler mismatched events; there was thus no "twenty-eight-year" conflict between the Sicilians and Neapolitans, and the Morellos had no part in ending the rule of the Brooklynites.[8]

Downey covered the business in just three pages by reproducing the sparse coverage accorded by newspapers of the day, in the context of a description of the Morello-Terranova family. The Camorra episode largely served as a convenient bridge between a discussion of the gangs of the latter 1910s and Prohibition.[9] Reflecting the press reportage, Downey confused fatalities associated with the Camorra with those related to the "Murder Stable."

Nelli linked the Camorra to the "rich economic opportunities" afforded by New York's illicit gambling market, before wrongly arguing that Giosue Gallucci was the inheritor of the Morello-Lupo territory. Like Chandler, Nelli assumed that the war between the Neapolitans and Sicilians, described below, began before Nicholas Morello and Eugene Ubriaco were shot dead, and that their demise was the outcome of a bogus "peace conference." Nelli's contention that the fight was over the legacy of Gallucci was also simplistic.[10]

City newspapers connected virtually every Italian gang assassination in East Harlem to the "Murder Stable." Assuming the existence of a single explanation for the local killings no doubt helped to increase newspaper sales, and excused the police from making more progress. In addition, they had no notion until late in the day of a "Brooklyn" dimension to the Harlem murders.

EARLY NEAPOLITAN CRIME IN NEW YORK CITY

Before the emergence of Brooklyn Neapolitan organizations, important individuals from Naples' organized crime milieu were active in Manhattan. Occupying a not dissimilar place in Naples to Vito Cascioferro in the Sicilian Mafia (Chapter 3) was Enrico Alfano.[11] In April 1907, Joseph Petrosino seized Alfano in the basement of a house on Mulberry Bend used for gambling;[12] he had been convicted of a crime involving moral turpitude in Italy and was returned.[13] In 1912, Alfano was incarcerated with 34 others at Viterbo, Italy, following their conviction for instigating the deaths of Maria and Gennaro Cuocolo, and for membership of the Camorra.[14]

Funds to pay Alfano's lawyers were reportedly collected from Neapolitan restaurants in New York. Giovanni Rapi, the Camorra's "treasurer," had an interest in a private bank in New York where the savings of immigrants were forwarded to Italy.[15] The New York defense fund treasurer was Andrea Attanasio, also sought in connection with the Cuocolo matter.[16]

RALPH DANIELLO

The background to some of the fatalities in Harlem and the Lower East Side, emerged when Raffaele "Ralph" Daniello (real name Alfonso Pepe), a member of an organization with headquarters in a Brooklyn coffee house at 113 Navy Street, gave a long confession to New York detectives. In Downey's exaggerated explanation of the event, Daniello cleared up 23 homicide cases "as well as naming New York City's top Mafioso."

Daniello did not say that the syndicates he exposed controlled "all the crime" in Italian New York[17] But the information the former gang member gave was as important for its intelligence value as for solving murders.

Daniello fled to California in early June 1917, and was arrested October 10 in Reno, Nevada, for the killing of Louis DeMaria on Navy Street, Brooklyn, in May 1916.[18] On the train back to New York, Daniello hinted that he might be prepared to cooperate, since it appeared that his buddies had ignored his pleas for money and equipment they owed. Daniello unburdened himself to police the following day.

Figure 5.1   Ralph Daniello. (Courtesy of the New York State Library)

According to Daniello, his former boss Andrea Ricci might also be persuaded to turn to the authorities. Detective Felix DeMartini believed that Ricci was shot dead in November 1917 to prevent him from talking ("they were taking no chances").[19] Several of Ricci's men were picked up at the Ricci funeral: Alessandro Vollero, Frank Clemente, Salvatore Costa, and John Esposito.

Members of the Brooklyn groups giving evidence for the state ultimately included Daniello, John Fetto, Esposito, Alfonso Sgroia, Tony Notaro, and John Mancini. Daniello only admitted to being involved in a secondary capacity in the Nicolo Morello, Eugene Ubriaco, and Giuseppe Verrazano killings. He learned the gangs' secrets either through direct participation in events he described, or via information gleaned from other gang members.[20]

The data that emerges sheds light on key East Harlem homicides stretching back to 1914. Although the information on the pre-1916 cases could not be used to bring the perpetrators to justice, they furnished the sole "inside" explanations of their causes. Statements given by the several former Brooklyn members who defected to the government were broadly consistent in content. An anonymous letter received by the Westchester District Attorney confirmed some of the basics.[21]

Accounts given by witnesses who were not personally involved in a murder were unexpectedly incomplete and occasionally confused. The motives for less significant deaths were also too often unexplained. But from the execution of Joseph DeMarco in July 1916, eyewitness testimony is available as to the actions and identities involved.

Most of those named as perpetrators, and the majority of the deceased, were of Neapolitan extraction. Gennaro "John" Russomano came from Campagna, as did Daniello, Giosue Gallucci, Aniello Prisco, and Generoso Nazzaro.

Heading the Brooklyn faction in Coney Island was Pellegrino Morano, the owner of the Santa Lucia restaurant. His counterparts along Navy Street were Andrea Ricci and Leopoldo Lauritano. Daniello and most of the others identified were allied with Navy Street. The two groups operated both independently and jointly.

Murders referred to by these witnesses as carried out by the Brooklyn Camorra were:

NICOLO DELGAUDIO

Nicolo DelGaudio was walking down First Avenue on October 19, 1914, when a shot came from an upper window, and he dropped dead. DelGaudio was characterized as "one of the lawless members of Harlem's Little Italy." His name was linked to an attack on the powerful Gallucci in 1913, in which Gallucci's bodyguard Tony Capalongo was killed.[22]

Vollero, one of the Navy Street leaders, later stated that DelGaudio had demanded a share from "Gesuele" (Gallucci) of the graft. Gallucci instead had DelGaudio eliminated. Gasparino Vincinenza, once sharing a cell with Vollero, similarly stated at trial that Vollero had told him that Gallucci had DelGaudio eliminated after DelGaudio complained of his share of the racket profits. Vollero went on to say, according to Vincinenza, "because we swore revenge, that is why we had to murder one after the other."[23] Lauritano married DelGaudio's widow.

Nicolo's brother, Gaetano DelGaudio, was killed after the murder of George Esposito, his bodyguard. Esposito was slain as he walked down East 108th Street on November 8, 1916, leaving DelGaudio exposed. On November 30, 1916, DelGaudio was executed by shotgun fire in his First Avenue café.[24] Esposito was a former Gallucci bodyguard identified by Daniello as a victim of the Navy Street crew.[25]

GIOSUE GALLUCCI

For Pitkin, the story of Giosue Gallucci demonstrated "the widespread, long-time, and diversified activities of as vicious a group of associated criminals as had often had their affairs aired in American courts."[26] To murder Gallucci required the combined resources of the Morellos and the Brooklyn organizations. Gallucci's death followed others that, while apparently not the responsibility of the Brooklyn Neapolitans, displayed the shaky and partial control that even the mighty Gallucci had on his East 109th Street terrain.

His brother Gennaro Gallucci was shot on November 14, 1909 in Giosue's home on East 109th Street, used as a bakery and coffee house. Complaints had been made against Gennaro in New York, but no prosecutions resulted. It was the second attempt on his life.

Antonio Zaraca, a Harlem gunman, was killed during September 1912 in the Café Degli at 336 East 109th Street owned by Giuseppe Jacko, who was mortally wounded in the attack.[27] It took place in Gallucci terrain and it was believed that Zaraca was a Gallucci bodyguard.

A theory held that Aniello "The Gimp" Prisco did the shooting.[28] "Prisco . . . was known to the police as one of the most dangerous Italian outlaws in this city," [29] and had been questioned over the Spinelli case in 1912 (Chapter 4).[30] Detectives considered that Prisco had shot Spinella at the behest of Gallucci because she gave the police information on the killing of her son-in-law.

Gallucci's nephew [31] John Russomano, born in 1888 in Naples,[32] confessed to killing Prisco in the Gallucci bakery on East 109th Street in December 1912, but only to save Giosue from being shot. Russomano depicted how Prisco had demanded a "big diamond stud" from Gallucci and $100. "So I looked around and I seen a revolver and I grabbed it and I fired two shots, and that is all I know."[33]

Figure 5.2 Outside Gallucci East 109th Street cigar business, ca. 1900.
Luca Gallucci (small boy to left) Giosue Gallucci and wife Assunta (centre)
John Russomano (right). (Courtesy of Anne Boyd)

A bullet in his abdomen and another in his neck felled Amadeo Buonomo
on April 9, 1913. Several men approached him; one shook his hand and two
others placed revolvers to his body and fired. The owner of a 114th Street
coffee saloon, it was supposed that Buonomo had vowed to revenge Prisco,
but that the Galluccis got to him first. Russomano had been wounded and
his bodyguard Tony Capalongo murdered in 1913 at the doorway of Russomano's home, perhaps by Buonomo, across the street from where Prisco
was shot in 1912.[34]

Giosue Gallucci was born in Naples in December 1864, emigrating in
1891 to seek his fortune in America. In Italy, Gallucci was known as "a
dangerous criminal," convicted nine times and kept under surveillance. His
other brother Francesco was portrayed as "a blackmailer like his brother,"
who had been convicted and sentenced on six occasions.[35]

In part alerted by the prefect of police in Naples, the New York police held
that Gallucci derived most of his income "from his control of the policy playing in Harlem, various gambling houses and houses of prostitution, all located
in that section of Harlem known as Little Italy." Victims of burglars went
first to Gallucci, since "more can be accomplished by applying to the said
Gallucci than by making complaint through official channels." "Gallucci's
consent was necessary," newspapers reported, "before anything out of the

way could be done in Harlem's Little Italy."[36] Gallucci was blamed for several deaths including that of Buonomo.[37]

Gallucci and his son Luca were gunned to death on May 17, 1915, in an East 109th Street coffee house that Giosue had bought for his son.[38] Once Gallucci and his bodyguards had sat down, strangers entered and fired at the party. Luca threw himself in front of his father in a vain attempt to shield him.[39] Giosue was shot through the neck and stomach. The assassins "leaped into a waiting automobile and were driven away."[40]

Gallucci, in the *Herald*'s view, "pays taxes on more than $350,000 worth of real estate and his friends say he is worth more than $1,000,000."[41] Notwithstanding this bold assertion, Gallucci only left cash to his beneficiaries amounting to $3,402, together with the property at 318 East 109th Street, which was rented out.[42]

According to Leopoldo Lauritano, Gallucci's bodyguards Generoso "Joe Chuck" Nazzaro and Tony Romano were instrumental in getting to him. Coney Island boss Pellegrino Morano was said to have supported the conspiracy to murder Gallucci, blaming Gallucci for the fate of his nephew Buonomo, and more importantly coveting the rewards that would accrue with Gallucci gone.[43] Daniello was told that Morano "paid the money to kill this man."[44]

The killing of Gallucci represented a joint venture, performed by the Morellos in Harlem acting with Brooklyn. Lauritano and Daniello heard the specifics from Nick Morello and Andrea Ricci, and Ciro Terranova, during the plot to kill Joseph DeMarco in 1916, said, "it will be the same thing that was in Harlem when Lucarillo was killed, no witness appeared against them."[45]

Lauritano was told: "Joe Chuck was out at the door on watch. Andrea (Ricci) and (Tony) Romano both entered in and did the shooting and then Joe Chuck helped them to make their getaway over the roof."[46]

Ricci's resentment against Gallucci may have related to his friendship with Prisco, subsequently slain by Russomano, in the horse stealing trade when Ricci lived on East 109th Street.[47] The prize to be had from Gallucci's death was control of the Italian lottery in that section of Harlem, which passed to the Morellos' Tommaso Lomonte and Steve LaSalle.[48]

JOSEPH DEMARCO

DeMarco formerly had an office near the notorious East 108th Street Stable, where he sold hay and grain to dealers.[50] He had "De Martini" shot on 108th Street, and the Morellos sought revenge.[49] DeMarco was shot at in April 1913, and a year later was slightly wounded, at which point he moved downtown to open a West 49th Street restaurant.

The Morellos and Navy Street appeared to want to open a gambling joint in the vicinity of DeMarco's own card game at 54 James Street, and were determined to eliminate the competition: "Nick Morello and Steve LaSalle says that it was impossible to control all the game, except that we should kill this DeMarco."[51] With DeMarco dead, the gang was free to open a card game at 167 Hester Street run by the Brooklynites Morano, Angelo Giordano and Vollero together with Nick "The Fixer" Canarelli (below).[52] Around 1912, Morano had a card game on Mulberry Street that was taken over by DeMarco, supplying another motive for Morano's eager contribution towards DeMarco's demise.[53]

The slaying of Joseph DeMarco represented the high water point of the collaboration between the Morellos and the Neapolitans. They had met in June 1916 at Morano's Santa Lucia restaurant, those present including Nick Morello, Steve LaSalle, and Eugene Ubriaco (for the Morellos) and people from Navy Street.[54] There was also a conference on 102nd Street between their representatives 3 days before DeMarco was slain.[55] A day prior to the hit, at Navy Street, Lauritano, Vollero, Ricci, Daniello, Esposito, Rocco Valenti, Bartolomeo Pagano, LaSalle, and the three Morello brothers (Ciro, Nick and Vincent Terranova) attended a final get-together.[56]

Giuseppe Verrazano would point out DeMarco to Navy Street gunmen once they got into the game DeMarco ran. To commit the act, Lauritano sent John Fetto, Esposito and Pagano, who were unknown to DeMarco. Rocco Valenti was also involved.[57] On the morning of the murder, the bosses said to Esposito, "Make a good job, Lefty, and don't miss them."[58]

Verrazano fatally wounded DeMarco in his James Street game on July 20, 1916.[59] Verrazano notified DeMarco as he shot him, "Don Pepe, this is a holiday for you."[60] The Navy Street gunmen mistakenly killed Charles "Three-Fingered Charlie" Lombardi, who looked like DeMarco. But Lombardi was "a mere spectator sitting in there, playing his game."[61]

Esposito recalled, "All at once, two shots were fired, the man in front of me jumped and I fired at him. Pagano seen the men falling and he fired at him . . ."[62] Fetto fired a shot but contended that he was there under duress, a claim upheld by other witnesses.[63] Valenti stood outside. Pagano and Esposito returned to Navy Street to meet Lauritano, Ricci, Vollero and Lauritano's brother. Nick Morello gave them $50.[64]

Fearing that he would seek revenge on those he held as responsible, DeMarco's brother Salvatore was shortly eliminated. His murderers were "Joe Chuck" Nazzaro, Frank "Coney Island" Clemente and Tony Medaglia, out to prove their worth to Brooklyn. On October 13, 1916, the mutilated body of Salvatore DeMarco was discovered in Astoria, Queens, in a clump of weeds in a vacant lot, almost decapitated. There were no signs of struggle.[65]

NICOLO MORELLO AND EUGENE UBRIACO

Pellegrino Morano originally came up with the idea of killing the Morellos, encouraged by Vollero.[66] Morano had managed a policy game in Harlem for several months in 1916, but could not make it pay enough to give Nick

Morello as gang leader the money he demanded for the privilege.[67] Eugene "Charles" Ubriaco, Morello's sidekick, wanted the money from Morano no matter what: "It makes no difference to me, if you had won ten thousand dollars you would have to put it in your pocket just the same."[68]

This, and the fact that he blamed Morello for $1,500 he lost during the period, furnished enough reasons for Morano's anxiousness to see Morello dead. If they would not return the policy game to him freely, he would take it back by force.[69]

Morano's interest in the Harlem policy racket was inherited from Tommaso Lomonte, LaSalle and Ubriaco.[70] Antonio Celentano subsequently had the game until Morano asked Morello if he could acquire it.[71] Morello agreed when Morano promised to pay him $25 weekly, as had Celentano. After Morano left the operation in the fall of 1916, Giovanni Tartaglione acquired it.[72]

Navy Street was evenly split over the wisdom of assassinating the Morellos, largely divided by their past experience of working with them and the importance given to maintaining peaceful relations with the "Sicilians." But once a decision was made to wipe out the Morellos, they acted as one. Vincenzo Parapalle, a Navy Street leader, for instance argued that the Morellos were in their debt and should live: "The Morellos are friends of ours, and you know that we had DeMarco killed to satisfy the Morellos."[73] They had done nothing wrong and had once even saved Ricci's life.

But Vollero wanted the Morellos' rackets, and to avenge the death of his "fellow townsman" Nicolo DelGaudio in 1914.[74] The Morellos, Vollero argued, made peace with DelGaudio, then "took him up to Harlem and had him killed."[75]

Morano reminded Tony Parretti, one of the Coney Island leaders, that "The Morello brothers kill my nephew (Buonomo) and I want revenge on my nephew, and also they make me move from uptown."[76] Eugenio Bizzaro added, "We can go up in Harlem and open up a saloon, and we can make a living there, and we can make also some money on the ice and coal."[77] These were Morello enterprises that were considered as ripe for a takeover. If the Morellos perished, Parretti believed, "We could all be wearing diamonds on our fingers."[78]

Morano threatened to kill Ricci if his consent was not forthcoming. Ricci was finally persuaded to go along, if the killing of the Morellos was done quickly and when as many of the 6 key Morellos as possible could be eliminated at a stroke.[79] A day before the event, a valise was given by their Philadelphia associates to take to Navy Street, thought to contain the guns used in the murders.[80]

Ricci would lure the Morellos on a pretext to Navy Street on September 7, 1916. It was hoped that more would come than the two that turned up. After being given drinks in the Panzoni restaurant by Ralph Daniello, Morello and Ubriaco went to find Ricci at his house on Johnson Street when they were ambushed.

Figure 5.3   Navy Street congregation. (Courtesy of the New York State Library)

"Bartolomeo Pagano drew his revolver and opened fire on Nicholas Morello . . . Tom Carillo drew his revolver as quick as a flash and opened up fire on this other man, Charles Ubriaco, and Lefty Esposito joined in the shooting of Charles Ubriaco."[81] "There was a fusillade of shots," the *New York Times* recorded, "which threw that densely populated neighborhood into an uproar."

Morello was found lying in a gutter with several wounds to his body, and Ubriaco was 50 feet away with a bullet through the heart.[82] The killers discarded their revolvers and ran off.[83]

Afterwards, Coney Island and Navy Street joined to make more money.[84] Eyewitnesses to the crimes were fixed.[85] At Baldo's restaurant on Coney Island, the combination had a dinner to celebrate the day's events. Up to 20 were present, drinking to the toast of "Health to the Neapolitans and death and destruction to the Sicilians."[86]

GIUSEPPE VERRAZANO

Giuseppe Verrazano was scheduled to die with the other Morellos on September 7, but failed to appear on Navy Street.[87] Verrazano had conducted gambling at 54 James Street, formerly DeMarco's joint, and his misfortune (like DeMarco's) was to be in the way of the planned 167 Hester Street game, to be conducted by Angelo Giordano and his pals.[88] The opening on Hester Street was also delayed by the need to pay off the precinct Captain in order to conduct the business unmolested.

"Pellegrino Morano was talking to Charlie Giordano and he talked about the killing of this Verrazano, so that they could get the game downtown."[89] Verrazano's killers—Alfonso Sgroia and Anthony Notaro—were selected because they were unknown to him.

A combined team from Brooklyn met on October 5, 1916 outside the Italian Garden restaurant at 341 Broome Street. Notaro walked up to the far side table Verrazano was sitting at and "opened fire." Verrazano "got up and staggered around and fell over behind the table."[90] Sgroia observed, "Everybody was hollering, the restaurant was upside down, everybody was hollering."[91] Two diners in the restaurant were wounded. At the doorway stood Daniello and Giordano, ready to slay Verrazano should he escape the gunfire inside.[92] But they were not needed. Notaro ran down Grand Street to be arrested in a doorway; Sgroia went along Elizabeth Street.[93]

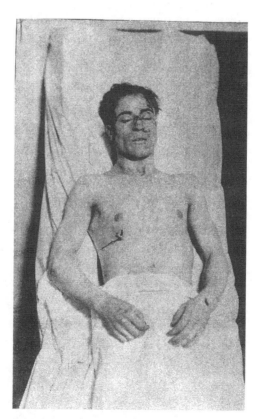

Figure 5.4 Generoso Nazzaro. (Courtesy of the New York State Library)

GENEROSO NAZZARO

Generoso "Joe Chuck" Nazzaro docked in New York in 1904 aged 19 from Avellino, Italy. Nazzaro's uneven journey through the underworld of East Harlem mirrored the constantly fluctuating dynamics and treacherousness of gang relations there.

Nazzaro's enmity towards Gallucci, leading to his participation in Gallucci's murder, probably stemmed from the time when he was held with Gallucci and Russomano in 1913 for carrying a concealed weapon. Publicly billed as a roundup of "the leaders in the policy blackmail outrages,"[94] Nazzaro was left to kick his heels in jail while the others were released on bail. When Nazzaro came out, moreover, Gallucci refused to buy tickets for a benefit to raise money for his freed bodyguard.

Because of problems that Gallucci's death generated him, Nazzaro swiftly departed Harlem for the neighborhood of 49th Street and Seventh Avenue, where he connected with DeMarco. Once DeMarco perished, Nazzaro transferred his loyalty to Brooklyn, with whom he had previously worked in removing Gallucci. To prove fidelity towards his new friends,[95] Nazzaro had helped to get rid of Salvatore DeMarco.

The causes of Nazzaro's own downfall were twofold. First, he wanted to kill ("trim") Navy Street member Frank Fevrola for a reason witnesses were unable to learn.[96] Second, Navy Street suspected Nazzaro and Frank Clemente of feeding the Morellos with the information they used in order to be able to shoot at Vollero and Daniello in February 1917 (see below).[97]

Tony Parretti conceived and arranged for the death of Nazzaro.[98] Sgroia and Aniello Parretti went on March 16, 1917 to Fevrola's home. From there, they traveled to a Yonkers saloon taking Nazzaro, who was told they were gathered to kill Fevrola. Walking down an isolated part of Nepperhan Avenue, Fevrola gave a signal and, as prearranged, Sgroia, Parretti and Fevrola fired at Nazzaro. Nazzaro dropped dead across trolley tracks.[99] "Joe Chuck didn't have a chance."[100] The three ran to a café in Mount Vernon and from there, made their way back to New York.

OTHER FATALITIES

Daniello named additional victims of the Brooklyn Camorra in trial testimony, but three could not be further detailed through research.[101] Murders divulged by Daniello, and whose deaths are substantiated by other sources, were those of Felicio Lacolla, on May 21, 1915,[102] Matteo Leone on September 9, 1915,[103] Michael Averna on July 23, 1916,[104] George Esposito on November 7, 1916,[105]and Giuseppe Chiarella on February 5, 1917.[106] The reasoning behind their deaths remains a mystery.[107]

The gang's principal subsidiary was a 735 Christian Street coffee store in Philadelphia. Ernesto Desiderio ran a game there for Eugene Bizzaro and Natale Bordonaro.[108] The money went to Navy Street, from where it was shared out, with Esposito receiving a piece.[109]

Daniello gave the names of three who died in Philadelphia following Verrazano's downfall. The same names were furnished in an anonymous letter to the Westchester District Attorney.[110] Salvatore Costa and Joe Vaccaro performed the Philadelphia "jobs," commissioned because the victims were allegedly "in correspondence" with the outstanding Morellos.[111]

THE MORELLOS REGROUP

As they were leaving the Hester Street gambling joint in February 1917, Vollero was shot in the back and Daniello wounded in his thigh.[112] The attacks were viewed as the first move by the remnants of the Morello outfit to regain the initiative. Lauritano asserted that Brooklyn would have to "kill them all before they kill us."[113]

A number of schemes were hatched to eliminate the Morellos.[114] They included ultimately abandoned plans to blow up the Terranova house on 116th Street,[115] to pick the Morellos off by sniper fire upon hiring a room in Harlem,[116] and to poison them.[117] The machinations came to an end when Vollero was incapacitated by his wound and could not direct the effort.[118]

BROOKLYN CAMORRA ORGANIZATION

Specifics of 20 members of the two Neapolitan groups active in Brooklyn were uncovered. Only two were U.S. born. There was a single Sicilian (Salvatore Costa); the rest came from the five provinces around Naples.[119] Although older members tended to be among the leaders (Ricci, Giordano and Lauritano), exceptions existed. Vaccaro was a lower level functionary, for example, as was Fetto and Fevrola.

Name	Birthplace	Year	U.S. immigration
Alberto Altieri	"Naples"	1890	unknown
Frank Clemente	Cervinara	1887	1906
Salvatore Costa	Castellammare	1893	unknown
Ralph Daniello	Pagani	1886	1907[120]
Ernesto Desidero	Angri	1885	1915[121]
Alberto Esposito	Avellino	1891	1905 ?
John Esposito	Brooklyn, N.Y.	ca. 1893	—
Giovanni Fetto	Cusano Mutri	1886	1910, 1913
Frank Fevrola	Avellino	1886	1901?[122]

Name	Birthplace	Year	U.S. *immigration*
Angelo Giordano	Avellino	1879	1890
Leopoldo Lauritano	Agerola/Gragnano	1872	1899
Pellegrino Morano	Prata	1877	1892, 1912
Antonio Notaro	Saviano	ca. 1892	unknown[123]
Aniello Parretti	Caserta	1892	unknown
Tony Parretti	Caserta	1891	1902
Lorenzo Romano	Prata	1889	1908
Tony Santulli	New York	1887	—
Alfonso Sgroia	Eboli	1886	1900
Giuseppe Vaccaro	Angri	1878	unknown
Alessandro Vollero	Gragnano	1889	unknown

In Coney Island, the boss was Morano, with Tony Parretti as his "under-boss." They were those from whom others took "direct orders."[124] That aside, there was little in the way of a hierarchy, specialization, or a division of labor within either of the organizations in Brooklyn. According to Sgroia, "There was two or three" Coney Island and Navy Street leaders, identifying Morano, Lauritano, Ricci, Vollero and Anthony Parretti.[125]

The Brooklyn "bosses" were simply those who paid the others and made the decisions. Daniello recalled, "they put us on a salary, when they were paying us twenty dollars, fifteen and ten dollars a week."[126] A family man got $20, a single man less.[127]

Prior to the 1916 slayings, "Every man was making a living by himself."[128] If they met, it was only as "friends." But Navy Street "was not officially a gang."[129] Esposito explained, "When I was a member I hang out there with them, I was friendly with them, I knew what they done, but I didn't take part in it."

Ricci, described as a Navy Street "boss," operated as late as 1915 as a front-line gunman against Giosue Gallucci. But as further killings were planned and took place, new men were taken on permanently and the bosses/workers dichotomy appeared. Recruits were placed on the gang's payroll to assure their loyalty and to make them readily available for future jobs.[130]

Like those joining the Mafia of New York City, Camorra members and associates did not receive payment for murder. Sgroia said, "If they told me to do it, I did it."[131]

There is no record of the two Brooklyn syndicates operating in a unified manner prior to the DeMarco murder, though Morano of Coney Island sponsored the Gallucci killing in which Ricci (Navy Street) was a participant. The two Brooklyn mobs called themselves from where they met.[132] It was likely that Morano's gang was formed only a couple of years before 1916, drawn from those who hung around his Santa Lucia. It is not known what happened to his group when the restaurant was closed, or when Morano was in Italy.[133] While Morano claimed to "know" people in other

U.S. cities who could help the Brooklyn based members, none were evident when Daniello was evading the police manhunt for him in 1917, further signifying the looseness of the ties within the network.

RITUAL

Commensurate with a Sicilian practice, the Camorra in Brooklyn had a ceremony. Notaro told the court how in the Easter of 1916, he was made a *Camorrista* in John Mancini's house on Coney Island. Three men were initiated (or "gained"): Ricci, Vollero and Notaro. Those in charge of the ceremony were Morano, Vincenzo Parapalle, Tony Parretti and Lauritano,[134] representing Coney Island and Navy Street.

Tony Parretti said to Notaro, "Now you are giving to make you a Camorrista and give you that title." He continued, "the leader of the society, the boss, is Pellegrino Morano and Vincent Paragallo is the second boss."[135] Notaro agreed to become a *Camorrista*. During the proceedings, orders were given to Notaro against talking; they must also obey the bosses, even if it meant killing. Tony Parretti gave them his penknife. Notaro cut Parretti on Parretti's arm and Morano sucked the blood. Morano said to Notaro, "You have gained."[136] Vollero and Ricci underwent the same process.

Previous participation in a murder was not a requirement to become a Brooklyn *Camorrista,* contrasting to a supposed Mafia practice.[137] But the ritual performed on Salvatore Mara by the White Plains "Black Hand" organization denoted in Chapter 2 in part consisted of a similar blood sucking element.[138]

For Daniello, becoming a *Camorrista* made them "a person among us criminals who is superior to other criminals."[139] In concrete terms, though, the advantages accrued by being made a fully-fledged member who underwent the ritual was unclear, except (for the bosses) to stiffen the resolve of hesitant underlings. When Notaro demurred over slaying the Morellos in September 1916, for instance, Morano reminded that they made him a *Camorrista* so that he should obey orders. "You must go. That is the reason why we gave you that title in the Camorra." Upon hearing that, Notaro carried through his mission.[140]

That the two Brooklyn groups could unite in the one ceremony suggested a common historical foundation, or the imposition on one of the parties of the ritual. On this question, the record is silent, since none of those conducting the ceremony except for Lauritano (who was apparently not asked) chose to admit their culpability in organized crime. The likeness of the two sets of recruitment procedures, hierarchies and bonds that connected members together on Navy Street and Coney Island also indicated a common experience in Brooklyn at least. The ritual may have been imported from one of the many towns and villages surrounding Naples from which the Brooklyn members came. It was not, however, that performed in the city of Naples as described in the 1911–12 Viterbo trial of leading "Camorrista."

CRIMINAL RECORDS

Pitkin remarked that the overwhelming majority of the Brooklyn *Camorristi* "brought their criminal habits, or at least proclivities, with them from elsewhere."[141] Several had criminal records in Italy before journeying to New York. But others did not; they found their niche on the streets of Manhattan and Brooklyn. Regardless of where they acquired their expertise, they were collectively more than a match for the Harlem Morellos.

Notaro and Aniello Parretti were two of the few to have stayed clear of the law before the murders of 1916. Tony Parretti was jailed twice for stabbings in Italy. Vollero was convicted of a shooting and jailed in Naples.[142] Daniello was arrested and served 2 years for cutting a woman's throat, escaping to America as Alphonse Pepe before he could stand trial for murder.[143] Desiderio was involved in stabbings in Italy and (allegedly) in a death in New York in 1906.[144]

Morano sold stolen horses for a living while residing in Harlem, and was fined for carrying a concealed weapon. Fevrola had been arrested in Yonkers for carrying a concealed weapon. In 1912, Esposito was convicted of shooting a man and received six months jail time for assault. Esposito was also wanted in Springfield, Massachusetts, for homicide.[145] Sgroia was convicted of a 1910 shooting.[146]

Lauritano was found guilty in 1913 and 1917 of carrying a dangerous weapon. Daniello and Ricci were jointly indicted in Brooklyn for robbery, larceny and assault in 1917. Daniello, furthermore, heard that Alberto Altieri had bumped off a man on Hester Street. Santulli was part of a "raiding party" that in 1914 fought with Jack Sirocco against Benjamin "Dopey" Fein outside the Madison Square Garden.[147]

CAMORRA IN NAPLES

Despite the seriousness of the crimes in which the Brooklyn members were involved, they were little more than a shadow of the Camorra in Naples in terms of their reputed scope and scale. Testimony taken at Viterbo in 1911 indicated that Naples was divided into 14 *Camorrista* districts, with 24 leaders (*capi'ntrine*) each in control of 48 *picciotti* (rank and file members). Complete with Grand Council of the local *capi*, each offshoot had its own committee to decide questions of general interest, and to hear appeals against the disciplinary code.

Enrico Alfano, arrested in 1907 by Petrosino, was described as the operational head in Naples, "a kind of president of the confederation of all the twelve sections." A "cashier" was available to take the place of the "head of heads" in the society if necessary. The head of heads and cashier were elected by a majority of votes.[148] The lowest level Camorristi (*picciotto di sgarro),* after a probationary period would undergo an initiation practice consisting of the swearing of obedience to the society, and the ordeal of a knife fight.[149] Whether the formal organizational structure reflected concrete relations is returned to.

NEW YORK ENTERPRISES

Before their takeover of Morello enterprises in 1916, the Neapolitans based in Brooklyn were active in policy gambling and retail cocaine sales. Daniello sold the stuff when he was a barber working for (or with) Vollero and Giuseppe (or Carlo) Simonelli, selling narcotics to "theatrical people and the waiters."[150]

Because this activity was "independent" of the gang's enterprises, Vollero refused to share any of the revenues accruing from it.[151] Cocaine trafficking apparently continued up to Vollero's arrest in 1917, and his operation was a source of friction with other gang members. (When Vollero agreed to a accept lower amount from reluctant artichoke dealers, for example, it raised a complaint from Tony Parretti speaking for those members who relied on the artichoke graft as their sole source of money.[152] Bizzaro had the same objection over the sum finally agreed with policy bosses.[153]) Esposito used to be a lookout man for cocaine dealers,[154] while Desidero was also a cocaine seller.[155]

His cocaine ventures brought Vollero into conflict with the Grimaldis, Frank, Fiore, John, Mike and Ralph, ending with the shooting of Frank Grimaldi in 1915.[156] They made peace at the Navy Street coffee house owned by the Lauritanos, when they "shook hands and kissed each other."[157] Vollero, according to Daniello, shot Louis DeMaria when he refused to respect territorial rights around Navy Street.[158] It was the crime that Daniello was indicted for in 1917 before he broke from the gang.

A comparable situation applied to gambling money. Marano kept the profits from his Harlem policy game to himself and his several partners. Moreover, when Esposito was considering opening a gambling den in Harlem on the suggestion of the Morellos, he kept the news from his Navy Street associates.[159] There was no sharing of the fruits from ventures started and operated by individual members, unlike the Mafia practice in which a part of the profits from criminal enterprises were "kicked upstairs" to the mob leadership.

On the legal side, discounting the Navy Street place in which the Lauritano brothers (Antonio and Leopoldo) and Vollero were interested and Morano's Santa Lucia, Daniello was a partner in a saloon and a restaurant with John Mancini on Skillman Avenue.[160] Eugene Bizzaro had a saloon at the corner of Johnson Street and Hudson Avenue with Carlo Cirillo.[161]

EXTORTION

The Navy Street organization following the removal of the Morellos from the equation, "collected by extortion and otherwise, from various enterprises, the sale of artichokes, the running of these various gambling houses which paid tribute."[162] According to the prosecutor in the Vollero case, "for some reason or other felt that they could not get possession of this coal and ice or cellar blackmail until the rest of the Morellos had been killed."[163]

Shortly after the fall of Nick Morello and Eugene Ubriaco, four East Harlem policy bosses were "invited" to see Eugene Bizzaro and Andrea Ricci at 328 East 109th Street in the heart of ex-Gallucci territory.[164] They refused to concede to a demand that they pay $1,000 a month to Brooklyn for the right to operate. They "were gamblers themselves and they were pretty hard characters themselves."[165] It was agreed that they would retain 40 percent of their earnings, with the Neapolitans getting the remainder.[166]

The policy bosses took the books and profits from Harlem to spots in Navy Street, Coney Island and Staten Island weekly.[167] One of those who made the journey, Giovanni Tartaglione, related, "On a Saturday, I would being down there (Navy Street) the policy game written. On the Monday or Tuesday I would bring down the money."[168] He later went to Staten Island, taking with him the policy registers and profits to Charlie Giordano's café there.[169] Other policy bosses Tartaglione knew from Harlem, such as Antonio Celentano, were observed there.[170]

The Brooklynites relinquished the Harlem policy game after about 3 months, when their compatriot Notaro was arrested in the Verrazano case and they needed bail money to release him.[171] In the end, they accepted $200 to return the game to its original owners. Vollero said "Give us $200 and you can give us the balance when you feel like it." That was the last money they ever received.[172]

Turning to the shakedown of artichoke sellers, which had provided another incentive to move against the Morellos, the initial plan was for the Camorra to open a store on Wallabout Market, and from there to drive other retailers out of business thereby cornering the market. Four key buyers were approached to put the scheme into force, and James Giordano, who knew the business, agreed to run the store.

But he pulled out, and Gaetano Migliaccio, a wholesaler, refused to sell his supplies exclusively to the Navy Street group. Migliaccio argued, "Are you crazy? To begin with, you need a capital of ten or eleven thousand dollars, and then the persons will go to the police and have each and every one of you arrested."[173] He said he could give them 30–40 boxes only.

Haggling left the parties agreeing that the Neapolitans would receive $25 per carload of artichokes arriving from California to the New York wholesalers, after they had originally demanded $50. Sellers insisted that was more than they could afford.[174] The threat that the Neapolitans would steal the dealers' horses and ruin their products if they demurred further was in the background to the negotiations.[175] Joe Conti, an artichoke dealer on East 29th Street, explained, "We were simply told to pay up, and that we could then keep in peace."[176]

The Camorra's predatory enterprises in late 1916 were comparable to those described by Block in his discussion of "power" syndicates. At their core, "power" groups have "no set tasks to perform except to menace and terrorize."[177] Schelling indeed considered extortion to be the most distinctive activity of organized crime.[178] In the business of selling protection, they were the polar opposite of those "enterprise" focused organizations denoted by Smith, Haller and Reuter, serving an otherwise untapped public demand without resort to coercion or intimidation.[179]

The predatory modus operandi was likely to eventually encourage victims to defect to law enforcement, especially where no quid pro quo for their compliance was forthcoming. The perils of trying to "shake down" gamblers were in the mind of Los Angeles Family boss Frank DeSimone in 1964. Other *borgata* members had warned him that it might "result in increased attention by law enforcement agencies." DeSimone contended that most bookmakers were also police informers, adding to the risk of attempting to take them on.[180] Successful prosecutions of Mafia leaders in Chicago and Boston, who turned to extorting local gamblers for income, showed the potential hazards.

The parade of aggrieved policy managers and artichoke dealers presented at the Camorra trials powerfully exemplified the difficulty for extortionists in securing the silence of their victims. The problem was most acute when a concerted police drive was on to convict their tormentors, threatening jail sentences against those refusing to cooperate. Giovanni Tartaglione, one of those testifying for the state, had worked for Ubriaco and (when Ubriaco lost money) for Morano. Tartaglione ran the game for Morano, working as his "secretary," for a time in 1916. Once Morano left, Tartaglione said he paid nobody,[181] though the Morellos had insisted that Morano give them $25 as a weekly sum.

Vulnerability to arrest and imprisonment may have encouraged a subtler type of extortion, especially taking the form of ostensibly freely given "donations" for a social event. On the last day of November 1916, Brooklyn police raided a "smoker" on Bridge Street organized by Andrea Ricci, in which 33 Italians were arrested as members of the Morello and Brooklyn factions. Complaints had been received from Italian merchants that they were forced to "lavishly buy" tickets.[182] The smoker was held, the police suspected, to raise money for a member of Ricci's gang in trouble with the law.[183] But they were unable to make headway.

There was also the matter of the perceived "fairness" of demands made of others when judged by the standards of the criminal underworld. Pellegrino Morano, for example, maintained that killing the Morellos to grab their operations was a justifiable reaction to the Morellos' previous behavior when he was in a client role. Vollero not too dissimilarly referred to the Morellos' killing of Nicolo DelGaudio as in some fashion legitimizing his decision to see them dead.

As the Brooklyn Camorra's history also established, a sharp division between the activities of power and enterprise syndicates was unrealistic. Morano and Vollero for instance ran market-driven ventures, while blackmailing those run by gang outsiders.

MUNICIPAL CORRUPTION

Interspersed through the trial materials were descriptions and allegations of official misconduct centered on bribes, furnished to guarantee that gambling was permitted to operate uninterrupted, and to ensure that *Camorristi* remained at liberty.

Official corruption was hardly a novel discovery, but the empirical link to organized crime was often elusive. In 1913, a "ex-saloonkeeper, stool-pigeon for the police, bribe-payer and bribe-collector," Ashley Shea, told the District Attorney how Harlem gamblers paid police up to the level of Captain for protection services, with a first payoff being of $1,300 "and half of the profits thereafter."[184] A year later, the ex Deputy Police Commissioner claimed that vice was widespread, "with the connivance of police officials."[185]

Ralph Daniello gave the Police Commissioner the names of detectives connected to the Neapolitan syndicates: Mike Mealli,[186] Charlie Carrao, attached to the First Branch Detective Bureau,[187] Bennie Grottano (who brought Daniello back from Reno) and "Castagnia."[188] Lauritano told Vollero, "we have to make a present to Mike Mealli" of a $100 purse, when Bartolomeo Pagano surrendered in the Morello affair, in order to secure his release.[189] "Lauritano put in $50 and Vollero matched it, saying, "I will put in $50 for Mike."[190] Joe Morone got $200 from Daniello to get Vollero out on bail after Vollero was held for the Morello and Ubriaco killings.[191]

Trial material outlined how Nicholas Canarelli, owner of a saloon or liquor store at 188 Grand Street, functioned as a middleman between the police and gamblers in the Hester Street quarter. One of the few Sicilians in the network,[192] Canarelli knew Morano, was involved in fixing the police,[193] and helped to divide the proceeds from the 167 Hester Street game.[194] A police captain was paid $200 per month, the money to be taken from the game's profits, in order to open the Hester Street operation after Verrazano was murdered.[195] "Nick had received the Captain's orders," Daniello testified, "that everything was ready, and that we could open up on the game."[196]

Samuel Martin, an Inspector of the Department of Licenses and formerly vice-chairman of the Democratic General Council, confirmed the importance of Canarelli. "Throughout the district," noted Martin, "(Nick) was known as the collector."[197] Canarelli saw police when a game was to be opened, usually in exchange for $100 a month.[198] Martin went on to describe how he personally helped someone to open up a crap game through Canarelli. The money was given to Nick and was presumed to have then passed to the police. Martin had helped "the Shoemaker" (Tony Parretti) to run a crap game.[199] Canarelli also handled liquor permits.[200]

Equally essential to the gang's longevity in lower Manhattan according to Daniello was Antonio Ferrara, the owner of a coffee shop or café at 195 Grand Street.[201] Ferrara was born like Morano in Prata, Avellino. Ferrara "was the man who used to fix our cases, either in New York or in Brooklyn."[202] Daniello explained, "Anything that has happened with this Navy Street gang (Ferrara) has fixed the police."[203]

James "Jimmy Kelly" DiSalvo, Hester Street saloonkeeper and restaurant owner, testified for the defense at Angelo Giordano's trial for murdering Verrazano. DiSalvio was a political power and the father-in-law of Frankie Yale's confederate Anthony "Little Augie Pisano" Carfano.[204] DiSalvio claimed to have known Giordano 20 years or more, and that Giordano was in his place when Verrazano was shot.[205] Giordano backed this assertion up; "I invited Mrs. DeSalvio to be a patroness of my Society, and I brought some tickets in a package."[206]

The Camorra network on the lower east side intermingled with political violence linked to the Mulberry Bend Italian vote. Gaetano Montimagno, of a rival political faction, shot down Michael Giamari, a Second Assembly District leader under sheriff Thomas F. Foley, on March 8, 1915. Giamari's brothers, Alfred and John, were earlier freed of a charge of shooting Vincenzo Candillo in revenge for Candillo's wounding of Mike.[207]

In 1916, Montimagno gave the names at Michael E. Rofino's trial of those he held responsible for the Giamari homicide, including Salvatore Zurica. Zurica was among the team that was to signal when Giamari approached his place of execution.[208]

Michael Grimaldi, one of the family once in dispute with Vollero over area cocaine territories, was connected in January 1917 to the Giamari slaying. James Licato allegedly shot Zurica to death. It was reported that Grimaldi, as a friend to both Licato and Zurica, had lured Zurica to the meeting where he was blasted. Licato was arrested in Grimaldi's coffee house on Carroll Street.[209] But in June 1917, Licato was acquitted, and charges against Grimaldi were dropped.[210]

ORGANIZATIONAL SECURITY

Descriptions of the Camorra in Naples highlighted its elaborate superstructure and means to bring in new blood. Higher group members' meetings were barred to "inferiors."[211] Communications between the bosses and other members were commonly conducted through trusted go-betweens (in the Mafia, by *caporegimes*).[212]

Yet it transpired in the Viterbo proceedings that the Naples Camorra chieftain Enrico Alfano dealt personally with the assassins who felled Gennaro Cuocolo and his wife Maria in 1906. It was this incident that was to prove Alfano's ruin, since a police undercover operative discovered the specifics. Scheming the removal of Cuocolo and his wife (who had performed unauthorized robberies and were suspected informers) also greatly excised the energies of "all the sectional Committees and all the members of the executive committee" of the Camorra, rather than the matter being dealt with as a relatively trivial matter at the local level.[213] Evidence from the Viterbo trial suggested something less than the imagery conveyed before and since of a supreme citywide conspiracy in Naples, in which the leaders were immune from prosecution.

In Brooklyn, the Neapolitans' organizational system permitted a free intermingling of members and bosses, posing identical dangers for the leadership's survival. No "buffer" function existed. Upon Notaro's arrest for murdering Verrazano in 1916, as a consequence, there was an immediate recognition that he might bring them down, if there was verification of his statements. Giordano sent him $15 a week ($5 more than usual), and tried to calm fears. The others were "keeping our mouth shut," so "what can he do?"[214]

How long the Neapolitans had known each other, either in Italy or New York, was crucial in determining levels of trust to be expected among the membership especially when the stakes were high. Sgroia knew Vollero in Gragnano when Vollero was a small boy.[215] Esposito had been acquainted with Ricci since about 1912, dating from their Harlem days.[216] Morano had known Ricci and Lauritano about a year before 1916, and knew Tony Parretti about 4 years.

Others knew the Brooklyn gang leaders for a much shorter duration, and were among the first to betray their paymasters under aggressive questioning. Sgroia for instance had known Aniello and his brother Antonio Parretti for under a year. Daniello was "friendly" with members only a matter of months (February–September 1916) before being placed on the payroll at Navy Street.[217] And Mancini knew Morano "to speak to" since 1916.[218]

Relations between some members were also based on the *comparaggio* or *compari* (godparenthood) custom. Vollero, Tony Parretti and Marano became *compares*,[219] when they "stood up" for Vollero's boy Raffaele at his christening.[220] Vollero was a *compare* of one of Pagano's children and[221] Pagano was Daniello's *compare*.[222] Daniello was a godfather to James Giordano, selected to run the Camorra's artichoke store.[223] Amelia Valvo, with whom Daniello had fled to California and Reno, was Giordano's daughter.

Esposito explained that before 1916, "you could not really call it a gang, because no one was actually getting paid by the bosses."[224] The cash nexus proved to be a weak foundation upon which to build trust and assure silence, when combined to a casually considered recruitment process and an apparently unplanned organizational structure that collapsed if one or more members talked to the authorities.

SENTENCES

Daniello, Sgroia, Esposito and Notaro were among Camorra members in Brooklyn giving evidence against their former cohorts in crime. Supplementing their testimonies was that of artichoke dealers and policy bosses. Leopoldo Lauritano made a statement supporting the information given by others, but he was not called to testify. When the dust had settled, the groups in Navy Street and Coney Island had been decimated.

For Verrazano's murder, Angelo Giordano was given the death sentence in May 1918 in the New York County Court of General Sessions. It was carried out in September 1921.[225]

Giovanni Mancini gave information on the Verrazano case to the Manhattan grand jury, was a witness against Morano in Brooklyn, and offered himself as a witness against Vollero. Mancini, furthermore, only heard of the conspiracy to kill Verrazano on the night of his murder. His role was to stand guard while Verrazano was slain. Because of this, Mancini was allowed to plead guilty to manslaughter.[226]

On the night of Verrazano's homicide, Anthony "Cheese" Santulli sent a messenger to find out where Verrazano was, and was outside the restaurant in which Verrazano was slain, according to a waiter. But there was no independent corroboration of the waiter's statement, and Santulli was freed.[227]

Charged with the gunning down of DeMarco and Lombardi were John Esposito, John Fetto, Leopoldo Lauritano, Bartolomeo Pagano, and Ciro Terranova. Esposito was selected as one of the shooting party, but gained nothing from it. He gave evidence against Terranova, Vollero, and Morano, and assisted in securing John Fetto's cooperation with the government. Esposito also helped to bring a guilty plea from Lauritano for the Morello murder. Esposito was consequently allowed to plea to a charge of manslaughter.[228]

Ciro Terranova was acquitted on June 6, 1918 of participation in the conspiracy resulting in the deaths of DeMarco and Lombardi, due to a lack of confirmation of the evidence given by Esposito and Fetto. Assistant District Attorney George Brothers concluded, "It was the unanimous opinion of everybody who heard the case that it was entirely hopeless to the jury . . . and that there was no likelihood or probability that the jury would convict."[229]

In 1937, Terranova was reported to be "broke," and his Spanish style mansion in Pelham Manor was foreclosed because he argued that he could not pay the rent. "He listed as his assets $200 owed to him, two shares of realty stock and a 'possible cause of action for false arrest'."[230] Terranova died February 1938 in Columbus Hospital of cerebral thrombosis.[231]

John Fetto made a full confession and testified against Terranova. Fetto was permitted to plead to first-degree manslaughter. Rocco Valenti was not present at the planning stage, and though selected to shoot DeMarco and

Figure 5.5   Ciro Terranova. (Courtesy of the Library of Congress)

Lombardi, he was not punctual. Similar to the Santulli case, there was no substantiation of assertions made against Valenti, who was released after spending 10 months in confinement.[232]

Alessandro Vollero was condemned to death on April 1, 1918, for the Ubriaco murder. In 1919, the sentence was reduced to a minimum of 20 years imprisonment and Vollero was released on parole in April 1933, returning to Italy.

Morano was convicted of the second-degree homicide of Morello, and sentenced to 20 years to life. Alfonso Sgroia was allowed to plead guilty to manslaughter. Because of his assistance, Sgroia was handed a reduced term of imprisonment of up to 12 years. He died in Italy in May 1940.[233]

Lauritano was locked up for 6–10 years in the New York State prison for the slaying of Morello, and paroled in 1926. In 1927, Lauritano received a further 5 years incarceration for perjury in relation to the trial of Tony Parretti for the killing of Morello and Ubriaco.[234] Tony Parretti was handed the death sentence in July 1926 for the Ubriaco fatality, being executed on February 17, 1927 in New York State prison.[235] He had fled to Italy, returning to New York mistakenly thinking most of the witnesses against him were gone.[236]

Figure 5.6   Alessandro Vollero. (Courtesy of the New York State Library)

On June 1, 1921, Frank Fevrola was found guilty in White Plains of responsibility for the slaying of Generoso Nazzaro; 9 days later he was condemned to death. Four attempts were made to free Fevrola from the State prison death house once his common law wife Tessie Bonaguar recanted her earlier testimony.[237] She declared that she gave "false testimony because of the threats and promises" made by the Westchester District Attorney, and the Yonkers Police Department, "as the policemen and detectives said they had a whole lot on me."[238] In 1923, Fevrola's sentence was commuted to life imprisonment.

In November 1921, Aniello Parretti was also convicted for the Nazzaro death and meted out the death sentence. He was freed in 1923 after his conviction was reversed on appeal and a new trial ordered. The Westchester District Attorney then dropped the indictment, and Parretti was released.[239]

Several of the former *Camorristi* met untimely ends. Alberto Altieri was present at a meeting with other gang members and artichoke dealers,[240] subsequently attending another, in which the killing of the outstanding Morellos was discussed.[241] The "millionaire bootlegger and Camorra chief" Altieri was killed in February 1921 in what the police depicted as a quarrel over the spoils from alcohol trafficking.[242]

After serving 9 years of a 15 year sentence, Giuseppe Vaccaro was shot down from a speeding sedan in June 1929 on a Brooklyn street.[243] John

Esposito's body was found at the back of a billboard along the Lincoln Highway, New Jersey, on December 31, 1924, shot by a .38 caliber automatic revolver. Esposito was out on parole.[244]

Ralph Daniello received a suspended sentence in June 1918 for manslaughter. In 1919, he was jailed for 5 years for shooting and wounding a man in Hoboken, New Jersey. (Daniello wrongly thinking, he contended, that the victim was sent from Navy Street to assassinate him.) Daniello, the star witness, was shot dead in front of his Newark, New Jersey, saloon on August 15, 1925, collapsing in front of the bar. The killer told Daniello before pulling the trigger, "I've got you now."[245]

MORELLOS

The Nick Morello organization was similar to that run by his half-brother Joseph Morello and by the Camorra outfits, in terms of its restricted size and in the absence of a developed hierarchy. Like the Brooklynites, the 1910s Morellos seem to have trusted in the power that carrying around a revolver gave them as the major way of deterring potential attackers. Inside the Navy Street headquarters was a secret panel or trap into which pistols were concealed, used by Nick Morello and Ubriaco on the day of their murders. The device was installed to prevent their being arrested on gun charges. Recruitment was, however, tighter and systematized in the Mafia.

Since Morano and Ricci had known and dealt with the Morellos many times, the *Camorristi* bosses were versed in the Morello's strengths and weaknesses. Morano admitted to knowing the Morellos 7–8 years, and was further informed about their operations from their visits to the Santa Lucia.[246] The Morellos, Ricci and Morano socialized together, and the Morellos attended the annual "smoker" given by Ricci at Bridge Street.[247] The Neapolitans calculated that even with the limited numbers at their disposal, it was possible to topple the Harlem "Sicilians."

The Morello/Terranova brothers (Nick, Vincent and Ciro), Steve LaSalle and Eugenio Ubriaco were the key figures targeted. Joseph Verrazano was sometimes included. Ubriaco was born near Cosenza, Calabria, in 1890. His father, Camillo, was a property owner on 114th Street.[248]

Stefano "Steve" LaSalle (real name LaSala) was probably born November 1889, in Corleone.[249] A long time resident of East 107th Street, LaSalle had the good fortune to be arrested on September 4, 1916 and was on remand at Raymond Street, Brooklyn, until his sentencing in October.[250] By a quirk of fate, he thereby avoided traveling with Morello and Ubriaco to share their fates on Johnson Street. LaSalle would become an influential member of the post Gaetano Reina organized crime Family under its various titles, reaching the post of *consiglieri*.

The question of why the 2 other Mafia *borgata* known to exist in Brooklyn or Manhattan in 1916 did not step to help their Mafia *amici* in Harlem arises. Despite their interests around Elizabeth Street (lower east

Figure 5.7 Stefano LaSalle. (Courtesy of the U.S. National Archives)

side), where the Morellos were a power, there was no sign of the D'Aquila Family intervening in the warfare to tip the balance of advantage in the Morello's favor. The Schiro Mafia in Williamsburg could have performed a mediation role, given its proximity to Camorra activities on Navy Street, particularly since Schiro and the Harlem group in trouble were earlier reported as "working together."[251]

To answer this seeming connundrum requires an understanding of the autonomous quality of relationships between *borgata*. Where a Family was in difficulties, it was left to resolve the problem. For this reason alone, the U.S. Mafia could never even approximate the nationwide conspiratorial role assigned to it by some commentators in the 1960s and beyond.

But perhaps there was a higher level that the Morello *borgata* could have appealed to in their deadly struggle with the Neapolitans? The Mafia "*assemblea generale*" (general assembly) was a fragile structure, exclusively dealing with relations between its constituents. It had no mandate—or ability—to intercede in matters involving non-affiliates.

The Commission, which replaced the general assembly, was as powerless to intervene where non-Mafiosi were involved, a constitutional feature manifested when the Cleveland Family was locking horns with the Danny Greene group in the 1970s.[252] Even when the matter involved other Mafiosi, as during the 1960s Gallo rebellion in Brooklyn, the Commission's authority to resolve matters was circumscribed.[253]

MAINLAND ITALIANS AND THE MAFIA

As the Neapolitan segment in New York City's organized crime was largely decimated, new opportunities for those still at liberty unfurled. Throughout the 1920s, non-Sicilians were slowly brought into formerly exclusively Sicilian crime organizations. The changed policy was caused by a reduction in Sicilian manpower sources, the demands of Prohibition, and the imminence of a Mafia war (Chapter 7), for which fresh recruits were required. Neapolitans disappeared as an autonomous factor in the city's organized crime.

THE "COMBINATION"

Until mainland Italians were accorded membership status in the New York City Mafia Families, some appear to have belonged to a "halfway house," composed of those ineligible because of their backgrounds to access Mafia membership. The FBI, in that context, overheard Genovese Family member Angelo DeCarlo referring to a *combaneesh* ("combination"). Those in the combination included the Calabrian and Neapolitan Guarino "Willie Moore" Moretti[254] and Ruggerio "Ritchie the Boot" Boiardo. They later joined the Mafia, in Boiardo's case in about 1944.[255]

The likes of Vito Genovese, Boiardo and Moretti were "sneaked into" the combination, DeCarlo argued, "before they got in here." According to DeCarlo, "Willie Moretti got sneaked in. They got sneaked in! Vito got sneaked in! I think he told me. In 1923."[256]

TONY PARRETTI'S VISITORS

These developments may have supplied the reason for a curious episode until now unnoticed. Condemned to die for the Ubriaco murder, Anthony Paretti in the New York State prison death house was allowed 17 visitors other than close relatives, "the largest ever permitted a condemned man in the thirty-seven years the electric chair has been in use in this State."[257]

Among those permitted to talk to Parretti by court order signed on July 20, 1926, were "Davido Prevetti" and Vito Genovese. Carmine Russo of Ozone Park, who also visited Parretti, was reportedly involved in an auto incident in May 1924 involving Genovese, after which Genovese was charged with homicide. Pasquale Ambrosino, another, had furnished part of the money to pay for Parretti's trial defence in 1926. By further order signed on October 14, 1926, Frank Amato and John "Volpo," from the Ozone Park, Queens, residence given by "Prevetti," were authorized to speak to Parretti.[258]

We have no idea what they discussed. But most were important names in the future Mafia. At least three came from the small village of Roccarainola, some 32km northeast of Naples. Genovese landed on American soil in June 1913 from Rigisliano, only a kilometer from Roccarainola.[259]

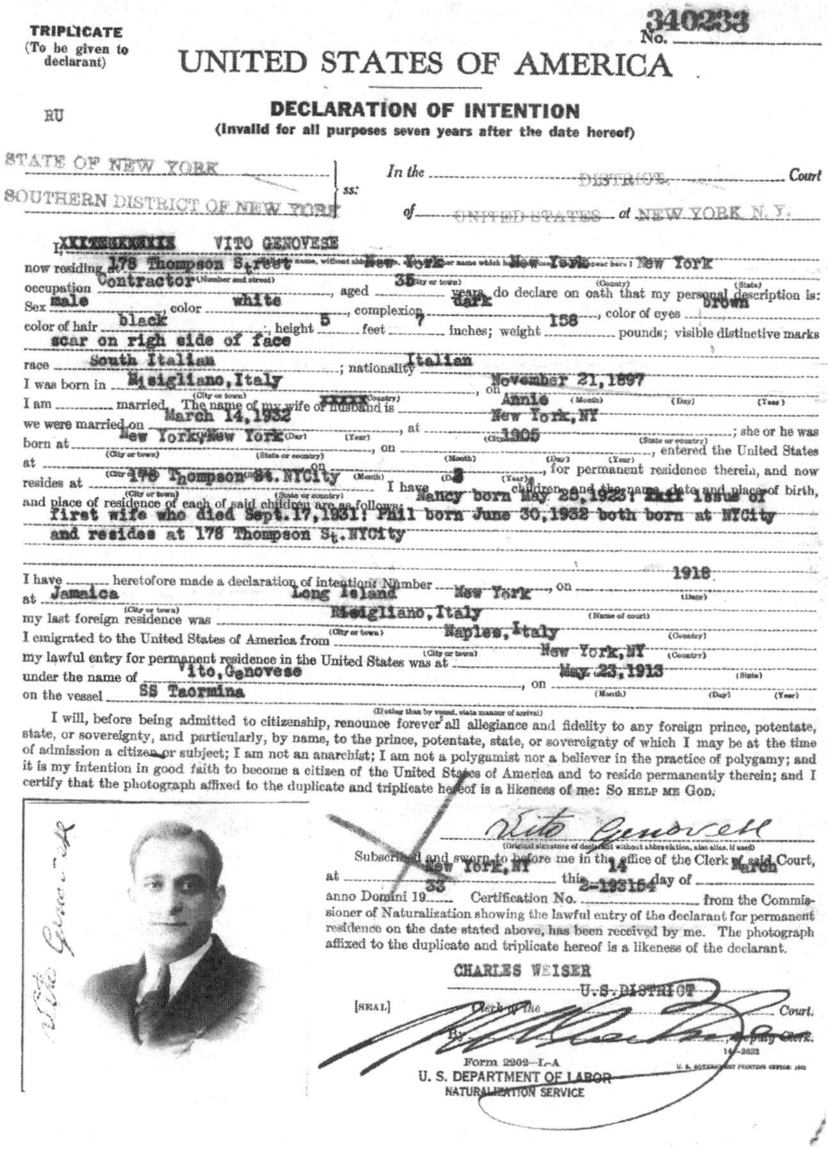

Figure 5.8 Vito Genovese naturalization record. (Courtesy of the U.S. National Archives)

Genovese, characterized by Joseph Valachi as the 1950s Mafia's "boss of all bosses under the table,"[260] is addressed in Chapter 6. Davide Prevete was born in Roccarainola in 1888, journeyed to New York twice. Prevete, who testified in some of the Camorra trials, died in July 1927 in an automobile accident in Queens."[261]

Working as a barber at 6 Mott Street in 1916, Prevete knew the leaders of both Navy Street and Coney Island Camorra factions.[262] He was a visitor to the Santa Lucia restaurant and occasionally went to Lauritano's place on Navy Street.[263] Tony Parretti "stood up" for one of Prevete's children.[264] During the Morano trial, Prevete denied that he had killed a man in 1907 on Skillman Avenue, and that he had collected money for "Dom Mimi DeFalco" in the Bronx.[265] Prevete knew Mike Giamari (above) well.[266]

Shortly before Verrazano died, the men involved in his murder met in a wine cellar in a basement next to "Ferrara's" on Grand Street. Angelo Giordano lived above the cellar. Prevete claimed not to know what his friends were discussing when he briefly socialized with them there.[267] Giordano's attorney argued however that Prevete "at least had knowledge of what was about to happen, if his testimony is true." He suggested that Prevete might have delivered to Notaro a message with respect to the plot against Verrazano.[268] Once Verrazano was gunned down, Sgroia met Tony Parretti in Prevete's shop.

Francesco "Frank" Amato, Parretti's third visitor, came to America in 1911 from Roccarainola. Genovese was Amato's *compare* in the Mafia,[269] and Amato went on to head the Pittsburgh Mafia in the 1940s.[270] "John Volpo" on Parretti's list may have been John Volpe, part of the same Pittsburgh *borgata* as Amato until perishing in 1932, for which act *capo* John Bazzano, Sr. died.[271]

Power in the Pittsburgh Family leadership oscillated between Sicilians (such as the Monastero brothers) and mainland Italians like Bazzano and Amato. Gentile explained how, in Pittsburgh, an initially powerful "Camorra" was "routed" by the Sicilians in the latter 1910s. In was Gentile's intervention that won the day for the Mafia, in his own telling.[272]

VALACHI'S PRISON CONNECTIONS

The backgrounds of Joseph Valachi's New York State prison associates illustrated the strength of those racial solidities that until the late 1920s blocked the admittance of non-Sicilians into the Mafia of New York City. Valachi, living on 109th Street during the period, recalled the likes of Gallucci, Zaraca and Russomano as men to be feared. During his imprisonment in the mid 1920s, his closest pal was Carmine "Dolly Dimples" Clemente, a fellow Neapolitan.[273] (Carmine's brother, Francesco "Coney Island" Clemente, was a member of the Navy Street organization.)[274] Valachi and Clemente "went around together all the time."[275]

Clemente was incarcerated for holding up, with seven others, the Starlight Amusement Park, Bronx, in 1925. For that, Clemente received 10–20 years.[276] As well as Clemente, Valachi was close in New York State prison to another Neapolitan, Alessandro Vollero.[277]

Vollero asked Valachi to intercede for him with Genovese, Neapolitan also, once Vollero was paroled; he was "fearful that (Ciro) Terranova would seek revenge" for the murder of Nick Morello. After speaking to Valachi, Genovese assured Vollero that he could "stop worrying."[278] Valachi's closeness to Genovese was confirmed by the presence of Vito and his wife Anna as witnesses to Valachi's marriage to Mildred Reina, a daughter of deceased Mafia chieftain Gaetano "Tommy" Reina, in 1932.[279] In 1931, Valachi joined the Family that would be led by Genovese.

CONSEQUENCES

Outside of New York State, those from mainland Italy were more influential in *Famiglia*. Frank "Ciccio" Milano, representing Cleveland as *representando officiale* in 1930, was of Calabrian stock, having been born 1891 in San Roberto. In Gentile's account (though not Bonanno's), Milano sat on the first "Commission" in 1931.[280]

The non-Sicilians' propensity, especially those inside the Masseria *borgata*, towards a broader scale of illicit operations may have been a by-product of their absence of exposure to the restrictive Sicilian tradition, together with a response to their lack of contacts in the other (mostly Sicilian) Families. Both factors led them to seek wider alliances in organized crime, frequently involving outsiders to the Mafia and its satellites.

Frank Costello, from Calabria, had investments in Manhattan real estate, the coin amusement machine industry and illegal gaming clubs in Louisiana and Saratoga, New York.[281] In Floridian casino enterprises, Costello's partners included Meyer Lansky, Frank Erickson, and Mert Wertheimer, a veteran Detroit gambling entrepreneur with ties to Nevadan gaming.[282] The Kefauver Committee followed Costello's trail in the placement of slot and coin machines in New Orleans, under the daily control of his Jewish associate Phil Kastel.[283]

Giuseppe "Joe Adonis" Doto another Masseria *borgata* non-Sicilian moved from bootlegging to a variety of regional gambling ventures, including the operation of a floating crap game and of a dog track in Atlantic City. Also in the Adonis business portfolio was an interest in restaurants in Miami and Saratoga with Costello, and a partnership with Vincent "Jimmy Blue Eyes" Alo, a Calabrian component of the Masseria Family.[284]

The polar opposite of these innovative Italian mainlanders was Sicilian conventionalists that still formed the bulk of the Mafia membership. One was Paolo "Big Paul" Palazzolo. Seized at the 1928 Cleveland meeting (Chapter 6), Joseph Guinta, and Frank Abbate used Palazzolo's Gary, Indiana, address when they were booked.

Born 1895 in Cinisi, Sicily, over the course of Prohibition Palazzolo financed dozens of speakeasies, provided bonds for suspects, and, through the Italian Food Products enterprise, supplied sugar to moonshiners. Palazzolo subsequently dabbled in the Gary policy racket. On April 4, 1935, in "a continuation of a long series of slayings dating back to prohibition days," he was gunned down at close range on the sidewalk of the home of his brother in law.[285]

RACIAL DIVISIONS

Nelli argued that regionalism was "repressed" in the U.S. Mafia by an awareness of the shared Italian heritage of members and by "the common quest for money."[286]But given the sharp sense of racial identity displayed during the 1916–1917 conflict, the formality of admitting to membership a handful of mainland Italian members did not entirely quell tensions with established Sicilians.

Navy Street mobster Salvatore Costa was sent to Coney Island when the demise of the Morellos in September 1916 was being planned for fear that he might give away the game.[287] Tony Parretti told Vollero, "I don't trust him. He is a Sicilian."[288] Valachi explained the similar outlook of Vollero, "Alexander told me, he expressed it this way, "If you hang out with a Sicilian 20 years and you have some trouble with another Sicilian, this Sicilian that you hang out with 20 years will turn on you."[289]

During the 1960s, a confidential FBI source complained that the Sicilian-mainland Italian schism remained a live issue within groups; "there is often a deep resentment, bias or prejudice among members who are Neapolitan for Sicilian, and vice versa."[290] Typical of the divisive attitude that persisted was Bonanno's belief that the non-Sicilians could never fully understand the "Tradition" ethically and culturally underpinning Families.[291]

The background of members had a substantial effect on the construction of coalitions. Even among the Sicilians, distinctions existed, based on place of birth. Those born in Agrigento province for instance formed a clearly defined "Manhattan" element in the primarily "Palermitani" Mangano *Famiglia* of the 1930s. Nicolo Gentile was appointed to arbitrate differences between the two wings.[292]

Regional identity affected Families away from New York. The St. Louis, Missouri, Mafia had "something of a caste system, and that makes a difference as to their standing within the organization as to where they or their families originated in Italy."[293] A faction of the Youngstown group (ostensibly part of the Cleveland Mafia setup) was divided into "Sicilian" and "Calabrian" blocs; "they have never been seen together as one group since one group could not trust the other."[294]

To stave off the potential for unrest from this source, a policy was sometimes enacted of "balancing the ticket," selecting a few non-Sicilians to higher-ranking positions in essentially Sicilian Families. In Philadelphia's organization, the "Sicilians" and "Calabrians" had their own underbosses.[295]

CONCLUSION

By late 1916, the Brooklyn Camorra organizations' territory encompassed part of Harlem (via its policy game), the lower east side (through the card joint), and the Washington Market (artichokes). Added to this were their original bases in Brooklyn. While they were briefly active in the locality, the Brooklynites injected a measure of "control" over the East Harlem territory, somewhat lowering the level of organized murders in the quarter.

The chaotic state of affairs evident in Italian Harlem until then broadly accorded with that described by Block in his study of Manhattan cocaine trafficking. The local cocaine market was comparably run "by criminal entrepreneurs who formed, reformed, split, and came together again as opportunity arose and when they were able."[296]

But Block's source mainly consisted of raw intelligence data viewed from the perspective of observers ignorant of the meaning of the sightings they recorded. Neither were they privy to events that took place perhaps several years earlier.[297] This information trial transcripts could provide for the particular group studied in this chapter.

The Morellos were atypical in the New York City Mafia community, in their selection of the Brooklyn Neapolitans as associates. Other New York Mafias conducted business with Sicilians. The multi-racial quality to East Harlem's population as it emerged was responsible for a large part of this difference.

Other Families' operations were also consensualistic. Ralph Daniello worked for several years in a barbers shop on Metropolitan Avenue, and his Skillman Avenue restaurant was but a few blocks from Roebling Street, both establishments sited near to the hub of Schiro operations in Brooklyn. Nonetheless Daniello, a normally sharp operator, was apparently unaware of his Mafia neighbors. Salvatore Costa was equally ignorant of the existence of the Williamsburg *borgata*, even though he was, like most Schiro members, from Castellammare.[298]

Chapter 6 explores aspects of the 1920s alcohol traffic run by men of honor in New York. It was neither as centralized, nor as dominant an activity inside Families, as the orthodoxy implies. A final theme explored in chapter six is the emergence of the Masseria and Profaci Mafia formations. The creation of the Masseria *borgata* in particular upset the balance of tradition and modernization in the New York City *Onorata Societa*.

6   New York City in the 1920s

INTRODUCTION

The Eighteenth Amendment to the U.S. Constitution, the Volstead Act or simply "Prohibition," became effective on January 16, 1920, at a stroke criminalizing the export of intoxicating liquors and the home brewing of beverages with over half a percent of alcohol. America was officially and comprehensively "dry." However, "The Volstead Act," as Behr remarked, "was hopelessly inadequate, because it grossly underestimated both the willingness of the law-breakers to risk conviction . . . and the ease with which the law-breakers would be able to subvert all those who job it was to enforce it."[1] "The job of the Prohibition Bureau," Sinclair similarly reported, "was to enforce the impossible."[2] The Bureau was hopelessly understaffed and became riddled with corruption.[3]

The New York State Legislature passed the Mullan-Gage Law to supplement the federal measure only to repeal it in 1923, "making New York the first state to confess to the utter failure of state prohibition enforcement."[4] "To all intents and purposes," said the World League Against Alcoholism in 1925," "anyone can now engage in the liquor traffic unmolested in the City of New York."[5]

For the standard historiography, the experience of alcoholic drinks distillation, packaging, distribution and retailing during Prohibition gave organized crime the capital and connections allowing for its later diversification into other markets. The Volstead Act, most alarmingly, encouraged the enlargement of organized crime in a fashion unheard of but a few years earlier. Lupsha for example argues, "We would not have organized crime as we know it in the United States, if not for the period of Prohibition."[6]

However, the "high seas" operations of legend, about which much was written and models were created, were not those that New York Mafiosi tended to participate in. In addition, a number of Mafia leaders did not become involved in the booze business at all. Prohibition did not lead to a higher degree of centralization of either of enterprise or of organization in the New York City Mafia.

HISTORIOGRAPHY

Gary Mormino made the key point, "The voluminous literature dealing with urban crime in general and the phenomenon of the 1920s in particular suffers from tabloidism."[7] The received analysis often encapsulates a dichotomous model, with Prohibition perceived as a watershed in the evolution of the American Mafia. "Organized crime was permanently transformed by thirteen years of Prohibition," Fox declared."[8]

Prohibition's major effect, in this paradigm, was to furnish the first opportunity for formerly isolated Mafias "to work together for power and profit."[9] Alcohol trafficking gave the Mafia "the opportunity to organize on a national scale, and to gain internal discipline on a national scale."[10] Jacobs' comment mirrored the same assumption: "The Italian-American organized crime groups became extraordinarily powerful during the period of national alcohol prohibition (1920–1933)."[11] Organized crime was "nationalized."[12] A 1929 Atlantic City conference revisited below was perceived as a defining moment in this history and as proof of its existence.

A second reported effect was less obvious. "Prohibition," argued Haller, "by bringing to the fore a group of particularly energetic criminal entrepreneurs, created a general phenomenon in American business history."[13] Alcohol trafficking was the primary means, it was contended, through which second-generation Italian-American gangsters gained access to the highest levels of power in *Cosa Nostra*.[14] The argument is addressed in Chapter 8.

"HIGH SEAS" IMPORTATION

Sea borne or "High Seas" "rum running" was technically distinct from "bootlegging," that denoting the overland manufacture and transportation of illegal alcoholic beverages. Importation of spirits was predominantly from Canada, whisky forming the majority of the stuff smuggled. Rum came from the West Indies.[15]

The primary method of getting liquor to the East Coast market was by means of ocean-going vessels anchored offshore in international waters. High-speed "feeder" boats landed the cargo. Otherwise, contraband liquor was brought in as legitimate goods. During the first years of Prohibition a divide emerged, with "high seas" importations making up the bulk of the liquor consumed, especially of the higher quality stuff, leaving the cheaper grade liquor to be manufactured by domestic producers.[16]

The escapades of colorful rumrunners such as William McCoy, Roy Olmstead and Arnold Rothstein were frequently chronicled, as the major operators in the sector.[17] Haller for example detailed the logistical and organizational intricacies of liquor importation, involving a large number of contacts across ethnic divides.[18] "Successful bootleggers . . . necessarily did business with other bootleggers and therefore joined in local, regional, and even international networks of economic cooperation."[19] Canadian distillery conglomerates colluding with American traffickers, headed by the Bronfman brothers of Montreal, were documented in depth.[20] The distilling of alcohol within the United States was barely mentioned.

Frank Costello was referenced as representing the Mafia presence in bootlegging alongside Lucky Luciano, John Torrio and Frank Yale in New York.[21] Costello "became known as the man to see in New York for anything connected to bootlegging."[22] He also became an important example of the purported trend towards "Americanization" in the Mafia, said to embody the "can do" attitude of younger generation Mafiosi who easily mixed with other races in furtherance of shared goals, "a key to their ultimate power and generalized authority."[23]

Frederick Pitts worked for Costello as an engineer on the vessel "California." In this capacity, Pitts "made many trips to sea in 1925, carrying out supplies and bringing back loads of liquor." Other illicit cargoes were transported back with Canadian liquor. Costello had several non-Italian partners in the venture including Frank Goss and Harry Sausser.[24]

Costello was one of 20 indicted in December 1925 for "the smuggling into the port of the greater part of the liquor that has reached New York in the last two years"[25] Late in 1926, Edward and Frank Costello were also charged with 27 others (among them four Coast Guardsmen) for conspiracy to violate the prohibition law. The smuggling ring was, according to the government, created in 1923 by the Costellos and operated a fleet of fast boats in order to bring contraband to thirsty Manhattan customers.[26]

ORGANIZATION OF BOOTLEGGING

Nelli read the evidence of Chicago's experience over Prohibition as indicating, "centralizing the chain of command, and controlling and directing the flow of money."[27] Within that history, formerly localized gangs were replaced by larger "businesslike" criminal organizations looking to the legitimate economy as their inspiration, and adopting "rational" methods of achieving their goals.

As proof of the apparent march towards consolidation and centralization in the booze supplying segment of organized crime, error-filled versions of a 3 days meeting in May 1929 in Atlantic City were referenced.[28] Nash summed up the popular belief by stating that this, the "first summit of US crime bosses ... galvanized the gangs of America into a powerful single unit which was directed by a board of directors ... whose influence would affect every American, in one form or another, for generations to come."[29] Among the many writers of the Atlantic City meeting were Gosch and Hammer. The objective of the gathering was "the start of an organization ... to develop a national monopoly in the liquor business."[30]

Meyer Lansky made a guest appearance in Eisenberg, Dan and Landau's book; however, old-time Mafiosi were shunned, "something which offended them deeply."[31] Nown and Powell were equally empathic about the importance of the Atlantic City congregation; it was "The biggest meeting in the history of American crime."[32] Out of the event, "grew the movement to modernize the underworld."[33]

The conviction that the 1929 Atlantic City was a national gathering of liquor barons even appeared in serious writings. Peterson detected the presence of mob kingpins Lepke Buchalter and Albert Anastasia from New York City.[35] Nelli opined that at Atlantic City were East Coast big shots, "led by a New York delegation that included Luciano, Costello, Lansky, Schultz, and Torrio (who apparently served as chairman)." The plan was to "coordinate activities between syndicates composed of a number of ethnic groups and to divide the market among them."[35]

For Lupsha, "the purpose of this meeting was to discuss ways of achieving cooperation, ordering markets, solving supply and distribution problems and ways to curtail the violence."[36] Albini's writing reflected the consensus ("Contrary to those who believe that the Apalachin meeting was the first meeting of syndicate leaders on a national scale is the fact that such a meeting had taken place at Atlantic City in 1928.")[37]

Also according to historians, the "Big Seven" was created out of the Atlantic City conclave, devised by Johnny Torrio and Meyer Lansky in "private talks." The Big Seven was alleged to be a prototype for later developments.[38] None of the published sources offered an alternative to the view that it was a meeting attended by a veritable "who's who" of top organized crime figures across America, in furtherance of a blueprint to expand their territory and to work together to avoid bloodshed.

Yet almost every newspaper of the day noted that the mobsters met in Atlantic City over May 1929 with the far more limited objective of ironing out differences in Chicago. Capone's presence had been quickly discovered in Atlantic City while he was attending the Dempsey-Tunney championship match. Since the local police had no charge on which to hold Capone, he was allowed to "go his way." Publicity around his presence was one reason that Capone left, on May 16.[39]

Al Capone unfolded the specifics of what occurred a day later to the Police Commissioner in Philadelphia.[40] The Atlantic City meeting was one of several that had been held to avoid further warfare in Chicago, an aim made more urgent in the wake of the St. Valentine's Day Massacre that February.[41] Meeting in the resort were "'Bugs' Moran and three or four other Chicago gang leaders, whose names I don't care to mention," Capone added.[42]

The Chicagoans were gathered in Atlantic City "to bury the past, and forget warfare in the future, for the general good of all concerned."[43] "Some of the biggest men in the business in Chicago were there," Capone continued,[44] in order to "stop all this killing and gang rivalry."[45]

Pasley, writing close to the event, echoed Capone's account,[46] as did Burns: "About thirty veterans of gangland wars answered the call . . . and representatives of every gang organization of the North, South, and West Sides of Chicago."[47] *Literary Digest* explained how the "peace conference," arbitrated by John Torrio, involved leaders of the Aiello-Moran mobs and Capone, at the end of which they agreed to "bury the hatchet" and to "sign on the dotted line" to end "gang warfare and murders in Chicago."[48] The *Chicago Tribune* identified those in attendance, "either in person or by proxy."[49]

Contrary to the assumption of a centralization of enterprises, cases indicated the transitory and makeshift characteristics of the majority of bootlegging engagements. Yasha Katzenberg, one of its founders, told a jury during the income tax trial of Torrio the real saga of the "Big Seven," a short-lived combination of smugglers active along the Atlantic Coast bringing in Canadian liquor. There were originally seven groups, but it "grew to be about a dozen." The elite of the booze running business was involved, including a contingent from New York (like Torrio and Joe Adonis), and several other East Coast cities.[50]

The purpose of the Big Seven was to stabilize the price of imported booze. Established in October 1932, it handled some 8,000 cases of rum monthly.[51] But despite its powerful membership, the Seven broke up in the spring of 1933.[52]

Reflective of the confusing impermanence characterizing most Prohibition engagements were shifting alignments within the New Jersey beer manufacturing and gambling sectors. Originally acting as a "strong arm" crew for a beer syndicate in Union and Essex Counties, a fraction of the Abner Zwillman, James Rutkin, Jerry Catena, and Angelo DeCarlo partnership split off to become importers and beer manufacturers for themselves. Willie Moretti, Lucky Luciano, Vito Genovese and Carmine Sabio, active in Bergen, Passaic and Hudson Counties, became the strong arm protectors of breweries in northern New Jersey, and Moretti and Luciano also operated illicit distilleries.

Moretti, Genovese and Sabio in addition also went into the numbers game in Bergen and Passaic Counties while financing distilleries. Zwillman and some of Luciano's associates also seem to have been involved in a former Waxey Gordon group brewery. DeCarlo and Catena, with others, started a gambling business in Union Township during this period.[53]

The alky syndicate run by Meyer Lansky and Lucky Luciano was reputed to operate on "big business" principles, "employing hundreds of people who frequently didn't have the faintest idea who their employers were." Wolf and DiMona claimed that Frank Costello's liquor running operation "was organized exactly like a corporation, with departments and staff for all phases of the business."[54] Yet Frederick Pitts was recruited to help Costello not via a secretive employment agency run by crime kings. Pitts' employment by Costello was secured when the Ocean Engineers Association sent Pitts, then looking for work, to see Costello because of his diesel engineering expertise. And when the Coast Guard seized the vessel used by Costello and his business partners, Pitts straight-forwardly hired a new crew from the same Association offices.[55]

Supplying alcohol over the duration of Prohibition produced complexities and diversity that did not gel with monolithic or bureaucratic perspectives. Huge numbers were involved at different stages of production, marketing and transportation, and the traditional historiography's concentration on a small number of cases and localities obscured the nature of organized trafficking in other areas. Moreover, "Compared with the legal liquor business," Haller asserted, "either before or after prohibition, bootlegging remained relatively small-scale and competitive."[56]

"MOONSHINING"

Domestically produced alcohol—"moonshine"—overtook other forms of illicitly consumed spirits in the last of the Volstead years. From around 1925, the sea-borne traffic subsided as "over-competition, murders by hijackers, the harrying of the Coast Guard" took their toll.[57]

It was announced in 1928 by Prohibition Commissioner James H. Doran that the Coast Guard had dismantled the rum-row off the Atlantic Coast, and that the amount of liquor shipped in from abroad had fallen from approximately 14,000 gallons in 1927 to 5,000 gallons.[58] Taking up much of the slack caused by effective Coast Guard initiatives was domestically produced moonshine spirits, utilizing "plants of a capacity fairly comparable to the old-time lawful distillery."[59] A thousand illicit distilleries were seized across the country in January 1930, of which nearly half were recorded as capable of producing up to 2,000 gallons of pure alcohol daily.[60]

There was "no organization or association of moonshiners; that phase of the illegal industry is highly decentralized," according to Doran.[61] It was, however, the field in which Mafiosi was most active. Growing to manhood in 1920s Brooklyn, Bonanno recalled, "there must have been two or three stills per block." The dangers to brewers from attempting to make the stuff were brought home to Bonanno when his partner, Giovanni Romano, "dozed off at the job" and died of his burns, after his basement 5-gallon still exploded on Withers Street in August 1925.[62] In 1922, a man was found dead in a room in Columbia Street, Brooklyn, in which a 75-gallon still was discovered. He had inhaled deadly vapors coming from tanks.[63]

On August 24, 1926, Sam and Frank DiMaria similarly lost their lives in Benton Harbor, Michigan, when they fell into a vat containing acid fumes. Frank tried to pull out Sam, but succumbed to the same fermentation process fumes that killed Sam. "Then there was an appalling silence and frantic cries no longer came from the interior of the huge circular container." Their father Stephen DiMaria was said to own the barn inside which the installation was discovered. At the rear was a 50-gallon still "with all its incidental equipment."[64]

SALVATORE MARANZANO

Salvatore Maranzano was no ordinary *Cosa Nostra* member.[65] Nominally a Schiro Family soldier, Maranzano's bootlegging operations stretched across Dutchess County, New York. But Maranzano's was by no means the only large volume distillery in the region. Another was discovered in December 1930, having a 2,500 gallon capability.[64] By the fall of 1931, nevertheless, Maranzano's was the most influential single voice in the United States Mafia. His place in crime history is assured as the alleged founder of "La Cosa Nostra."

Maranzano was born on July 31, 1886 in Castellammare del Golfo, Sicily, to Antonina Pisciotta and Domenico Maranzano.[67] Salvatore's marriage to Elizabetta Minore,[68] sister of "don Toto of Trapani,"[69] gave Maranzano standing in the Trapani Mafia establishment. Former Secret Service agent Joseph Palma claimed that in 1915, Maranzano ("a man of violent character") was accused and acquitted of having participated in the death of a policeman. After a spell training as a priest in a seminary, Maranzano became a cheese merchant in Palermo.[70]

Maranzano was the former "chief warrior" in Castellammare del Golfo, Sicily, to Joseph Bonanno's uncle Stefano Magaddino, and was once a follower of Bonanno's father Salvatore. They had fought the Buccellatos, who reappear in Chapter 8.[71] Once the pressure exerted by the Fascists in government became intense, Maranzano left Sicily.[72]

Confusion has marked attempts to ascertain when Maranzano landed on American soil. Various dates ranging from 1918 to 1927[73] have been cited, the uncertainty perhaps caused by the co-existence of three males named Salvatore Maranzanos from Sicily of roughly the same age and each living in New York. However, the Mafioso Maranzano's family minus Salvatore arrived in New York on the SS America in October 1923. They were headed for 93 Truxton Street, Brooklyn, where one of Salvatore's brothers, Nicolo (born 1866), lived.[74]

Sicilian *uomo di rispetto* Dr. Melchiorre Allegra subsequently related how Maranzano, as "chief" of the Mafia in Trapani province, backed him for political office in 1924, showing Allegra around the city of Palermo "and the boroughs." According to Allegra, "April 6, 1924" was "the day I presented my political candidacy."[75]

Maranzano must therefore have left Sicily for North America between April 1924 and 1925. Maranzano at one hearing intimated that he had been in America since about March 1925. Bonanno stated, "My life took a decisive turn at the end of 1925 when Salvatore Maranzano, a hero of mine in Sicily, immigrated to the United States."[76] Joseph Palma also gave the year 1925 to the Kefauver Committee as the year Maranzano moved (to Canada) from his native Sicily.[77] Yet even 1925 may be too late.[78] In any event, by May 1927, Maranzano felt secure enough in the United States to feel able to buy the house at 2706 Avenue J, Brooklyn that was to be his main residence when he died.

Maranzano was registered as entering Ontario province from Niagara Falls on February 5, 1926 for the first time, giving his occupation as the owner of a Saltfleet Township farm, nearby Hamilton.[79] The profession cited by Maranzano might have been determined by recently (1923) introduced restrictions on who was allowed to reside in Canada.[80]

Maranzano was likely to have been biding his time, and his Canadian sojourn was but an expedient until he could feel sufficiently secure to apply for U.S. citizenship. Maranzano may have been under the protection of the Buffalo or Niagara Falls Mafia at this stage, with the Niagara Falls contingent including a strong contingent of *amici nostri* from Castellammare del Golfo revolving around the Mazzara, DiBenedetto and Palmeri families.[81]

Rocco Perri, a major Calabrian crime figure resident in Hamilton, Ontario, was a supplier of bootleg liquor to Anthony "Nino" Sacco in Buffalo. Sacco lived in Buffalo in the 1920s, near Angelo Palmeri, a ranking Niagara Falls and Buffalo Mafioso, and knew Palmeri from at least 1914.[82]

This huge still on the Harrican brothers farm at Gayhead, raided by federal officials in January, 1929, was on a parcel of land immediately adjoining the Little Binnywater where the body of a murdered man was found last Sunday.

Figure 6.1 Maranzano Distillery, Dutchess County, 1930. (Courtesy of the *Poughkeepsie Journal*)

Sacco may have furnished a link between Maranzano's sojourns in southern Ontario and Buffalo.

Bonanno described the significance of Dutchess County in Maranzano's American ventures. "One of our numerous transfer points—where whiskey shipments were stored for pickup and distribution elsewhere—was at a barn near Wappingers Falls, New York."[83] Maranzano bought a Colonial style house there, almost certainly where Mafia initiation ceremonies were held in November of 1930.[84]

Maranzano managed to maintain a low-key operation until March of 1929, when Rocco Germano, a Poughkeepsie real estate dealer, fired upon a liquor truck traveling on Main Street. Its driver and mate abandoned the vehicle, which had been stolen in the Bronx. Detectives looking into the matter were convinced that Germano was employed by a liquor ring, later identified as Maranzano's, to collect money, and that the men in the truck had failed to hand over what they owed.[85] Germano was jailed for a month and 15 days and fined for 3rd degree assault.[86] A 5,000-gallon plant was uncovered as a result of the investigation, depicted as "the most elaborate ever seized in this region."[87]

Next, John and Thomas Harrigan were charged in January 1930 with the ownership of large-scale distillery installations found on their Gayhead farm.[88] Two 2,500-gallon stills, 350 gallons of thinner, alcohol and mash were confiscated. Local residents had complained that the heavy trucks used to transport the alcohol to New York City were tearing up the roads.[89] Germano had rented the property on which the still was seized on behalf of the Maranzano organization, but fear made the Harrigans reluctant to say who they leased the barn in which the plant was discovered to, or who paid their legal expenses.[90]

A partly decomposed and strangled body nicknamed "John the Painter," bound with chains and weighed down with cast iron, was found on April 19, 1931 in the Binnewater pond, also owned by the Harrigans.[91] Twine binding the corpse was similar to that found in Maranzano's New Hamburg farm; but proof positive of his involvement was lacking. Detectives worked on the theory that the man was strangled in Wappingers Falls and his body taken to where it was discovered.[92]

CONTEXT

Although Maranzano's liquor operations appeared to have been wound down before the Castellammare War began, his residence in Wappingers Falls was occupied until at least April 1931, when he applied for and received a pistol permit using this address.[93] Maranzano's success in evading arrest before and after his bootlegging enterprise was dismantled was due to his shrewd manipulation of legal loopholes and care in selecting associates.

The Maranzano case suggested that within the bootlegging field, the business of supplying drink was far from the racial melting pot activity implied by accounts of high seas smuggling. Chief among the figures that worked with Maranzano in Dutchess County were the Sicilian transplants Pietro "Peter" Sciortino,[94] Vito Mule,[95] Santo Vultaggio[96] and Nick Guastella.[97] Mule and Vultaggio were, like Maranzano, from Castellammare del Golfo, and were related by marriage. The non-Sicilian in the set, Rocco Germano, operated in an ancillary function.

New York was by no means the only state where Italian-Americans associated with the *Onorata Societa* worked together almost exclusively. A similar situation appertained in Cleveland.[98] The Kansas City sugar syndicate of the 1920s was an "Italian" operation.[99] The notorious Dragna family (Chapter 4) was caught operating another plant, this one in Walnut, California, in 1923. Eight people of Italian stock were arrested, after equipment was found that had the capacity to turn out 100 gallons of white corn whisky daily.[100] Where Mafiosi were absent from an area, bootlegging was frequently patterned according to a comparable common ancestry or nationality.[101]

Trust was a vital commodity in bootlegging as in other illicit enterprises, and men of honor tended to select as business partners those known to them, either as members or associates in *borgata*. Joint Mafia membership furnished a sound structure in which illicit deals could be consummated, but at the cost of limiting those with whom business was conducted.

Given the narrow base of Mafia recruitment and perceived problems when working with those outside of the Family system, the end product usually entailed *amici nostri* working with other Italians associated with Mafia organized crime. This was especially so in moonshining where, by contrast to the seaborne side of the business, partnerships with non-Italians were often unnecessary until the goods came to market.

WHITE-COLLAR OPERATIONS

Some Mafiosi eschewed the liquor trade altogether. Business and real estate investments typified a faction of the Reina Family's activities in the 1920s, which no doubt preferred the relative tranquility of a "business" career to the dangers of liquor running. They were also following, in many cases, a trade they already knew. Like those running Maranzano's distilling activities, the white-collar operations run by the Rao and Gagliano groups of the Reina Family were ethnically contained.

The Bronx lathing industry in which the Raos and Gaglianos had lasting interests was periodically accused of anti-competitive practices. The structural characteristics of the business closely accorded to the model furnished by analysts of a typically racketeer susceptible industry (see Chapter 4). It was thus concentrated in an "unorganized, high risk, low prestige service," serving a local market in which a "low standard of ethics seem generally to prevail."[102]

VINCENT RAO

Among those foremost in creating a legitimate business portfolio was Vincent John Rao, a brother-in-law of Angelo Gagliano arrested in the Baff case. Vincent's Rao's brother Calogero "Charles," born 1898 in Corleone, worked in the Greco-Gagliano saloon when Barnet Baff was slain.[103] Vincent Rao surmounted early brushes with the law[104] to become an investor in properties in East Harlem, including in the home he shared with his wife Millie at 235 East 107th Street.[105] Rao worked in 1931 for the Automint Vent Company, putting up bail money and furnishing lawyers to storekeepers renting their slot machines.[106]

Allegations of price fixing and organized crime influence sporadically emerged in the Bronx lathing and hoisting marketplaces. In 1938, Vincent Rao was accused of having a "virtual monopoly" on the lath-hoisting business in the city, but nothing came from it.[107] Partners in the Five Boro Hoisting Company, established in 1926, were later Joseph "Pip the Blind" Gagliano, a narcotics trafficker, and his cousin Rao.[108]

The Rao brothers were stockholders in the United Lathing Company[109] (below) and in the Westchester Lathing Corporation, set up in 1955. In 1959, Charles Rao replaced the murdered Genovese Family mobster Anthony "Little Augie Pisano" Carfano in the Ace Lathing Company, which did the lathing and plastering work on the Yonkers Raceway. Lucchese group member Nunzio Arra (Chapter 4) was an Ace Lathing investor. According to the New York Commission of Investigation, contractors and subcontractors on the project made "shockingly exorbitant" profits.[110]

Ace Lathing shared offices with Westchester Lathing, formed in 1951 by Carfano and his brother August. Stockholders in Westchester included agents of firms who agreed that all "nail-on lathing work" secured by their firms "would be assigned to Westchester." Because of it "the State was deprived of the benefit of genuine competitive bids."[111]

TOMMASO GAGLIANO

Tommaso "Tommy" Gagliano made the most comprehensive movement into the lathing and hoisting industries. Gagliano was the underboss of the Reina Family until[112] 1930, when he took it over.[113]

Joseph Valachi stated that Gagliano "was born into "Causa Nostra" in Italy.[114] The precise date of Gagliano's birth in Corleone is unclear, varying in official records between 1884 and 1885.[115] Via marriage to Giuseppina "Josephine" Pomilla, also of Corleone, Gagliano became the brother-in-law

Figure 6.2   Tommaso Gagliano. (Courtesy of the U.S. National Archives)

of Nunzio Pomilla, his partner in several Bronx businesses.[116] Pomilla, born in 1893, was identified in the 1960s as part of the Lucchese Family, the successor to the Gagliano organization.[117]

Chart 6.1 details the major business connections. Tommaso's wife Josephine was a partner in the Central Lathing Company, incorporated in 1956 with Ben Nicolosi and James Saia. Nicolosi and Saia married the daughters of Thomas Valente, another Lucchese Mafia member. (Gagliano was a former owner in the Company.) A construction and lathing investor of Nunzio Pomilla's, Gaetano "Tommy" Lucchese, took the *borgata* over upon Gagliano's death on February 16, 1951.[118]

Gagliano's most controversial, and ultimately ruinous, investments were made with another immigrant from Corleone, Antonio Monforte. They started out in the lathing business in 1925 with capital of $3,000.[119] Their major involvement was in August 1926. The United Lathing Company was incorporated with seven directors, among them, alongside Gagliano, was Anthony Cecala, Ignazio Milone—and the former Mafia "boss of bosses" Joseph Morello.[120]

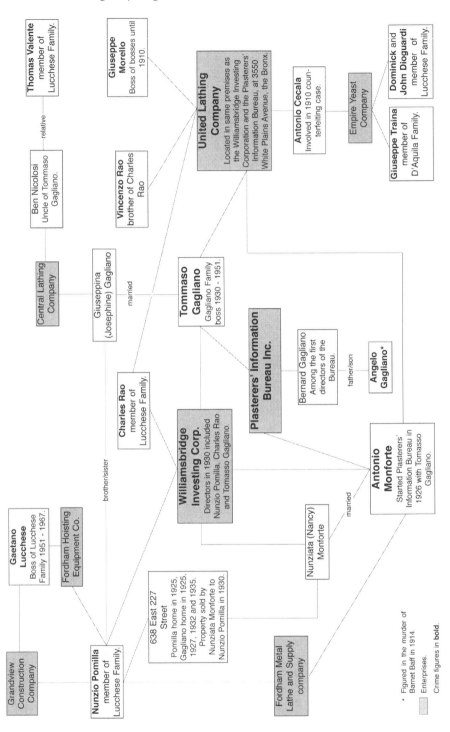

Chart 6.1   Gagliano related businesses.

In addition, Cecala—one of Morello's 1908–9 forgers—was president of the Empire Yeast Company with premises at 159 Chrystie Street, Manhattan.[121] In 1929, Dominick Dioguardi worked for Empire Yeast and his son, the renowned John "Johnny Dio" Dioguardi, got his first legitimate job there, as a yeast deliverer. On May 26, 1928 Cecala was gunned down while on his way to the company's office. He had been expecting trouble but was caught by two gunmen firing from a front apartment across the street from where he was walking. Cecala "slumped to the sidewalk with the top of his head almost blown off by a charge of shot."[122] D'Aquila Family underboss Joseph Traina subsequently became Empire Yeast's president.

Most of the stockholders in United Lathing were Corleonesi immigrants. Morello and Gagliano came from different Mafia organizations but were bound together by this common affinity and by experience of lathing and plastering.[123] The Williamsbridge Investing Corporation (in the same offices as United Lathing) and the Plasterer's Information Bureau featured, in various phases of its operation, Pomilla, Gagliano, Calogero Rao, Monforte and his wife Nunziata (Nancy).[124]

Monforte and Gagliano established the Plasterers' Information Bureau in 1928, with the ostensible aim of furnishing information on costs to its Bronx based members, who paid it a percent of the gross contract prices awarded.[125] In reality, the Bureau turned the Bronx lathing industry into a price fixing and customer allocating monopoly, enforced by the threat of strikes by the local lathers' union, to be used against recalcitrant contractors. For organizing the cartel, Monforte took a rake-off on each job secured.[126] Monforte himself "never used violence at all. The presence of four or five plug-uglies in his train may have constituted so plain a threat that violence was unnecessary."[127]

Leading Bronx lathers joined United to pool their resources, receiving huge return on capital invested in return for their collaboration. United Lathing, the Plasterers' Information Bureau and the Williamsbridge Investing Corporation, came under the spotlight of the Bronx District Attorney in 1929 when a fire was started in a Bronx apartment house connected to "building racketeers reported to be 'shaking down' contractors." Other fires followed and a plasterer was burned to death. Joseph Alberti and Giuseppe Sindona of United Lathing were questioned.[128]

The arson inquiry eventually exposed Monforte's part in colluding with Mike McCluskey, the lathers' union local 308 delegate in the borough, to make the scheme work. Enough evidence was amassed to sentence Monforte to a term of imprisonment of 7½ to 15 years in March 1930, and McClusky was jailed for 5–10 years.[129]

The file was then turned over to federal authorities. In February 1932, a federal grand jury charged that between 1928 and 1929, corporate and income tax was evaded amounting to a total of $1,270,000, the proceeds of extortion partly laundered through the Plasterers' Information Bureau. Prices quoted by members to builders were rigged by the Bureau, with the

Bureau raking off 1 to 2 percent on every contract awarded to its members. The fires starting the investigation were purportedly set to force independent contractors out of business.[130] Gagliano failed to declare over $245,000 gained from the racket on his 1928–9 tax returns.

Five indicted included Monforte (United Lathing president), Gagliano (acting secretary and employee), Giuseppe Alberti (secretary), and Frank Casella and Antonino Marziano, stockholders.[131] Unindicted co-conspirators were Lena Morello—the widow of the murdered Joseph Morello (Chapter 7)—and Charles Rao.[132] Found guilty of income tax evasion, perjury and conspiracy on May 21, 1932, Gagliano was handed a 15 months federal penitentiary sentence.[133]

CONTEXT

New York City Mafia leaders became involved in legitimate businesses long before the 1960s, when the phenomenon of Mafia "penetration" of legitimate industries first hit the headlines.[134] It was then argued that the entry of Mafiosi injected a sinister dimension into an affected industry. Using its reputation for violence, evidence was presented that Mafiosi performed a powerful stabilizing function that made the chance of a profitable cartel collapsing less likely, a reason given as to why Mafia overtures were seldom rejected by those contractors approached.

But the history of the industry demonstrated that the Raos and Gaglianos did not play a "rationalizing role" in Bronx lathing of the sort observed in the New York City building industry in the 1980s, bringing with it "coordination and predictability to the construction process."[135] Neither did the Raos and Gaglianos "seize control" of Bronx lathing and construction businesses, deploying either the threat or reality of violence.

Nor were, so far as is known, funds from organized crime used to finance the Rao and Gagliano enterprises. Nothing in the record exists, either, that companies were utilized to "launder" the profits of criminality. There was no evidence, lastly, of the lathing participants, despite their exalted position in the Mafia, deploying a wider *Cosa Nostra* network to extend their influence.

Most Bronx lathers joined the United Lathing cartel to receive excess profits on capital invested.[136] During Monforte's trial, "in one instance, a contractor estimated that he could make a fat profit at ninety thousand dollars. Monforte told him to put in a bid of a hundred and twenty-five thousand. He got the job, and the extra thirty-five thousand,"[137] acting as a powerful disincentive for employers to expose the conspiracy. Bernard Lyons, a contractor pressured by Monforte to come across with $800 for a job, at first went along. A strike called by McClusky was also called off. For his cooperation, Lyons received $1,700 more than originally expected.[138]

Gagliano was a contractor first and Mafia boss second.[139] Valachi said about Gagliano "up to today I know he never got a nickel back and never had a piece of any racket."[140] Valachi's observation, matching other materials, implied a permanency of Gagliano's involvement in the sector that went considerably beyond that noted in a conventional model of racketeering, in which Mafiosi solely sought to enter an industry for ulterior reasons, solely related to the extortion of industrial stakeholders.[141] Yet the financial rewards from Tommaso Gagliano's short racketeering escapade were negligible. In 1935, Gagliano petitioned for bankruptcy with liabilities of $352,676 and assets of $79,800.[142]

Gagliano had long years of experience as a lathing contractor before he moved into racketeering between 1926–32. According to a descendant of the Raos, "all the Gaglianos/Raos came over as lathers or plasterers."[143] Upon his release from Atlanta penitentiary in 1933, and following his 1935 bankruptcy,[144] Gagliano became as committed to the industry as before.[145]

Gagliano's lathing partner Joseph Morello, known to crime historians as a renowned Mafia leader (Chapter 3), when away from organized crime was a plastering contractor, a sector allied to lathing. About 1896–7, Morello became an ornamental plasterer, with the Terranova brothers helping out (Ciro Terranova followed him into the trade). Morello's financial interest in United Lathing in the 1920s was therefore probably something more than a cynical stratagem used to extract what he could from a segment of the industry through illegal means before the house of cards collapsed.[146]

The presence of New York City Mafiosi in the Bronx lathing and hoisting markets had variable effects on levels of recorded criminality in the business, despite the Raos and Gaglianos being ranking members of the same *borgata*. First were those enterprises against which there were no allegations made; second were those instances where an allegation was made but ended without arrest or prosecution (involving the Rao brothers). Third was Tommaso Gagliano's racketeering.

Those who chose to invest in Gagliano's businesses were more notable for their Corleone backgrounds, several also being related (corresponding to the ethnic dynamic noted in Chapter 4), than for any organized crime links they may have had.[147] The assumption made within the orthodoxy was that Mafiosi entered businesses for anything other than legitimate objectives. Convention has it that Family members sought to "obtain market power in an industry, or even dominate that industry."[148] According to Nelli, "once they gained a foothold, racketeers had every intention of staying on, not as hired specialists but as partners."[149] The "penetration" of legitimate industries by organized criminals was frequently linked to their need to create a "front" for their illegal enterprises, or as a way to drain the industry concerned by criminal methods.

But Jester noted, "There would appear to be some indications that businesses operated by organized crime associates do manage to operate within the law."[150] Mafiosi sometimes entered a field for similar reasons to those found in the general population, not least to follow in fathers' footsteps. There was no evidence that Mafia leaders such as Gagliano added a distinctive *Cosa Nostra* aspect to the proceedings, or that outsiders to the industry were even partially calling the shots from the shadows.

THE NEW YORK CITY MAFIA OF THE 1920s

At the outset of Prohibition, three New York City Families existed. They included the remnants of the Morellos in Manhattan, and the Schiro organization lodged in Brooklyn. A possibly larger Mafia formation, led by Salvatore "Toto" D'Aquila, had offshoots in Brooklyn and Manhattan. By the last years of the 1920s, the numbers involved in Italian-American organized crime had risen, and two new syndicates were established.

THE RISE OF THE MASSERIA FAMILY

Overshadowing the history of the New York Mafia in the 1920s was that of Giuseppe "Joe the Boss" Masseria. Many fallacies surround his ascent in organized crime, notably that he took over in Harlem.[151] Emerging from seeming obscurity, he forged an alliance that challenged the established order in the city's Mafia. Masseria became the head of the most influential New York syndicate by "gobbling up" smaller alcohol organizations.[152] While his syndicate was in its infancy and he fought alongside his men, Masseria was as yet unable to insulate himself from attacks on his life. Any bodyguards he employed were either nowhere to be seen when the shooting started, or proved ineffective.

Masseria was born about 1887 in Marsala, Sicily,[153] the son of Joseph Masseria and Vita Marthera.[154] His first criminal undertakings included an alleged foray into the Black Hand and kidnapping.[155] For almost eighteen months, Masseria led a burglary gang robbing stores in the Bowery until he was caught in 1913 while trying to break through the rear wall of a pawnshop. (Those captured with Masseria included the brothers Ruffino, discussed in Chapter 7.)[156]

On May 23, 1913, Masseria was sentenced to from 4 to 6 years imprisonment for third-degree burglary. Via their suspected use in early 1912 of a Lima-Lomonte owned saloon (p. 54) as a base, his robbery team may have encountered the Morellos. But there is no support for Chandler's claim that Masseria broke from them by "gunning down their cousin."[158]

Until the 1920s, Masseria lived in a Forsyth Street saloon.[159] Prohibition virtually overnight made Masseria's territory valuable, embracing as it did the "Curb Exchange" situated along Kenmare Street, Broome and Grand Streets,[160] where liquor wholesalers met to match supply with demand.

Famed during its existence, the Curb Exchange was dissolved in 1922 when shootings related to its activities forced the police to act.[161]

Fully exploiting this coincidence of history and geography, Masseria expanded from his lower east side territory and secured a lock on an important portion of the Italian-American underworld extending from Brooklyn to the Bronx, operating primarily through Salvatore Lucanio and the West Side based Vito Genovese. Masseria's alliance with the recently released Joseph Morello, "Masseria's brain trust, his chief adviser and chief strategist,"[162] gave Masseria leverage in Italian Harlem, where Morello knew the major players if a showdown loomed. Key Luciano men such as Gaetano Pennochio, David Petillo, and Mike Miranda headquartered on Mott or Broome Streets, and their reputed political patron, Albert Marinelli, had his club on Lafayette Street.

When his sentence for forgery was commuted in October 1921, the former Morello counterfeiter Ignazio Lupo told the government that he was planning to return to Italy to settle the family estate after his father died. Lupo's sister (who administered the estate) had become terminally ill, and Lupo was asked to return to Palermo in order to help her identify his share of the family's assets. Although the U.S. Attorney General was "doubtful whether the purpose for making the trip to Italy as stated by Lupo is the real one," Lupo was allowed to go.[163]

But Nicolo Gentile supplied another reason for Lupo's anxiousness to make the trip. According to Gentile, Lupo, Morello, Umberto Valenti,[164] and 9 others were condemned by the U.S. Mafia's general assembly, "following a tumultuous meeting."[165] Problems with Salvatore D'Aquila, the post-Morello "boss of bosses," lay behind the friction. The group asked Gentile, then living in Sicily, to intercede. Gentile promised to do what he could upon his return to New York. Until then, they should be on their guard and "trust nobody."[166]

Former "boss of bosses' Morello's decision to join Masseria may have been a reaction to D'Aquila's move against him. Valenti was recorded returning from Italy to New York in mid January 1922.[167] To regain D'Aquila's confidence, Valenti agreed to remove D'Aquila's chief rival, Masseria.[168] That Masseria and Valenti vied for control over the area embracing the Curb Exchange was a further reason for the hostility existing between the two.

On May 8, 1922, "Within a block of Police Headquarters," five men on Grand Street began firing a fusillade of bullets at each other. "When the battle was ended," the *New York Herald* recorded, "the gunmen had shot four men and two women, but had not harmed each other." Masseria threw his gun aside and was running away when he was arrested.[169]

The Grand Street fighting was believed linked to the shooting a day earlier of Vincent Terranova.[170] Terranova had made a fortune from bootlegging, and was on his way to his home at 338 East 116th Street when a car filled with gunmen drew up on the curb and fired.[171] A few hours later, Silvio

Tagliogambe staggered into his East 4th Street accommodation with a bullet lodged in his back, but on his deathbed refused to discuss the matter.

The warfare continued. On August 8, 1922, Masseria "fell to his haunches although unarmed," when he was shot at by two gunmen laying in wait on Second Avenue and Fifth Street. He was shot at three times at "point blank" range, but "by astounding agility" dodged the bullets. The shooters ran off and escaped in a car. Two innocent bystanders were seriously wounded after they tried to halt it on Fifth Street.[172]

The struggle ended on August 11, 1922 when, at 12th Street and Second Avenue, Umberto Valenti was assassinated. "Valenti, said to have been strong in his hatred for Masseria, was killed coldly and with as little compunction as one would swat a fly," contended the *Herald*. Valenti was seen stumbling towards a taxi but collapsed, mortally wounded, on the running board.[173]

As he gained in prestige, Masseria extended his reach to other cities in competition with D'Aquila, by encouraging those who would challenge established local bosses backed by D'Aquila. Masseria sponsored Salvatore "Black Sam" Todaro, the Cleveland *consiglieri*, against the Lonardos, the dominant bootlegging chiefs in the city.[174] The move seems to have been a crude attempt to embarrass D'Aquila backing the Lonardos.[175] (Gentile judged Cleveland as dangerous for Valenti while he was on the outs with D'Aquila, because of the presence of the Lonardos[176]).

Todaro eventually rowed with the Lonardos and joined the Porrellos. Joe and John Lonardo were shot down in October 1927; Todaro was believed to be the instigator, acting for the Porrellos who gained most. But Masseria's sponsorship failed to save Todaro himself from death in June 1929 at the hands of Angelo Lonardo, Joseph's son, and his cousin Dominick Sospirato.

SALVATORE D'AQUILA

Masseria's elevation in the U.S. Mafia was thereafter based upon the assassination of D'Aquila. Eventually to become the largest of the nation's Families, the D'Aquila organization is, however, the least known about. Gentile furnished the bulk of the information presently available to researchers. Notwithstanding that, D'Aquila members would make an important contribution to the growth of the New York Mafia. Like the Masserias, kin connections were unimportant in organizing relationships. Those from Agrigento tended to operate in Manhattan; D'Aquila members from Palermo were more active in Brooklyn.

Identified D'Aquila members did not make the journey from Sicily until the 1900s, and D'Aquila himself only came across in 1906 at the age of 29 (born November 1877 in Palermo).[177] D'Aquila lived near to Joseph Morello in his first years in New York.[178] Upon Morello's incarceration in 1910, D'Aquila acquired much of his authority, initially based in East Harlem. "The position of (Morello) as a consequence of his having received a 25 years prison sentence," Gentile noted, "had been entrusted by the General Assembly to Mr. Toto D'Aquila."[179]

Secret Service reports encapsulated fragments of D'Aquila's gradual assumption of influence, though not without resistance. In February 1912, Salvatore Clemente tipped off his Secret Service handlers that he had "attended a meeting at 115 Lewis Street Thursday night . . . it seems that (Grisafi) is to become a member of the Toto de' Aquila (sic) gang" Clemente later advised that a meeting was called at Vincenzo LoCicero's store by D'Aquila.[180]

If Gentile is to be believed, power went to D'Aquila's head. As "a man exceedingly ferocious and crafty," D'Aquila had his agents shadow Gentile, and arranged for men in his "black book" to be condemned to death.[181]

D'Aquila was gunned down beside his car on Avenue A, Manhattan on October 10, 1928, after driving his wife and children from the Bronx to consult a doctor.[182] "Jim Carra" supplied a version of who was behind the slaying. Carra, a self-proclaimed "70-year-old veteran of organized crime, once high in the Mafia," claimed to belong to the "D'Aguila" family.

D'Aguila was, Carra informed readers, shot down by his underboss, Salvatore "Mambrao," who himself was shot down in the Castellammare War, a likely reference to Manfredi Mineo, D'Aquila's successor as boss of the *Famiglia*.[183] Gentile believed however that responsibility for D'Aquila's fate ultimately lay with Masseria, with whom Mineo was aligned.[184] Salvatore Maranzano would use this to argue for Masseria's murder (Chapter 7).

The top leadership of the D'Aquila Family was often Palermitani in origin, among them Manfredi Mineo, born 1880, Giuseppe Traina, and Frank Scalise (real name Scalisi).[185] Shortly after arriving in New York, Mineo was questioned after visiting a counterfeiter, Carmelo Cordaro. Mineo and the Harlem group identified with Nick Morello were connected to the murder of Joseph Fontana, "who served thirty years in Italy for murder and who had been a leader of the Black Hand in Palermo." The Secret Service heard that the murder was part of a feud between D'Aquila and the other factions. As Chapter 3 notes, Mineo appears to have reached an accord with D'Aquila.[186] Another slaying, that of Giuseppe Fanaro also in 1913, was laid at the door of the Mineo and Harlem organizations.[187]

According to latter day *borgata* member Michael "Mikey Scars" DiLeonardo, his paternal grandfather Jimmy DiLeonardo was a D'Aquila soldier.[188] Gentile supplied the names of a handful more of those aligned to D'Aquila, but without giving specifics. Included were Giuseppe Parlapiano from Sciacca, and Calogero DeLeo from Porto Empedocle. Aside from those named elsewhere in the text, others identified with the D'Aquila network included Domenico Arcuri, Stefano LoPiccolo, and Luigi Marciano. D'Aquila's lower east side interests were represented by, among others, Joseph Biondo[189] and (for a time) Umberto Valenti.

Vincenzo "Vincent" Mangano, born on December 1888 in Palermo, Sicily, would take over the Family from Frank Scalise in 1931. Like D'Aquila, Mangano and his brother Philip[190] were linked to the Buffalo Mafia hierarchy.[191] Umberto Anastasio, commonly known as Albert Anastasia, was unusual for his non-Sicilian heritage. Born 1902 in Tropea, Anastasia's closest associates were fellow Calabrians. Aside from Joseph Florina, they numbered Giacchino "Jack" Parisi, a brother in law to Vincent Mangano.

Anastasia and Florina (alias Speranza), was sentenced to be executed for the May 16, 1920 killing of George Terrillo, gunned down on Union Street, Brooklyn. Overlooked in later books, which typically laid the blame for their successful appeal in 1921 on the intimidation or murder of witnesses,[192] was the fact that the chief prosecution witness, Marguerita Vicchi, had a police record and was hopelessly biased against Florina, having previously attempted to have him arrested for robbery on false evidence and had once tried to run Florina down.[193] Her trial testimony was also contradictory.

As he was driving down Sackett Street in Brooklyn in April 1923, Biaggio Giordano, the early Black Hander noted in chapter two, and Anastasia were fired upon from a ground floor window. Giordano died and Anastasia was badly wounded. That March, Anastasia had been booked after the slaying of Joseph Busardo, himself arrested for the death of a man in his home. Like Anastasia subsequently, Busardo was released.[194]

Figures 6.3 Participants at Cleveland assembly, December 5, 1928. (Courtesy of the U.S. National Archives)

CREATION OF THE PROFACI FAMILY

On the morning of December 5, 1928, Patrolman Frank Osowski observed a number of "tough looking" men enter the Statler Hotel in Cleveland from two cars. Reinforcements were called, checking the hotel register and raiding rooms occupied by 23 Italians, who "virtually all wore new silk underwear and fine linen."[195] They were arrested on suspicion.

None of the arrestees would admit to even knowing each other. But all were carrying pistols and the majority had criminal records. Ten days later, 15 plead guilty as "suspicious persons," and were threatened with fines or jail sentences if they did not leave town. On the same day, the rest were found not guilty on the same charges but quickly exited the city.

Cleveland was likely as not selected because it was perceived as a venue where Mafia delegates could go about their business in peace, and without becoming embroiled in local problems. Their choice was though an implicit vote of confidence in the Porrello family's stewardship of the Cleveland mob.

The planned 1928 conference was not "the first Mafia Grand Council meeting ever held in the United States."[196] Gentile noted others. Yet since none of the participants gave a credible explanation of why they were gathered, several theories rapidly surfaced.

They came together to "work out differences and arrange greater cooperation;"[197] or to discuss Unione Siciliana matters.[198] Others contended it was "to work out a solid Mafia front in preparation for an upcoming national bootleggers' meeting in Atlantic City;"[199] to fix territorial boundaries, or to settle quarrels. For Chicago law enforcement, the men were preparing to discuss a replacement for the slain Chicago *capo* Tony Lombardo, pointing as evidence to the presence in Cleveland of Pasqualino Lolordo, the brother of Lombardo's bodyguard Joseph when Lombardo was shot dead. But the majority in attendance was non-Chicagoans who had no overpowering stake or interest in the seemingly perpetual inter-mob bloodletting that took place there.[200]

Moreover, only a handful of those questioned in Cleveland were leaders of the Mafia in 1928, their representing the three cities of Brooklyn (Joseph Profaci, Joseph Magliocco, Vincent Mangano), Chicago (Joseph Guinta, Pasquale Lolordo) and Tampa (Ignazio Italiano). The rest were in the nature of supporting actors. Since the mob situation in Tampa was calm, Chicago and Brooklyn were likely as not on the Cleveland agenda before the planned conclave was broken up.

Within Chicago and Brooklyn, 3 assassinations occurring in July, September and October 1928 were probably the key to understanding why Cleveland was called. Antonio Lombardo's loss in 1928 was more than likely on the minds of those present in Cleveland from greater Chicagoland specifically.

In addition, Bonanno remarked that a "boss of bosses," like D'Aquila, was a "figurehead" around whom "most of the other leaders, by necessity, had to cluster and align themselves."[201] Given his importance, D'Aquila's killing barely two months beforehand had reverberations across the U.S. Mafia, and must have been central to the Cleveland schedule.[202] Strengthening the proposition of a D'Aquila tie was the presence there of Giuseppe Traina. Traina, born 1883 in Belmonte Mezzagno, functioned as D'Aquila's "substitute," speaking for D'Aquila when he was unavailable[203]

With the removal of D'Aquila, a power vacuum occurred in Brooklyn, his former bailiwick, which required resolving. Up for discussion, lastly, was perhaps the position of Joseph Profaci, who would come to lead the "fifth" Family of New York City.

Profaci had only lived in Brooklyn a matter of 3 years prior to 1928, about when he became head of his own *Famiglia*. Neither Profaci nor his second in command Magliocco (so far as is known) was a member of a Brooklyn crime organization before 1928 that they could rise through in the traditional manner, to gain enough experience to become leaders of men. Profaci and Magliocco thus came to Cleveland as bosses, yet apparently without serving an "apprenticeship" in organized crime.

Cleveland was partially arranged, in this analysis, in order to recognize or to acclaim Profaci as heading a newly formed Family in Brooklyn in order to restore equilibrium in the borough following the D'Aquila killing. Those identified with Profaci's hometown of Villabate were also the biggest single group in attendance at Cleveland.[204]

Chicago's acquiescence with Profaci's elevation was vital because of Chicago's contacts with Brooklyn through the celebrated Frankie Yale (see below), part of whose territory was acquired by Profaci. Italiano's presence in the Hotel Statler reflected his personal connections to Profaci. Because of his advanced age and therefore experience, Italiano may also have been selected as an advisor to the assembly.

JOSEPH PROFACI

Attempts to trace with any degree of completeness or certainty the history of Joseph Profaci are fraught with practical difficulty. A native of Villabate, Palermo, born in October 1897, Profaci admitted having been released by Sicilian police in 1916 from a charge of theft, attempted rape and "violation of the domicile." Profaci was less fortunate in 1920, imprisoned for a year while on bail for theft and false witness of a public document in Palermo.[205]

Upon his discharge, Profaci decided to make a new start in America. On September 4, 1921,[206] he set foot in New York, to soon set up a grocery store and bakery in Chicago.[207] In 1925, with their not making the expected profits, Profaci upped sticks for Brooklyn, where he worked in the olive oil business.[208]

Profaci recalled his Cleveland arrest to the Kefauver Committee. He went to Cleveland to meet Italiano, a friend of his and of his father in Sicily.[209] In about 1927, Profaci had sold 150 cases of oil to Italiano in Tampa, and was in Cleveland to sell more. Going to the Hotel Statler with his brother in law Magliocco, "as soon as I walked in, they pinched me." Other links between Profaci, Magliocco and Italiano have been established for this book.[210] Joseph Traina also had a connection to Italiano, in his case through York Street (Brooklyn) real estate.[211]

Profaci's puzzling ascent in the Brooklyn Mafia may have been through Sicilian connections. Profaci was purportedly "the son of a very well-to-do business man in Sicily,"[212] who came "from the same home town" as the father of Joseph Barbara, Sr., an important upstate New York *amici nostri*.[213] Profaci's American olive oil enterprises, furthermore, stretched to cities like Cleveland, where Profaci supplied Cleveland Mafia power Frank Milano's import company.[214]

Profaci's otherwise mysterious rise may have been originally linked to those contacts, and to his family's possible ties to the Villabate Mafia.[215] Giulio D'Agati, Mafia boss of Villabate in the mid 1920s, was a relative of Frank D'Agati, a Profaci member in New York.[216] During a trip to Sicily in 1956, additionally, the son of Bonanno Family patriarch Joseph Bonanno and his bride were warned to stay away from Villabate, since "friends and distant relatives" of Profaci were involved in a Mafia war in the town.

FRANKIE YALE

Regardless of the source of Profaci's authority, he appears to have led a organization or coalition that was still fragile in 1930, accounting for Profaci's decision to stay on the sidelines during the Castellammare War. As his primary power base, Profaci obtained a segment of the slain mobster Frankie Yale's territory.

Francesco Uale or Ioele—usually known as Yale—was born in 1893 in Longobucco, Calabria.[217] Over his years as a Masseria organization "group leader,"[218] every manner of crime was linked to Yale, ranging from narcotics trafficking, to the laundry and ice rackets and the taxing of gamblers and "panderers."[219] Yale was also written about as involved in labor rackets.[220] The distribution of imported Canadian whiskey was a major Yale venture.

Yale was "known to every criminal lawyer, detective and newspaper man in Brooklyn."[221] In February 1921, he was wounded walking past the Duane Field Club on Park Row.[222] He was fired on again that year, this time in Bath Beach, and his brother Angelo was wounded.[223] Frank Forte, Yale's chauffeur, was cut down in a probable case of mistaken identity.[224]

Yale's Chicago connections were strong. His "playmates included Johnny Torrio," the future Chicago boss.[225] Yale was partly identified as the killer of James Colosimo in 1920,[226] and as one of those who murdered Torrio's Irish competitor Dion O'Banion in 1924.[227] Police, in addition, believed that the Lombardo murder of September 7, 1928, was a settling of scores for the murder of Yale by Capone's people.[228] "Two men fell in step behind him, pulled out .45-caliber revolvers, and fired dumdum bullets into his head."[229] Joseph Ferraro, one of Lombardo's two bodyguards, died a day later of the wounds he sustained. The shooters disappeared in the crowds.

Yale's ruin came, it was considered, after he hijacked Capone's whiskey shipments on Long Island, and short-changed Capone on an alcohol deal for

$17,000.[230] Others concocted a theory that depended on the flawed assumption of Yale being national head of the Unione Siciliana (refer to Chapter 8).[231]

On July 1, 1928, a black sedan car passed Yale's new Lincoln automobile on 44th Street. As the two cars drew alongside one another, "there was a burst of firing."[232] Yale, shot on the left side of the head, lost control of his machine, which crashed against steps leading to the ground floor room of 923 44th Street. Yale was found dead, slumped over the wheel of his car with a revolver in his pocket.

The black sedan car used in the slaying, bearing Illinois or Indiana license plates, was found nearby. Inside were a pistol and shotgun (both used), and a fully loaded Thompson machine gun traced to Peter Von Frantzius, a Chicago sporting goods dealer. Von Frantzius told of selling several of these weapons to Frank Thompson from Elgin, Illinois, who "peddled them to Chicago gangsters."[233] One of the pistols used supplied a tie to Capone.[234] Parker Henderson, a Miami hotel owner, bought Capone 12 of them, which were delivered to Capone's Palm Island mansion.[235]

If he was not the most powerful Italian gangster in Brooklyn, Yale was surely the most newsworthy. Yale's funeral mirrored the widespread respect—and fear—he engendered in Italian communities in Borough Park and Bath Beach. A holiday was declared and thousands thronged the church where Yale's requiem mass was held [236]

Michael Abbatemarco with roots in Sassano, Salerno, tried to take up the slack caused by Yale's murder. But on October 6, 1928 on 83rd Street, Abbatemarco was fatally wounded at the wheel of his car. It was suspected, but never proven, that Abbatemarco had "cheated the combination in a business deal," and that former Yale henchman Anthony "Little Augie Pisano" Carfano had ordered his execution.[237]

Yale and later Profaci operated in approximately the same territory of Brooklyn, embracing Bensonhurst and Bay Ridge.[238] Yale's removal meant a transfer of some of his men to the Profaci Family. Mainland Italians chiefly headquartered in South Brooklyn around Union Street (e.g. Anthony Carfano and Joe Adonis) stayed with "Joe the Boss" Masseria and Carfano continued to supply a link to Masseria in Manhattan.[239] Profaci's "Sicilians"[240] tended to operate further south in Brooklyn. Nonetheless, Mike Abbatemarco's younger brother Frank "Frankie Shots" and Frank's son Tony "Tony Shots," became Profacis.

Joseph "Clutching Hand" Piraino, the last person known to have seen Yale alive,[241] was at the time of his own death (March 27, 1930) a partner of Carfano in a policy game, and was reputed to have taken over some of Yale's operations.[242] Piraino's sons, Anthony "Big Tony" Piraino and Joseph S. Piraino, went with Profaci.

The 1963 McClellan Committee understood that the Profaci group was an offshoot of the Maranzano Family, perhaps basing this verdict on a 1962 statement made by Joseph Valachi.[243] Yet Valachi confused the issue, by also testifying that Profaci "was formerly boss of the Gagliano family."[244]

Bonanno was clear that the Profaci Family predated the Castellammare War. If the Profaci organization were an offshoot from Maranzano's, Bonanno would have known. The Valachi contention also failed to account for Joseph Profaci's presence at the December 1928 meeting.

The purpose of the Cleveland meeting cannot be known with a high degree of confidence or sureness. But the theory that it was there to realign the Mafia after the downfall of the mighty D'Aquila, and to sponsor Profaci as head of his own syndicate in Brooklyn, explained the calling of an assembly in the context of wider U.S. Mafia politics.

CONCLUSION

The domestically produced side of the illicit alcoholic beverages market, where Mafiosi were commonest, was ethnically differentiated, localized and competitive. Block's assertion that the Prohibition era bootlegging market was centralized because of the consolidated ownership of breweries in New Jersey lacks broader applicability.[245]

The chief hazard confronting entrepreneurs in the field was the danger of hijacking of the end product, necessitating the deployment of armed guards on liquor-laden trucks. A syndicate's reputation for toughness and for defending its territory and assets ruthlessly and without compromise was a vital requirement in order to deter this form of attack. In this manner, territorial boundaries were clarified and strengthened.

If prohibition was the Italians' route to power in organized crime, as regurarly argued, it paled in significance to Jewish enterprises serving the East Coast marketplace.[246] The predominantly Jewish beer syndicate of which Waxey Gordon was head for instance "controlled at least thirteen breweries distributed in Pennsylvania, New York, and especially New Jersey."[247]

Led by the Reinfeld brothers in Newark, operating in tandem with such Jewish crime luminaries as Abe Zwillman and Joseph Stacher, the "high seas" Reinfeld operation was believed to have been responsible for approximately 40 percent of the illicit liquor consumed in America sourced from Canada and Europe. Between 1926–33, the syndicate "showed deposits under fictitious names in 6 different banks, totaling $21,067,643.25," stashed in banks in Newark, Union City and New York City. After Repeal, the partners bought into a nationwide liquor importer and wholesale liquor dealer, Browne-Vinters. Their interest was sold in 1940 for $7,500,000 to Distillers-Seagram Corp.[248]

Chapter 7 describes and analyses the Castellammare War. Notions of centralization within the criminal underworld, based on the misreading of events occurring during Prohibition, supplied the inspiration for conceptions of an overarching Mafia "command center" (the La Cosa Nostra Commission) emerging in the wake of the Castellammare War. But the Castellammare War was fought for other reasons, and its effects were radically at odds with the imagery with which it became associated.

7 Castellammare War and "La Cosa Nostra"

INTRODUCTION

Large scale bootlegging and the smuggling of alcohol had profound effects on the New York Mafia, by contributing to an expansion in the number of Mafiosi and Families, and in propelling new Mafia leaders to the forefront.[1] Out of the ferment, according to its adherents, came La Cosa Nostra (LCN), the major effect of a legendary conflict known as the "Castellammare War" of 1930 and 1931. But Mafia power and structure was as diffuse and occasionally factious after the War as before it, with no dominant leadership type, power source, or developmental pattern subsequently emerging. The War was also far from the bloodbath usually portrayed.

The warfare primarily involved Mafiosi gathered around Salvatore Maranzano, from the Sicilian town of Castellammare del Golfo (its participants were known as Castellammaresi), and those from sundry Italian sources aligned with the 1930 *capo di capi* Joseph "Joe the Boss" Masseria. Because the LCN paradigm refers to a reading of the War in New York City, and because the LCN framework continues to exert a major effect on the received historiography, both the War and the LCN's origin are explored in depth.

The discourse surrounding the existence of the LCN, occurring in the absence of original research, has become stale and polarized. Since confusion and exaggeration characterize histories of the War, little confidence can be placed on expositions of the LCN's commensurate rise. Attempting to portray a faithful account of the Castellammare War therefore serves not only to correct and expand the historical record, but also functions as a prelude to a discussion of the LCN. The group incorrectly viewing the events of the Castellammare War as a defining point in American Mafia history encompasses every level of published resource.

The LCN approach, based on a misreading of the small amount of empirical material available at its time of formulation, lacks a solid factual base, mainly consisting of a series of untested assertions. The War was predominantly a revolt by several U.S. Families against trends towards the informal consolidation of power that had built up, centered on the *capo di capi's* patronage powers. Propaganda played an important part in the ensuing battle, complicating the task of later disentangling myth from reality.

HISTORIOGRAPHY

Distinguishing the orthodoxy on the War has been confusion and error over basics, caused by a dependence on a small number of published sources. In part because elementary questions have been left unanswered, and serious factual mistakes have been allowed to linger unchallenged, two perspectives on the War and therefore the LCN emerged. This chapter addresses organizational issues. Chapter 8 discusses supposed sociological changes within the Mafia leadership coming to fruition after the War.

The first asserted that the Castellammare War "led directly to the evolution of syndicated crime."[2] Cressey and others explained how it created the "current structure of confederated crime."[3] Supportive of the concept of the War in creating the LCN super-government of crime was the entire corpus of journalistic work, and a number of comments from within the scholarly community.[4]

Given their view on the Mafia issue as fundamentally irrelevant to a discourse on the sources of organized crime, it was unfortunate that those favoring the "contextual" approach, described in Chapter 1, were virtually the only authors to have given the War and the history of the LCN any measure of critical attention. Woodiwiss made the perspective's point "Gangsters have only ever been continuously replaceable players in a much bigger game."[5]

It thus declined to engage with the history of the Castellammare War, despite acknowledging the War's importance to a preceding narrative, except by exposing purported flaws and limitations in Joseph Valachi's evidence on the matter.[6] By otherwise ignoring it, or by failing to show interest in any of the particulars, the inference created was that the Castellammare War was inconsequential to the real history of American organized crime.

The absence of further research has permitted "two" non-interactive histories of both the War and of the LCN to run parallel to one another. Jacobs most recently represented the earlier "pro" Castellammare War convention via his concentration on the LCN paradigm as representing the reality, though mostly focusing on post-1970 events.[7]

EYEWITNESS SOURCES

Vaguely drawn hints of a "Sicilian" conflict were aired at the time of the Castellammare War's killings.[8] But what had been missing until the 1963 "Valachi" hearings was a perceived "national" dimension.[9] To construct a reasonably coherent and accurate version of the events, this chapter refers primarily to the experiences of three participants in the Castellammare combat active in New York City: Joseph Valachi, Nicolo Gentile, and Joseph Bonanno.[10]

JOSEPH VALACHI

Outlines of the War's events were originally presented before the American people by Joseph Valachi, the first Mafia member to appear in a public forum confessing to his life in *"Cosa Nostra."*[11] Aside from his role in propagating a selective view on the Mafia's history and structure that could be exploited by political leaders, Valachi gave valuable intelligence information. Without Valachi's help, for example, it was doubtful that the historical chart shown during the 1963 Senate hearings, which encapsulated key elements of the changing balance of power from 1930, could have been compiled (Chart 7.1). Valachi's reliability as an observer has been since questioned, but other sources uphold in its general form his reconstruction of events in 1930 and 1931.

Critics were, above all, incorrect to assert that Valachi's public evidence "was not corroborated on any essential point."[12] Nor was Valachi's testimony noticeably marred by any "coaching" he allegedly received from his FBI handlers.[13]

A meticulous comparison of Valachi's public testimony with his autobiography, "The Real Thing," not intended for public use and therefore hardly part of a conspiracy to deceive the public, reveals no substantial differences in the story lines offered.[14] Moreover, the recollections of Gentile and Bonanno substantiate those of Valachi where they intersect.

FOR OFFICIAL USE ONLY

NATIONAL LIST

NO. 409

NAME : Joseph VALACHI

ALIASES : Joe Cago, Cargo, Kato, Joseph Siano, Anthony Sorge, Charles Charlano, Joe from the Bronx.

DESCRIPTION : Born 9/22/03 in NYC; 5'5"; 195 lbs.; brn eyes; grey hair; heavy build; dk complexion; dyes hair blk on occasion.

LOCALITIES FREQUENTED : Resides: 45 Shawnee Ave., Yonkers, N.Y. Owns: Lido Bar, 1362 Castle Hill Ave., Bronx, N.Y. Frequents: Delmar Bar, 180th St., and Belmont Ave., Bronx; Construction Workers Social Club, 420 E. 116th St.; all in NYC.

CRIMINAL ASSOCIATES : Anthony Strollo, John Stoppelli, Vincent Mauro. Knows every important racketeer in NYC.

FACSIMILE OF SIGNATURE : See reverse

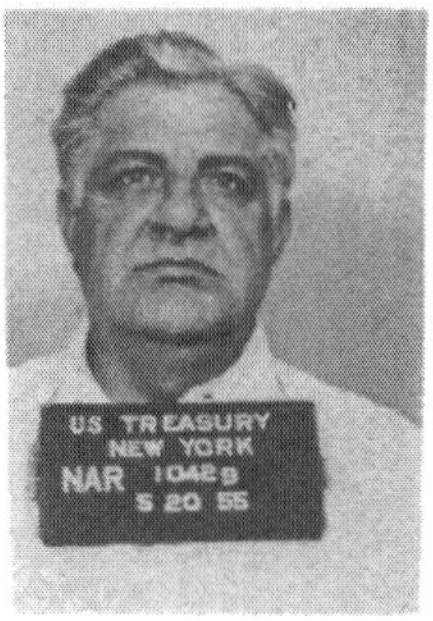

Figure 7.1 Joseph Valachi. (Courtesy of Lennert van't Riet)

Queries have properly been raised over the political uses to which Valachi's testimony were put, in order to mobilize support for an ongoing Justice Department campaign for "more laws and more police manpower."[15] The FBI's patchy performance against the Mob is frequently mentioned within the context of Attorney General Robert F. Kennedy's desire to get the Bureau more deeply involved against organized crime. The issue of political undertones associated with Valachi's public appearance will be returned to at the end of the chapter.

Valachi was careful to distance himself in his proclamations from any suggestion that he was directly involved in Castellammare War murders, except to concede that he was driving the getaway car in question, and to acknowledging that he performed reconnaissance work before and after the fact.[16] Some of Valachi's claims were based on hearsay and, as Bonanno and others have since argued, "Valachi did not see the entire picture,"[17] a limitation he shared with other informants.

But Valachi could supply first hand information as to who was involved in murders, which subsequent research has failed to undermine. As the only storyteller on the War from the Gagliano Family side, his information is also unique as a counterpoint to the Maranzano dominated version given by Joseph Bonanno.

NICOLO GENTILE

Gentile operated on a higher plane, shedding new light on events described by Valachi, who was shown Gentile's reminiscences by the FBI. Gentile's memoirs, available to the FBI since about 1961 and to the Federal Narcotics Bureau earlier, were less headline grabbing than were Valachi's but historically more significant. In 1937, Gentile was one of two wholesalers in the largest narcotics ring "in the history of the United States."[18] Jumping bail to return to Italy, Gentile was tricked in 1958 into revealing himself to an undercover narcotics agent. Gentile readily assisted the Federal Narcotics Bureau by writing his life-story.[19]For this act of betrayal, the Catania, Sicily, Mafia *cosca* was asked to murder Gentile by their "American cousins," but they declined and Gentile was "allowed to waste away."[20]

Born June 1885 in Siculiana, Sicily, "Gentile's account of the Mafia's development in the United States parallels that of Valachi's," said the *New York Times*.[21] Dickie, who correctly suggests that Gentile has been "seriously undervalued" by researchers, notes that he was "the best witness" to the pre-1937 U.S. Mafia, and unlike Valachi, Gentile moved "in elite criminal circles."[22] Two versions of Gentile's work, which matched in almost every respect, were obtained for this book.[23]

Similarly to Valachi and Bonanno, Gentile operated "in a very Sicilian world," and often lost sight of developments outside of the Mafia.[24] His version was as self-serving as theirs, like Bonanno and Valachi portraying

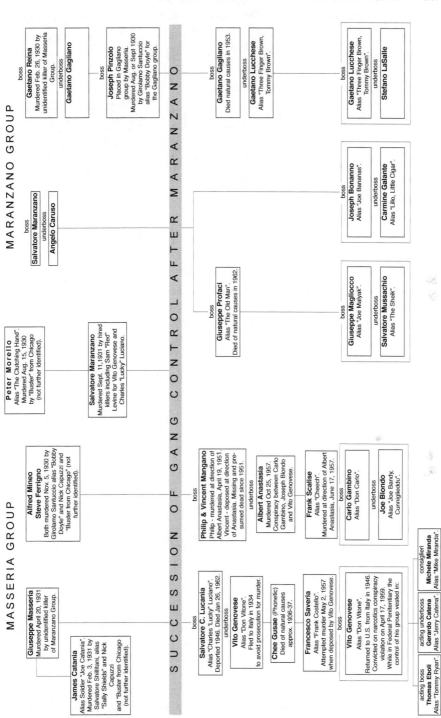

Chart 7.1 Masseria-Maranzano war and evolution of gang control, 1930 to present.

RESTRICTED—FOR OFFICIAL USE ONLY   INTERNATIONAL LIST

NAME   : Nicola GENTILE

NO. **133**

ALIASES   : Zio Cola; Nick; Don Cola; Cola Gentile.

DESCRIPTION   : Born in Sicily on June 12, 1885;
                  61 years old; 5'6" tall; weight 146 lbs.;
                  eyes chestnut; hair mixed gray, partly
                  bald.

LOCALITIES   Resides at No.8 Via Bari, Palermo, Sicily.
FREQUENTED   : Frequents 90 and 120 Elizabeth Street,
                  New York City when in the United States.

CRIMINAL   Pasquale Siracusa; Joseph Parlapiano;
ASSOCIATES   : Mimi LiMandri; Alfonso Attardi and
                  members of the Mafia.

FACSIMILE OF
SIGNATURE   :

Figure 7.2   Nicolo Gentile. (Courtesy of the U.S. National Archives)

himself always in a positive light. Gentile also suffered from the handicap that he was in Italy from January 1927 to early November 1930, during the build-up to the Castellammare War.[25]

JOSEPH BONANNO

Our final primary resource is Joseph Bonanno. Due to his higher stature in the Mafia than Valachi, and his earlier involvement in some of the events than either Gentile or Valachi, Bonanno's overview was arguably broader.

His exposition of the reasoning from the Maranzano camp is, furthermore, invaluable. Counterbalancing this, Bonanno was not privy to some of the peace conferences that included Gentile. More than Gentile, Bonanno tended to idealize the aims of the struggle.

ORIGINS OF THE WAR

Most that has passed for a faithful explanation of the causes of the War can be contested. The orthodoxy, exclusively focused on Massera's assumed personality flaws, masked other factors in igniting the War.

Convention has it that Masseria became power-hungry, and that this character defect "got the better of him."[26] In scheming to extend his influence across the U.S. Mafia by force and intimidation, Masseria was solely responsible for starting the War as groups out of favor with Masseria united in their own defense.

Masseria was said to be "bidding for absolute supremacy in the Italian underworld."[27] Gentile concluded, "The actions of the administration of Masseria were imposed in dictatorial and exasperating commands which did not allow reply."[28] Bonanno's distain for Joe the Boss came through clearly in his account: he achieved power "through a combination of intimidation, strong-arm tactics, bullying and tenacity."[29] Beyond such caricatures, analysis has been absent.

To trace the tensions between Families that erupted in the Castellammare War, Bonanno and Gentile similarly focused on Chicago. Gentile's interpretation differs in crucial respects to Bonanno's. But both argued that fundamental to understanding why the War occurred were the figures of Joseph Aiello and Alphonse "Al" Capone.[30]

A central figure in the violent history of Chicago's Prohibition era gangs, Joseph and the Aiello family upped sticks to Chicago in the first years of the 1920s after partaking in a shooting affray in Utica, New York. There, Aiello joined forces with Antonio Lombardo, named as the Chicago *capo* by Gentile.[31] Unlike his sponsor Capone, Lombardo was Sicilian,[32] and could therefore exert influence in the Chicago lodge of the Unione Siciliana, a mutual aid society catering to mainly Sicilian immigrants (see Chapter 8).[33]

The Irish gangster George "Bugs" Moran and Aiello combined forces once "ambition struck" Aiello. Aiello parted from Lombardo, thereby losing Capone's protection.[34] Forced by Capone to leave Chicago "trembling for his life" in late 1927, Aiello retained an influence in the city by proxy.[35]

At about the same time, in Gentile's analysis, Masseria attempted to force Capone, the non-Mafioso, to hand over $50,000 in tribute. After it came to the notice of the Mafia general assembly through Lombardo, Capone was brought into the Masseria Family's orbit to avoid the payment.[36] Capone was given "the privilege of becoming part of the family" of Masseria, on condition that he would eliminate Lombardo and Aiello. This obligation was duly discharged.[37]

Yet the story offered by Gentile made no sense if the standard history of Chicago's organized crime, locating Lombardo under Capone's wing and Lombardo's 1928 homicide actually being by Aiello gunmen (Chapter 6), is maintained. Capone, moreover, showed loyalty to those like Lombardo who had proved their worth.[38]

There are other problems. Why the general assembly should devise a way of helping the non-member Capone out of the jam is a mystery, particularly since its resolution involved a radical break from the past by admitting a Neapolitan into their ranks. And Aiello survived long enough to supply money to Maranzano's war chest until October 1930, far later than Gentile's chronology allowed for.

Bonanno's recollections were equally at odds with the established narrative, in his case by having Masseria approach Aiello rather than Capone, and proposing they fight Capone together. But "Aiello told Masseria that he considered Capone an intruder in his city," and sent him packing back to New York with nothing to show for his entreaty.[39]

After this rebuff, Masseria courted Capone. Intersecting at this point with Gentile's tale, Capone would be given command of his own Family in Chicago if he followed Masseria's instructions. Bonanno remarked, "It was all too much."[40] As the price of his admission into the Mafia, Capone was required to rub out Aiello and to relinquish his brothel-keeping interests, perceived by the Sicilian leaders as "unseemly and immoral."[41] Capone, already at loggerheads with Aiello over territorial encroachments, agreed with relish.

Bonanno continued. Gaspare Milazzo, "the Castellammarese stalwart from Detroit,"[42] resisted pressure from Masseria to betray Aiello, as did Stefano Magaddino, the Castellammaresi Buffalo Mafia chieftain. In spurning Masseria, Milazzo and Magaddino laid the basis for the War, since it caused the tempestuous Masseria to make inflammatory remarks against all *amici nostri* from Castellammare which could not be over-looked. "Now he was disparaging the honor of Castellammare itself," Bonanno recalled.[43]

Again though, the case as presented collides with other information. The Detroit Italian syndicate leader, until his death from influenza in February 1930, was likely as not Salvatore "Sam Sings in the Night" Catalonotte.[44] Milazzo was in no position to speak for the Detroit Family, hence to take advantage of Masseria's offer in 1929 to "split the country" with him, or to swing Detroit Masseria's way, "if he would betray Aiello."[45]

Masseria, the Family head and patron extraordinaire over the U.S. Mafia, would also have been among the first to understand the grave danger he was putting himself in by backing different bosses in turn, and in such an obviously scheming manner. And why would Masseria want to risk antagonizing the pre-eminent Chicago gang figure, Capone, by making overtures to the weaker Aiello?

Aiello was permanently removed as a source of strife for Capone and Masseria on October 23, 1930, when two machine gun posts at Kolmar and West End Avenues, Chicago, slammed "thirty-five steel coated bullets" into his body.[46] Peterson, the foremost authority on Chicago's gangland, dismissed claims that the downfall of Aiello was related to the Castellam-mare War. "For an explanation of Aiello's murder" he asserted, "it is illogi-cal to look beyond the local Chicago gang wars of the period."[47] Peterson's argument notwithstanding, Aiello's contribution to financing the campaign against Masseria in New York is undeniable.[48] The totality of the evidence suggests that Chicagoan factors were not the sole reason for Aiello's mur-der, but that they were predominant.

The underlying problem was one of motive. Neither of the two infor-mants—Bonanno and Gentile—offered a convincing explanation as to why Masseria singled out Mafiosi with roots in Castellammare del Golfo for removal. "They didn't tell me why they were sentenced to death," said Valachi, but "they decided to get together and fight; so long as they are all going to die they had nothing to lose."[49] "All I understand," he added, "is that all the Castellammarese were sentenced to death."[50] Bonanno fell back on the argument that the Castellammarese clan in America "refused to kowtow to him,"[51] an interpretation that only made sense if Bonanno's description of the causes to the War was credible.

The perils of attacking that particular faction of the New York Mafia were great. Danilo Dolci noted, "Before the First World War, the Mafia of Castellammare and that of Monreale were probably the most powerful in Western Sicily."[52] "Castellammare has an evil reputation in Sicily," Maxwell wrote; "it vies successfully with Montelepre, the home town of Giuliano, as a place of blood and violence."[53]

In America, the Castellammare group in the Schiro Family demonstrated the extraordinary lengths they would go to in order to avenge a slur through their participation in the events surrounding Camillo Caiozzo's death, an event explained in Chapter 8. The Castellammare-born in the New York City Mafia also had kinship connections to other American cities that could also be mobilized in an emergency.

Among Masseria's former companions in crime were the Castellammare born Ruffino brothers, Giuseppe and Salvatore, who were apparently well known to Schiro members in Williamsburg, Brooklyn, where they resided.[54] Salvatore Ruffino was a one-time bartender in a Lomonte saloon in Harlem. A team including the Ruffinos and Masseria pulled off burglaries in the Bowery until their capture and imprisonment in 1913 (see p. 154).[55] Across the 1920s, a number of newcomers from Castellammare also lived on East 11th and 12th Streets inside Masseria's lower east side territory, yet without suffering harassment from Masseria's men.

Explanations of why the fighting began given by Bonanno and Gentile seemed designed to demonstrate why Masseria was the guilty party, and why it was imperative to stop him through force of arms. By attempting to force through an expansionist agenda, Masseria was signing his own death warrant.

But Gentile's account also contained a previously forgotten comment, that Masseria "forced all the representatives of the United States to approve" the death sentence on the Castellammarese.[56] What arguments Masseria used to achieve this end are lost to history. Despite this, that the Mafia as a whole concurred with at least some of the reasons for Masseria's policy towards the Castellammaresi suggested the likelihood of another story of why the War began, perhaps casting Masseria in a better light, but that was conveniently shelved once his opponents came to power.

NEW YORK CITY MAFIA, 1930

On the threshold of the Castellammare War, the Masseria Family was the most powerful, described as "the A & P of bootleggers."[57] Masseria's associates were sited in Brooklyn and the Bronx, complementing a powerful Manhattan contingent. Gentile noted Masseria's contacts with Mafia syndicates in Chicago, Detroit and Cleveland.

The former Salvatore D'Aquila organization, now headed by Manfredi "Alfred" Mineo, was "an avowed ally of Masseria's." A third Family, headed by Gaetano Reina of the Barnet Baff case, was primarily active in East Harlem and the Bronx. The *Onorata Societa* faction under Joseph Profaci stayed officially neutral in the War and functioned as "an intermediary with other groups."[58] (Though Valachi and Bonanno referred to Profaci as sympathetic to the cause of the Castellammaresi.) Last was the Schiro syndicate based in Williamsburg (Brooklyn). Most of the Families had interests in Manhattan and Brooklyn.

REINA'S FALL

Capeci, Peterson and Chandler are mistaken in thinking that the Castellammare War began with the Gaetano Reina homicide.[59] Nonetheless, it spurred the first opposition to Masseria in New York.

Figure 7.3   Gaetano Reina family. (Courtesy of Tammy Reina)

One of two gunmen in front of the Sheridan Avenue, Bronx, house of Marie Ennis, apparently his mistress, cut Reina down on February 26, 1930. "Reina's assailant," the *New York Times* reported, "used a double barreled shotgun which sent ten slugs into the ice dealer's body." [60]

Interpretations viewing Masseria as the puppet master behind Reina's death are contained in both Valachi and Bonanno.[61] But Masseria normally operated discretely, acting through nominees and extending his power through the means of alliances and understandings, particularly in his dealings with out of state groups.

The obvious suspects in the Reina killing were not anticipating retribution. Joseph Morello, "the second most important man in Masseria's Family,"[62] for instance gave the April 1930 census-takers his and his family's correct whereabouts. Masseria was discovered relaxing in Miami.[63]

Chandler reasoned that the former Reina Family membership initially made no moves to avenge the killing of their *capo*, since it was felt that it was in some measure "justified."[64] The argument explained subsequent events, for Valachi stressed that only a minority of the old Reina Family at first conspired to see Reina's replacement, Joseph Pinzolo, dead.[65] "There was about 15 of them that trust one another," Valachi said; "They couldn't trust everybody" in the Reina *Famiglia*.[66]

Police enquiries into the Reina homicide focused on his ice business, unsurprising given the amount of mayhem affecting the industry. Maas believed that Masseria ordered the gunning down of Reina because he had resisted a move to "muscle in" on this "lucrative" racket. Scaduto likewise perceived Reina as controlling "most" of the ice activity "in New York City." Downey presented an identical case, despite the absence of any evidence to buttress it.[67]

Violence in the ice business was pervasive. In the Bronx where Reina was based, the "ice-selling business became a struggle for vantage spots and a battle of price cuts that threatened the patience and the pocketbooks of the rival competitors and their allied icemen."[68] A high level of industrial competitiveness could be perceived as indicative of the lack of a Mafia presence that could exert tight control over the local market. In Reina's car, detectives found evidence that he was planning for the possibility of an assault once a "loaded rifle and two boxes of cartridges" was discovered. A pistol was also found on Reina's body.[69]

In 1927, a "city-wide trust" was exposed, the objective of which was to regulate ice prices through fixing the market. If "strong arm" tactics failed against interlopers attempting to "poach" customers from trust members, they were ruined via economic levers. But a multitude of small-scale dealers were involved, and coordinating them for mutual profit was a perennial annoyance.[70] Those holding out against cartel rules were, however, no doubt chastened by the brutal July 19, 1929 slaying of Jacob Stoffenberg on East 137th Street by an ice rival.[71]

Masseria remains the prime suspect in the slaying of Reina largely by default; no other suspects have been identified. But the alternative, of

Reina's demise being at least partly related to business competition, cannot be excluded. In the event, no arrests were made.

STIRRINGS OF REVOLT

Difficulties lay in Reina's replacement, Joseph Pinzolo, viewed by dissidents in the Family as a Masseria stooge. His promotion particularly angered underboss Tommaso "Tommy" Gagliano, who may have expected to take over from Reina. Gagliano led those like Dominick "The Gap" Petrelli who were bitter that they "didn't have anything to say" about Pinzolo's elevation, "so we killed him."[72]

Pinzolo was apparently unfamiliar to the group, not having lived or been active in the East Harlem territory populated by the Reinas. Nor was he related to others in the syndicate, fuelling disquiet about where his allegiance lay.[73] Uniquely among the New York Family heads, Pinzolo had been captured in the act of committing a Black Hand activity, as noted in Chapter 2. But his decision to inform on Giuseppe Costabile suggested a lack of backbone in Pinzolo that Masseria may have perceived and exploited.

The Gagliano team plotted to strike Pinzolo on a "sneak" basis. As Valachi put it, "They were trying to get all they could get before (Masseria) found out" their identities and thus their affiliation.[74] Through Morello, who had operated for years in Harlem, Masseria may also have known the regular Reina membership, making it imperative that Gagliano recruit strangers to Morello to his cause.

A coterie of "made" and proposed Mafiosi aligned with Gagliano's splinter group would plot the overthrow of Pinzolo, and subsequently join with Maranzano in a general war against Pinzolo's patron, Masseria. The Castellammare War in New York City amounted to a series of opportunistic engagements; murders outside of New York were the outcome of chiefly localized dynamics exploding or simmering just below the surface before the War began, while being influenced by personalities and events as they emerged in New York.

GASPARE MILAZZO'S EXECUTION

The trigger that "officially" set off the Castellammare War was the shooting in Detroit of Gaspare Milazzo[75] and Rosario "Sam" Parrino.[76] Milazzo had risen to assume the top job in the Detroit Mafia unknown to law enforcement.[77]

Like the Reina execution, that of Milazzo and Parrino was accomplished efficiently and without fanfare. As they were eating in the back room of a fish market at 2739 East Vernon Highway on May 31, 1930, two armed men burst in and blazed away. Milazzo died instantly; Parrino lingered on for three hours before succumbing to his wounds.[78] There it might have ended, but for the fact that Milazzo had strong links through his place of birth in Sicily (Castellammare) and via Vito Bonventre to the Schiro Family.

Responsibility for the two killings, as reported in the 1930 Detroit press, fell on the "downtown" or West Side crime faction led by Chester LaMare.[79] Once "Sam" Catalonotte died that February, a "mad scramble for the leadership" had divided the Detroit Italian underworld into two blocs.[80] In an effort to assuage tensions, East Side mob leader Angelo Meli dispatched Milazzo and Parrino to negotiate a peace agreement. But LaMare had no intention of sharing power.[81]

After the demise of Milazzo and Parrino, LaMare became a marked man when the remaining East Siders demanded his head. LaMare was permanently removed from the equation on February 6, 1931 in the kitchen of his Grandville Avenue home; he was found fatally wounded by his wife Anna. "From Detroit," Bonanno remarked with satisfaction, "we heard that the man whom Masseria had backed to lead the former Milazzo Family, Cesare LaMare, was no longer among the living."[82]

Parrino's brother Joseph had a desire, nurtured by Masseria, of taking over the Williamsburg Family, then led by Maranzano. "For a chance at becoming Father, Parrino was willing to serve a tyrant."[83] Parrino was killed in January 1931, succumbing to bullet wounds fired by one of 3 men he was sharing a West 40th Street restaurant table with.[84]

Salvatore Maranzano used the murders of Milazzo and Parrino as a platform to launch his bid for power. Maranzano "profited from the situation," by encouraging Milazzo's compatriots from Castellammare, together with *paesani* from Palermo of the slain former *capo di capi* Salvatore D'Aquila, to avenge themselves on Masseria.[85]

But other data sits uneasily with Maranzano's interpretation perceiving Masseria as directing LaMare's actions in Detroit from afar. Two men who eventually stood trial for ambushing Milazzo and Parrino were not Masseria's New York hitmen but Joe Amico, LaMare's bodyguard, and Joe Locano, another local man and a LaMare ally. Their Recorders' Court trial opened in October 1930. Prosecution witnesses were vague on the stand as to whom they saw leaving the fish market and Philip Guastello, the owner, was among those who gave them an alibi. Amico and Locano were acquitted on October 23.[86]

LaMare was apparently fearful for his life even before Milazzo and Parrino were riddled with bullets.[87] Their slayings could not be the only cause of his murder. The theory consistently pursued by the police was that LaMare's own men shot him in an act of betrayal devised by the East Siders. Enough evidence to support the case was gathered to bring three former LaMare associates to Recorders' Court trial in 1932, though they too were acquitted.[88]

No doubt Masseria's patronage was useful to LaMare, by connecting him to a leader with friends across the U.S. Mafia. But its translation into practical assistance in Detroit was pitiable. In spite of his influence, Joe the Boss could not save LaMare from the wrath of his East Side opponents.

MARANZANO'S ELEVATION

As the supposed founder of La Cosa Nostra, Maranzano's place in U.S. organized crime history is assured. Yet there was nothing in his background to infer that Maranzano's plans ever extended to a reorganization of the American Mafia. While officially only a rank and file member of the Schiro Family, Maranzano had built up an independent power base that would serve him admirably during the upcoming contest.

Maranzano's high Sicilian Mafia status was familiar to Masseria through Morello who was, Bonanno claimed, acquainted with Maranzano in Palermo.[89] Given his previous position in Sicily, it was apparent that Maranzano would have aspirations beyond that of serving as a loyal "soldier" for Nicolo Schiro.

Prior to the shooting of Milazzo and Parrino, Schiro had adopted a conciliatory posture towards Masseria, even if it meant the payment of $10,000 in "tribute." Schiro thereafter "went into hiding," leaving the field open for Maranzano, who emerged as his successor after his version of why Milazzo and Parrino were killed was widely accepted and acted upon. Upon the demise of Vito Bonventre in July 1930, Maranzano was formally elected as the "commander for the upcoming fight."[90]

PREPARATIONS

Because of the perceived dangers in taking on Masseria, Joseph Bonanno, a Maranzano loyalist, postponed his wedding to Fay Labruzzo, daughter of Bonanno's friend Calogero Labruzzo.[91] Maranzano's family was also reported to be living in Montreal in mid 1930.[92] With the Salvatore Maranzano family absent, his brother Giuseppe and his own family rented Maranzano's house on Avenue J., Brooklyn. Bonanno would be Maranzano's "chief of staff." A clear chain of command was created and an effective communications system established. The intelligence apparatus used by Maranzano proved its worth time and again.[93]

On September 17, 1930, three Maranzano men (Bonanno, Sebastiano Domingo and Charlie DiBenedetto) were waiting in front of Brooklyn city hall for "fresh" machine guns to be delivered when they were arrested.[94] Detroit detectives believed that the firearms were headed in the opposite direction, from New York to the Capitol Coal Company in Detroit owned by Angelo Meli, and that DiBenedetto and Bonanno were agents of Capitol Coal in New York. After interrogation, the men were released and a raid was conducted on the premises of the coal company, during which nothing was found.[95]

Financing the War against Masseria was a major challenge. Gagliano gave according to Valachi's Senate testimony, by far the most ($140,000),[96] while Magaddino and Aiello gave $5,000 weekly apiece. Valachi gave an alternative figure to his FBI debriefers of $150,000 from Gagliano.[97] In Maas's book, however, Maranzano enters the picture; "Maranzano and Gagliano" put up "$150,000 each for the war against Joe the Boss."[98]

But Maranzano only left behind after his death a mortgage on his Sea Isles, Brooklyn, and Wappingers Falls properties. Stocks and bonds worth $18,302 and $12,784 in cash on deposit in the Banco di Napoli were uncovered. Another $30,640 cash was on deposit at the Italian Savings Bank.[99]

Valachi complained that the men doing the fighting were paid a pittance, $25 each week, in his case split between himself and three companions. He conducted "a couple of burglaries . . . so we could have some money in our pocket."[100]

The issue arises as to why Maranzano did not use the profits from his liquor enterprises to fund and equip the War, reducing the burden placed on Gagliano especially. Valachi did not question the information he was given, and because of the casual way in which it was transmitted, he may have exaggerated (or mistakenly recalled) a wholly unrealistic figure for the money aspect of the Castellammare War, which does not appear in either Bonanno or Gentile.

OTHER CITIES

Aside from New York City, Detroit and Chicago, Celeste Morello and Valachi mention two other U.S. cities as contributing to the War. One source (probably Valachi) led the FBI to understand that the Buffalo group sent "at least" 12 men to help out Maranzano and that they "participated in a very active manner" in the War.[101] Valachi named three.[102]

Like Gaspare Milazzo, Salvatore Sabella, the late 1920s head of the Philadelphia Family, had solid connections to Bonventre and to Magaddino before he too left Brooklyn.[103] How the arrivals from Philadelphia and Buffalo spent their time in New York is undetermined, and Enrico "Harry" Riccobene, the source for the Philadelphia angle, gave contradictory accounts as to whether his contingent went to New York at all.[104]

THE DEATH TOLL

Because of discrepancies over the number of homicides that took place over the course of the Castellammare War, a painstaking search was performed to ascertain and to confirm the identities of the dead. The number arrived at was far smaller than expected. But in order to give the LCN model credibility, it would have to emerge as a logical answer from a titanic struggle involving scores of Mafiosi, and in which Mafias nationwide were affected to the extent that the demand for structural change became irresistible.

There was no evidence that Maranzano "had an army of about six hundred men under his command,"[105] or that (Chandler) "in New York alone more than one thousand members had taken to mattresses."[106] We have no information on who the gunmen working for Masseria were, though Bonanno contended, "almost everyone involved in the war" recruited "fresh soldiers."[107]

Valachi quoted a bloodcurdling "from 40 to 60" homicides on the Masseria side alone.[108] According to Maas, "before the bloodletting was over, some sixty bodies would litter US streets"[109] Salvatore "Bill" Bonanno argued, "There were bodies all over the streets of several major cities;"[110] the Castellammare bloc had "a force of approximately 400 men."[111]

But including Milazzo and Parrino, only 9 shooting deaths were linked to the warfare, together with the accidental murder of a "civilian" uninvolved with the Mafia. Five other killings, 3 in Detroit and 2 related to Maranzano in New York, were uncovered that may have had a link to the War.[112]

Complicating the task of calculating the proper number of War losses was "run-of-the mill" turmoil tied to the notoriously unstable alcohol racket. As Sifakis observed, "it was hard to tell which corpse belonged to the Castellammare War and which to the ordinary booze wars raging in the underworld."[113] After the early deaths of Milazzo, Parrino and Bonventre, Castellammare War fatalities were almost all on the Masseria side, making his defeat inevitable.

VITO BONVENTRE

Vito Bonventre was a second cousin of Bonanno,[114] and a key figure in the "Good Killers" affair (Chapter 8) who had retired from his bakery business a wealthy man.[115] But on July 15, 1930, he was shot in the back in a garage behind his home at 60 Orient Avenue, Brooklyn.

There were no witnesses to the Bonventre shooting.[116] Selected by Masseria as an early target because of his ability to help Maranzano in funding a War, Bonventre's demise and the abdication of Schiro led to Maranzano assuming control of the Schiro Family.[117]

JOSEPH MORELLO AND JOSEPH PIRAINO

Gosch and Hammer incorrectly named Frank Scalise and Albert Anastasia as the assassins of the one-time "boss of bosses" Joseph Morello.[118] Sebastiano Domingo told Valachi that he had gunned down Morello with "some other guy in the office."[119]

The New York dailies reported that on August 15, 1930, two gunmen burst into the 352 East 116th Street office where Morello was meeting his real estate partner Joseph Piraino[120] and Gaspare Pollaro. Morello was shot to death, left lying on the floor. Piraino, wounded twice, fell to his death through another window. Pollaro was wounded.[121] "The Gagliano group knew that they didn't do it," but their Steve Rannelli discovered the truth through his contacts in the Maranzano Family,[122] laying the basis for collaboration between the organizations.

JOSEPH PINZOLO

Perceiving the strength of the Masseria organization, Gagliano took time before attacking Pinzolo. Possibly galvanized into action by the knowledge that they now had an ally in Maranzano, Girolomo "Bobby Doyle" Santuccio shot Pinzolo.[123]

Pinzolo's body was found on September 5, 1930, "riddled with five bullets" in a room occupied by the California Dry Fruit Importers. Gagliano underboss Gaetano "Tommy" Lucchese had leased the office 4 months earlier. "I got the break of my life," Santuccio was quoted as saying, "I caught him alone in the office."[124] Lucchese may have set Pinzolo up.[125]

Valachi mentioned a meeting subsequently held on Staten Island by the whole of the former Reina *borgata* to find out who was responsible for executing Pinzolo. "Steve" (probably Rannelli) said, "Now they are calling a meet they figure that whoever don't show up is guilty, but we are going to fool them as we are going to show up." It appeared that the bulk of the Pinzolo membership remained reluctant to do anything that might antagonize Masseria. They need not have worried; after it, the full membership was no wiser as to the perpetrators of Pinzolo's execution.[126]

MURDER CONTRACT

Not long after the Staten Island conclave, the former Reina Family came round to the idea that they needed to kill Masseria. We do not know the particulars, or what arguments were used to sway them from their previous position, only that it happened.

A question arises at this point of how Maranzano would have hoped to resource the War if Gagliano had fortuitously not began to plot Pinzolo's overthrow several months before Maranzano entered the fray, Gagliano thereby being available to Maranzano as a cash cow. Equally, the small Gagliano faction of whom Valachi was a part could hardly have expected to win a battle against Masseria alone. A merger of the Gagliano and Maranzano groups was essential.

Representatives of the Gagliano and Maranzano organizations met to devise a way forward. It was agreed to give one another the name of a Masseria "boss" to eliminate. If all went according to plan, they would amalgamate under Maranzano's leadership. Domingo told Valachi, "they made a deal between them, after all they got to be sure of one another." He continued, "so your people gave us a name for us to kill and the old man gave Tom Gagliano a name for you guys to kill, and when that was done we got together."[127]

Valachi left historians with the problem as to the identity of the two selected by Gagliano and Maranzano for death, which research has failed to resolve.[128] Valachi himself never knew their names. He admitted, "I don't know the name, one gave one name, the other gave another name."[129] A number of authors misread Valachi on this, even his biographer Peter Maas.[130]

CLEVELAND

Valachi believed that the Castellammare War "was made national" in late 1930. Chicago, Cleveland and California were cited.[131] As Chapter 6 explained, the power play between Masseria and his predecessor as *capo di capi*, D'Aquila, extended to Cleveland.

In the latter half of 1930, Masseria's unidentified "brother" attempted to contest the position of the official boss of the Cleveland Family, Frank Milano.[132] For this affront to the established Cleveland hierarchy, Masseria in New York threatened his brother and a supporter, Angelo Antona, with death if they further disobeyed Milano.[133] That was the end of dissent in Cleveland.

The situation may have been staged by Masseria to test Milano's authority in Cleveland. Alternatively, Masseria's reaction to the challenge posed by the 2 Cleveland upstarts may have been calculated to send a message to Milano and other *Famiglia* bosses that Masseria had no plans to usurp them in the manner that his opponents had predicted.[134]

MANFREDI MINEO AND STEFANO FERRIGNO

The deaths of Manfredi "Alfred" Mineo and Stefano "Steve" Ferrigno[135]in a courtyard of the Alhambra apartments, 760 Pelham Parkway (Bronx), effectively sealed the War for Maranzano in November 1930. The Manfredi and Ferrigno contracts were the first fruit of the Gagliano-Maranzano collaboration, performed by individuals from both groups.

The assassination of Ferrigno and Mineo was conducted with "all the efficiency of a Chicago gang war ambush," three gunmen firing through the closed windows of a first floor apartment.[136] After leaving a conference attended by Masseria, the back of Mineo's head was almost blown

Figure 7.4 Stefano Ferrigno and Manfredi Mineo, November 5, 1930. (John Binder Collection)

off.[137] "Ferrigno lay with his face to the ground," the *Bronx Home News* reported, "his head toward the windows from which the slayers had fired, and Mineo dropped at Ferrigno's side."[138]

Through his contacts, Masseria at last learned who was behind the assassinations, and realized the weight and scale of the opposition facing him.[139] Within a few months, he would sue for peace. Masseria had "made too many false moves, sought too many needless confrontations and offended too many people."[140]

PEACE OVERTURES

The Mineo (former D'Aquila) group was visibly splintering under the pressure exerted by Maranzano. Near the end of the War, the Mafia general assembly at last asserted its formal authority, stepping in to "demote" Masseria, and to create a forum to investigate his actions.[141] It was, of course, a pragmatic reaction to the waning fortunes of Masseria, and the need to end the crisis by appealing to Maranzano's sense of where the common good lay.

Bonanno noted a party around Christmas 1930 near Hyde Park, New York, held to celebrate developments and to renew friendships with out of towners like Magaddino of Buffalo and Joseph Zerilli of Detroit. Another purpose was to welcome latecomers to the Maranzano cause from the Mineo camp such as Vincent Mangano, Frank Scalise[142] and Joseph Traina, who responded positively to Maranzano's entreaties.[143]

Figure 7.5   Gaspare Messina. (Courtesy of Frances E. Messina)

Gentile attended near the end of December 1930 or into early 1931 a summit in Boston at which the respected local *capo* Gaspare Messina was elected the provisional *capo dei capi* in place of Masseria. Traina was entrusted with the task of forming a commission to discuss with Maranzano how to end the War, and to arrange for new elections to be held to choose who would become the next "boss of bosses." With Traina on the commission were Gentile, Vincent Troia,[144] Salvatore "Toto" Loverde (Chicago),[145] and Joseph Siragusa of Pittsburgh.[146]

To present a show of impartiality, none on the commission came from either Castellammare or from Marsala, birthplaces of Maranzano and Masseria. But Troia was reported to be under the influence of Maranzano, as was Traina. Loverde acted for the Capone syndicate, formally aligned with Masseria but now wavering in its alliegance. It was apparent that Maranzano was "the stronger of the two," and persuading Maranzano to stop the fighting was the focus of the commission's work [147]

Maranzano arranged for them to be driven about ninety miles upstate to a secluded location (probably to his base in Wappingers Falls) where the commission was presented with a show of force and a reiteration by Maranzano of why Masseria should be liquidated. But Gentile persuaded the group to remain neutral and no decisions were arrived at. The death sentences that Masseria had imposed were revoked at a later convention attended by Maranzano. "Immediately afterward," a third and final deputation saw Maranzano in a futile attempt to ask him for a two months' ceasefire.[148]

The failure of negotiations involving the commission reflected the permissive system of consultation and mediation between U.S. Mafia organizations. Parties in dispute were "encouraged" to discuss solutions to problems, but it was ultimately left to Family heads to accept or to reject them. The system left the general assembly during the War in the difficult position of aiming to restore peace but without the means to enforce it.

Fearing police intervention if the gunplay continued, Masseria gave orders for his members to abandon the use of firearms. Upon hearing this, Masseria's men gave him "the ultimatum" to "rearm" or else.[149] When Masseria refused to listen, they began to plot his downfall.[150] Maranzano added fuel to the fire by promising that if they were to eliminate their leader, the bloodshed would end.[151]

Realizing the hopelessness of his position, Masseria "offered himself to be a plain soldier," but was snubbed.[152] The War was essentially over before February 1931, when Joseph Catania, a Masseria man, was slain. Catania's fate was not directly part of the War, but Valachi commented that Maranzano "would never make peace unless he gets Joe Baker." Catania was going about his daily business without a bodyguard when he was cut down.[153]

The fall of Catania served a triple aim. It underlined Maranzano's dominance as of early 1931, functioned as a means of settling an old score under the guise of "business,"[154] and acted to further diminish the status of Ciro Terranova.[155]

MASSERIA'S DEMISE AND THE END OF THE WAR

Shortly after the Mineo and Ferrigno homicides, Masseria moved house and "never went out except in his steel-armored motor car and was reputed to keep a bodyguard always with him."[156] It was in this automobile that he was driven to his death.[157]

In the early afternoon of Wednesday, April 15, 1931, Masseria drove to a garage nearby the Nuovo Villa Tammara restaurant on West 15th Street, Coney Island, and entered the premises. Perhaps lulled into a false sense of security by the expectation that the war could be ended peacefully, a get-together planned there was, so far as Masseria was concerned, nothing out of the ordinary. Gentile explained, "One day, among others, we all decided that we would eat at a Coney Island restaurant."[158]

"What happened after that," the *New York Times* reported, "the police have been unable to learn definitely."[159] Masseria was "seated at a table playing cards with two or three unknown men" when he was fired upon from behind; he perished from gunshot wounds to his head, back and chest.

No witnesses came forward, though "two or three" men were observed leaving the restaurant and getting into a stolen car.[160]

SUMMARY

By virtue of it encompassing several Mafia Families, the War was considerably more than the routine gangland strife that Albini noted as "common to other syndicates throughout the history of syndicated crime in the United States."[161] But it was a great deal further away from the type of grand contest that marked "an important turning point in Italian-American groups."[162]

What Valachi called the "undeclared war" lasted from September to November 1930. It was during this that the important casualties were inflicted, mostly on the Masseria side. The intention was to remove as many Masseria men as possible without Joe the Boss being able to identify (and so counter-attack) his opponents.

The relationship of the killings to the War was at times contestable. Whether for example Reina's "early" shooting should be included is open to argument. And Catania's was a by-product of Maranzano's desire to send a message out that he was in control.

Politically, the Castellammare War solidified the position of the chieftains of Mafia syndicates in Buffalo and Chicago. Capone, a "group leader" at the start, was especially favored by events as they unfolded, being included in the decisions to remove both Masseria and Maranzano. Chicago's new-found status influenced the choice of venue for the most important meetings. The Castellammaresi faction in the U.S. Mafia made gains, openly recognized by their prominent position on the Commission.

Masseria was caught wrong footed by the reaction of his opponents to the Reina and Bonventre murders and had made no preparations. Masseria's recruitment of Capone, of Neapolitan parentage, may have been for his traditionalist opponents another provocation that would lead to a showdown. Masseria's aloofness also left him friendless once the majority Sicilians in other Families combined to assert their weight.

Maranzano's genius lay in bridging those fissures that existed in the New York Mafia in the cause of removing Masseria. Maranzano had the inestimable advantage of having been a *representando officiale* in Sicily at a time when Sicilian developments and identities remained important in America.

Maranzano may have been positioning himself to take over from Schiro or even Masseria before the warfare began. Maranzano's success afterwards was chiefly attributable to a highly successful campaign attempting to connect Masseria to the Milazzo and D'Aquila murders, knowing that if his account was accepted their compatriots would seek justice Mafia style.[163]

MAFIA ORGANIZATION AFTER THE WAR

Once the fighting stopped, there was no appetite among the membership at large for a restructuring of the *Onorata Societa* along LCN lines to prevent a repetition. Solutions to prevent a renewal of conflict focused on the abolition of the "boss of bosses" system, on the role of Sicilian men of honor in the American honored society and membership restrictions.

The Castellammare War's effect on Mafia organization was minimal. Dual membership of Mafias in Sicily and the United States was forbidden and new enrollment was suspended. The dispensing of the highest-level patronage was parceled out among individuals sitting on the Commission.

New York City Family heads recognized after Masseria perished, as Bonanno shrewdly declared, were "either allies or supporters of Maranzano during the war."[164] As a result of the fragmentation of the Mineo organization, Maranzano was able to impose his nominee as head, Frank Scalise, on a demoralized membership. No such maneuver was possible within the old Masseria Family, which through the enhanced Luciano remained independent of Maranzano's power plays.[165] The situation in Newark, New Jersey, was also spelled out.[166]

LA COSA NOSTRA

Borgata members welcomed the return of peace. Because of the modest scale of the fighting, involving few Families, there was no reason to create the revolutionary organization of La Cosa Nostra in 1931. Assertions made that the LCN was instituted following Masseria's fall have their roots in a slanted and partial interpretation of Valachi's statements of a spring 1931 meeting held in a Washington Avenue, the Bronx, "dance hall," attended by "about four hundred members."[167]

Speaking before the assemblage, Maranzano purportedly "set up a table of organization for the New York Mafia; which was eventually adopted by all groups in the country," modeled on the military chain of command of a Roman legion.[168] Maas concurred: "The table of organization set forth by Maranzano was subsequently adopted by Cosa Nostra Families across the country."[169]

Valachi recited 32 years later how Maranzano explained in the Bronx why the War was fought, "of how Joe the Boss Masseria and his buddy Peter [Giuseppe] Morello were killing members and shaking them down." Maranzano also identified and recognized the New York City leadership.[170]

Maranzano, according to Valachi, additionally outlined at the Bronx gathering the New York City organizational hierarchy. It was this facet of the meeting that was to be misconstrued as the outlining a new organizational structure that would be adopted by Mafias nationwide.[171]

188 The Origin of Organized Crime in America

Yet a close examination of the original sources reveals something entirely different. Neither Bonanno nor Gentile, high enough in the Mafia hierarchy to have known differently, mentioned any change of structure after Masseria's death. Nor was there a suggestion by the 3 eyewitnesses to the War that the future trajectory taken by the American Mafia was at stake during, or after, the conflict. In his initial debriefing by the Narcotics Bureau, moreover, Valachi was reported to have said that Maranzano had only "recognized" the other New York City heads in the Bronx assembly.[172]

Other contradictions surfaced between accounts. Gentile reported that Maranzano "reorganized the most important borgate of New York" and was "elected capo dei capi" in a May 1931 Chicago get-together. But Bonanno, who was there, depicted it—"our first national conference"—merely as a chance for participants to recognize Maranzano's informal "supremacy on the national scene." Maranzano "apprised us of the reconstitution of leadership in New York, introducing the new Fathers one by one."[173]

Maranzano was evidently reiterating in the Bronx what experienced members did not have to be told, but that had to be explained to those new to the New York City honored society, like Valachi.[174] Bonanno and Gentile failed to mention the Bronx gathering because there was no reason for them to attend it.

Chandler reported that the decentralized Family hierarchy was modified during the War when Valachi joined, to echo the need for speed of response. It was a "wartime structure of government."[175] Valachi reflected that argument: "at this time, during the trouble, there is nothing like lieutenant or anything like that."[176] Once the fighting stopped, the former organizational setup—with which Valachi et al. were unfamiliar—was restored.

The Washington Avenue meeting also decided into which *Famiglia* the newly recruited members wished to belong, another reason why Bonanno and Gentile, settled in their own organizations, were not invited. (During the War, fresh faces had moved between the Gagliano and Maranzano Families freely.) Valachi elected to stay with Maranzano.[177]

Bonanno mentions a meeting in "a resort near Wappingers Falls," New York, in May 1931. The heads of other *Famiglia* joined to discover "how matters stood in New York," and to hear Maranzano's justification for the War.[178] Later that month as noted, a conclave was held in Chicago, "mainly to allow everyone to identify and place himself within the new political constellation." Capone, formally recognized as leader of the Chicago "outfit" was the host.[179]

"BOSS OF BOSSES"

Cressey believed that a "boss of bosses" of the stripe of D'Aquila, Masseria and Maranzano had "absolute control over Mafia members."[180] Among others, Cressey named Maranzano as the last of this kind. Gentile represented Masseria (and his predecessor D'Aquila) as accumulating dictatorial powers, operating through "secret agents" in "every city."[181]

But inconsistencies abounded. The *"capo di capi"* arrangement was, Gentile argued, a mirror of that in Sicily, when we know that nothing comparable existed there.[182] "Apart from arrangements within the framework of a definite action," recorded Hess of Sicily, "each separate cosche enjoys complete freedom of movement."[183] The Sangiorgi report of the late 19th century showed that Palermo-based *cosche* "had formal rounds of consultation and a unified system of trials," but they had no overall command system.[184] Anton Blok concurred; inside Sicily, "The various local cosche maintained loose relationships with each other without, however, yielding their relative autonomy to any overarching or sovereign power."[185] Melchiorre Allegra's writings as a former man of honor revealed a system of cooperation in the 1920s Sicilian setting, yet with no suggestion of a predominant figure armed with despotic powers.

Bonanno asserted that the American *capo di capi* was no more than the most powerful or esteemed figure in the Mafia constellation. "In Sicily," Bonanno adds, "we would refer to such a man, one who has gained the respect of all the other Fathers, as a *capo consiglieri*—a head counselor, a chief adviser."[186]

The relationship of the individual in question to the rest of the American Mafia was multifaceted. He needed not head the largest Mafia organization, although three of the four incumbents were from New York City.[187] Neither did his influence peddling necessarily equate with command over a large quantity of armed resources, as Masseria discovered to his cost. There was no explicitly allocated firepower available to buttress a "boss of bosses" authority, but ideally by virtue of the high esteem in which he was held, he was entrusted to help maintain the peace between American Mafia leaders.

The influence of the "boss of bosses" was by no means unlimited. Because of the dispersed characteristic of Mafia relations, sufficient space was created for rivals to mobilize localized coalitions to challenge his power. After *consiglieri* Salvatore Todaro died in 1929, for instance, Masseria supported Todaro's employer Joseph Porrello as Cleveland *capo*.[188] In May 1930, despite Masseria's patronage, Porello and Sam Tilocco were shot to death, followed in July by the slaying of Joseph's brother Vincente "James" Porrello. Masseria's backing was insufficient to win the day.

But by narrowing patronage powers in the hands of a "boss of bosses," decisions became highly personalized, creating distrust, partiality and encouraging players to jockey for position around him. Some members sought to curry favor with a *capo di capi,* while others attempted to challenge his authority.

Gentile seems to have been among the latter, perceiving himself to his biographer as a contestant for power with D'Aquila when functioning as "a great counsellor, intermediary, mediator."[189] At the time he described his American adventures, Gentile was retired, and happy to talk about his supposed prowess in the Mafia before listeners who were not able to contradict his interpretation of events.[190]

The volatility caused by individualizing power was the main reason for the abolition of the *capo di capi* system in 1931. The divisive manner of Maranzano's ascension made the system appear more dangerous and open to abuse than ever.

MARANZANO'S "CORONATION"

With Masseria in his grave, the former protagonists alive could afford to relax together. Luciano, Lucchese and Biondo, once on opposing sides, were seized attending the Stribling-Schmeling boxing bout in Cleveland on July 4, 1931.[191]

From August 1–3, 1931,[192] representatives of the U.S. Families assembled in the Nuovo Villa Tammara restaurant in Coney Island to celebrate the return of peace, and to witness the rise of Maranzano as the foremost figure in the American Mafia. It took place where Masseria had been murdered and was thus a highly symbolic setting.[193]

The gathering sought to rub in the victory of Maranzano, or was a means of healing wartime divisions.[194] Brooklyn detectives frisked those entering the restaurant after receiving information that a successor to "Joe the Boss" would be elected there.[195]

"The search was made," as the *New York Sun* reported, "after the police learned that four men arrested on Saturday were bound for the affair." They were Joseph Barbara, Natale Evola, Vincenzo "Jim" Coppola, and Nicolo Gruppose (or Gruppuso), arrested outside Santo Vultaggio's Ocean Avenue, Brooklyn, house. Joseph Barbara described how, "I was going to Coney Island and was stopped on Ocean Parkway, a motorcycle cop stopped us and asked if we had a gun, so we also had a gun, and I showed it to him, and showed him permit . . . But he didn't want to believe permit. He took us in for investigation and as far as I know, that's what it was."

All except for Gruppuso were from Castellammare, and Barbara and Evola would become Mafia leaders in their own right. Gruppuso was gunned down in September 1935, inside a Bowery seafood restaurant [196]

Held under the auspices of the "Societa Sciacca Maritima" (Maritime Society of Sciacca),[197] the banquet lasted three days. Tickets were sold, the proceeds from which were supposed to go towards "fireworks and decorations" for the annual Feast of the *Madonna del Soccorso* ('Our Lady of Help,' the patron saint of Sciacca) held on Elizabeth Street in lower Manhattan.

The Sciacca Maritime Society had been organized in 1899 "for benevolent and charitable purposes."[198] But Maranzano's use of the festival demonstrated the Mafia's influence in the broader Sicilian community of New York that was replicated later.[199] Gentile, who was present, says, "A group of high spirited boys provided to receive guests, accompanied the guests, greeted them with 'Long Live Our Capo'."[200]

Most American Families were untouched by the War. Nonetheless, they were required to "realign themselves within this new reality."[201] "As representatives of various families arrived at the banquet," Maas wrote, "each threw his contribution on the table,"[202] with Frank Scalise collecting it.[203] In total, between \$100,000 and \$115,000 was officially received,[204] though a sum of "well over the 150 thousand dollars mark" was rumored as donated.[205]

DOWNFALL OF MARANZANO

Even before the celebrations had ended, the wartime coalition Maranzano had fashioned was crumbling. Bonanno afterwards considered that Maranzano "became somewhat of a misfit" in the peacetime environment.[206] Magaddino became distrustful of Maranzano's "cheapness," "speculations" and "dishonesty," and refused to contribute \$10,000 asked of him for Maranzano's private fund.[207]

At the close of the Coney Island assemblage, Maranzano had hinted, at a meeting attended by Capone, Magaddino and two others, "very strongly [at] the possibility of the outbreak of a war." Magaddino urged moderation and an attempt to "pinpoint responsibilities."[208]

Part of the money raised at Coney Island was supposed to go towards compensating those who made the most sacrifices in the conflict.[209] Yet Maranzano kept it.[210] He explained to Valachi, "we must get the mattresses again, by that he meant that we are going to war again." They would need the proceeds from the feast as a war chest.[211]

Maranzano went on, "We have to get rid of" big-time New York gangsters like Capone, Luciano, Dutch Schultz, Vito Genovese, Frank Costello, Vincent Mangano and Joe Adonis. There were ten to twelve he couldn't "get along with."[212] It was perhaps no coincidence that those Maranzano identified had either actively opposed Maranzano or had remained aloof during the War.

Valachi's reaction was, "who wants to control everything?"[213] He was instructed to report to Maranzano on the Gagliano men who hung around East 112th Street, and Girolomo "Bobby Doyle" Santuccio, who occupied an office next to Maranzano's, was not to be told.[214]

Schultz' name may have been included because of his previous ties to Masseria by way of Ciro Terranova and Joseph Catania. Catania in turn was associated with Anthony Iamascia in the Bronx bail bond business. Schultz's bodyguard in mid 1931 was Iamascia's brother Daniel, "an important guy" in the former Masseria (now Luciano) syndicate.[215]

Catania was shot to death in 1931 purportedly for hijacking Maranzano's liquor trucks that were presumably moving from Dutchess County through the Bronx territory controlled by Catania and Schultz to get to the New York City market. The inclusion of Schultz's name on Maranzano's list may have been related to the same issue.

Figure 7.6   Dutch Schultz. (Courtesy of the Library of Congress)

Maranzano had helped to install Frank Scalise in charge of the Mineo Family on condition that he arrange for the assassination of Vincent Mangano, who had been slow in Maranzano's view to come over during the War. Scalise failed to carry out his instructions. Worried for his life, Scalise "went to the house of Joe Biondo to whom he confided all that had happened. Biondo called in Mangano, Lucky Luciano and from Chicago Al Capone."[216] A plan to eliminate the new *capo di capi* was hatched.[217] In the meantime, fearing for his life, Luciano "never came alone when he was invited to Maranzano's house."[218]

GARMENT RACKETEERING

Apparently for this reason, Luciano arranged for the assassination of Salvatore Maranzano on September 10, 1931. But another explanation was available of why Maranzano died, centered on garment district racketeering. Bonanno wrote, "A likely bone of contention was New York's garment district."[219] Powell's book filled in some of the particulars, followed by an enhanced version in Turkus and Feder's "Murder Inc."[220]

This interpretation illustrated the dangers for conventionalist Mafia leaders such as Maranzano when they chose to embroil themselves in predatory schemes involving non-Italians. Bruno Belea, a general organizer in the Amalgamated Clothing Workers of America, sought to enlist Luciano to fend off the racketeering advances of Louis "Lepke" Buchalter and Jacob "Gurrah" Shapiro, not knowing of their friendship, and was rebuffed.[221] Maranzano apparently took the contract on a once-only basis, naively assuming that he could exit as quickly as he had entered. Maranzano assured Luciano, "We're just going for the payday. We won't make trouble."[222]

The move occurred in the middle of delicate discussions involving the Lepke-Luciano combine and top-level garment district union officials. Cutters' Local 4 of the Amalgamated that had become entangled with Buchalter and Luciano through its business manager Philip Orlofsky. Orlofsky was occupied in a bitter struggle with Sidney Hillman, president of the parent union, over control of the Local, which Hillman won once Local 4's offices were raided on August 29.

According to both Block and Kavieff, Hillman gave Lepke $25,000 for his contribution in ridding the union of the Orlofsky rebels, also securing Lepke's position inside the Amalgamated.[223] Hillman paid Buchalter $350 weekly from 1932–1937; for that, Buchalter "performed various kinds of muscle work" for Hillman. The struggle over cutters' Local 4, in this analysis, was a carefully crafted gambit designed to force Hillman into dealing with Lepke.[224]

"Civil war" broke out in July of 1931 within the Amalgamated. An estimated 40,000 union members came out, "principally against employers who were violating union standards and who were employing gangsters to help fight the union."[225] Interspersed with acts of violence and accusations of gangster control of the clothing industry were attempts by non-union employers using strong-arm tactics to keep the Amalgamated out of their plants.[226]

At the city, union officials and mob bosses were trying to regain control, Anthony Froise, an Amalgamated official, was shot and wounded by the Lepke-Orlofsky crowd. Maranzano was assigned to even the score. Guido Ferreri, a clothing manufacturer, was gunned down by Maranzano men "within sound of his family" on the driveway of his Ocean Parkway home on July 31, 1931.[227] Worse, Guido was confused for his brother John, the real target, who had an ongoing dispute with the Amalgamated over his "open shop" garment factories in Brooklyn and New Jersey.[228]

In Scaduto's unsubstantiated report,[229] following Ferreri's shooting, a top-level get-together was called, composed of a mixture of the Italian and Jewish mobsters: Lepke, Luciano, Meyer Lansky, Frank Costello, Ben Siegel, and Dutch Goldberg.[230] The decision to slay Maranzano was made after Lepke warned Luciano that Maranzano was not only in danger of disrupting their joint clothing sector plans, through the botched Ferreri assassination. Maranzano's actions were also calculated to demean Luciano before his Mafia peers.[231]

A preoccupation by historians and politicians with events in the Mafia causing Maranzano's downfall failed to appreciate other contributing factors. Throughout his years in America, few if any non-Italians became part of Maranzano's circle. Bonanno, reared in the same traditional environment as Maranzano, knew of the pitfalls from entering a field with which he was unfamiliar and where other powerful players were entrenched. Because of that, Bonanno refused to be tempted by Luciano into an involvement in garment area graft.[232]

Lacking Luciano's grasp of the dynamics inside Jewish organized crime especially, Maranzano's excursion into the garment district—a "Jewish" gang territory in the 1930s—was fraught with risk. For their part, Jewish garment racketeers were bound to have been suspicious of Maranzano's behavior and motives, given his studied isolation from non-Italian organized crime since arriving in America.

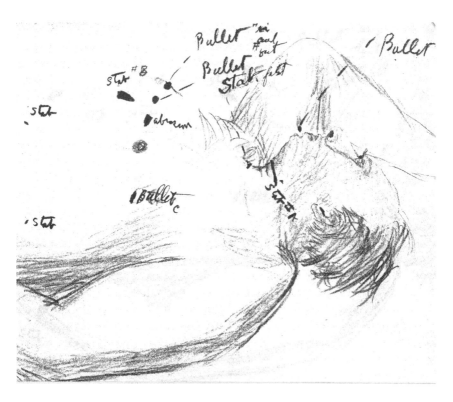

Figure 7.7 Salvatore Maranzano's body, September 10, 1931. (Courtesy of the NYC Municipal Archives)

END OF MARANZANO

Scaduto described how the assassins waited "for about a week" in a vacant apartment across the street from Maranzano's home, "to get a shot at him."[233] Only after Maranzano failed to appear there—or the timetable was moved forward—did they resort to the hazardous plot to get to Maranzano in the middle of the day in his office at 230 Park Avenue, situated in a busy office building.[234]

What happened on the afternoon of September 10, 1931 has been detailed in a number of books.[235] Leading the execution squad was Abe "Bo" Weinberg, a Schultz shooter, followed by Sam "Red" Levine of the Lansky-Siegel organization,[236] another (un-named) Lansky-Siegel member, and two unidentified "trigger men from the Newark mob."[237] One held up those waiting in the anteroom, while the others killed Maranzano by stabbing and shooting him to death.[238]

In exchange for their help in removing Maranzano, Italians helped Lansky and his associates in their 1933 "Jewish War" against Irving "Waxey Gordon" Wexler.[239] Family head Tommaso Gagliano owned a garage in which Murray Marks (a Gordon man) parked. Gagliano tipped off Luciano, and that was how they "got" Marks on June 29, 1933.[240] A man ran up to Marks and fired 5 shots at him as he alighted from a bus. The shooter was "whisked away from the scene in a sedan."[241]

Luciano had, says Bonanno, "taken responsibility for Maranzano's death," acting before Maranzano could strike against him and his lieutenant Vito Genovese using the renegade Irish gunman Vincent "Mad Dog" Coll. Operating outside of the New York City Mafia structure, which Maranzano distrusted, Coll was unlikely to betray his paymaster.[242] Coll was not known to be connected to Maranzano, thus was an ideal candidate to take the contract.

Weinberg's crew "made it by minutes." As Coll was entering the building "to kill Vito and Charley," who "never showed up,"[243] Weinberg's men, who had just killed Maranzano, waved him away.[244]

The extent of the conspiracy against Maranzano became clear as the day wore on. Valachi was due to meet his boss, but was told by "Charlie Buffalo" "not to bother."[245] Valachi was also saved from sharing Maranzano's fate by Dominick "The Gap" Petrelli's (a Gagliano) timely intervention.[246] Valachi remarked, "Now I realize they were all in on this."[247] Petrelli, among others in the Gagliano Family, had been informed of the planning against Maranzano, and may have been involved in it.

CONCLUSION

Histories of the Castellammare War have been marred by constant references to outdated and unproven information that failed to explain the meaning of the fighting. Valachi, Bonanno, and Gentile had the most rudimentary and incomplete knowledge of the sources of hostility that emerged as the Castellammare War. But they left explanations that could be tested through other sources. Their respective identification of Castellammare War victims encapsulated their different positions in the struggle and when they entered the fray.[248]

Embellished numbers of those who died in the War and took part in it were priceless if picturing the War in terms that hit the headlines, and in underscoring the argument since made that it had transforming effects on the U.S. Mafia. But assertions since made of the Castellammare War as "nationwide" in its scope and as marking the end of the old, fragmented system of Mafia governance, failed to match the historical evidence.

Cosa Nostra was not created with the Commission in 1931.[249] And there was equally no master plan contrived by Luciano to take over the Mafia in New York City (see Chapter 8). Maranzano was a victim of his own erratic behavior, and Luciano stayed loyal to Masseria until it was obvious that he was on the way out.

The Castellammare War was a watershed in Mafia history insofar as it prompted changes in the admissions criteria, resulted in the abolition of the *capo di capi*, and through its ban on Sicilian Mafia members joining American groups. The internal organization of Families was unaltered, as was the relationship between heads. Far reaching, though, was the political uses made of the unsound narrative on the War, grossly inflating the scope and significance of the fighting and the post-war settlements.

The Justice Department under Robert F. Kennedy exploited Valachi's appearance before the Senate Permanent Subcommittee on Investigations in 1963 to buttress its case for new laws.[250] Since 1961, under Kennedy, who had served for the McClellan "Rackets Committee" in the latter 1950s,[251] combating organized crime had become a priority.

Both at the 1963 hearings and in interviews, Kennedy stressed the importance of Valachi as showing the wealth and power of Italian-American criminals in La Cosa Nostra, "resting on a base of human suffering and moral corrosion." A selective adaptation of Valachi's testimony was crucial to the cause of proselytizing the Department's argument for extending the federal jurisdiction over organized crime.[252]

The concept of a highly disciplined, super-organization of crime with offshoots ("tentacles") in every U.S. city, that reached its apogee in the LCN model, had antecedents in flawed depictions of Chicago and New York's underworld over the Prohibition and New Deal eras.[253] The commensurate vision presented to the American public from 1963 was of Maranzano's LCN pursuing an aggressively expansionist agenda that only strong remedial policies could stymie.

The LCN was accused of endangering "the economic infrastructure of the United States, threatening the integrity of the governing process, escalating taxes, increasing the costs of goods and services to the consuming public, and jeopardizing the personal safety" of U.S. citizens.[254] Yet the Castellammare War was significant for what it sought to conserve, chiefly in the localized nature of decisionmaking that was equally a characteristic of the pre-1930 Mafia system. The fissures that developed also graphically illustrated the power of "Sicilian" values and loyalties, that negated the assumption of the U.S. Mafia from 1931 as increasingly mirroring the organization of American society at leadership levels.

The Castellammare War remains a cornerstone to explanations of the "Americanization" process in the Mafia. As La Cosa Nostra signified the organizational dimension to the historiography, proponents of the Americanization scenario argue that after 1931 a new kind of Mafia leader assumed control of the Families. To this we next turn.

8   Americanization and the Families

INTRODUCTION

The Castellammare War has been given an unwarranted status in attempting to explain how the Italians purportedly became the top dogs in America's organized crime structure. But if the Castellammare War did not alter the Mafia's structure and organization, did it alter the character of the Family leadership, making it more attuned to the "American" setting?

The La Cosa Nostra model was but one of a two-strand paradigm unified by the belief that an "Americanized" class of Mafia leaders staffed the new La Cosa Nostra syndicates. There was a measure of disagreement over the time scale this involved, but the outcome was not in doubt. Similarly to the LCN framework in being devoid of a robust empirical support, the Americanization proposal supplies the most commonly used paradigm to understand holistic changes in the Mafia.

In place of a wide-ranging investigation of the backgrounds of Mafia figures, the concentration has been on a few well-publicized individuals who have supplied a factual underpinning for the hypothesis. Yet there was no evolution towards a single type of leadership, in New York or elsewhere. Furthermore, how an "American" Mafia boss might be identified, and the operational impact that such identification might have, remain open questions.

Tales of an upsurge in the number of "American" Mafia leaders tended to emerge in those accounts that stressed a growing threat from organized crime. Since the fresh leadership of Families understood rational business practices and principles, that could maximize the potential of the LCN, these influences would be used to expand the reach of the Mafia. The elevation of the "Americans" to positions of responsibility inside Families represented a step change in the danger to society posed by the Mafia, in this hypothesis.

HISTORIOGRAPHY

Speculation surfaced that the slayings of Giuseppe Masseria and Salvatore Maranzano in 1931 had generational implications. Particularly noting the relative youth of Salvatore "Charlie Lucky" Luciano (real name Lucania), who emerged as one of the major winners from their murders, Nelli asserted, "The conflict between old and new resulted in the triumph of the Americanizers."[1] In the favored scenario, Masseria and Maranzano embodied traditional values and attitudes imported from Sicily that functioned as a brake on the growth of Families. Their elimination was therefore a prerequisite if the Mafia was to move from its ghetto base.

The concept of an Americanizing direction to organized crime's leadership predated the Castellammare War. Smith remarked that the 1920s gangster was commonly viewed as "the criminal equivalent of a modern businessman, whereas his predecessors had been regarded simply as ruffians."[2] In 1928 it was said, "Those who are strange to the mobman's ways might have some trouble in picking him out."[3] Dr. William Hickson of the Chicago Municipal Court argued in 1929 that for the modern gang figure, "shootings are merely his businesslike way of keeping competitors balanced with himself."[4] Sociologist Daniel Bell perceived the same blueprint: "As American society became more 'organized,' as the American businessman became more "civilized," and less "buccaneering," so did the American racketeer."[5]

Thompson and Raymond connected the revolution in organized crime's management to the need for bootleggers to deal with people outside of the immigrant community. It meant sharing resources and power with those in the wider population displaying the same stance on how to conduct business. Those who denied the new reality were removed; "Before that could happen there was a lot of murder, and there had to be."[6] Cressey's comparable belief was that the destruction of the "Old World Mafia" was a necessary precursor for a "new leadership" to emerge, with different "principles and policies."[7]

The historiography of the Americanization project in the Mafia was given an apparent empirical backing by the "Purge" thesis. It argued that in September 1931, a massacre of older conservative Mafiosi occurred in order to make way for a younger generation of leaders impatient to make their mark. The influence of the Purge theory was greatest from the late 1930s to the mid 1970s, when it was finally discredited. The Americanization theory lives on in an attenuated form, however.

Salerno in 1969 made no mention of either a Purge or the generational question.[8] Neither did the Senate Committee that reported on Valachi's testimony in 1965.[9] Nonetheless, while the Iannis could find no evidence of a sharp historical break within the Mafia in their observational study of the "Lupollo" faction, they assumed that Americanization and the Purge had occurred in other Families.[10] "The old "Moustache Petes," the custodians of the Mafia tradition," the Iannis asserted, "were either killed off or passed into obscurity."[11]

By the time the Nelli and Dickie works were released, original research had been conducted exposing the fallacy of the Mafia Purge thesis. It followed that there could be no dramatic transformation of the leadership in control of *Cosa Nostra* Families. Yet while exposing the Purge myth, Nelli and Dickie were faithful to the broader theme of a generational changeover at boss level, with ramifications for the manner in which Mafia organizations were run. The changeover to an Americanized Mafia leadership was now presented as a non-violent process, conservative leaders retaining a degree of power after 1931.[12] Nelli remarked, "The one correct point—and also the major point—of the story was the fact that Maranzano's death marked the victory of the Luciano 'Americanizers' in New York over the 'Greaseballs.'"[13]

"MOUSTACHE PETES"

With or without the Purge component, counterposed against the Americans in the argument was first generation Mafioso, always pictured as clannish and insular in outlook. Variously nicknamed by their detractors as "Moustache Petes," "Greasers," "Greaseballs" or "Greenhands," those in this category were ill-suited to U.S. conditions.

Valachi was unimpressed by their inability to speak English well.[14] The Profaci Family's Charles "Charlie Sits" LoCicero, for example was unable "to read or write the English language."[15] Bill Bonanno singled out the "old-world people" by their gait and manner. Positively, they were said to carry themselves "with more circumspection" than did the Americans in the Mafia,[16] to follow orders without question,[17] and adhered to the Mafia "code of silence" rigidly.[18]

Mafia traditionalists were criticized from this viewpoint for moving in narrow circles and refusing to adopt a "businesslike" approach to organized crime,[19] preferring to leech off their immigrant compatriots than make their own way by seizing the multiple opportunities to hand.[20] Moustache Petes were "loath to associate with non-Sicilians," no matter how productive such a collaboration might prove to be.[21] Joe "the Boss" Masseria was portrayed as the classic case of a leader who held onto "outmoded" and dysfunctional practices.[22]

As Valachi put it, "The Americanized usually stole for their money, where the Italian born since he is a kid he has racketeering on his mind." They were considered by other members as Black Hand variety "nobodies", without a proper organizational base and committing the kind of unnecessary violence ("kill crazy") that would land them in jail.[23] Because of their inability or refusal to see the wider picture, the rewards the Moustaches reaped from organized crime were modest.

LUCIANO

By virtue of his close connection to the assassinations of Masseria and Maranzano, Salvatore Luciano's personality became central to the Americanization case, as he sought to "rationalize proceedings and organize crime

Figure 8.1   Salvatore Lucania. (Courtesy of the U.S. National Archives)

as an efficient business operation."[24] Leading "a generational revolt against the bosses of New York's Italian gangs,"[25] Luciano and his young acolytes were ideally positioned to gain from Masseria's demise, "solidifying his own position of primacy" and starting the modernization process.[26]

Luciano was perceived as the archetypal modern American gangster, "essentially a 'loner' who was "more businesslike and also more democratic than the old-style Sicilian leaders."[27] Reared in the American big city environment, Luciano was materialistic, innovative and individualistic. A probation report compiled on Luciano in 1936 pointed out: "His ideals of life resolved themselves into money to spend, beautiful women to enjoy, silk underclothes and places to go to in style."[28]

The creation of the *Cosa Nostra* Commission in 1931 solidified and extended Luciano's project, according to this analysis.[29] Luciano both devised the concept of a Commission and decided who would sit on it.[30] "In effect, a board of directors," the Commission embodied the "American Way" of conducting crime.[31]

PREVIOUS RESEARCH

Attempts to explore the validity of the Americanization proposal have been compromised by the deployment of unrepresentative information and confusion as to how the "American" leaders were to be identified. A third difficulty lay in the presumption that the ascent of Americanized bosses would have radical effects on the activities of underlings.

The Americans were, however, linked in the literature with youthfulness as their one enduring empirical characteristic. "With the extermination of

Masseria," wrote Turkus and Feder, "the younger element was dominant in 'the family' for the first time."[32] Two articles from Haller dealt with the age of a select group of bootleggers in the years coinciding with the Castellammare War and with the Americanization debate.

Haller indeed concluded that the 1920s bootlegging market was "seized by newcomers: ambitious, yet relatively unknown men." But that conclusion was based, for his New York sample, on the specifics of the newsworthy but atypical Luciano, Frank Costello, Frankie Yale and Johnny Torrio.[33]

A table Lupsha presented in 1981, purporting to demonstrate a takeover by "young Americans" of "organized crime" in 1931 conflated those with a link to the Castellammare conflict with the majority who were without any connection.[34] An identical error undermined Nelli's survey of 58 "top or middle-management syndicate leaders" in 1931, "in ten cities."[35]

Dickie discarded the notions of the Purge and of the Commission as Luciano's creation. But similarly to Nelli, Dickie clung onto the essentials of the Americanization approach, causing confusion at both the conceptual and operational levels. Thus while the "Americanized" Mafia leaders in control from 1931 were nearer to approaching the businesslike ideal, according to Nelli, "working relationships" were "far more personalized than in a legitimate American corporation."[36]

Dickie followed Nelli in seeking to steer a course that attempted to reconcile the Americanization theory with the evidence. Muddle was the result. Dickie thus correctly discounted differences at one point between Greasers and the Americanizers as an artificial construct. A page later, though, the dichotomy reappears as a real one, and with Mafia traditionalists apparently still in the driving seat. Undefined "Sicilian methods" were argued as persisting in the Mafia "long after the young guns of the Prohibition era-Luciano, Capone, and their like were gone."[37]

Focusing on a few headline-grabbing Mafiosi as somehow representative of the majority of the Mafia elite after 1931 was an unsound methodology. A broader range of empirical material in fact suggests that traditionalists were almost as dominant in the New York City Mafia after 1931 as during the preceding years. There is no reason to believe that the situation in other cities was different.

1928 CLEVELAND MEETING

Although the theoretical outlines of the traditionalistic and the modernized types of men of honor are reasonably clear, which individuals belonged in which camp was often difficult to fathom. At which stage a Mafioso became "Americanized" enough in the discourse to be labeled as a Luciano ally was a particularly tricky task to uncover.

The centrality of age to the debate was obvious. If not born in America, the Americanizers were argued as coming to the New World at a young enough age to assimilate "American" values and goals, either through the educational system or informally.

The group of pre-Castellammare War Mafiosi seized in 1928 at the Hotel Statler, Cleveland, noted in Chapter 6, is excellently placed to compare against those "American" members supposedly emerging to greater influence from 1931, and who were presumed to have youth on their side. The expectation for the Americanization hypothesis to hold was that the members gathered in 1928 would be substantially older than Luciano. It was these older men and others like them who would be overthrown or decline in influence after the War, according to convention.

Helping to resolve this question was the fact that those in Cleveland were from a variety of U.S. cities. Findings based on the Cleveland sample can therefore be generalized to Mafias beyond New York City.

In terms of their places of birth, those seized in 1928 were, to a man, Sicilian. At Mafia assemblies, Gentile observed, members spoke "Our language, Sicilian."[38] The largest group in Cleveland came from around the city of Palermo; the rest came from towns scattered throughout western Sicily. None came from Castellammare del Golfo or thereabouts, notwithstanding its subsequent importance in U.S. Mafia history.

The largest single contingents in Cleveland lived in Brooklyn and Chicago, and over half in the sample were subsequently slain.[39] The handful of bosses present were older than the mean at the time of their entry into America, a feature to be expected from a "traditional" Mafia organizational hierarchy.

Name	Birth Year	Birthplace	Immigration	1928 Age
Philip Bacino	1902	Ribera	1923	26
Emanuel Cammarata	1903	Villabate	unknown	26
Samuel DiCarlo	1904	Vallelunga	1906	22
Ignazio Italiano	1860	Santo Stefano Quisquina	1903	68
Pasqualino Lolordo	1887	Ribera	unknown	42
Andrew Lombardino	1904	Newark	n/a	24
Salvatore Lombardino	1891	Gibellina	1907	37
Joseph Magliocco	1898	Villabate	1914	30
Vincent Mangano	1887	Palermo	1905–1906	41
Giovanni Mirabella	1904	St. Louis	n/a	24
Salvatore Oliveri	1895	Corleone	1912	33
Paolo Palazzolo	1895	Cinisi	1920	33
Joseph Profaci	1897	Villabate	1921	30
Michael Russo	1893	Cerda	1906	35
Calogero Sanfilippo	1899	Casteltermini	1907	28
Joseph Scacco	1901	Camporeale	1920	27

Name	Birth Year	Birthplace	Immigration	1928 Age
Salvatore Tilocco	ca. 1892	Licata	1909	37
Joseph Traina	1883	Belmonte Mazzagno	1901	45
Joseph Vaglica	1893	Monreale	1894	ca. 35

Luciano was born in 1897, arriving in New York in 1907; in 1928, he was therefore 31 years of age. Of those attending the Cleveland event for which we have data (19), nine were younger than Luciano in 1928, one was of approximately the same age as Luciano (Profaci) and nine were older. This therefore located Luciano in the middle of the Cleveland group in terms of his age in 1928.

The mean age of the 19 identified for Cleveland was 34, slightly older than Luciano was in 1928, but that figure included the elderly Italiano. Without Italiano, the mean age dropped to 32, almost exactly the same age as Luciano.

As noted, age at the time of their immigration was critical in the discourse, since an early entry to America gave the assimilation process more time to work. Again excluding Italiano to avoid skewing the results, the mean age at entry into America of the 14 Cleveland names for which years of immigration were found was around 15, somewhat older than Luciano's age when he set foot in New York (nine) but not grotesquely so. The Cleveland dataset, in a nutshell, failed to uphold the Americanization model's prediction that those arrested in 1928 would be markedly different from Luciano when measured by the key age of birth or immigration indicators.

CASTELLAMMARE WAR MAFIA

Pursuing the argument to the Castellammare War period, when the Americanization case had most theoretical resonance. Comparing information on the Maranzano and Masseria sides (1930–1), the former were somewhat older when incoming to America, but younger by age in 1930. Maranzano was the oldest in the sample to arrive from Sicily in his New York Mafia group, as were Morello and Masseria in theirs.

Luciano (part of the Masseria organization) was indeed younger than the mean of those identified in both Castellammare War camps at the time he came to America. But Luciano was not as young as Ciro Terranova, often perversely identified with the traditionalists. And youth was no guarantee of Americanization; Bonanno became a boss at a relatively young age (26 in 1931) yet remained resolutely conservative in his outlook.

Maranzano Family and Castellammare War affiliates

Name	Age at Immigration	1930 Age
Giuseppe Aiello	17	40
Giuseppe Bonanno	19	25

Name	Age at Immigration	1930 Age
Vito Bonventre	30	55
Frank Callaci	7?	30
Gaspare DiGregorio	16	25
Sebastiano Domingo	3	21
Tommaso Gagliano	21	46
Gaetano Lucchese	12	31
Stefano Magaddino	18	39
Salvatore Maranzano	39	44
Angelo Meli	16	33
Gaspare Milazzo	unknown	43
Giuseppe Parrino	24	44
Rosario Parrino	20	40
Dominick Petrelli	11	29/30
Stefano Rannelli	unknown	28
Dominick Sabella	16	31
Salvatore Sabella	21	39
Girolamo Santuccio	8	30
Salvatore Shillitani	U.S. born	24
Giuseppe Valachi	U.S. born	27

Masseria Family and Castellammare War Affiliates

Name	Age at Immigration	1930 Age
Giuseppe Adonis	7	28
Albert Anastasia	15	28
Alfonse Capone	U.S. born	31
Anthony Carfano	U.S. born	36
Frank Costello	ca. 4	ca. 39
Carlo Gambino	21	30
Vito Genovese	16	33
Nicolo Gentile	18	45
Frank Livorsi	U.S. born	27
Salvatore Lucania	9	33
Vincent Mangano	17	42
Giuseppe Masseria	14 ?	43
Manfredi Mineo	31	50
Giuseppe Morello	unknown	63
Giuseppe Pinzolo	19	43
Saverio Pollaccia	17	43
Giuseppe Rao	U.S. born	29
Giuseppe Rosato	16	26
Frank Scalisi	17	37
Ciro Terranova	5	42

Focusing on Maranzano and Masseria, who were significantly older than Luciano, may have influenced writers in their formulation. Yet aside from Luciano, the chief beneficiaries from the Castellammare War were the traditionalists. Furthermore, most of those who stuck by Luciano after the War as members of his Family were older than Luciano himself, presumably qualifying them as "Moustaches." Moreover, Luciano's underboss, Vito Genovese, was younger in 1930 than the mean, implying his Americanization on that scale. Yet Genovese was older than the average when he first stepped foot in New York. Underlings with mixed characteristics surrounded Luciano. And it was Luciano who was atypical of the norm, before or after the Castellammare War.

Age of birth, or age of immigration to the United States, were not reliable predictors as to which Mafiosi in New York City could be categorized as "Americans" or "traditionalists." Moreover, most members sought to join a *borgata* to "command respect" (in the traditional style) as much as to make money (in the "American" fashion).[40] Focusing instead on the types of illicit enterprises conducted in New York City, the "conservative" Bonannos were little different from their "American" opposites in the Luciano-Genovese organization.[41]

Masseria adopted a surprisingly liberal recruitment policy, working with a number of non-Sicilians, among them the Calabrian Frankie Yale and the Neapolitan Gaetano "Tommy the Bull" Pennachio. In March 1930, Masseria was found in the company of not only Luciano and his Italians, but also "Nig" Rosen of Philadelphia and Harry Brown from Chicago.[42]

None of the three witnesses to the Castellammare War and to its settlements, Bonanno, Gentile and Valachi, explained the conflict in terms of generational differences or leadership models.[43] Since local conditions varied, the suggestion that Luciano could impose his style of leadership across the Mafia was unrealistic, in the same way that Maranzano had no hopes of imposing an LCN organizational form.

Bill Bonanno posited a larger role for him in the establishment of the Commission. Far from being an invention of Luciano, though, Gentile recalled that the concept of a Commission came from himself. Gentile was by his age (born in 1885) and date of arrival in America (1903) a traditionalist.[44] But at a Chicago conference in May 1931, Maranzano, who would lose the most if the Commission were created, managed to scupper the idea.

Luciano was simply one of a number of Commission members with no special status or powers within the Mafia elite. As Woodiwiss argued, the concept of Luciano as a criminal mastermind was first engineered and mythologized by Thomas E. Dewey to further Dewey's political ambitions. Compliant journalists who did "little investigating of their own" further embellished the Luciano legend.[45]

The question of the type of leadership in Mafias that took up so much attention was marginal to the real outcome of the War. The orthodox Family structure and leadership cadre was resilient to reform, and most members associated chiefly with their own ethnicity as before.

"THE PURGE"

The Mafia Purge theory explained, in a neat and simple package, how the Americans managed to wrest control from diehard Moustaches. Yet "not one shred of evidence has turned up" to buttress it.[46]

The Purge account signified the mass murder of "members of the Sicilian Castellammare group in New York, and Sicilian 'greasers,' 'handlebars,' and 'moustache Petes' all over the country."[47] Assuming that Salvatore Maranzano was at the head of the Moustaches, at "the very same hour" that Maranzano was eliminated, "about ninety guineas were knocked off all over the country." The casualties were "unassimilated Sicilians," or "old-time mobsters." Powell stated that 'at least' thirty Maranzano loyalists were wiped out on or shortly after Maranzano.[48] Turkus and Feder similarly asserted, "Some thirty to forty" old timers were dispatched, "all over the United States."[49] The removal from positions of power of the "Old World Mafia" was a precondition for the "new leadership" to surface under Luciano.[50]

Valachi did not mention the Purge, nor did others appearing before the 1963 hearings that laid the basis for the LCN paradigm.[51] Although Block is generally credited with exposing the myth of the Purge in 1978, seven years earlier Albini noted that sources were unable to give even the names "of these so-called victims."[52] "We keep hearing," Albini asserted, "of the number of victims ranging from 30 to 90, yet we were unable to find any source that gave the names of these so-called victims."[53] Talese had alluded in 1971 to "several" deaths related to Maranzano's,[54] and Nelli's debunking exercise appeared in 1976.[55]

Block and Nelli shattered the Purge thesis by searching major American newspapers for the few weeks after Maranzano's demise, when the assassinations were supposed to have taken place.[56] They discovered virtually no correlation between Maranzano's and other killings recorded that month.

But their methodology was imperfect. They rejected newspaper accounts that did not meet a prior expectation of what they "should" have contained. Reports making no mention of Maranzano or of New York City were automatically discarded. The process generated a self-fulfilling outcome, which did not explore the full range of possibilities.[57] No evidence, nonetheless, has emerged since the 1970s in support of the Purge story. The Bonanno Family, which contained the most Maranzano loyalists and therefore would have been hit first and hardest in any massacre, suffered no reprisals after Maranzano's end.[58]

Even disbelievers in the Purge have stated that three murders mentioned by Joseph Valachi were coupled to Maranzano's demise, those of Luigi Russo, James LePore, and Samuel Monaco. LePore was fatally wounded on September 10, 1931 by bullets shot from a car on Arthur Avenue in the Bronx. Russo and Monaco were subject to beatings before their bodies were thrown into Hackensack River and Newark Bay, New Jersey, where they were found on September 13.[59]

But no proof has unfolded since Valachi's statements which show a connection between the Russo, Monaco, and Maranzano deaths. The Newark
newspapers tied the fates of Monaco and Russo to an alternative scenario.[60]
Because they were important New Jersey *amici nostri*, and due to the coincidence of their perishing when Maranzano did, Valachi jumped to the
conclusion that the Russo and Monaco homicides were part of a Maran-
zano-related conspiracy.[61]

Only those who were part of Maranzano's inner circle were under
threat of attack. Since Valachi was a Maranzano confidant, his pals were
shot at on the day of Maranzano's execution. Peter "Petey Muggins"
Mione, Steve "Buck Jones" Casertano and John "Johnny Dee" DeBellis,
were fired upon just after Maranzano's removal.[62] They had conducted
surveillance for him.[63]

Block cited the gunning down of Joseph Siragusa in Pittsburgh as a possible Purge event because the slayers escaped in a car bearing New York
license plates.[64] According to Gentile, Siragusa, the Pittsburgh Mafia representative, "in his time, had done everything possible to have me killed."
Once they heard of Maranzano's death, Gentile and John Bazzano (functioning as either the Pittsburgh *representando officiale* or the Family underboss) thought of "eliminating Siragusa."[65] Siragusa was shot down in his
home on September 13, 1931.[66]

It was postulated that many, if not most, of those eliminated in the Purge
were from an "army" of Sicilians that Maranzano was reported to have
smuggled in from Sicily during the 1920s, fleeing from Fascism to fight
his corner.[67] "At the very minimum," Chandler elucidated, "five hundred"
Sicilians made the journey to New York.[68] The *Sun* spoke of Maranzano
bringing in over 8,000 aliens to replenish his forces "in recent years." That
figure was also quoted in the *New York American* and in the *New York
Times*.[69] Dickie, Nelli and Block repeated it uncritically.[70]

Yet almost every New York City Mafia figure known to participate in
the Castellammare War was established in New York years before 1925,
when the campaign against the Sicilian Mafia gained momentum under a
new Prefect of Palermo, Cesare Mori. Only Maranzano and Bonanno (who
took over from Maranzano), departed from Sicily in the right "mid 1920s"
time frame needed to validate the argument.

Moreover, the chief of the New York Police Department's Alien Squad
said in September 1931 that "he is quite certain that there is no connection
between the death of Maranzano and immigration activities." Efforts by federal agents to track down Maranzano's imported soldiers led nowhere.[71]

UNIONE SICILIANA

The Purge story first unfurled via a distorted understanding of the Unione
Siciliana's history. The Unione became, in the older narrative, the means

used by Luciano to achieve his Americanization goal.[72] "Ever since the purge of '31," observed Feder and Joesten, "Unione has been no more Mafia than a processed shot of heroin is the original poppy."[73] New York was "its seat of power."[74] The "national president" of the Unione was named as the former Morello organization's Ignazio Lupo and subsequently Brooklyn hoodlum Frankie Yale.[75]

Cressey repeated statements taken from the 1930s and 1950s on the Unione Siciliana's role in the inter-generational takeover, believing them to be true.[76] The Iannis similarly considered the Unione as a vehicle for those Sicilian traditionalists who would be overthrown by the "achieving, second-generation Italian-American mobsters who were now moving into leadership roles in the gangs."[77]

Unione Supreme President Judge Bernard Barasa added to the air of mystery surrounding the Chicago lodge of the Unione by attending the funerals of James Colosimo, Antonio D'Andrea and Dion O'Banion; notorious "mob" figures.[78] Capone mobsters like the Gennas and Antonio Lombardo were associated with the lodge.

Schiavo gave the earliest critique of this analysis, terming it as "drivel."[79] Albini noted contradictory information on the subject.[80] Dwight C. Smith found, "The lack of clear evidence about the Unione Siciliana could lead to the suspicion that there might have been two organizations with the same name having no real connections."[81]

The Unione Siciliana was one of the "thousands of fraternal organizations which the Italians established in America along the lines of mutual benefit societies."[82] The Unione's own records for the period in question are lost, but its official history is clear. Founded in 1895 in Illinois, it was one of the "thousands of fraternal organizations which the Italians established in America along the lines of mutual benefit societies."[83] Through a process of consolidation, the Unione emerged as a political broker in turning out the "Italian" vote at municipal elections, particularly in Chicago.[84]

The organization was renamed the Italo-American National Union (IANU) in 1925, in order was also to accommodate a small non-Sicilian membership, and was also licensed to sell insurance in Illinois, Indiana, Michigan and Ohio. However, there were no lodges in New York[85] for Lupo or Yale to join or lead. Since the Unione was largely a "Sicilian" phenomenon,[86] the idea that the Calabrian Yale was its "national head" was far fetched.[87] Especially when, according to legend, the Neapolitan Capone was denied membership precisely because of his non-Sicilian ancestry.[88] (Believers in the Unione-Yale link having wrongly assumed that Yale was Sicilian.) Lupo spent most of his life after 1910, furthermore, in jail.

A "very reliable informant" told Kefauver investigators in the fall of 1950 that the Unione was organized "over 30 years ago" by one Joseph LaPorta. LaPorta was considered by a Committee source to belong to the Unione's inner council, "comparable to the Grand Council of the Mafia."[89] FBI agents interviewed LaPorta in 1960. While living on

East 107th Street, LaPorta came into contact with the likes of Gaetano Lucchese and his Mafia lieutenant Joseph Rosato.[90] LaPorta even gave Lucchese a half share in his Bronx fabrics business, for which service Lucchese promised to secure orders.[91] Yet nothing afterwards surfaced indicating that LaPorta was "made" into the Mafia, or that he belonged to the Unione.

Outside of its recognized gangland connections in Greater Chicagoland, the Unione appeared to abide by its legitimate objectives of supplying "a subsidy during sickness, a return ticket to Italy for the chronically ill, aid in securing employment, and often other benefits—all for a small monthly fee."[92] And nowhere could it be equated with an Americanization project.

CONCLUSION

The Unione was invaluable to authors attempting to picture the Mafia in exaggerated terms, as "one strong link among the many in the national chain of crime."[93] Erroneously connecting the Unione, which was written of as nationwide in scope, to a mythical Luciano project explained why the Americanization process was thought to have happened across areas with divergent characteristics.

The American Mafia had no ability to carry out coordinated carnage on anything like the scale of a Purge; and Buffalo's Steve Magaddino boasted that, "when Maranzano died, I was the one who managed things so that no one got killed."[94] Likely as not, the violent death of the powerful Maranzano was expected by the underworld to cause ruptures leading to more killing. In the cause of restoring calm, an institution promoted by Luciano, as Valachi claimed, was a "council of six" composed of the *consiglieri* within each of the New York *Cosa Nostra* Families.[95]

The Purge was an archetypal product of second hand rumor and hyperbole; as Block says, "standard fare in the secretive oral culture of the underworld."[96] Journalistic imperatives to tell a saleable story did the rest. What was remarkable was that the Purge invention lasted unchallenged for so long.

THE NEW YORK MAFIA AFTER 1931

Further conditioning perceptions of a "modernization" campaign in the New York Mafia was the vast quantity of material devoted to the syndicate run in Chicago by Al Capone. Chicago was universally portrayed as multiethnic, coldly efficient, businesslike, and aggressively expansionary.[97] Landesco reported, "The Capone gang was formed for the business administration of establishments of vice, gambling, and booze."[98] This model of Chicago's story was reiterated almost ad infinitum, with entire books devoted to the subject.[99]

"Chicago" style imagery heavily affected, for example, the description accorded to Frankie Yale's assassination in 1928, viewed as the first importation of "gang war tactics of Chicago" onto the streets of Brooklyn.[100] "Chicago gang warfare tactics" were also pointed to in contemporary descriptions of the 1930 murders of Stephen Ferrigno and Manfredi Mineo.[101]

By contrast to the undifferentiating "Chicago" gang paradigm, a range of membership sources and internal relations distinguished New York City *Famiglia* before and after the Castellammare War. Two ideal types are presented as representing the majority "Sicilian" kinship-oriented groups in New York, and the Masseria faction which fitted key characteristics of an "Americanized" Mafia organization in which kin connections were insignificant, and non-Sicilians powerful.

MASSERIA FAMILY

Marsala, Sicily, Joseph Masseria's birthplace, was not a source for U.S. Mafiosi. Nor did Marsala have a Mafia tradition that Masseria could import to America.[102] Without a power base in Sicily, or later in New York, Masseria was at a decided disadvantage in dealing with others in the New York Mafia fraternity. That misfortune of birth forced the ambitious Masseria to turn, whilst in New York City, to an amalgam of individuals native to Sicily and—in a break with orthodoxy—the rest of southern Italy, in order to build up an organization. Masseria's members were scattered throughout the boroughs for an identical reason.

From 1937, a succession of Italians from Calabria or Campagna were bosses of the former Masseria *borgata*. A similar pattern of non-Sicilian involvement as members was detectable lower down the hierarchy.[103] Masseria Family constituents included Frankie Yale (Chapter 6) and:

SAVERIO POLLACCIA

Instructive of the easy intermingling of mainland Italians and Sicilians in the Masseria syndicate, Saverio "Sam" Pollaccia, Masseria's *consiglieri*, was identified with the Calabrian Frankie Yale. Pollaccia was born in 1887 in Villafrati, Sicily and entered New York in 1905.[104] Salvatore D'Aquila and his wife were made godparents to Rosalia Pollaccia, one of Saverio's daughters, in 1920. He attended the Chicago funeral of the city's *capo* Mike Merlo, and was questioned alongside Yale for the murder of Dion O'Banion.[105] Pollaccia's name and Brooklyn residence were found in an address book held by Orazio Tropea, a Chicago mob character killed in 1926.[106]

Police supposed that Pollaccia was in attendance at the Pelham Parkway meeting from which Mineo and Ferrigno were walking when they were shot

Figure 8.2   Saverio Pollaccia. (Author's possession)

dead (Chapter 7).[107] It was believed by detectives that Pollaccia had also attended the Coney Island meeting at which Masseria was murdered.[108]

Pollaccia was in grave danger with Masseria dead, since Vito Genovese harbored a grudge against him. "Now, with a change in the leadership," Gentile explained, Genovese "wanted to avenge himself in a cowardly way."[109] Pollaccia disappeared in about 1932,[110] while on his way to Chicago, at the hands of the Chicago syndicate's Paul Ricca and Genovese.[111]

SALVATORE LUCIANO

"Charlie Lucky" Lucania and Vito Genovese had a disproportionate effect on the fortunes of the Masseria syndicate. Like Marsala, Luciano's town of birth was not a hub of Sicilian Mafia operations that Luciano could tap into when seeking advancement in New York.

Luciano was born in Lercara Friddi on November 24, 1897 as Salvatore Lucania (Anglicized to Luciano) to Antonio and Rosalie Lucania.[112]

He arrived in the United States with his parents and siblings in October 1907.[113] The Lucanias settled on 10th Street and First Avenue, an ethnically heterogeneous area with a "a smattering of immigrants of other nationalities."[114] Luciano lived on East 10th Street for most of the next 20 years.

Leaving school at 14, he won a job as a shipping clerk in a hat factory lasting a few months[115] before being enticed into street gambling as a more exciting alternative. Luciano was jailed for a year—serving six months—in June of 1916 for possession of a half-dram of heroin.[116] Fondly reminiscing about those days, he recalled how he lived in a furnished room with Joseph Biondo on East 14th Street picking the pockets of Italian immigrants, averaging "three hauls a day."[117]

On June 2, 1923, Luciano sold two ounces of heroin to a Secret Service informer, and three days later another ounce. Faced with a long jail term as a second offender, Lucky bargained for his freedom by informing the agents where a trunk of narcotics could be found on Mulberry Street.[118]

He operated gambling dens in the mid 1920s, and by his own admission derived an income from betting and bootlegging.[119] In 1929, Luciano was found wandering about badly beaten in the early hours of the morning on Staten Island.[120] He stated to a grand jury that four men picked him up in a car on 50th Street and 3rd Avenue claiming to be police officers. Luciano had no idea why they attacked him.[121]

VITO GENOVESE

Luciano's underboss between 1931–1936, when Luciano was jailed for 30–50 years as the overlord of a "$12,000,000 a year vice ring,"[122] was Vito Anthony Genovese, born in November 1897. Genovese was alleged to have been a driver for Paul Siciliano, the 1920s "King of Ravenswood" from Campagna, during which time Siciliano was tried for a murder that Genovese was said to have committed. As observed in Chapter 4, Genovese had ties to the 1910s Brooklyn Neapolitans. On the West Side of Manhattan, Genovese was the leader of the "Thompson Street Mob," which "traditionally operated an Italian lottery in the Neapolitan communities in New York and neighboring cities."[123]Genovese's criminal record began in 1917 for carrying a concealed weapon, his only conviction until 1958 despite 12 arrests.

GUARINO MORETTI

Most known members of the Masseria Family were unrelated to each other. Guarino "Willie Moore" Moretti, of Calabrian heritage,[124] was an exception. Frank Costello and Joe Adonis were godfathers to two of Moretti's daughters; Costello was also Moretti's best man when he married. Moretti was best man at Adonis's wedding. One of Moretti's daughters married Frank Palmeri, a son of Paul Palmeri, brother of Buffalo member Angelo Palmeri. The other daughter wed Dominick LaPlaca, Moretti's bodyguard/driver.[125]

SCHIRO-MARANZANO FAMILY

The differences from the Schiro *Famiglia* could hardly be starker. Exclusively Sicilian,[126] led by Nicolo "Cola" Schiro in Williamsburg, Brooklyn, it became heavily attuned to inter-related Mafiosi from Castellammare del Golfo (Chapter 7) featuring familial links to Mafiosi in other American cities (Chart 8.1). Schiro made the journey to Brooklyn in 1902 from his native Roccamena, Sicily, by way of Boston.[127]

The bulk of the future Schiro Family membership arrived within a few years of Schiro's arrival, making it the "second" Family of New York City after the Morellos.[128] A minority of Schiro members came from other areas in Sicily, including Nicolo Gentile (for a time) and Angelo Caruso, the latter figure representing a non-Castellammarese element.[129]

Interstate criminal networks were thereby created through shared kinship and birthplace affiliations. In Williamsburg, Castellammaresi immigrants

Figure 8.3 Nicolo Schiro. (Courtesy of the U.S. National Archives)

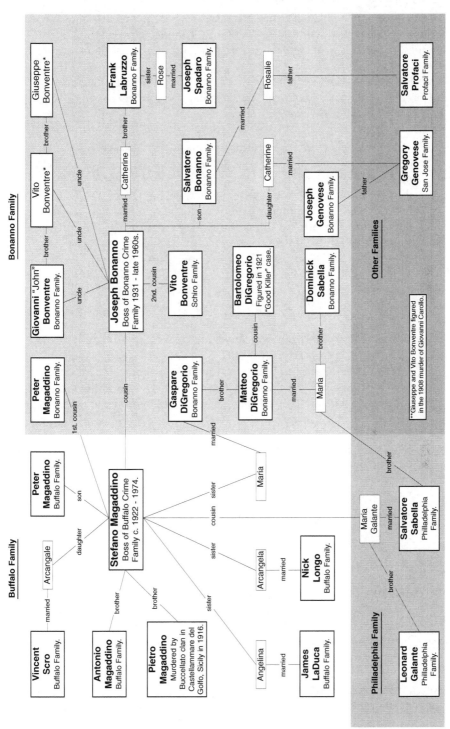

Chart 8.1 Castellammaresi kinship connections.

settled within a few blocks of one another, replicating the pattern displayed in East Harlem and denoted in Chapter 2. Among those giving addresses within a few streets of each other in Williamsburg were the future leaderships of the Philadelphia (Salvatore Sabella), Detroit (Gaspare Milazzo), Buffalo (Stefano Magaddino) and Brooklyn (Vito Bonventre) Mafias. Others occupying tenement houses in the neighborhood were rank and file Buffalo and Brooklyn *Onorata Societa* members.

- *105 Roebling Street.* The brothers Dominick and Salvatore Sabella, of the Bonanno and Philadelphia Families respectively, used the accommodation after arriving in New York in the 1910s. Stefano Magaddino and Salvatore Sabella listed it as their home in 1921 and 1931. During the Castellammare War, 105 Roebling Street housed Matteo DiGregorio, a brother of Bonanno Family member Gaspare DiGregorio, and his family.
- *115 Roebling Street.* Schiro *caporegime* Vito Bonventre, born in 1875,[130] and his family, lived at 115 Roebling Street at least between 1915–1921, where he had a bakery/saloon.[131] Both that and a 222 North Fifth Street residence associated with Bonventre were stayed at when Gaspare Milazzo married Rosaria Scibilia in November 1914. Stefano Magaddino gave it as his home address in 1920 and 1921.
- *222 North Fifth Street.* Dominick Sabella and his sister lived at 222 North Fifth Street in about 1915, the same dwelling as that occupied by Rosaria Scibilia, the wife of Gaspare Milazzo, and by Vito Bonventre. Maria Sabella lived there, a sister of Dominick and Salvatore Sabella and the future wife of Matteo DiGregorio. Castellammare-born Antonio Mazzara (below) stayed at 222 North Fifth Street in 1912 with his brother Philip Mazzara.[132]
- *242 North Fifth Street.* This was Vito Bonventre's first destination in 1905, staying with his brother Antonino. Francesco Finazzo (below) headed there in September 1905, as did Vito Mule in 1904. Santo Vultaggio, Mule's brother in law, later joined him (Chapter 7).

THE "GOOD KILLERS"

By the 1920's, Schiro stood out in the predominantly "Castellammaresi" Williamsburg organization. Unlike Masseria members, from disparate backgrounds, those from Castellammare del Golfo under Schiro maintained strong links to their Sicilian hometown. A glimpse into the ramifications was furnished in 1921, when a Castellammare-based *vendetta* spilled onto the streets of Detroit and New York. Several of those identified above were involved in the affair.

The investigative papers in the case were destroyed many years ago. This account is based on newspaper reports and the few other public records that have survived. Adding to the problems encountered in accurately and precisely portraying the events was the uneven quality of some of the reporting.[133] The focus is on those events and individuals for which consistent information was secured.

Three aspects of the American side of the *vendetta* quickly emerged. The first was that the majority of the recorded victims of the feud lived in Detroit. Second, that our knowledge of the events is generally limited to 1917–1921. And while some of the murders cited were apparently connected to the blood feud, others were committed in America for a variety of less obvious reasons, be it for robbery or for control over lotteries.[134]

The chief protagonists in New York and Detroit, as in Castellammare, were the Buccellato family and the Bonanno/Magaddino families. Joseph Bonanno contended that the Buccellatos were, "archenemies in Castellammare, and archenemies they remained in Brooklyn."[135]

On August 8, 1921, the body of an unidentified male was found by crabbers, "bound with ropes and weighted at feet and rocks" in Tucker's

Figure 8.4 Stefano Magaddino. (Courtesy of the Library of Congress)

Cove near Belmar, New Jersey. Death was by gunshot wounds. A paper was found on his body that helped to identify the dead man as Camillo Caiozzo. Caiozzo was born November 1894 in Castellammare, docking for the last time in New York in June 1920. Caiozzo had left New York for New Jersey on July 30, 1921, and was reported as missing. Until recently, the murdered man had been living on East 12th Street on the lower east side with Bartolomeo Fontano.[136]

The Caiozzo case broke when Carmela Pino, a jilted sweetheart of Fontano's, told Captain Michael Fiaschetti of the Italian Squad about Fontano's role in the Caiozzo shooting. Fontano "spilled everything."[137] A combination of bad conscience and Pino's information seem to have prompted Fontano's confession. Fontano's decision to spill the beans was perhaps also influenced by the threat of the electric chair if he refused to cooperate.[138]

Figure 8.5　Pietro Magaddino grave. (Author's possession)

The New Jersey killing was in retaliation for the Castellammare murder of a Stefano Magaddino brother. Magaddino, born 1891 in Castellammare and steeped in Sicilian Mafia tradition, was "schooled" in the ways of the New York City Mafia at some point after his arrival in February 1909. "A representative came," he affectionately remembered, "who was fond of me; he was always taking me along and telling me all these discourses." After a week his mentor, "always in a cloud of smoke," had told Magaddino about "everybody."[139]

Pietro Magaddino, Stefano's brother, was slain on July 19, 1916 in Castellammare, "the first child in the family."[140] It seemed intertwined with the death of "peacemaker" Salvatore Bonanno and to charges of cattle-rustling; a Magaddino narrowly escaped murder at the hands of the Buccellatos. Stefano suspected Caiozzo of having a hand in the slaying of Pietro. As Caiozzo's closest friend in America, also from Castellammare, Fontano was selected to set up and to shoot him. The conspiracy to get rid of Caiozzo was formulated in Vito Bonventre's saloon at 115 Roebling Street.[141]

At the gang's suggestion, Fontano persuaded Caiozzo to travel with him to Asbury Park with a story that they were to buy a brothel. But it was in a marshy and overgrown area along Shark River on August 2, 1921, that "Fontano put the muzzle of the shotgun against his old friend's back and jerked the trigger." Salvatore "Rose" Cieravo, from whose Riverview Inn they had rested and left, had egged on Fontano to shoot Caiozzo, loaned Fontano the murder weapon (a shotgun) and helped Fontano to dispose of the body.

Cieravo saw Giuseppe Lombardi. The next day, Lombardi, Francesco Puma, Fontano and Cieravo found the body of Caiozzo, tied stones to it and sank it in Tucker's Cove, from where it was recovered on August 8. Cieravo, Lombardi and Puma were consequently named as accomplices before and after the Caiozzo homicide.[142]

Fontano arranged for the other gang members in New York City to be picked up by detectives, either at Grand Central Station or at their homes. All except DiGregorio were charged with participation in the Caiozzo execution.[143] Arrested on August 16, 1921, besides Fontano, were:

Vito Bonventre, 115 Roebling Street
Bartolomeo DiGregorio, 117 Roebling Street
Mariano Galante, 198 Orchard Street
Giuseppe Lombardi, 217 Elizabeth Street
Stefano Magaddino, 105 Roebling Street
Francesco Puma, 504 East 12th Street

Puma had been charged in 1913 with assault and attempted robbery, when 3 Italians stopped a messenger carrying cash for the Nathan Manufacturing Company on Fifth Avenue. Shots were exchanged and Puma was

Figure 8.6   Vito Bonventre. (Courtesy of the U.S. National Archives)

caught fleeing the scene.[144] But the big catches in August 1921 were Magaddino and Bonventre, Joseph Bonanno's cousins.

To Fontano, the gang that ordered the Caiozzo murder was called the "Good Killers." There was no evidence that the Killers were the "enforcement arm" of "A Castellammarese criminal syndicate that later evolved into crime families in Brooklyn, Buffalo and Detroit."[145] Joseph Bonanno's otherwise informative book ignored the matter altogether, giving a false explanation of why Magaddino got into difficulties and left Brooklyn[146]

In August 19, it was reported that Detroit detectives had gone to New York to question Fontano about seven Detroit fatalities.[147] Four days on, the head of the Black Hand Squad in Detroit announced that Fontano had solved the killings of Detective Emmanuel Roggers in 1917 and Detroit hoodlum Tony Giannola. Andrea Licato and Mariano "Mimi" Cruciato, "members of the Good Killers Society," were identified; Licato was indeed an original suspect in the Roggers slaying.[148]

The New York arrests were signaled as "the most important capture ever made" by the New York Police's Italian Squad.[149] Hunt and Tona persuasively asserted, "It seems likely that police departments perceived

ARRESTED IN NEW YORK FOR BLACK HAND KILLINGS

Several men are under arrest in New York under suspicion of having been connected with the slaying of eight Italians and Sicilians in Detroit, eight in New York and one in Jersey City. Their arrest followed the confession at New York last Sunday of Bartolo Fontana, a barber, who is quoted as having said he confessed in order to get into prison, where he would be safe from threats of death made against himself.

More than 50 violent crimes of the last 15 years bear the marks of this so-called "Bonventrist Band," according to New York police. Thhose in the above photograph taken in New York following the arrests are, from left to right:

Stefano Magadïnno, Brooklyn; Detective S. A. Repetto, one of the officers who made the arrests; Francisco Tuma, Giuseppe Lombardi, a barber; Vito Bonventre, a door maker, said to be the leader of the gang; Mariano Galane, a painter, and Fontano.

Figure 8.7 "Good Killers." (Courtesy of the *Detriot News*)

an opportunity to dispense with a number of high-profile unresolved murder cases"[150]

Wildly fluctuating numbers of "Good Killers" victims cited (with "over 125 murders" recorded on August 19[151]) was an important aspect of newspaper reporting.[152] But the NYPD's 1921 Annual Report only noted Caiozzo's murder. A statement given by Fiaschetti in his memoirs, that "Good Killer" members paid the price for their crimes, was also wide of the mark.[153]

PROSECUTIONS

The Black Hand Squad in Detroit declared on August 24 that no search would be made for the graves of victims in their city. "The Detroit Sicilian colony," it concluded, "is extremely quiet now and free from reports coming to this office."[154] Thus officially ended the Detroit phase of the investigation.

Magaddino, Bonventre and Galante were freed when it was decided that the evidence against them was poor. Francesco Puma was murdered on November 4, 1922.[155] A month later, charges against Lombardi were dropped.[156]

Fontano entered a plea on March 22, 1922 of "non vult" in Freehold, New Jersey, to the charge of participation in the first-degree homicide of Caiozzo, and was sentenced to life imprisonment with hard labour.[157] He was found dead on February 8, 1956, at 229 Third Avenue, Manhattan while out on parole, apparently a suicide victim.[158]

Immediately following his sentencing, Fontano told the court how Cieravo had urged him to shoot Caiozzo in the woods at the behest of the Bonventre gang. Forensic evidence tied Cieravo to the case, but with only Fontano's word against him, Cieravo's denials were enough to secure his acquittal on March 24, 1922.[159]

GIOVANNI CAROLLO

Fontano asserted that the first "Good Killers" leader, Vito Bonventre, was a baker. Bonventre was slain and his body either cremated in his own oven,[160] or "hewn to bits and crammed into a bag" in Brooklyn, about 15 years earlier.[161] "The killings started" when his murder was avenged.[162] In one account, the Vito Bonventre arrested in 1921 was a nephew of the founder.[163]

No evidence has since materialized that agrees in every respect with Fontano's narrative, and this area is no exception.[164] Because Fontano joined years after the formation of the "Good Killers,"[165] his description of its origins was sketchy and (like the Purge myth) no doubt twisted over the years. What follows is therefore offered as no more than a plausible depiction of the homicide described by Fontano that began the bloodletting in New York City.

In April 1908, the strangled body of Giovanni Carollo, a recently arrived immigrant from Castellammare, was found in two flour sacks in a lot at 52nd Street and Fort Hamilton Avenue.[166] Police believed that Carollo "had the poor judgment to seek a repayment" of $100 he loaned to Giuseppe (aged 27) and Vito Bonventre, bakers on 22nd Street. They were held as suspects, as was Jasper "Gelente" (Gaspare Galante) and "Stadler Lisante," who worked for the Bonventres,[167] but the case petered out.[168]

Castellammare-born Giuseppe (born 1881) and Vito Bonventre (born 1891) were brothers of Pietro Bonventre, living on 4th Street, Brooklyn,[169] and Giovanni Bonventre, identified in 1963 as part of the Bonanno Family. Pietro was a brother-in-law of Salvatore Bonanno, the father of Joe Bonanno, making him Joe Bonanno's uncle. Galante, another of Pietro's brothers-in-law, came to New York on the same vessel as Giuseppe, boarding it from Naples.[170] Vito Bonventre[171] by the 1920s was indeed a baker, operating the Lincoln Bakery.[172]

The death of Carollo may have been what Fontano alluded to in his account in an obtuse and confusing fashion. The year of the Carollo homicide was about right, a baker named Vito Bonventre was involved (as Fontano stated) and an incident occurred in which a body was found crammed in a bag. The Carollo case also had overwhelming Castellammare connotations, and was coupled to the Bonanno and Magaddino clan at the core of the "Good Killers" clique.

Fontano had not met the "second" Vito Bonventre, who died in 1988. Although Bonventre's subsequent reputation was as a legitimate businessman, during the 1960s "Banana War," he let his Troutman Street home be used for a DiGregorio faction meeting.[173] Bonventre may have been dragged into the Carollo murder against his better judgment, but he felt compelled to participate because of his connection to the Bonanno-Magaddino Mafia coalition in Sicily and America.

LATER FATALITIES IN NEW YORK CITY

New York City victims of the "Good Killers" reported by Fontano fell into two classes. First were those murders committed in Brooklyn, which were apparently an outcome of the Castellammare-based *vendetta*. Other homicides identified by Fontano (primarily on the lower east side) involved a variety of Italian-Americans with no apparent connection to each another, or to Castellammare.

Lower east side, Manhattan, fatalities named by Fontano were:

- That on April 20, 1913 of Vito Buccellato at 194 Chrystie Street. Buccellato was stabbed to death in what police then considered to be a "Black Hand" case.[174] Vito Caradonna and Frank Puma were arrested and discharged for the murder in 1921.[175]
- Rosario Briganti and Antonio Curatolo in 1919 (see below).
- Salvatore Messina in June 1920. It was believed by investigating officers that Messina was slain in a narcotics dispute.[176]
- Salvatore Mauro, a cheese merchant on Elizabeth Street, was shot dead "in broad daylight on a crowded New York Street" on December 29, 1920. Mauro was fired upon at point blank range. Detectives could only guess at the cause.[177]
- Known locally as an unofficial mediator, poolroom owner Joseph Grantello was felled in Chrystie Street on February 28, 1921,

the fatal shots fired from "basement steps across the street."[178] A newspaper reporter tentatively identified Mariano Galante as the killer.[179]

- Vincenzo Alfano from Castellammare was shot dead on Delancey Street on June 16, 1921, in what the police depicted as a drugs-related fallout. Two gunmen were seen firing at Alfano from behind.[180]

Besides the murders of Buccellato and Alfano, no link with Castellammare could be found, and those of Briganti and Curatolo, about which more is known, were generated by other causes. Joseph Ales, a "Good Killers" associate, was indicted for the June 1919 homicide of Briganti on Chrystie Street. In a disputed statement, Ales said that Curatolo and Vito Giallo asked him to act as a lookout man while they robbed the victim. When Briganti put up a fight, he was shot. Fontano was able to speak to Ales while Ales was in jail.

Yet Ales claimed to know "nothing about it" at his trial. The police had battered him "In every place they could get me" to make Ales sign a statement written in English that he did not understand. Nonetheless, Ales changed his plea to guilty and was sentenced on March 2, 1922, to eight to sixteen years.[181]

Carlo Barbara was arraigned in September 1921 for the shooting of Curatolo.[182] Frequently using the alias of "Charles" Barbara, Carlo proved to be the Castellammare-born brother of Joseph Barbara Sr., "host" of the famous 1957 Apalachin meeting of Mafiosi (Chapter 1).[183] Curatola was alleged to have been blackmailing Barbara and had ruined him financially, causing Curatola's murder in July 1919 outside a place owned by Barbara.

Barbara never stood trial, perhaps because of the disputed confession wrung from Ales. Antonio Martinico turned up as an elevator operator in 1954 San Francisco, where he had settled. Ales had identified Martinico in his admissions as killing Curatolo, acting with Barbara. He successfully fought extradition to New York, having been a "law-abiding resident" of California since 1921.[184]

But four more homicides identified by Fontano that took place in the heart of the Schiro Mafia territory in Brooklyn had a Sicilian "feud" component. Brooklyn victims were to a man from Castellammare.

- Antonio Mazzara and Antonio DiBenedetto were killed on November 11, 1917 at Roebling and North Fifth Streets. Mazzara was found lying face down on a pavement, shot through the heart. DiBenedetto, hit three times, was seen "clinging to a lamppost and slipping slowly to the sidewalk."[185]Fontano noted these murders as starting a new series of tit for tat killings in Brooklyn and Detroit. Mazzara and DiBenedetto had testified in 1913 for the Ruffinos.

DiBenedetto's brother Joseph was the brother-in-law of Mazzara's older brother Philip, "leader of a powerful faction of Buffalo's Italian colony," gunned down there in 1927.[186] Joseph DiBenedetto, in whose car Philip Mazzara was driving, was Mazzara's "trusted first lieutenant and confidant." Joseph DiBenedetto was Buffalo-slain in early 1929.[187]

- The owner of a poolroom, Frank Finazzo, was shot at the corner of Roebling and North Fifth Streets on the morning of December 10, 1917, in what the police announced as the "work of a gang."[188]
- Giuseppe Ponzo was slain on January 14, 1918 on Metropolitan Avenue. Ponzo was born around 1886 in Castellammare.[189]

DETROIT

A majority of the Detroit homicides linked by Fontano to the "Good Killers" revolved around a Brooklyn-Detroit axis that re-emerged in the Castellammare War. More is known about the context of these fatalities. The *vendetta* aspect was powerful but did not account for every murder. Identified by Fontano in Detroit were the killings of:

PIETRO BOSCO, AND SAM AND TONY GIANNOLA

The Giannolas—Salvatore ("Sam") and Antonio ("Tony)—had been active in Detroit's organized crime since 1912, when the body of Salvatore Buendo was found.[190] As of 1917, the Giannolas had "been arrested more often in connection with Sicilian outrages than any other men."[191]

Bullets fired into his back on January 3, 1919 as he stepped from his car ended the life of Tony Giannola, the "brains" of the Giannola mob.[192] Salvatore, "King of the Sicilian Underworld," perished on October 2, 1919 while leaving a bank on Russell Street and Monroe Avenue. Sam had vowed revenge on Tony's slayers. Giovanni "John" Vitale, the Giannolas' mob nemesis, was murdered on September 28, 1920. Vitale's body was found after residents heard firing and saw two cars driving from the murder scene.[193]

These deaths may have been associated with that of Peter Bosco. Bosco, whom Fontano recognized as a further "Good Killers" victim, was cornered and fatally wounded in October 1918 in his Trumbull Avenue and Ash Street garage.[194]

The Giannolas were from Terrasini[195] and Vitale was Cinisi-born.[196] Crucially though, Bosco was born in Castellammare del Golfo.[197] Bosco's dealings with Tony Giannola dated from before May 23, 1915, when Tony and Lena Giannola became godparents to Anthony Bosco, the son of Peter and his wife Mary.[198] Tony Giannola and Bosco were arrested that August in relation to the kidnapping in Detroit of a four-year-old child, Patrina Mazzola, for ransom.[199]

Bosco became Giannola's partner in a bakery or grocery store. When the profits were not up to expectations, Bosco was forced out. Recriminations followed, and after Bosco was slain—some supposed by the Giannolas—[200-] gossip held that Bosco loyalists would exact retribution.[201] Others argued that John Vitale, who had been friendly with Bosco, united with disgruntled ex-Bosco associates to kill their common foe, Tony Giannola.[202]

In a confused fashion, Fontano's identification of Bosco did have a Castellammare perspective. But in 1919, "probably the most feared and hated Sicilian gang leader since the Giannola eclipse," Tony Alescio, whose origin is unclear, was accused of shooting the two Giannolas and Bosco. After Sam Russo was found innocent of killing Bosco in December 1919, charges were dropped against Alescio, Andrea Licato and Mariano Melita.[203] Calogero Arena was also tried and acquitted as one of Sam Giannola's assassins; he had lived with Giannola at his Ford City house during the Giannola-Vitale war.

The primary cause of these three Detroit murders probably lay less with revenge slayings transplanted from Sicily than with treachery in Detroit's underworld. Like the four Brooklyn victims, though, two other murders Fontano designated were indicative of a struggle with an extra-Detroit basis. They were of the Buccellatos from Castellammare, and their fates were linked to the Schiro Mafia in New York. A third case in Detroit, missed by Fontano but highly pertinent, has now been revealed.

FELICE BUCCELLATO

In August 1913, Carlo Callego (or Calegro) was gunned to death on his doorstep. Before dying, he named Felice (Filippo) Buccellato and Vito Adamo as his attackers.[204] Adamo and Buccellato were released when Callego's wife and a boarder testified that Callego had told them that he did not recognize his assailants.[205]

Callego was reported to be friendly with the Giannolas, but against the Adamos,[206] who were allied with the Buccellatos. The threat from the Adamos to Giannola rule was removed when Vito and Salvatore Adamo were slain in November 1913 "in a fusillade of slugs from a sawed-off shotgun."[207]

An associate of the Giannola group, Salvatore Cipriano, and a chemist, Vitorio Cusmano, died in April 1914 when a package Cipriano was holding in the Cusmano drugstore exploded in his face.[208] It was thought that Tony Giannola was the intended target.[209] Nineteen men were arrested at the home of Felice Buccellato, sited above the grocery store belonging to the slain Vito Adamo.[210] Buccellato was one of eight ordered to leave the city.[211]

Felice Buccellato's end came from bullets fired at him on March 17, 1917, by one or more gunmen at Orleans Street and Lafayette Avenue.

The murderers scattered after slamming three lead slugs into his body. Police credited the slaying either to "a revival of the feud among East Side foreigners,"[212] or to a "vendetta which may have had its origin in Sicily."[213]

JOSEPH BUCCELLATO

On May 4, 1919, Joseph Buccellato and Mike Maltisi, a boarder, were put to death in their apartment on Newport Avenue. Three men were seen leaving the house after pistol shots were heard. Detectives concluded it was another outcome of a feud.[214] Seeking the slayers, detective Harold Roughley was killed.

Figure 8.8 Giovanni Torres. (Courtesy of Debbie Duell)

PIETRO BUCCELLATO

Pietro "Peter" Buccellato's was the only murder in the Detroit series furnishing information on a probable gunman. Buccellato was unconnected to either his killer or to organized crime—except through his Buccellato relatives and birthplace, Castellammare.

Pietro Buccellato was bumped off near his home on December 22, 1917, while boarding a streetcar on his way to work.[215] Joseph Brucia (another Castellammare immigrant) and Vincenzo Ilado were arrested but freed two days later. Brucia and Ilado were related and had links to the Schiro Family territory in Brooklyn. The police probe uncovered Buccellato's ties to Ilado and to the Schiro territory in Brooklyn, before Buccellato moved to Detroit.[216]

Giovanni "Angel Face" Torres was arrested in March 1918 for the homicide. Torres had been a suspect in the gunning down of Felice Buccellato.[217] Displaying a dogged determination to get the right man, according to the police, Torres wounded Joe Constantine and slew Paul Mutoc (who lived next to Constantine) in December 1917 when Torres had "gotten them confused with Buccellato."[218] (They resembled Pietro and were shot near to where Buccellato was slain.)

Given the supposition that "Good Killer" members came from Castellammare (in Trapani province), the fact that Torres was born 1897 in Palermo was anomalous. Torres, though, was normally found on East 11th Street, Manhattan, which was similar to Williamsburg in being heavily populated by Castellammaresi settlers. (Puma and Fontano lived in the quarter.) It may have been where "Good Killer" leaders recruited Torres, precisely because he was a stranger to those selected to die in Detroit.[219]

During the Recorder's Court trial of Torres, police officer Louis Oldani testified how the dying Buccellato told him that, "the same man that killed his cousin was the one that shot him." (Another version has Buccellato saying his demise was caused "on account of his cousin."[220]) Oldani thought that Joseph Buccellato might be the cousin referred to.

Joseph Buccellato, Pietro's cousin, had shot Mazzara and DiBenedetto only a month previously in Brooklyn (above). But Pietro's reference to his cousin could as easily have been to the violent Felice. Both Felice and Joseph were involved in the Detroit and Brooklyn killings and were named by Fontano as fatalities of the New Yorkers. Felice and Giuseppe Buccellato were brothers, and Pietro was their cousin.[221]

In June 1918, Torres was acquitted of Pietro's murder following the jury's acceptance of alibi evidence provided by his relatives in New York.[222] Deported to Sicily "for a killing" after the verdict was announced,[223] Torres returned to America in the 1920s, when he moved operations to Baltimore, then briefly to Brooklyn. It was there that Torres died on March 28, 1930 "under withering fire," in front of 128 Kane Street, a house belonging to the deceased Joseph Piraino and occupied by Piraino's brother-in-law.[224] Three men were seen fleeing in a car.

IN PERSPECTIVE

The Detroit killings only stopped after the Giannola brothers and their archrival John Vitale perished, though the consequences lasted into 1920 and implicated Angelo Meli and Joseph Zerilli, who would help to rule the post-Castellammare War local underworld.[225] Akin to the Brooklyn murders blamed by Fontano on the Good Killers, a number of the deaths in Detroit were better explainable by a Sicilian sourced struggle.

Of the ten Good Killer members identified, eight were born in Castellammare.[226] The rest, Joseph Ales (from Paceco [Trapani]) and John Torres (Palermo) had definite (Ales) or likely (Torres) Castellammare connections in New York City. There is no evidence that Sicilian Mafiosi were specially brought over to help those in conflict; established immigrants in New York City and Detroit performed the murders, partly in a continuation of events occurring in Sicily.

Five Manhattan deaths named by Fontano were not correlated to Castellammare. These may have been ones identified by Fontano as committed independently of the Brooklyn led group Fontano caused to be arrested.

Homicides committed in Detroit, aside from those of the three Buccellatos, were difficult to categorize. There was a Castellammare edge to the Bosco murder, but given the availability of another perspective for why Bosco died, no firm conclusions can be drawn. In Detroit, the Giannola fatalities were the least likely to have been Sicily related, since they had stored up other enemies over the years.

Fontano's account, "not all the parts of which were quite plainly related on first examination,"[227] reflected his secondary importance in the "Good Killers." As a self-admitted "outsider" to the group who joined several years after the mob was formed, Fontano's declarations on events in which he was not personally involved gave a partial and jumbled understanding of why things happened as they did.

The manner in which Caiozzo perished showed an unprepared side to the gang's activities that belied the reputation of the Mafia for battle-hardened efficiency and attention to detail. As a result, Caiozzo's body was quickly found, and an investigation began. The absence of a tiered hierarchy within the Bonventre-Magaddino faction that could insulate the leadership from prosecution was another unexpected characteristic, but did reflect a similar feature found in the Morello organization (Chapter 3).

CONTEXT

Paoli's model was of a Sicilian Mafia curiously bereft of those family connections that Naylor recognized as the Mafia's chief leverage in organized crime, instead depending upon "bonds of artificial kinship created through the ceremony of initiation of new members."[228] But Bonanno rejoined, "it is impossible to understand events—whether they are marriages, political alliances, or killings—unless there is some understanding—literally—of just who was related to whom."[229] Cressey asserted, "genuine family relationships play an important part in determining one's status in American 'family' units—one cannot move very high in the organization unless he is somehow related to the Boss."[230]

Similarly to the situation with the Schiros, kinsmen formed the backbone of the Iannis' Mafia organization; "The power structure in the business mirrors the family genealogical chart."[231] Kinship had the potential to supply a lasting bond between members that the *compari* relationship favored by the Neapolitans, for example, could not match. Such connections could, on the other hand, be a source of strife. The Gallo brothers rebelled in the 1960s over a perception of nepotism and favoritism within the Profaci syndicate, leaving non-relatives of the bosses to "fend for themselves."[232] The Los Angeles Mafia organization had comparable difficulties.[233]

POST–1931 NEW YORK CITY HEADS

Luciano gained in status from his role in the Castellammare War, influencing—though not dictating—the selection of the new Mineo Family head. "With Lucky's rise to power," recorded Bonanno, "Scalise became a liability to his Family, which didn't want to antagonize the powerful Luciano and his cohorts."[234]

Once the dust had settled, New York City *borgata* after Maranzano's fall were headed by:

Joseph Bonanno (former Maranzano Family)
Tommaso Gagliano (former Pinzolo Family)
Salvatore Luciano (former Masseria Family)
Vincent Mangano (former Mineo Family)
Joseph Profaci

The pre-1931 Sicilian preponderance in the upper levels was maintained, with the major exception being the Masseria arrangement:

Maranzano/Bonanno Family

Joseph Bonanno	Sicilian
Giovanni Bonventre	Sicilian
Frank Garofalo	Sicilian
Giovanni Tartamella	Sicilian

Gagliano/Lucchese Family

Tommaso Gagliano	Sicilian
Stefano LaSalle	Sicilian
Gaetano Lucchese	Sicilian

Masseria/Luciano/Genovese Family

Joe Adonis	Non-Sicilian
Frank Costello	Non-Sicilian
Vito Genovese	Non-Sicilian
Salvatore Lucania	Sicilian
Michele Miranda	Non-Sicilian
Guarino Moretti	Non-Sicilian
Antonio Strollo	Non-Sicilian

Mineo/Mangano/Anastasia Family

Alberto Anastasia	Non-Sicilian
Giuseppe Biondo	Sicilian
Vincent Mangano	Sicilian
Giuseppe Riccobono	Sicilian
Frank Scalise	Sicilian
Giuseppe Traina	Sicilian

Profaci Family

Giuseppe Magliocco	Sicilian
Salvatore Musacchio	Sicilian
Giuseppe Profaci	Sicilian

In other American cities, a traditional Sicilian hegemony was unaltered. Buffalo's Stefano Magaddino was reinforced. Boston's *capo* Gaspare Messina and his Prince Street partner Frank Cucchiara, from Salemi, Sicily, carried on unchanged.[235] Messina retired from active Mafia affairs in the 1930s to care for his sick wife and died, aged 78, in June 1957 at his Somerville home.

Santo Volpe was another case in point. The Pittston, Pennsylvania, boss, Volpe came from Montedoro, Sicily, the place of origin for several members of his organization. From 1914, Volpe began the business of building a coal empire, until he was "among the largest producers of anthracite coal" in the country, and considered respectable enough to be allowed to join government committees and cultural societies.[236]

TOP LEVEL MAFIA PATRONAGE SYSTEMS

The existence of a "supreme" U.S. Mafia authority was long the subject of speculation. In 1940, the U.S. Treasury representative in Milan, Italy, received a list of "Grand Council" members, with Brooklyn dominating the body.[237] Without reliable information, the Federal Bureau of Narcotics (FBN) was successful in propagating the Grand Council model.[238]

The Federal Bureau of Investigation uncovered the facts. For in September 1959, as Chicago outfit bosses Tony Accardo and Sam Giancana were discussing a visit Sam had made to New York, FBI "bugs" were recording everything.[239] The history supplied by Gentile was added to the information gleaned in Chicago.

"GOVERNO CENTRAL"

The system that was shaped in late 1931 dispersed top-level patronage among several Mafia leaders, and was more regularized in its operation than the "general assembly" (*governo central*) depicted by Gentile. Noted in Chapter 4, neither it nor the subsequent "Commission" system was designed to interfere with the ability of Mafia groups to respond according to local conditions.

THE "COMMISSION"[240]

The Commission system that followed was never intended to serve as a means of extending *Cosa Nostra* power across the underworld.[241] "The Commission," Bonanno explained, "was an American adaptation," with the objective of maintaining order through its mediation role.[242] "In an internal revolt," according to Bonanno, "the matter is normally resolved within the Family."[243]

When conflict threatened the common weal, the Commission would intervene if asked to, but only when the parties in dispute agreed to accept its authority and recommendations. Individual members of the Commission might also be available as contacts for non-New York bosses. Representing the most powerful *borgata*, mostly centered in New York City, other Families found it wise to heed Commission advice nonetheless.

The Commission fixed the future size of American Families at their 1931 levels, in part to prevent ambitious bosses like Masseria from enlarging their own membership at the expense of other organizations. Closure of Mafia enrolment (the "books") to new members for over ten years by the Commission also strengthened the grip of the conservative leadership across the country.[244]

How the Commission interacted with specific situations and problems is a matter of controversy. It was erratically used even for important matters.[245] "The mechanisms of commission and Cosa Nostra decisionmaking are . . . obscure," argued Jacobs et al.[246] The circumstances in which a "genuine" Commission meeting occurred are another area of contention and ambiguity.[247]

The predominant influence of Sicilian traditionalists was evident on the first and later Commissions. Those Bonanno perceived as being on the "Conservative" (traditional) wing, operating in New York City, were himself,

Joseph Profaci, Vincent Mangano and Tommaso Gagliano. They were of Sicilian extraction and widely related to other Family members and, less so, to the leaders in other Mafia organizations. The Commission's New York "Liberals" (otherwise known as "Americanized") were Gaetano Lucchese, Albert Anastasia and Vito Genovese, non-kinship focused and in most instances of Italian mainland extraction.

CONCLUSION

There was no "Americanization" of the Mafia in the way often described. Traditionalist *amici nostri* held most of the important posts into the 1960s, way beyond the period that could validate an Americanization paradigm that sought—as it did—to link the process to the Castellammare War. As the Purge has been discarded, so the Americanization hypothesis should be consigned to the same category of empirically unsupported myth. Additional confirmation of the "conventional" character of New York Mafias came from admonitions against its members becoming involved in "pimping" (managing houses of prostitution), an activity abhorred by the Sicilians as being "unmanly."[248]

U.S.-born ("American") Mafiosi gradually assumed positions of authority. But the changeover owed nothing to the Castellammare War and everything to the death of first generation immigrant bosses, the slowly acting acculturalisation process, and the curbing of immigration from Mafia heartlands in Sicily.

What the Americanization model highlighted was the perception of a growing menace from organized crime. Lupsha, a subscriber to the case, observed that "organized crime is constantly innovative and reaching out for both new markets and new talent to maintain its basic competitive edge."[249] Nelli, another enthusiast, saw the 1930s as when "millions poured in from loan-sharking, from syndicate-controlled whorehouses, and from expanding traffic in narcotics."[250]

Italian mainlander members were not always sympathetic to the use of family connections by their Sicilian counterparts to give them a lead.[251] For their part, Sicilians could adopt a snobbish attitude towards the new group of entrants.[252] It was arguably from non-Sicilian members facing prejudice and antagonism in Mafia organizations that the concept of the "Moustache Pete" or "Greaser" had the most resonance, as a term of abuse to be used against those Sicilians who refused to fully accept their claim to equality in the mob.

Chapter 9 opens up the findings made for New York City. Diversity between Mafia organizations is underlined. There was no nationwide Mafia ring even as a goal for Families to strive for, or a unified Family structure to make it happen. Neither did Families attempt to expand their market share in the manner of legitimate firms.

9 Localism, Tradition, and Innovation

Since the 1970s, attention has focused almost entirely on questions that dealt with neither the U.S. Mafia specifically, nor with its forms of organization. Also strikingly absent is reliable material by which to compare the imagery with the reality. The present research attempts to redress these issues.

Much of our current knowledge of the New York City Mafia's formative history is founded on speculation, exaggeration, hearsay evidence and ideological preconception. Multiple and often conflicting priorities have confused the task of accurately identifying the threat posed by the Mafia in America, and of arriving at the appropriate level and type of response.

The way that Mafias were visualized and functioned as economic units partially depended on federal and state interventions. The creation of illicit markets, together with the perceived size and the definition of organized crime, were issues that were suffused with "politics." And the strategic threat from "non-traditional" crime syndicates was contrasted against a skewed history of the Mafia, which embodied caricatures and embellishments radically at odds with case studies.[1]

Variations within and across Mafia formations were evident in New York City, a feature that indiscriminate paradigms of Mafia organization failed to adequately capture. At one end of the spectrum was the Schiro Family, conservative and insular. Co-existing with it was the archetypal "American" organization originally headed by Giuseppe Masseria emerging from a different set of environmental factors.

"Viewed this way," Albini remarked, "syndicates became a series of very complex and interwoven relationships."[2] The economic underpinnings of *borgata* could be dynamic and innovative, while the Family structure and hierarchy—the "political" component—remained conservative. The political aspect was particularly noticeable as a group became large enough for a multi-layered "career ladder" to develop within it. Some *amici nostri* were uninterested in advancement through the ranks, preferring to make money. Others, like Salvatore Maranzano, were less content to view their membership exclusively in terms of the economic pull it conferred.

Eight chapters have engaged with themes appearing in the corpus of previous work on the U.S. Mafia. Chapter 2 explained how the Black Hand was frequently no more than a series of independent groups with few links to crime networks. Akin to their Italian-American equivalents, Sicilian Mafia groups were seemingly not, at this time, involved in the extortion of smaller legitimate enterprises. Calabrians were an under-estimated source of organization, having no cultural qualms over participating in the Black Hand. But Black Hand operators impacted on Mafias by stymieing their efforts to create and to solidify territorial control.

Black Hand extortion had fizzled out by the time Prohibition came into effect. What happened to former Black Hand operators is unclear, though none made a significant contribution to subsequent organized crime.

Chapter 3 dealt with Sicilian Mafia influence in New York City. Similarities between the structure of American Mafia organizations and practices in Sicily permitted an interchange of members between American and Sicily. Nonetheless, there was no grand plan for Sicilian Mafias to export their brand of organized crime to U.S. shores. Men of honor in Sicily and New York City had connections to other U.S. cities, but on an individual level.

Beyond the specifics of the Baff investigation of 1914 described in Chapter 4 were important questions around Mafia admission practices. Where the easiest, quickest and less conditional route into Mafia organized crime was unavailable, an aspiring Mafiosi might create an opportunity for himself by alternative means that tested his criminal skills and character. Those from mainland Italy faced the most difficulties to making it into Mafia crime.

Chapter 4 also highlighted an ethnic facet to labor racketeering. Unsurprisingly given the ethnic basis of much of the economic activity across New York City, Mafiosi racketeers usually selected for infiltration those industries where Italians, as workers or employers, were a force. Industries varied in their vulnerability to Mafia racketeering also according to factors beyond the economic marketplace. The metropolitan kosher poultry sector was perceived as an unpromising ground for Italian racketeers. Furthermore, the Baff murder investigation exposed the truth that employers could form and enforce a cartel without inviting or welcoming professional racketeers into the industry.

As explained in Chapter 5, assistance to the embattled Morellos from other Mafias was conspicuous by its absence, belying any suggestion that the *Onorata Societa* could form a united front even during a crisis. From the 1920s, Sicilian groups, partly to assuage tensions, began admitting Neapolitans and Calabrians on a limited basis. Yet most New York City Mafiosi continued to be resolutely "Sicilian" by birth or heritage.

Over the thirteen years of prohibition, the magnitude and number of Families in New York City grew. Yet while being an important source of revenue, the liquor trade did not transform the structure of the 1920s New York City's Mafias. Less observed, moreover, were Mafia factions that eschewed the traffic altogether, similarly to the Gaglianos and Raos. Furthermore, the lathing industry that Tommaso Gagliano participated in, for instance, did not have a deeply engrained and lasting problem with racketeering, while

encouraging cartel creation. Rather than seeking to corrupt economic institutions, the way in which lathing businesses were run by the Raos and Gagliano additionally reflected a wider tolerance of malpractices. Those involved
in the lathing sector did not enter it for ulterior reasons, and the extent of
the industry's problem with predatory crime was limited and is historically
uneven. The findings undermine the assumption that Mafia intrusions generated a uniformly active racketeering problem.

Overblown claims have marred accounts of the Castellammare War.
Whether judged by the number of confirmed victims or by its outcome, the
legends around the War far exceeded the proven record. Out of the War
came absurd notions of La Cosa Nostra, with its own youthful devotees, a
"board of directors," and hegemony over most other forms of syndicated
crime. The LCN conception appeared to be modeled on Chicago's "Strictly
Business Gang" as depicted by Landesco and a multitude of others.[3]

Aligned with the fallacy of La Cosa Nostra's creation was the notion that
the Castellammare War was a battle between generations of Mafiosi. The
conclusion in this unsubstantiated paradigm was never in doubt. Luciano
and his Young Turks surfaced, on schedule, to command the Mafia. The
emphasis, in the Americanization model, with cooperation between ethnicities contradicted the LCN framework, furthermore, with its focus on
the takeover of rival organizations. As Chapter 8 demonstrated, anything
resembling corroborated evidence to back up the grandiose assertions made
of the LCN and the Americanization process was absent.

Mafia *borgata* operated in most cities with larger Italian communities;
but that did not translate into a nationwide Mafia organization. Aside from
the disjointed manner in which Mafias were constitutionally arranged, Paoli
explained that "due to the constraints of product illegality," fragmenting pressures were inevitable.[4] Haller added that criminal entrepreneurs "generally
have had neither the skills nor the personalities for the detailed, bureaucratic
oversight of large organizations."[5] "Even when members of Italian crime families operate ongoing illegal enterprises, they are often small scale and informally organized."[6] Reuter attributed this in the illicit bookmaking field to
"Narrow profit margins, the high cost of credit, difficulty in collecting debts,
law enforcement, and poor entrepreneurial judgment."[7]

Mafia membership, Bonanno reminds us, merely meant an expanded
range of "connections."[8] It was never an entry point into control of the
underworld, or effortless access to the millionaire lifestyle. Sicilian men of
respect were, like their American cousins, "free to make business deals with
whomever he wants."[9] Edelhertz and Overcast contended, "To be "made"
one has to be a producer, not a mouth to feed."[10]

What membership of a *borgata* bestowed was a level of protection
against interlopers. "Nobody would ever bother you, whatever you did,"
Fratianno said, "you more or less had a free ride, carte blanche, let's put
it."[11] Naylor argued that, "it gave some assurance that members in their
business dealings would not cheat each other."[12] Where a Mafia member
ran a venture, "no one, whether it be another member of the organization

or an outsider, can infringe upon his territory, contact any runners or harm his business in any manner."[13]

Haller listed other benefits, ranging from "bonding and social prestige for members," to the finding of business contacts.[14] There was, as well, a greater possibility for the success of an activity if another member was involved. Based upon their membership, Mafiosi could offer "arbitration" services to those functioning outside of the law, with the parties at logger-heads knowing that any agreement struck would probably be adhered to.[15]

The localized, ethnically determined basis to Mafia recruitment ensured that later expansion could be problematic. Emerging throughout this history is the role of the place of birth of New York City Mafiosi or their parents. A majority of social and business interactions involving Mafiosi were conditioned by ethnic factors, setting limits on how far Mafiosi could readily expand their influence. Unsurprisingly, given the restrictive criteria for Mafia membership, and the supposed advantages conferred by working with other Italians connected in some fashion to Families, racial factors were a powerful factor in the organization of enterprises, market-driven and predatory.

The 1930s narcotics ring in which Gentile took a part, for instance, was skewed at the management level towards *paesani*. In "one of the most important narcotic smuggling and distributing" cases of the age, Vincent Carriera, Al Mauro and Dominick Visco handled the distributing end, while the principal wholesalers were Gentile and Vincent DiMaggio. Sam Maceo, a Galveston crime figure, organized most shipments to the Southwest.[16] Intercepted conversations between U.S. men of respect illustrated an identical ethnically biased trait.[17] Names found in address books seized from Mafia leaders displayed an identical characteristic.[18] Chicago's multiethnic leadership, in which tradition was marginalized, was able to move into wider fields of endeavor.

No Mafia Family existed in the majority of American states, although organized crime did.[19] While admitting the longevity of form and relative strength of Families in licit sectors of the New York economy (Chapter 1), even in its Manhattan "stronghold," Italian hegemony over organized crime was partial.[20] Belief in Mafia supremacy was especially articulated when discussing its alleged role in the illicit gambling field. Cressey expressed the opinion of most of the law enforcement establishment, that "The members of this organization control all but a tiny part of the illegal gambling in the United States."[21]

But Justice Department statistics confirmed that as of 1975, most illegal gambling was independent of what it termed "organized crime," the percentage cited ranging from 53 percent controlled by syndicates in the Northeast, to a miniscule 2 percent in the U.S. Southwest. "A substantial—perhaps a major—share of gambling is controlled by persons only slightly, if at all, connected with organized crime."[22] The Commission on the Review of the National Policy Toward Gambling in 1976 equally clearly refuted the suggestion of overarching Mafia control.[23]

"Authoritative" estimates cited by Caputo of the profits from illegal gambling ran from "six to fifteen billion dollars per year."[24] Cook likewise argued that organized crime "has probably made more millionaires than the Harvard Business School."[25]

Yet since the American Mafia's monopoly over gambling, the believed "bedrock" of its revenue stream, was far from airtight, the profits accruing to *borgata* members from the activity were not nearly so large as predicted. Outside of narcotics, there was no recognized case of Mob figures making the transition from crude cash transactions to the stereotypical command over million-dollar portfolios funded from secret Swiss bank accounts.[26] John Gotti, the head of the Gambino Family (the nation's largest; the old D'Aquila organization), enjoyed a middle-class lifestyle—but nothing more.[27]

Anna Genovese, the former wife of "mob kingpin" Vito Genovese, sought a $350 weekly temporary alimony in 1953 at the Freehold Superior Court in New Jersey. Anna made a claim, repeated by authors since as yet more proof of the huge profitability of Mafia controlled activities, that Vito had bank deposits in places as far flung as New York, New Jersey, Naples and Switzerland.

Genovese countered by saying that his only income was $107 weekly from the Colonial Trading Company. Anna admitted under cross-questioning to previously lying under oath and she was hazy about the details. Other witnesses flatly refuted the substance of her testimony. Upon hearing both sides, Superior Court Judge Donald McLean awarded her an order of only $800, to be paid for by the sale of the family home and its furnishings at Atlantic Highlands, New Jersey. (That Anna said was worth $250,000, but was valued at $55,000)

The Internal Revenue Service pursued Anna's allegations and found them baseless.[28] A sample of wills or probates left by deceased Mafia figures in New Jersey-Pennsylvania likewise uncovered their generally leaving few or no assets.[29]

The Wharton Econometric Forecasting Associates in 1986 noted, "someone's previous speculation and often casual estimate is reported as if it were the result of careful and complete analysis."[30] They found that the total net income of illegal gambling nationally was a modest $4.48 billion yearly.[31] Reuter also pointed out that most estimates made of organized crime's profit margins were untenable.[32] "His analysis suggested "the Mafia may be a paper tiger, rationally reaping the returns from its reputation while no longer maintaining the forces that generated the reputation."[33]

Cummings and Volkman explained, "illegal gambling operations require a huge overhead, swallowing up large percentages of the gross. Mafia crews tended to use gambling profits as "work" money, i.e. putting that cash back onto the street to capitalize the much more profitable enterprises of hijacking and loansharking."[34] After reading about the DeCavalcante Family's New Jersey numbers game of the 1960s, Murray Kempton dryly commented, "Any given DeCavalcante soldier can hardly sit in his presence without giving way to confessions of indigence."[35]

The aim of this book has been to test and assess the validity of contrasting perspectives and factual claims and to propose fresh insights. The received history "has often made it difficult to separate the fact from the fiction . . . and it has discouraged many criminologists from seriously studying the problem."[36]

Where distinctive "stages" of evolution in Mafia-style crime have been identified,[37] it has been achieved by discarding information that indicated the intricacy of crime networks, and by ignoring environmental limits to their authority. "The history of the phenomenon of organized crime in American society," Block cautioned, "contains numerous pitfalls, although none quite so precarious as the presence of a standard historiography."[38] Utilizing a reductionistic historiography and stereotypical constructions could not hope to capture the diversity and modesty of scale and outcomes that characterized New York City's Mafia in its formative years.

Notes

NOTES TO CHAPTER 1

1. The Iannis differentiated the noun "Mafia," referring to forms of criminal organization, from a "the cultural attitude of mafia," deploying the lower case "m" (Francis A. J. Ianni with Elizabeth Reuss-Ianni, *A Family Business* [London: Routledge and Kegan Paul, 1972], p.43; Luciano J. Iorizzo [ed.] *An Enquiry into Organized Crime*, The American Italian Historical Association, 1970, 8) This book follows that convention.
2. *Time*, August 22, 1969.
3. *Forbes*, September 29, 1980.
4. James B. Jacobs et al., *Busting the Mob* (New York: New York University Press, 1994), 244.
5. Herbert E. Alexander and Gerald E. Caiden (eds.) *The Politics and Economics of Organized Crime* (Lexington: Lexington Books, 1985), 3.
6. Alan A. Block and William J. Chambliss, *Organizing Crime* (New York: Elsevier, 1981), 117–8.
7. Letizia Paoli, *Mafia Brotherhoods* (New York: Oxford University Press, 2003), 223.
8. A good example is Peter Lupsha's article "Organized Crime in the United States," in Robert J. Kelly, ed., *Organized Crime: A Global Perspective* (Totowa, New Jersey: Rowman and Littlefield, 1986), 32–57. Refer also to William D. Falcon (ed.) *Organized Crime in the United States: A Review of the Public Record* (Washington, DC: Department of Justice, 1987), Chapter 1.
9. Donald R. Cressey, *Theft of the Nation* (New York: Harper and Row, 1969), 4.
10. Consult the pronouncements is the U.S. President's Commission on Organized Crime, *The Impact: Organized Crime Today* (April 1986) 35–50.
11. Hood represented the first perspective—"It is best defined as a sentiment of opposition to social and moral obligations, and to legal restraint." (*Fortnightly Review*, 77 [January 1902] 102–11. *The Times* impressed upon its readers in 1875 that in Sicily, the Mafia was but a "feeling of sympathy which induces the idle, vicious and discontented to make common cause for their mutual advantage against law, order, and morality."(*Times* [London] June 21, 1875).
12. FBI guidelines define cooperating witnesses as those individuals who have left organized crime and testified against their former cohorts in crime. Informers are regarded as individuals who remain in organized crime, supplying information but with no plans to have them testify in public.

13. The Narcotics Bureau considered that the Mafia was tightly disciplined and "organized along clan lines," with its members "absolutely obedient to the officers of the organization." During the 1950s, the FBN apparently believed that the American organization was run from Palermo, Sicily (U.S. Congress, Select Committee on Improper Activities in the Labor or Management Field, *Investigation of Improper Activities in the Labor or Management Field*, hearings 85ᵗʰ Congress 2ⁿᵈ Session 1958, 12220).

14. William F. Roemer, *Roemer: Man Against the Mob* (New York: Donald I. Fine, 1989), Chapter 15, *FBI Criminal Intelligence Digest*, November 8, 1961 to SAC, New York. FBI report of September 12, 1960 from Chicago office titled *Changed Samuel M. Giancana, AKA. Sam Flood*.

15. U.S. Congress, Senate, Committee on Government Operations, Permanent Subcommittee on Investigations, *Organized Crime and Illicit Traffic in Narcotics: Report*, 89ᵗʰ Congress 1ˢᵗ Session 1965, 5.

16. *Organized Crime and Illicit Traffic in Narcotics: Report*, 5, 117.

17. Joseph Volz and Peter J. Bridge, *The Mafia Talks* (Greenwich, Conn.: Fawcett Publications, 1969); Henry A. Zeiger, *Sam the Plumber* (New York: New American Library, 1970); Henry A. Zeiger, *The Jersey Mob* (New York: New American Library, 1975).

18. John Dickie, *Cosa Nostra* (London: Coronet, 2004), 195. Its population rose from 4,766,883 in 1910 to 7,454,995 in 1940. Immigration from Italy to New York swelled over the period in question from 12,223 recorded in 1880 to 390,832 in 1920 (U.S. Bureau of the Census figures; Ira Rosenwaike, *Population History of New York City* (Syracuse University Press, 1972), 58; Edwin Fenton, *Immigrants and Unions, a Case Study* (New York: Arno Press, 1975), 9.

19. Humbert S. Nelli, *From Immigrants to Ethnics* (Oxford University Press, 1983), 63.

20. In Chicago, for example, powerful non-Italian mobsters working with the Italians were classed by the McClellan Committee as a separate unit from "Chicago's branch of the Mafia." (*Organized Crime and Illicit Traffic in Narcotics: Report*, 119).

21. The President's Commission on Organized Crime in 1986 reported that half of "the total strength of La Cosa Nostra nationwide" was found in New York City's five boroughs (President's Commission on Organized Crime, *The Edge* [March 1986]191).

22. Peter Reuter, "Research on American Organized Crime," in *Handbook of Organized Crime in the United States*, Robert J. Kelly et al. (Westport, CT: Greenwood Press, 1994), 91–2.

23. Albini, *The American Mafia*, 7–9; Gary W. Potter, *Criminal Organizations* (Prospect Heights, Ill.: Waveland Press, 1994), 27.

24. Margaret E. Beare and R. T. Naylor, *Major Issues Relating to Organized Crime: Within the Context of Economic Relationships*, April 1999.

25. Merry Morash, "Organized Crime," in *Major Forms of Crime*, ed. Robert F. Meier, (Beverly Hills, CA.: Sage Publications, 1984), 215; Albini, *The American Mafia*, 7–9; Peter A. Lupsha, "Individual Choice, Material Culture, and Organized Crime," *Criminology*, 19, no.1 (1981):10.

26. Humbert S. Nelli, *The Business of Crime* (New York: Oxford University Press, 1976), ix.

27. Alan Block, *East Side West Side* (Cardiff: University College Cardiff Press, 1982), 10.

28. John F. Gallagher and James A. Cain, "Citation Support for the Mafia Myth in Criminology Textbooks," *The American Sociologist* 9 (1974):72.

29. Thomas A. Firestone, "Mafia Memoirs," *Journal of Contemporary Criminal Justice* 9, no.3 (August 1993):197.
30. Dickie, *Cosa Nostra*, 5.
31. Virgil W. Peterson, *The Mob* (Ottowa: Illinois: Green Hill Publishers, 1983), 442.
32. "When dealing with subordinates," according to Zeiger, when discussing the contents of intercepted conversations involving New Jersey leader Ray DeCarlo, "he exaggerated his prowess, and put the fear of himself in them."(Henry A. Zeiger, *The Jersey Mob* (New American Library, 1975), 7.
33. *FBI Criminal Intelligence Digest*, March 11, 1963.
34. Refer to Chapter 8 (Nicolo Gentile, *Translated Transcription of the Life of Nicolo [E] Gentile, Background and History of the Castellammarese War and Early Decades of Organized Crime in America* (no date) 108; Nick Gentile, *Vita di Capomafia* [Rome: Editori Riuniti, 1963], 116.)
35. Jacobs, *Busting the Mob*; James B. Jacobs et al. *Gotham Unbound* (New York: New York University Press, 1999); James B. Jacobs, *Mobsters, Unions and Feds* (New York University Press, 2006).
36. Block, *East Side West Side*, 256.
37. Joseph L. Albini, *The American Mafia* (New York: Appleton-Century-Crofts), 1971.
38. Ianni, *A Family Business*.
39. Peterson, *The Mob*.
40. Peter Reuter, *Disorganized Crime* (Cambridge, MA: MIT Press, 1983), Chapter 7; Mark H. Haller, "Illegal Enterprises: A Theoretical and Historical Interpretation," *Criminology* 28, no.2 (1990):226–7.
41. Craig Thompson and Allen Raymond, *Gang Rule in New York* (New York: The Dial Press, 1940).
42. Burton B. Turkus and Sid Feder, *Murder Inc.* (London: Victor Gollancz, 1952).
43. Patrick Downey, *Gangster City* (New Jersey: Barricade Books, 2004). The *Library Journal* observed, "The serious Mob collector may want Downey's book as a comprehensive who-fell-where source, but as a thing to read it is an uncompelling catalog of gangster killings"(*Library Journal*, April 15, 2004).
44. Block, *East Side West Side*, 12.
45. Margaret E. Beare, *Structures, Strategies and Tactics of Transnational Criminal Organizations*, Paper presented at the Australian Institute of Criminology, Canberra, March 9–10, 2000.
46. Michael Woodiwiss, "Transnational Organized Crime," in *Critical Reflections on Transnational Organized Crime, Money Laundering, and Corruption*, ed. Margaret E. Beare (University of Toronto Press, 2003), 25; Michael Woodiwiss, *Crime Crusades and Corruption* (London: Pinter, 1988), 146–7; Albanese, *Organized Crime in America*, 47–8.
47. Doubters should examine the mountain of uncensored FBI reports, some dated from the period before Joseph Valachi confessed and which were therefore unaffected by his statements, in the U.S. National Archives' John F. Kennedy Assassination Records Collection. A letter dated May 10, 1962, to the Rome legal attaché making "reference to a number of titles of importance in this organization," was written about 3 months before Valachi began to speak. Above that, dozens of "made" American Mafiosi up to and including "bosses" have since refuted the skeptics' position in countless trials.
48. Refer to Joseph L. Albini and Bronislaw Bajon, "Witches, Mafia, Mental Illness and Social Reality," *International Journal of Criminology and Penology* 6 (1978); Joseph L. Albini, "The Mafia and the Devil: What They

have in Common," *Journal of Contemporary Criminal Justice* 9, no.3 (1993): 242; Jay S. Albanese "God and the Mafia Revisited," in *Career Criminals*, ed. Gordon P. Waldo (Beverly Hills, CA.: Sage, 1983): 43–58; Philip Jenkins and Gary Potter "The Politics and Mythology of Organized Crime," *Journal of Criminal Justice* 15 (1987): 473–484.

49. Albanese, *God and the Mafia Revisited*, 43–4.

50. Basing their judgment on secondary sources and on an interview with "one of Angelo Bruno's "capos," or so the Pennsylvania Crime Commission tells us," nicknamed "Freddy," whose main contribution to the book was, not surprisingly given his reputation, to deny the existence of a local Mafia. Potter and Jenkins concluded, "the existence and the history" of the Philadelphia Family "largely represented the work of myth-makers." (pp. 5–6). Since 1985, those who have "flipped" to the government from the Philadelphia Mafia include Ralph Natale (the boss), and Philip Leonetti (underboss). At the *caporegime* level were Peter Caprio, George Freslone and Robert Luise Jr. Up to 10 Philadelphia Mafia "soldiers" have also defected.

51. For instance in Potter's *Criminal Organizations*, and *The City and the Syndicate*, William Howard Moore, *The Kefauver Committee and the Politics of Crime 1950–1952*, (Columbia, Missouri: University of Missouri Press, 1974).

52. Judith Hybel's research showed for example that "contrary to popular belief, the introduction of a state lottery appears to increase participation in the illegal numbers game."(Maureen Kallick-Kaufman and Peter Reuter, "Introduction," *Journal of Social Issues* 35, no.3 [1979]:5). The Commission on the Review of the National Policy Toward Gambling suggested that far from eradicating the illicit market for bookmaking, the decriminalization of off-track betting in New York in 1970 led to a "small net increase in illegal bookmaking operations in New York." Decriminalized lotteries in Connecticut and New Jersey have not damaged the illegal side as predicted (Commission on the Review of the National Policy Towards Gambling, *Final Report* Washington, DC, [1976], 138) Due to a lesser scale of infiltration into the gambling world by Mafiosi than is often assumed, Reuter found that organized crime Families "will not be much affected by efforts to suppress illegal gambling"(Reuter, *Disorganized Crime*, 187).

53. *New York Times* (hereafter *NYT*) October 18, 1980.

54. In Sicily, control over the local state's regulatory process was a distinctive basis of Mafia power (cf. Arlacchi, *Mafia Business*; Giovanni Falcone, *Men of Honour* [London: Warner Books, 1992]).

55. The New York City construction industry's history is a classic example. Allegations of criminality "in all phases of the industry" have been current since the 1920s. But the later day entry of Mafiosi presented the city with a seemingly intractable problem, to which it has yet to provide a sustainable solution (New York State Organized Crime Task Force *Corruption and Racketeering in the New York City Construction Industry: Interim Report* [June 1987]). Following a tougher regulatory regime imposed in the wake of earlier scandals, Mafia influence was expected to wane. These hopes have been dashed (*NYT*, January 10, 1999, August 8, 1999, September 4, 2000).

56. Reuter, *Disorganized Crime*, p. 175.

57. Robert J. Kelly, *The Upperworld and the Underworld* (New York: Kluwer Academic Publishers, 1999), 3.

58. Dickie, *Cosa Nostra*, 2.

59. Paoli, *Mafia Brotherhoods*, 155.

60. Consult U.S. Congress, Senate, Committee on the Judiciary, *Organized Crime in America*, hearings 98th Congress 1st Session 1983, 189–275.

61. Joseph Bonanno with Sergio Lalli, *A Man of Honour* (London: Andre Deutsch, 1983), 79.
62. Paoli, *Mafia Brotherhoods*, 8.
63. FBI *La Causa Nostra*, New York Office, January 31, 1963.
64. Tom Behan, *See Naples and Die* (London: I.B. Tauris, 2002), 184.
65. Valachi noted that in his own Genovese Family, they never met "as a whole" for the 30 years he was a member (U.S. Congress, Senate, Committee on Government Operations, Permanent Subcommittee on Investigations, *Organized Crime and the Illicit Traffic in Narcotics*, hearings 88th Congress 1st Session 1963, 82).
66. U.S. Congress, Senate, Committee on Government Operations, Permanent Subcommittee on Investigations, *Organized Crime and the Illicit Traffic in Narcotics*, hearings 88th Congress 1st Session 1963, 66; Ralph Salerno and John S. Tompkins, *The Crime Confederation* (Garden City, NY: Doubleday, 1969), 156–8.
67. *Organized Crime and Illicit Traffic in Narcotics: Report*, 2 and 7.
68. *FBI Criminal Intelligence Digest*, March 11, 1963; FBI, *La Causa Nostra*, New York Field Office, July 1, 1963.
69. Utilized in upper case to differentiate it from the familiar biological family unit.
70. FBI, *La Cosa Nostra*, Milwaukee Office, December 23, 1963.
71. Even Cressey admitted that the "skeletal structure" he noted omitted "the many "unofficial" positions any organization must contain."(Cressey, *Theft of the Nation*, 126).
72. Stephen Fox, *Blood and Power* (New York: William Morrow, 1989), 70.
73. *L'Ora*, September 19, 1963.
74. Quebec Police Commission, *The Fight Against Organized Crime in Quebec*, Editeur Officiel du Quebec (1977), 51.
75. Kenneth Allsop, *The Bootleggers* (London: Four Square Books, 1966), 16.
76. "It still forms the basis for much of the thinking and writing about organized crime today."(Jay Albanese, *Organized Crime*, [2nd ed] [Cincinnati, Ohio: Anderson Publishing, 1989], 92).
77. Kelly, *Organized Crime A Global Perspective*, 47–8.
78. Mark H. Haller, "Bureaucracy and the Mafia: An Alternative View," *Journal of Contemporary Criminal Justice* 8, no.1 (1992).

NOTES TO CHAPTER 2

1. New York Municipal Archives, *WPA Italians of New York*, MN # 21258, roll # 259.
2. Francis A. J. Ianni with Elizabeth Reuss-Ianni, *A Family Business* (London: Routledge and Kegan Paul, 1972), 43; G. E. Castiglione, "Italian Immigration into the United States 1901–4," *American Journal of Sociology* 11, no.2 (Sept 1905): 185; Edwin G. Borrows and Mike Wallace, *Gotham: A History of New York City to 1898* (New York: Oxford University Press, 1999), 1122.
3. Robert Anthony Orsi, *The Madonna of 115th Street* (New Haven, CT.: Yale University Press, 2002), 34.
4. Giuseppe Selvaggi, *The Rise of the Mafia in New York* (Indianapolis: The Bobbs-Merrill Co., 1978), 7.
5. Joseph Valachi, *The Real Thing*, U.S. National Archives and Records Administration (hereafter referred to as NARA) RG 60, MLR Entry no. 306H 60.10.3, 1.

6. Ibid., 8.
7. Ibid., 22.
8. The cases of Vincent Mangano and Nicolo Gentile, for instance.
9. Howard Abadinsky, *Organized Crime* (3rd ed.) (Chicago: Nelson-Hall, 1990), 51.
10. Jacob A. Riis, *How the Other Half Lives* (New York: Dover Publications, 1971 [reprint of 1901 ed.]), 47.
11. U.S. Works Progress Administration, *The Italians of New York* (New York: Random House, 1938), 19.
12. Orsi, *The Madonna of 115th Street*, 14–7.
13. Robert E. Park and Herbert A. Miller, *Old World Traits Transplanted* (New York: Arno Press and the New York Times, 1969 [1st ed. in 1921]), 151.
14. Joseph Bonanno with Sergio Lalli, *A Man of Honour* (London: Andre Deutsch, 1983), 62.
15. Thomas Monroe Pitkin and Francesco Cordasco, *The Black Hand* (Totowa, NJ: Littlefield, Adams and Co., 1977), 2.
16. *New York Times* (hereafter *NYT*), December 30, 1922, January 20, 1923.
17. Email from Tammy Reina, February 10, 2003.
18. Email from Catherine Campbell, May 26, 2003.
19. *NYT*, June 9, 1912.
20. Herbert Asbury, *The Gangs of New York* (New York: Paragon House, 1990 [1st ed. 1927]), 253.
21. Illustrating the closeness of ties between Kelly and Timothy Daniel "Big Tim" Sullivan, the Tammany leader in the Bowery and East Side districts, was Kelly's purchase of Sullivan's former home on East Chester Road.
22. *NYT*, June 9, 1912.
23. 1920 Bronx census; WWI draft registration record. Not in 1871 as Jay Robert Nash charged (Jay Robert Nash, *World Encyclopedia of Organized Crime* [London: Headline Books, 1992], 409). Nor was he therefore Neapolitan (Humbert S. Nelli, *The Business of Crime* [New York: Oxford University Press, 1976], 107; John Dickie *Cosa Nostra* [London: Coronet, 2004], 206).
24. Asbury, *The Gangs of New York*, 273.
25. Nick Tosches, *King of the Jews* (New York: HarperCollins, 2005), 213.
26. Asbury, *The Gangs of New York*, 287.
27. Nelli, *The Business of Crime*, 107.
28. Asbury, *The Gangs of New York*, 292.
29. Craig Thompson and Allen Raymond, *Gang Rule in New York* (New York: The Dial Press, 1940), 361.
30. FBI, *Girolomo Santuccio* New Haven Office, February 18, 1963.
31. Humbert S. Nelli, *The Italians in Chicago 1880–1930* (New York: Oxford University Press, 1970), 134.
32. Pitkin, *The Black Hand*, 228.
33. Numbers refused entry to America as "convicts" were 49 in 1903, and 25 in 1904, virtually all coming from the south of Italy (G. E. Castiglione, "Italian Immigration into the United States 1901–4," *American Journal of Sociology,* 11, no.2 [Sept 1905]: 191). In 1908, only 16 deportations were implemented, with a further 8 cases "pending."
34. *NYT*, August 15, 1904; September 13, 1904.
35. Nelli, *The Business of Crime*, 79.
36. Pitkin, *The Black Hand*, 137.
37. Albert Fried, *The Rise and Fall of the Jewish Gangster in America* (New York: Holt, Rinehart and Winston, 1980).

38. Robert A. Rockaway, *But—He Was Good to his Mother* (Jerusalem: Gefen Publishing, 1993).
39. Jenna Weissman Joselit, *Our Gang* (Bloomington: Indiana University Press, 1983).
40. Patrick Downey, *Gangster City: The History of the New York Underworld 1900–1935* (New Jersey: Barricade Books, 2004), 20; Hank Messick and Burt Goldblatt, *The Mobs and the Mafia* (New York: Thomas Y. Crowell, 1972), 11.
41. William J. Flynn, *The Barrel Mystery* (New York: The James A. McCann Co., 1920), 15.
42. *NYT*, March 3, 1907.
43. Robert M. Lombardo, "The Black Hand," *Journal of Contemporary Criminal Justice* 18, pt. 4 (2002): 401.
44. John Landesco, *Organized Crime in Chicago* (Chicago: University of Chicago Press, 1968), 109.
45. *St. Louis Republic*, August 5, 1911.
46. *St. Louis Post-Dispatch*, March 19, 1911.
47. *NYT*, December 31, 1911.
48. *NYT*, August 5, 1911.
49. *Pueblo Chieftain* May 11, 1922. Scaglia's untimely demise brought about a fissure in the Pueblo Mafia, and three of Scaglia's relatives fled to Kansas City seeking the protection of the local *capo*, at that time Nicolo Gentile. Accusations made against them that pitted the Kansas City and Pueblo Families against one another, prompted the Mafia general assembly to meet, at which Gentile saved their lives (Nick Gentile, *Vita di Capomafia* [Rome: Editori Riuniti, 1963], 83–5).
50. *St. Louis Post-Dispatch*, December 25–27, 1910.
51. Joseph L. Albini, *The American Mafia* (New York: Appleton-Century-Crofts, 1971), 191; Dickie, *Cosa Nostra*, 208; Pitkin, *The Black Hand*, 3; Lombardo, *The Black Hand* (2002), 394.
52. New Castle Public Library, "The Black Hand Society," a collection of articles that appeared in the *New Castle News* in 1907.
53. Nelli, *The Business of Crime*, 75–6.
54. *New York Tribune*, September 14, 1903; Pitkin, *The Black Hand*, 15–6; Nelli, *The Business of Crime*, 75–6. Giordano was to reappear in newsprint in 1923 as the friend of Albert Anastasia's who was murdered on Sackett Street (Chapter 6).
55. *NYT*, September 14, 1904.
56. *NYT*, March 9, 1908, December 31, 1911.
57. Extortion narratives' "emphasis on vulnerable victims" is noted in Vincent Sacco, "The Black Hand Crime Wave," *Deviant Behavior*, vol. 24 (2003), 60.
58. *NYT*, January 6, 1908.
59. *New York Herald*, August 23, 1914.
60. *Literary Digest*, April 5, 1919.
61. Nelli, *The Business of Crime*, 84. Broader uses of the Black Hand technique are discussed in Sacco, "The Black Hand Crime Wave," 69.
62. *NYT*, August 8, 1904.
63. *NYT*, October 12, 1912; January 29, 1914.
64. *NYT*, September 11, 1905; *New York Tribune*, September 11, 1905.
65. *NYT*, April 5, 1908; Humbert S. Nelli, "Italians and Crime in Chicago: The Formative Years, 1890–1920," *The American Journal of Sociology* 74 (1969): 373–391; Lombardo, *The Black Hand* (2002), 394–409.
66. Nelli, *Italians and Crime in Chicago*, 388.

67. *NYT*, January 6, 1908; Arrigo Petacco, *Joe Petrosino* (London: Hamish Hamilton, 1974), 27.
68. *Cosmopolitan Magazine*, June 1909.
69. *World*, March 15, 1909; *New York Herald*, July 5, 1914.
70. *NYT*, October 12, 1913.
71. *NYT*, January 29, 1914.
72. Westchester County Archives, Elmsford, NY: District Attorney files, statement of Salvatore Mara, March 20, 1913.
73. Peter Edwards and Antonio Nicaso, *Deadly Silence* (Toronto: Macmillan Canada, 1993), 18.
74. *Times* [London] October 26, 1901. Such was Musolino's popularity that while he was on trial, he received "fruit, flowers, and other presents from feminine admirers, and hundreds of love letters, the senders only waiting for his release to marry him" (*NYT*, January 15, 1911).
75. The Secretary apparently served as a generalist who performed any task asked of him outside of slayings and, with the head man, he organized the recruitment of new members.
76. Westchester County Archives, District Attorney files box T 187–the People of the State of New York against Raffaello Bova (1913); *NYT*, May 28, 1913; *Sun*, March 22, 1913.
77. U.S. Congress, Senate, Committee on Government Operations, Permanent Subcommittee on Investigations, *Organized Crime and the Illicit Traffic in Narcotics*, hearings 88th Congress 1st Session 1963, 1047. Pellegrino was born 1889 in Calabria.
78. Edwards, *Deadly Silence*, 17–19.
79. Including the towns of Hillsville, Youngstown and New Castle.
80. James D. Horan and Howard Swiggert, *The Pinkerton Story* (London: Heinemann, 1952), 222–7.
81. *New Castle News*, March 15, 1907, June 14, 1907, July 23, 1907, July 24, 1907, July 29, 1907, July 20, 1907, July 31, 1907.
82. In the worst case uncovered, a merchant and hotelkeeper, Dominick Tutino, paid $3,600 to keep the gang from harassing him (New Castle Public Library, *The Black Hand Society*).
83. *Cleveland Plain-Dealer Magazine*, March 28, 1909.
84. *New Castle News*, October 7, 1907; James D. Horan, *The Pinkertons* (London: Robert Hale, 1967), 446.
85. *Cleveland Plain Dealer*, March 28, 1909.
86. Nelli also touches on the Mahoning Valley story in his 1976 book (92, 137–9).
87. Horan, *The Pinkertons*, Chapter 35.
88. *New Castle News*, July 23, 1907.
89. Romeo died in Campbell City, Ohio, his base of operations, in 1976.
90. Mallamo was close to the Gambino Family-linked Corbi brothers, Tony and Frank of Baltimore; Mallamo and Tony Corbi were the joint owners of the Yo Hio social club in Youngstown in 1958. Mallamo was born 1904 in Calabria, dying April 1987 in Youngstown.
91. FBI, *La Cosa Nostra*, Cleveland Office, June 15, 1964.
92. The proposed member was instructed to kneel several times before a statue of the Virgin Mary, repeating of an oath of loyalty. The pouring of glasses of wine to drink, together with the lighting of candles before the statue, was part of the procedure. The initiate was told to consult Mallamo if he had problems; but "you must never get mad." "At no time during the initiation ceremony did (he) use the words "La Cosa Nostra" (FBI *La Cosa Nostra AKA*, Cleveland Office, June 15, 1964). Several men were reported in attendance at a 1964 ceremony including Mallamo and Joseph "Blackie"

Gennaro, who created and was head of the Ohio Boxing Commission and later of the International Boxing Council. Gennaro managed several boxers including Ernie Shavers, who in 1977 fought Mohammed Ali.

93. Walter S. Bowen and Harry Edward Neal *The United States Secret Service* (New York: Chilton Company, 1960), 45—6.
94. *New York Herald*, June 14, 1914; Flynn, *The Barrel Mystery*, 198–202.
95. *New York Herald*, June 14, 1914.
96. *Sun*, December 26, 1910.
97. Alberto Verrusio Ricci, "Black Hand Exposed at Last," *True Detective Mysteries*, X111, no. 6 (September 1930); *The Olean Evening Times*, July 5, 1928.
98. No trace of this individual could be found, but the Pettenelli surname is often found in the Naples region (www.gens.labo.net).
99. *Paterson Evening News*, August 12, 1907.
100. Petacco, *Joe Petrosino*, 26.
101. FBI *La Causa Nostra*, San Francisco Office June 31, 1963; Bill Bonanno, *Bound by Honor* (New York: St. Martin's Paperbacks, 1999), 19–20.
102. Giovanni Falcone, *Men of Honour* (London: Warner, 1992), 116.
103. Pino Arlacchi, *Men of Dishonor* (New York: William Morrow, 1992), 53—4.
104. Celeste A. Morello, *Before Bruno Book 2—1931–1946* (2001) 29.
105. The "oldtimers" according to hoodlum Ray DeCarlo, "wouldn't breathe a word to you and let them know they were in it" (Henry A. Zeiger, *The Jersey Mob* [New York: New American Library, 1975], 151).
106. In spite of Guardalabene's arrest in 1913 as a suspect in the shooting of Felice Lazara. Rumors spread that he was "King of the Black Hand Society" in Milwaukee, and that "the Italians were all afraid of him because his word was law" (Bureau of Investigation, *In Re: Angelo Guardalabene* , May 20, 1918).
107. *Milwaukee Journal*, February 7, 1921; March 19, 1952.
108. Morello, *Before Bruno Volume 1*, 40.
109. Ed Reid, *Mafia* (New York: Random House, 1952), 121; U.S. Congress Senate Special Committee to Investigate Organized Crime in Interstate Commerce, *Investigation of Organized Crime in Interstate Commerce*, hearings part 4, 1950–1951, 318 and 369. The FBI file on DiGiovanni notes that because of a reluctance of witnesses to testify against him and the absence of confessions, DiGiovanni and his co-accused were released.
110. Antonio Napoli, *The Mob's Guys* (College Station: Virtualbookworm.com Publishing, 2004), 56.
111. *Springfield State Journal*, June 26, 1914.
112. *Springfield State Journal*, June 3, 1914.
113. *Charleston Daily Mail*, November 2, 1923.
114. Born January 1887 in Serradifalco, Sicily.
115. *NYT*, July 15, 1908; *New York Herald*, July 15, 1908. Pinzolo was "the first of the only two bomb throwers ever caught in the act in the history of the New York Police Department" (*NYT*, September 24, 1911).
116. *New York Herald,* July 15, 1908; *NYT* July 15, 1908; *The Outlook*, August 16, 1913; New York Municipal Archives, case no. 67581 (1908).
117. *NYT*, September 24, 1911.
118. *NYT*, September 6, 1911.
119. *New York Tribune*, September 6, 1911.
120. *NYT*, September 6, 1911.
121. Pinzolo set foot on American shores in August 1906.
122. Arthur Train, *Courts, Criminals and Camorra* (New York: Charles Scribner's Sons, 1912), 233.

123. General Sessions Court, County of New York, The People of the State of New York against Giuseppe Costabile, case no. 84659 [1911]. Notwithstanding the removal of Costabile, the harassment of Spinelli continued, to the extent that in 1913 he was reported to be "a ruined man. He has not paid anything to the Black Hand, but his decorating business has failed, his houses are mortgaged up to nearly their full value, and he and his wife and children are working out by the day to pay the interest on the mortgage" (*Outlook*, August 16, 1913).
124. *NYT*, April 3, 1910.
125. Bowen and Neal, *The United States Secret Service*, 37–8.
126. Flynn, *The Barrel Mystery*, 26.
127. *NYT*, April 17, 1903; *New York Herald*, April 16, 1903.
128. Annual Report of the Chief of the Secret Service Division for the Fiscal Year Ended June 30, 1910, 7.
129. *NYT*, December 31, 1911.
130. *Baltimore Sun*, April 2, 1908, April 16, 1908, April 23, 1908.
131. *New York Herald*, August 13, 1904.
132. *New York Tribune*, August 13, 1904.
133. *Newark Advocate*, August 13, 1904; *NYT*, August 14, 1904; August 16, 1904; *New York Herald*, August 14, 1904; Pitkin, *The Black Hand*, 54.
134. The $20,000 demand nearly caused a run on John Bozzuffi's bank when a story emerged that the kidnapping affair was prearranged (*New York Herald*, March 8, 1906). Bozzuffi was convicted of grand larceny in 1916 and sentenced to State Prison for up to 3½ years imprisonment (*NYT*, February 2, 1919).
135. New York Police Department Prisoner's Criminal Record, Ignazio Lupo.
136. *World*, March 15, 1909.
137. *NYT*, March 17, 1909; NARA, RG 204, 230/40/1/3 box 956—Ignazio Lupo, 6.
138. "A certain Manzella a merchant in New York," was noted by witness Antonio Comito as owning a "sick horse," on the property where counterfeits were produced in 1908. Research has failed to uncover whether this Manzella was the Elizabeth Street importer.
139. *NYT*, November 16, 1909.
140. *Washington Post*, February 5, 1922.
141. Hess noted a Sicilian case in 1880, when the Baron Antonio Callotti received a blackmail note demanding 8,000 lire, but the matter was settled for 370 lire (Henner Hess, *Mafia and Mafiosi* [Farnborough, Hants.: Saxon, 1973], 143–5).
142. Bonanno, *Bound by Honor*, 6; Robert M. Lombardo, "The Black Hand" *Global Crime*, vol. 6 (2004), 272.
143. Bonanno, *A Man of Honour*, 40.
144. Gioacchino Lima, the husband of Morello's sister, was one of Morello's relatives treated by Dr. Romano free of charge.
145. *New York Herald*, June 14, 1914; Flynn, *The Barrel Mystery*, 174–182, 221.
146. Albini, *The American Mafia*, 193; Secret Service daily reports, January 30, 1913.
147. Ianni, *A Family Business*, 52.
148. Lombardo, "The Black Hand" (2004), 270. Fentress describes how *lettere di scrocco* were sent to "squeeze the purses" of landowners, "or, to keep them from performing an unwelcome surveillance, prevent them from even visiting their own lands. . . ." (James Fentress, *Rebels and Mafiosi* [Ithaca: Cornell University Press, 2000], 166. Refer also to Hess, *Mafia and Mafiosi*, 130; Albini, *The American Mafia*, 192.) In the 1890s, over 219 letters demanding

money with menaces were handed to the police in Palermo (Francis Marion Crawford, *The Rulers of the South* [New York: The Macmillan Company, 1900], 377–8).

149. *NYT*, July 28, 1904.
150. *NYT*, September 3, 1908; *New York Tribune*, March 9, 1908.
151. *NYT*, March 9, 1909.
152. *NYT*, January 17, 1913.
153. *Boston American*, July 31, 1904.
154. *Detroit Journal*, November 11, 1911; *Detroit Free Press*, November 12, 1908.
155. *Detroit News*, July 25, 1917; July 26, 1917.
156. *Detroit News*, March 7, 1918.
157. *Detroit News*, May 5, 1919.
158. Press articles do not support the idea that Johnny Torrio, a purported relative of Colosimo, was brought from New York in about 1910 to rid Colosimo of the Black Hand. According to this version, Torrio killed 3 Black Handers to end the problem (Jack McPhaul, *Johnny Torrio* [New Rochelle, New York: Arlington House, 1970], 73–8; F.D. Pasley, *Al Capone* [London: Faber and Faber, 1966], 13; Nelli, *The Business of Crime*, 78). The *Chicago Tribune* made no mention of the 3 murders until 1929, and then only in a retrospective and abridged form.
159. *Chicago Tribune*, May 15, 1920, December 14, 1920. In the 1920 interpretation, a friend of Colosimo's was the intended victim, but Colosimo arranged for the slaying of the blackmailers. Only after this did Colosimo become a "marked man" (*Chicago Tribune*, May 15, 1920).
160. U.S. Circuit Court of Appeals for the Second Circuit, The United States of America vs. Giuseppe Calicchio et al., *Transcript of Record*, 451–3.
161. Nelli, *The Italians in Chicago*, 219.
162. Pitkin, *The Black Hand*, 5; Lombardo, "The Black Hand" (2004), 279.
163. Dickie, *Cosa Nostra*, 205.
164. Diego Gambetta, *The Sicilian Mafia* (Cambridge, MA.: Harvard University Press, 1993), 251.
165. *L'Ora*, September 21, 1963.
166. Giovanni Schiavo, *The Truth About the Mafia and Organized Crime in America* (New York: The Vigo Press, 1962), 135.
167. Lombardo, "The Black Hand" (2002): 395.
168. Ibid.
169. Ed Reid, *Mafia* (New York: Random House, 1952), 5–6; *St. Louis Star,* November 21–22, 1927.

NOTES TO CHAPTER 3

1. David Chandler, *The Criminal Brotherhoods* (London: Constable, 1976), 112–3.
2. Bill Bonanno, *Bound by Honor* (New York: St. Martin's Press, 1999), xviii.
3. Arriving on May 9, 1911.
4. U.S. National Archives and Records Administration (hereafter referred to as NARA), RG 87, daily reports of agents, vol. 41, reel 593, November 11, 1913.
5. Ed Reid, *Mafia* (New York: Random House, 1952), 44.
6. NARA, RG 129, Inmate Case No. 2882, Giuseppe Morello assorted years of birth have been assigned to Giuseppe Morello. Chandler gives 1863. Downey agreed with 1870 (Patrick Downey, *Gangster City: The History of the New York Underworld 1900–1935* [New Jersey: Barricade Books, 2004] 18).

7. Chandler, *The Criminal Brotherhoods*, 113.
8. NARA, RG 129, Inmate Case No. 2882; Dino Paternostro, *L'antimafia Sconosciuta Corleone 1893–1993* (Palermo: La Zisa, 1994), 28.
9. William J. Flynn, *The Barrel Mystery* (New York: The James A. McCann Co., 1920), 244–61.
10. NARA, RG 59, File 13495 (decimal file 092.65) frame 0606, roll # 845.
11. Streva was also a benefactor to Jack Dragna, discussed in the next chapter.
12. Archivio di Stato di Palermo Fondo, "Sottoprefettura di Corleone" (1860–1929) Busta n. 15 Fascicolo 1. The case is recounted in *New York Herald*, June 14, 1914; *Washington Post*, June 7, 1914; Downey, *Gangster City*, 19–20; Flynn, *The Barrel Mystery*, 244–61. One Paolo Streva is recorded entering the port of New York in 1902, journeying to his brother in Chicago.
13. Archivio di Stato di Palermo, Serie: Archivio Generale—Questura di Palermo Busta 1584 Fascicolo 352, report of April 2, 1909; NARA, RG 59, file 13495 (decimal file case no. 092.65). The trial transcript in the 1894 case was destroyed in the 1908 Messina earthquake (NARA, RG 129, Inmate Case No. 2882, Giuseppe Morello).
14. Ellis Island records show a Giuseppe Morello born around 1867 as an incoming passenger to New York in 1890, 1892 and 1896.
15. U.S. Circuit Court of Appeals for the Second Circuit, The United States of America vs. Giuseppe Calicchio et al., *Transcript of Record* (hereinafter 1910 trial transcript) 456.
16. David R. Johnson, *Illegal Tender* (Washington: Smithsonian Institution Press, 1995), 27–31; James Fentress, *Rebels and Mafiosi* (Ithaca, N.Y.: Cornell University Press, 2000), 178–9.
17. Chandler, *The Criminal Brotherhoods*, 71.
18. *NYT*, June 3,1865; *Brooklyn Eagle*, March 16,1875.
19. *Times* [London] June 21,1875; *Brooklyn Eagle*, March 16,1875.
20. Thomas Pitkin and Francesco Cordasco, *The Black Hand* (Totowa, NJ: Littlefield, Adams and Co., 1977), 38–9.
21. *NYT*, October 16,1888; October 22, 1888; *New York Tribune* October 23,1888; *Sun*, April 19, 1903.
22. An informant for the Secret Service, John Gleason, confided how Mollie Callahan, a servant in the Morello household, "saw the plates and described them as copper plates." She later vanished and was believed to have been murdered (NARA, RG 87, daily reports of agents 1875–1936 [microfilm publication T-915] roll 116).
23. According to the *Times* and *Herald*, she was the "widow of an old counterfeiter who died in prison," and had been in the racket "since her girlhood" (*NY Herald*, May 23, 1902; *NYT* November 28, 1902). Frauto's origin is murky, but she appears to have come from Sicilian stock, born in 1866.
24. NARA, RG 87, microfilm publication T-915, roll 108, report of April 24, 1902.
25. *NYT*, February 17, 1895.
26. *The Evening Record*, May 22, 1902; *Bergen County Democrat*, May 23, 1902; *NYT*, November 28, 1902.
27. *The Evening Record*, May 22, 1902.
28. NARA, RG 87, daily reports of agents 1875–1936 (microfilm publication T-915) roll 108.
29. *World*, May 23, 1902; *New York Herald*, May 23, 1902; NARA, RG 87, microfilm publication T-915, roll 108, report of May 27, 1902.
30. Archivio di Stato di Palermo, Serie: Archivio Generale—Questura di Palermo Busta 1584 Fascicolo 352, report of May 16, 1909; Archivio di Stato

di Palermo, Serie: Archivio Generale—Questura di Palermo Busta 1584 Fascicolo 352, report of April 2, 1909; Arrigo Petacco, *Joe Petrosino* (London: Hamish Hamilton, 1974), 92–3.

31. *Bergen Record*, July 8, 1902; *Trenton Times*, July 9, 1902.
32. *Chicago Tribune*, February 8, 1916; *Niagara Falls Gazette*, December 8, 1902.
33. *Chicago Tribune*, December 5, 1921.
34. *NYT*, July 25, 1902; *Brooklyn Eagle*, July 24, 1902, July 25, 1902, October 5, 1902.
35. Chandler, *The Criminal Brotherhoods*, 114.
36. *Brooklyn Eagle*, July 24, 1902, July 25, 1902.
37. NARA, RG 87, daily reports of agents 1875–1936, microfilm publication T-915 roll 108.
38. *NYT*, April 20, 1903; 1910 trial transcript, 462–470.
39. Manhattan death certificate no. 12640 (1903); John Dickie, *Cosa Nostra* (London: Coronet, 2004), 200–203; Walter S. Bowen and Harry Neal, *The United States Secret Service* (New York: Chilton Books, 1960), 39; Flynn, *The Barrel Mystery*, 1–8; Petacco, *Joe Petrosino*, 1–14.
40. Flynn, *The Barrel Mystery*, 18–19.
41. NYMA, DA Record of Cases, NY County Case no. 42841 (1903); Flynn, *The Barrel Mystery,* 13–14.
42. An identical barrel was found in Inzerillo's establishment, and sawdust on the floor of the joint matched that in the base of the barrel used to conceal the cadaver. Burlap was also discovered, which was the same as that discovered in the barrel. A wagon seen in front of Zarcone's shop was used, it was thought, to carry away the corpse (*NYT*, April 17, 1903).
43. *NYT*, April 16, 1903; *New York Herald*, April 17, 1903; Arthur A. Carey with Howard McClellan, *Memoirs of a Murder Man* (London: Jarrolds, 1931), 101–109.
44. *NYT*, April 21, 1903; December 31, 1911.
45. Flynn, *The Barrel Mystery*, 20–1. Madonia and DePriema had lived in Lercara, Sicily.
46. *NYT*, April 17, 1903, April 20, 1903.
47. *NYT*, April 28, 1903; Pitkin, *The Black Hand*, 50.
48. *New York Tribune*, April 27, 1903.
49. *New York Tribune*, May 2, 1903; *NYT*, May 8, 1903; Flynn, *The Barrel Mystery*, 14–15; Bowen and Neal, *The United States Secret Service*, 40; Joseph W. Gavan, "The Clue of the Crucifix," in *Strange and Mysterious Cases* (London: Hutchinson and Co., 1929), 106–121; Carey, *Memoirs of a Murder Man*, 101–109.
50. New York Municipal Archives, DA Record of Cases, NY County Case no. 42841 (1903).
51. Inzerillo pleaded guilty to a naturalization offence in 1903, and was questioned in 1909 over a "Black Hand" bomb explosion. It was reported that Inzerillo had been "more or less under the surveillance of the police" since the Madonia business (Circuit Court of the United States of America for the Southern District of New York, U.S. v. Pietro Inzeriello CRM D-3555, October 11, 1904; *New York Tribune,*March 16, 1909; *Sun*, March 17, 1909).
52. *NYT*, February 24, 1908; *Washington Post*, February 23, 1908; *Stevens Point Daily Journal*, June 14, 1909.
53. *New York Herald*, April 26, 1914, May 24, 1914, July 19, 1914; *Sun*, March 14, 1909; NARA, RG 87, daily reports of agents, vol. 4, reel 593, November 27, 1913.
54. Zarcone's death certificate could not be found in the Danbury municipal archives.

55. *Danbury Evening News*, July 31, 1909. Pietro Zarcone, a son of Giovanni's brother Antonino, and a godfather to Ignazio Lupo, was questioned in April 1909 for the shotgun killing in Brooklyn of Andrea Gambino, an Italian barber "known to the police as a Black Hand man." It was said that Gambino had tried to extort $50 from Zarcone; they fired on each other and Gambino was shot and his head smashed in (*NYT*, April 15, 1909). Domenico Zarcone, brother of Giuseppa Zarcone, Giovanni's wife, was brought to Police Headquarters in 1914 for having extorted a ransom for the return of 5 years old Giuseppe diFiore (*NYT*, July 3, 1914). Carlo Zarcone, also related to Giovanni Zarcone, was a convicted counterfeiter in Milwaukee (*Milwaukee Sentinel*, January 15, 1909).
56. *Danbury News*, July 29, 1909.
57. Information supplied by Marina Riggio.
58. New York Municipal Archives, DA Record of Cases, NY County Case no. 42841 (1903); *World*, February 2, 1904.
59. *Wilkes-Barre Record*, October 24, 1905, October 27, 1905. Flynn believed that a "kinsman" of DePriema slew Petto, avenging the murder of Madonia (Flynn, *The Barrel Mystery*, 22).
60. *The Wilkes-Barre Record*, October 24, 1905.
61. Named after Ignatz Florio, the son of Vincenzo Florio, a businessman with broad interests in Sicily Florio inherited "the greatest fortune in Italy," but also a cadre of Mafiosi who protected his villa in Palermo (Dickie, *Cosa Nostra*, 113).
62. Division of Old Records, Surrogates Court, Manhattan, Certificate of Incorporation.
63. Flynn, *The Barrel Mystery*, 29–31; *Washington Post*, May 3, 1914.
64. 1910 trial transcript, 302; Flynn, *The Barrel Mystery*, 32.
65. *NYT*, December 11, 1910.
66. Lawrence Richey Papers, *Black Hand Confessions 1910*, Herbert Hoover Presidential Library, box 1 (hereafter Richey Papers), 76 (new pagination).
67. In March 1909, Giglio sold his share of Cina's farm to Giuseppe Palermo.
68. 1910 trial transcript, 89–119.
69. Richey Papers, 68 (new pagination).
70. 1910 trial transcript, 89–119.
71. Thomas Hunt, "'Clutch Hand' Confusion" www.onewal.com/ Peterson also believed that Lupo was the chief of the group (Virgil W. Peterson, *The Mob* [Ottowa, Illinois: Green Hill Publishers, 1983], 127).
72. Richey Papers, 55 (new pagination).
73. *NYT*, April 3, 1910.
74. *New York Times* (hereafter *NYT*) December 5, 1908.
75. Richard Hammer, *The Illustrated History of Organized Crime* (Philadelphia: Courage Books, 1989), 11.
76. Herbert Asbury, *The Gangs of New York* (New York: Paragon House, 1990 [1st ed. 1927]), 267–8.
77. His Declaration of Intention said March 1878. Pitkin replicated Flynn's error in thinking that Lupo came from Corleone (Pitkin, *The Black Hand*, 210). Neither was his surname Saietta; that was his mother's maiden name.
78. The Italian police were unable to ascertain if Salvatore was "in any way related" to Giuseppe Morello of Corleone.
79. 1910 trial transcript, 462–470; Archivio di Stato di Palermo, Serie: Archivio Generale—Questura di Palermo Busta 1584 Fascicolo 352, report of April 2, 1909. In Liverpool, Lupo may have stayed in the now demolished "Italian" quarter (for its history, read Terry Cooke, *Little Italy* [Liverpool: The Bluecoat Press, 2002]).

80. 1910 trial transcript, 22–82.
81. Flynn, *The Barrel Mystery*, 111–168.
82. 1910 trial transcript, 22–82.
83. Ibid., 205–6.
84. *NYT*, November 16, 1909.
85. *Poughkeepsie Evening Star*, January 6, 1910.
86. NARA, RG 204, section 29 page 46 box 681—Giuseppe Palermo.
87. NARA, RG 60, entry 112, straight numerical file / file no. 145199.
88. 1910 trial transcript, 22–82.
89. Ibid., 89–119; Bowen and Neal, *The United States Secret Service*, 41–4.
90. *New York Herald*, May 10, 1914.
91. Richey Papers, 1, 20 (new pagination). Yet Comito's story of being tricked into traveling to Highland when he assumed he was going to Philadelphia, in another direction entirely, rings hollow. He was trusted enough, moreover, to be allowed to travel to New York and to learn the secrets of the gang. Furthermore, Comito's regard for the safety of his common-law-wife, who remained with the forgers as a form of "hostage," evaporated once he was arrested.
92. *NYT*, February 20, 1910.
93. *NYT*, February 20, 1910; Bowen and Neal, *The United States Secret Service*, 47.
94. NARA, RG 60, entry 112, straight numerical file / file no. 145199; NARA RG 204, 230/40/1/3/Box 956—Ignazio Lupo.
95. FBI, report *La Causa Nostra*, New York Office, January 31, 1963. Philadelphia's ceremony, forbidding counterfeiting, was one example.
96. John Cummings and Ernest Volkman, *Goombata* (Boston: Little, Brown, 1990), 138.
97. United States Penitentiary, Atlanta, Georgia, admission registers, Manhattan death certificate no. 14831 (1924); NARA, RG 204, Section 29, page 46, box 681—Giuseppe Palermo; NARA, RG87, daily reports of agents, reel 590, July 1911.
98. U.S. Penitentiary, Atlanta, Georgia, admission registers.
99. *NYT*, July 16, 1936.
100. NARA, RG 204, 230/40/1/3 box 956—Ignazio Lupo, 16.
101. *NYT*, February 23, 1938.
102. *NYT*, July 16, 1936. Not for running "a grape racket, as well as running a lottery" (Downey, *Gangster City*, 40).
103. *NYT*, July 16, 1936. For the documents used in building this case, consult NARA, RG 204, 230/40/1/3 box 956—Ignazio Lupo.
104. Flynn for instance was said to have traced "sixty murders to Lupo's gang . . ." (Asbury, *The Gangs of New York*, 268).
105. Archivio di Stato di Palermo, Serie: Archivio Generale—Questura di Palermo Busta 1584 Fascicolo 352, report of April 2, 1909.
106. Salvatore Canale, a shoemaker, was found dead in January 1907 on East 106th Street. He was believed to be a victim of the Black Hand (*NYT*, January 20, 1907). Canale was a member of the Corleone branch of the Order of Foresters.
107. No trace of Sperizza could be found on databases. But Salvatore "Svelazo," the owner of a "tawdry little groggery" on Forsyth Street, was shot down on December 11, 1906. Petrosino "had reason to believe" that Svelazo was a cousin of Madonia murdered in 1903 (RG 204, 230/40/1/3 box 956; *NYT*, December 12, 1906).
108. Dickie, *Cosa Nostra*, 205.
109. Flynn, *The Barrel Mystery*, 97.
110. Fred J. Cook, *Mafia!* (London: Coronet, 1973), 39.

111. FBI *Mafia Monograph* Section 1, Sicily, July 1958, 97.
112. Diego Gambetta, *The Sicilian Mafia* (Cambridge, MA.: Harvard University Press, 1993), 111; Fentress, *Rebels and Mafiosi*, 173.
113. NARA, RG 87, daily reports of agents, March 15, 1903.
114. NARA, RG 87, daily reports of agents, reel 117, vol. 30, February 22–3, 1912.
115. 1910 trial transcript, 47–50; Richey Papers, 54 and 57 (new pagination).
116. Richey Papers, 72 (new pagination).
117. Thomas Hunt, "Caged Wolves" www.cagedwolves.com.
118. Fred D. Pasley, *Muscling In* (London: Faber and Faber, 1932), 146; Giuseppe Selvaggi, *The Rise of the Mafia in New York* (Indianapolis: The Bobbs-Merrill Company, 1978), 44–5. One particular allegation persists. Antonio Morello was, according to Chandler, the elder brother in the Morello family, and "credited with some thirty New York murders in the 1890s," among them that in December 1892 of Francesco Meli, "a Neapolitan member of the city's only Camorra family, which held sway in Brooklyn."(Chandler, *The Criminal Brotherhoods*, 111–113). But Antonio Morello was no relative of Joseph Morello, and Mele was not a *Camorrista*. Antonio Morello told the police in 1892 that a crippled Mele had insulted his wife, provoking him to shoot Mele. Morello was sentenced in February 1893 to 20 years for the manslaughter of Mele (New York Municipal Archives newspaper clippings, unattributed article dated December 5, 1892; *New York Tribune,* December 5, 1892; *NYT* February 4,1893; John Jay College, New York Court of General Sessions, The People of the State of New York against Antonio Morello, case no.33).
119. Downey, *Gangster City*, 18.
120. Passenger manifest, series M237, roll 603, frames 566–567.
121. Dino Paternostro, *L'antimafia Sconosciuta Corleone 1893–1993* (Palermo: La Zisa, 1994), 28; Dickie, *Cosa Nostra*, 160–1.
122. Materials supplied by Rosanna Rizzo. Angela Terranova (nee Piazza) died in June 1941 in Queens, New York, of diabetes mellitus. She had been living with Salvatrice Lupo, the wife of the imprisoned Ignazio (Queens, New York, death certificate no. 4526 [1941]).
123. Uncorroborated evidence suggests that when the Morello family were Louisiana-resident, their first child by named Calogero died and a second infant, born a few years later, was given the identity (information supplied by Mike Dash). In the event, Calogero was shot to death in 1912 in a quarrel on East 114th Street, by a lieutenant of the "Kid Baker" gang, in retribution for the murder of his nephew Benedetto Madonia in 1903. It resulted in the retaliatory murder by Nick Morello, Tommaso Lomonte and others of Rocco Cusano or Osano (*NYT*, April 17, 1912, June 5, 1912; *New York Herald*, April 17, 1912). Downey asserted that Charles Morello was killed with Charles "Charlie Baker" Marrone, getting Marrone confused with Charles "Kid Baker" Barlo or Barles (*Gangster City*, 32–3). Marrone, a former bodyguard for Amadeo Buonomo (Chapter 5), was shot down early December 1913 in a saloon on East 115th Street (*NYT*, December 6, 1913; *New York Herald*, December 6, 1913).
124. Lena Morello's sister, Mary Salemi (1909–1995) was married to Charles Sberna, executed in January 1939 for the first degree homicide of policeman John Wilson in 1937 during a botched hold up (*NYT*, November 23, 1938).
125. Petition for Naturalization, November 1911; Declaration of Intention no. 2579 (1907); NARA, RG 129, Inmate Case No. 2882, Giuseppe Morello. Lima died 1922 in California.
126. New York County Declaration of Intention, no. 120119; Petition for Naturalization, no. 105297: Vincenzo Terranova.

127. Manhattan marriage certificate no. 18591 (1913); 1910 trial transcript, 404–5.
128. Manhattan marriage certificate no. 251 (1903).
129. Teresa Catania entered America in 1904 with her mother, Marianna "Anna" Mendolia, the mother of Antonio Catania, father of "Joe the Baker," and his brother James "Jimmy the Baker" Catania. Their mother, the wife of Antonio Catania, was Francesca "Francis" LaScala. It made "Joe the Baker" Catania a nephew to Ciro Terranova through his marriage to Tessie Catania.
130. Gleaned from Ellis Island arrival records, the 1910 Manhattan census and Giuseppe Catania's 1931 death certificate. "Jimmy the Baker" Catania (born 1900) acquired a piece of the Italian bakery racket from the murdered Giuseppe in the 1930s, and remained an influence in the Mafia around Arthur Avenue in the Bronx.
131. Antonio Saltamaggio was born in Corleone, 1873.
132. Marriage certificate, Pointe-a-La-Hache, Louisiana, February 1894.
133. *NYT*, June 20, 1923.
134. 1910 trial transcript, 456–460.
135. Flynn, *The Barrel Mystery*, 33.
136. Ibid., 210–211.
137. NARA, RG 87, daily reports of agents, reel 591, New York, 34, February 14, 1912.
138. Flynn, *The Barrel Mystery*, 207–11.
139. NARA, RG 87, daily reports of agents, reel 591, New York, 34, February 25, 1912.
140. Said to be a "Black Hand Leader," Dispenza was shot three times through the head in the Chicago "Black Hand Belt" of Milton Avenue and Hobbie Street in January 1914 (*Chicago Tribune*, January 24, 1914; Chicago death certificate no. 5071 [1914]).
141. *New York Tribune*, November 16, 1909.
142. *NYT*, November 16, 1909.
143. The twists and turns were reported in great depth in the *Daily States-Item*, July 5, 1902; *Daily Picayune*, June 13, 1902; *Daily States*, June 12, 1902 and *Sun*, August 23, 1903.
144. *Daily Picayune*, June 14, 1902.
145. *Times-Picayune*, May 7, 1903.
146. Flynn, *The Barrel Mystery*, 212–4.
147. NARA, RG 129, Inmate Case No. 2882, Giuseppe Morello.
148. Other information showed him as born from 1878 to 1880, yet his mausoleum gave 1876. DiGiorgio's Declaration of Intention stated his year of birth as 1880, which was consistent with the census data.
149. *Daily Picayune*, June 12, 1908.
150. DePeche, or DiPicki, had only been in New Orleans for about two weeks. The case against him was abandoned when DiGiorgio testified that he did not recognize the accused as his assailant (*Times-Picayune*, May 14, 1916, January 31, 1917).
151. *Los Angeles Times*, July 19, 1921; *Chicago Daily Tribune*, May 14, 1922; *Times-Picayune*, May 14, 1922; *New Orleans States*, May 14, 1922. Indicative of ties between DiGiorgio and the Los Angeles Mafia elite, in 1923 the DiGiorgio family sold their Menlo Park, California, property to the wife of Rosario DeSimone, another Los Angeles Mafia boss, for $10,000.
152. *Chicago Daily Tribune* and *Chicago Journal-American*, May 14, 1922.
153. *New York Herald*, May 8, 1903; Flynn, *The Barrel Mystery*, 9–11.
154. John S. Kendall, "Blood on the Banquet," *Louisiana Historical Quarterly*, XX11 (1939): 819–22.

155. Kendall, "Blood on the Banquet", 832.
156. NARA, RG 87, daily reports of agents 1875–1936 (Microfilm Publication T-915) roll 116, report of June 19,1900.
157. Flynn, *The Barrel Mystery*, 214.
158. *Times-Picayune*, January 12, 1932.
159. Texas Crime Investigating Committee records, 1950–1953 Special Reports, "History of the Mafia, 1950".
160. *Daily Picayune*, July 10, 1902.
161. *NYT*, May 8, 1903; *New York Herald*, May 8, 1903.
162. NARA, RG 87, daily reports of agents 1875–1936, (Microfilm publication T-915) roll 108, report of March 23, 1903.
163. Proven by his November 5, 1905 marriage certificate, the June 21, 1908 baptism record of Rosalie Marchese, and Coroner's office record no. 485, Parish of Orleans Coroner's Office; *Daily Picayune*, July 22, 1910.
164. *Daily Picayune*, April 15, 1910, July 22, 1910.
165. *Daily Picayune*, July 22, 1910.
166. Flynn, *The Barrel Mystery*, 212–4.
167. *Times Picayune*, November 21, 1915.
168. The 1891 New Orleans City Directory shows that Charles Matranga lived at 150 S. Basin, and his henchman Rocco Geraci at 165 S. Basin. Vincent Moreci and his brothers also lived there (Soards' 1891 *New Orleans City Directory*).
169. Kendall, "Blood on the Banquet", 833 and 836.
170. *Daily Picayune*, March 13, 1910.
171. *Daily Picayune*, March 12, 1910.
172. *Times Picayune*, November 20, 1915.
173. US District Court Eastern District of Louisiana, Declaration of Intention, 1924; Metairie Cemetery, New Orleans records.
174. NARA, RG 129, inmate case no. 2882 (Giuseppe Morello). On November 7, 1919; November 30, 1919; January 4, 1920; January 15, 1920.
175. FBI report dated July 11, 1967, Bureau File no. 92–6054.
176. Chandler, *The Criminal Brotherhoods*, 185.
177. Flynn, *The Barrel Mystery*, 213.
178. U.S. Congress, Senate, Special Committee to Investigate Organized Crime in Interstate Commerce, *Third Interim Report*, 82nd Congress 1st Session 1951, 77; Michael Kurtz, "Political Corruption and Organized Crime in Louisiana," *Louisiana History* 29 (1988): 243–8.
179. Mark H. Haller, *Bootleggers and American Gambling 1920–1950*, in Commission on the Review of the National Policy Toward Gambling, Appendix 1 (1976) 113.
180. U.S. Congress Senate Special Committee to Investigate Organized Crime in Interstate Commerce, *Third Interim Report*, 82nd Congress 1st Session, 1951, 147.
181. New York State, *Interim Report of the Joint Legislative Committee on Government Operations on the Gangland Meeting in Apalachin, N.Y.* (1958) 113.
182. U.S. Congress, Select Committe on Improper Activities in the Labor or Management Field hearings, 85th Congress 2nd Session, 1958, 12221.
183. Donald R. Cressey, *Theft of the Nation* (New York: Harper and Row, 1969), 25.
184. Joseph L. Albini, *The American Mafia* (New York: Appleton-Century-Crofts, 1971), 154–5.
185. Anton Blok, *The Mafia of a Sicilian Village 1860–1960* (Cambridge: Polity Press, 1974), xxi; Robert M. Lombardo, "The Black Hand" *Global Crime*, vol. 6 (2004), 271.

186. Humbert S. Nelli, *The Italians in Chicago, 1880–1930* (New York: Oxford University Press 1970), 152–3.
187. United States Senate, Select Committee on Improper Activities in the Labor or Management Field, *Investigation of Improper Activities in the Labor or Management Field* hearings 85th Congress 2nd Session 1958, 12220–1.
188. Dickie, *Cosa Nostra*, 196.
189. Edwin Fenton, *Immigrants and Unions, a Case Study* (New York: Arno Press, 1975), 1.
190. Bonanno, *Bound by Honor*, 6.
191. Referring to the Morello and Williamsburg, Brooklyn, groups. A third organization, bossed by Salvatore D'Aquila, is far less well known about (see Chapter 6).
192. FBI, *Mafia Monograph,* July 1958, Section 1, Sicily.
193. Blok, *The Mafia of a Sicilian Village*, 137.
194. Henner Hess, "The Traditional Mafia," in *Organized Crime: A Global Perspective* Robert J. Kelly (ed.) (Totowa, New Jersey: Rowman and Littlefield, 1986), 120.
195. Fentress, *Rebels and Mafiosi*, 173.
196. Ibid., 179.
197. Ibid., 174.
198. Cressey, *Theft of the Nation*, 142.
199. Henry A. Zeiger, *The Jersey Mob* (New York: New American Library, 1975), 151.
200. For the Sicilians, read Giovanni Falcone, *Men of Honour* (London: Warner Books, 1992), 89.
201. In the Bonanno Family of Brooklyn, a simple show of hands at a meeting of the full membership decided who should become the "Father." For groups in Sicily, ordinary members elected the *caporegimes*, and the upper layer bosses selected the *capo* (Bonanno, *A Man of Honour*, 139; *Paese Sera,* September 19, 1963; *L'Ora*, January 22–23, 1962).
202. *Paese Sera*, September 19, 1963; confirmed in Bonanno, *A Man of Honour*, 139; and Peter Maas, *Underboss* (New York: HarperCollins, 1997), 205–6.
203. *L'Ora*, January 22–23, 1962.
204. *Paese Sera*, September 19, 1963.
205. *Paese Sera*, September 21, 1963; Nicolo Gentile, *Translated Transcription of the Life of Nicolo (E) Gentile, Background and History of the Castellammarese War and Early Decades of Organized Crime in America*, 33 and 35.
206. Gambetta, *The Sicilian Mafia*, 146, 262–70.
207. NARA, RG 60, Joseph Valachi, *The Real Thing*, 303–4.
208. U.S. Congress, Senate, Committee on Government Operations, Permanent Subcommittee on Investigations, *Organized Crime and the Illicit Traffic in Narcotics* hearings 88th Congress 1st Session 1963, 183–4.
209. *Newsday*, May 13, 2006; U.S. Congress, Senate, Committee on Governmental Affairs, *Organized Crime: 25 Years After Valachi* hearings 100th Congress 2nd Session 1988, 223–4; Bonanno, *Bound by Honor*, 20; Celeste A. Morello, *Before Bruno Book 2—1931–1946* (2001), 70. The revelations of Lenny Strollo of Youngstown are printed in the *Cleveland Scene*, April 8–14, 1999.
210. FBI, New York Office, October 20, 1967.
211. *L'Ora*, January 22–3, 1962.
212. James Fentress and Chris Wickham, *Social Memory* (Oxford: Blackwell, 1992), 195.
213. Dickie, *Cosa Nostra*, 35–6, 81–2; Fentress, *Rebels and Mafiosi*, 215–6.

214. Dickie, *Cosa Nostra*, 157–161.
215. Pino Arlacchi, *Men of Dishonor* (New York: William Morrow and Co., 1992), 69.
216. Leonid Kolosov, "Rome," in *Undercover Lives*, Helen Womack (ed.) (London: Weidenfeld and Nicholson, 1998), 24.
217. FBI, Chicago Office, September 25, 1967.
218. See for example the Chicago charts prepared by the Federal Bureau of Narcotics in the 1960s contained in NARA, RG 170 Accession No. 170–74-4, BNDD "Subject Files of the Bureau of Narcotics and Dangerous Drugs," box 52.
219. Humbert S. Nelli, *The Business of Crime* (New York: Oxford University Press, 1976), 139.
220. Fentress, *Rebels and Mafiosi*, 217–8; Dickie, *Cosa Nostra*, 36, 82, 161.
221. Letizia Paoli, *Mafia Brotherhoods* (New York: Oxford University Press, 2003), 113.
222. Dickie, *Cosa Nostra*, 36.
223. FBI *La Causa Nostra* New York Office, January 31, 1963; Henry A. Zeiger, *The Jersey Mob* (New York: New American Library, 1975), 157. Larasso was too young, born 1926 in Elizabeth, to have known of this from direct experience. His parents were from Ribera, Sicily, as was the leadership of the Elizabeth *borgata*.
224. Richey Papers, 58, 70, 81 (new pagination). Lieutenant Antonio Vachris and his Italian Squad colleague Crowley finished Petrosino's mission in Italy, collecting and bringing back to New York criminal certificates and photographs of hundreds of Italian ex-convicts who had transferred recently to America (Pitkin, *The Black Hand*, 125). However, they arrived in New York too late to be of use.
225. Richey Papers, 58–9, 70 (new pagination).
226. Richey Papers, 81 (new pagination).
227. *Sun*, March 14, 1909; *NYT*, March 14, 1909; Reid, *Mafia*, 172; Nelli, *The Business of Crime*, 97.
228. *NYT*, March 16, 1909; *Sun*, March 16, 1909; *Sun,* February 20, 1909.
229. *NYT*, February 20, 1909, March 14, 1909.
230. Petacco, *Joe Petrosino*, 31.
231. *NYT* March 14, 1909; *New York Tribune*, March 14, 1909.
232. Finazzo was accused in 1907 of the death of Epifanio Arcara, but the case was dismissed (Archivio di Stato di Palermo, Serie: Archivio Generale—Questura di Palermo Busta 1584 Fascicolo 352, report of May 16, 1909; Petacco, *Joe Petrosino*, 191). Acara, the owner of a skirt factory at 339 East 107th Street where Angelo Gagliano was to establish his laundry (Chapter 4), was found on September 22, 1907 with stab wounds to his body. One theory the police advanced was that he was murdered because of an affair with a woman who had recently married (*NYT*, September 23, 1907; Manhattan death certificate no. 30845 [1907]).
233. Archivio di Stato di Palermo, Serie: Archivio Generale—Questura di Palermo Busta 1584 Fascicolo 352, report of May 16, 1909. In 1949, the Federal Bureau of Narcotics had Enea under investigation as a narcotics smuggler from Italy, where he lived "as a wealthy man and frequents daily restaurants and other public places." (NARA, RG 170, records of DEA Office of Enforcement Policy Classified Subject Files 1932–1967) Reid called Enea "Don Pasquale in Palermo," the "High priest of the world Mafia," and indicated that he died in 1952, "going blind" (Reid, *Mafia*, 44).
234. U.S. Senate, U.S. Immigration Commission, *Report*, [1911] XXXVI, 282–3.

235. Emmanuele Notarbartolo was slain on February 1, 1893, but a warrant for the arrest of Fontana and Raffaele Palizzolo was issued in 1899. Palizzolo, a member of the Palermo provincial and municipal councils, a leading member of the Bank of Sicily's general council, and on the boards "of a number of civic committees and charities," had links to four Mafia *cosche* in Palermo province. Palizzolo and Fontana were tried in Bologna and convicted, Palizzolo for organizing both murders, Fontana for executing Notarbartolo. But at a retrial in 1903, both of the accused were acquitted (Fentress, *Rebels and Mafiosi*, 236–245; Dickie, *Cosa Nostra*, 135–52).

236. Archivio di Stato di Palermo, Serie: Archivio Generale—Questura di Palermo Busta 1584 Fascicolo 352, report of April 2, 1909.

237. *New York Herald*, July 19, 1914.

238. Archivio di Stato di Palermo, Serie: Archivio Generale—Questura di Palermo Busta 1584 Fascicolo 352, report of April 2, 1909.

239. The court of appeal declared the charge annulled, for lack of evidence, in 1890.

240. Archivio di Stato Palermo, Serie: Archivio Generale-Questura di Palermo, Busta 1584 Fasciolo 352.

241. Archivio di Stato di Palermo, Serie: Archivio Generale-Questura di Palermo Busta: 1584 Fascicolo: 352, report of April 2, 1909. Petacco argues that Carlo Costantino "changed his name to Giovanni Pecoraro" in America (Petacco, *Joe Petrosino*, 13), but their ages do not match, nor do their towns of birth.

242. *New York Tribune*, April 30, 1903; Petacco, *Joe Petrosino*, 13.

243. *World*, March 15, 1909.

244. Richie Papers, 45–6.

245. *NYT*, March 8, 1923. His son Michele Pecoraro was a Gambino Family member who moved to California, dying there, of natural causes, in 1967.

246. Petacco, *Joe Petrosino*, 169. Ceola's "final report," as detailed by Petacco (170–4), differs in several respects from the report presently available in the Archivio di Stato, Palermo. The original report is used here.

247. Petacco, *Joe Petrosino*, 176.

248. Archivio di Stato di Palermo, Serie: Archivio Generale—Questura di Palermo Busta 1584 Fascicolo 352, report of April 3, 1909. Salvatóre Brancaccio, according to Petacco, appeared in a letter of September 1901 that was found among Cascioferro's papers. In it, Brancaccio invited Cascioferro, Morello, Costantino, Fontana, and two others "to eat a plate of macaroni together." Census records show Brancaccio residing on Navy Street, Brooklyn, born in 1850. A family man, he died in 1923 of natural causes (1900, 1910 Brooklyn censuses, Brooklyn death certificate no. 398 [1923]).

249. www.ellisisland.org/.

250. Archivio di Stato di Palermo Serie: Archivio Generale—Questura di Palermo Busta 1584 Fascicolo cc. 196, report of April 29, 1909.

251. Archivio di Stato di Palermo, Serie: Archivio Generale—Questura di Palermo Busta 1584 Fascicolo 352, report of April 2, 1909; *NYT*, April 7, 1909.

252. In 1911, Morello was reported to have given his lawyer information "in regard to Petrosino's murder," but that he had refused to sign a deposition or statement (*Atlanta Constitution*, January 7, 1911; January 12, 1911; Petacco, *Joe Petrosino*, 185–6). This was denied by Flynn, the Warden of Atlanta Penitentiary, and by the legal firm in charge of getting Morello's depositions. The New York Police Department and the Secret Service also had no information to that effect either. Efforts by this writer to find the alleged confession were unsuccessful. Fulton County (Atlanta) Superior Court files contained an uninformative Petition for Commission to take deposition of G. Morello, "In the matter of Carlo Costantino, et al. charged with murdering Giuseppe Petrosino, now pending in the Court of Appeal, Italy." (Minutes of Fulton

Superior Court, Book 66, 1910–1912, 150–151, Civil Records Room, Fulton County Court House).

253. Richey Papers, 59 (new pagination).

254. Richey Papers, 60 (new pagination); *Washington Post,* June 21, 1904; Flynn, *The Barrel Mystery,* 52–101.

255. Richey Papers, 30–1. A probable reference to the bandit Francesco Paolo Varsalona, who then operated in the area.

256. Flynn, *The Barrel Mystery,* 52–101.

257. 1910 trial transcript, 352–3.

258. Giglio married Giovanna Cina, Salvatore Cina's sister, and Cina married Vincenzo Giglio's sister Rosalia. Rosalia Cina (nee Giglio) was the daughter of Ignazio Giglio, and the brother of Angelo S. Giglio, who became a future power in Tampa, Florida, organized crime. Angelo Giglio, a nephew of Tampa Mafia bosses Santo Trafficante Sr. and Jr., was shot to death in 1952. Ignazio Italiano was from Santo Stefano Quisquina, Sicily (Chapter 6).

259. 1910 trial transcript, 442–9.

260. Richey Papers, 87 (new pagination); Flynn, *The Barrel Mystery,* 142.

261. Denoting a relationship to the Minore family of Castellammare del Golfo (NARA, RG 204, section 29, page 46, box 681, Giuseppe Palermo). Palermo's alias may have originated from the Castellammare born Giacoma Saracina, who in 1906 stayed with Palermo in Manhattan. Never-married Palermo used the Saracina pseudonym throughout his life in New York, and it was the name he was buried under. A photograph in Joseph Bonanno's book of "Turi" Saracino may or may not be of Palermo, though Palermo was incarcerated when the photograph was supposedly taken (1910).

262. Certificate of Incorporation, index no. 792/1906C.

263. NARA, RG 204, section 29, page 46 box 681, Giuseppe Palermo.

264. Richey Papers, 77 (new pagination).

265. Richey Papers, 86 (new pagination); Flynn, *The Barrel Mystery,* 141.

266. Richey Papers, 51. (new pagination).

267. Cressey, *Theft of the Nation,* 46.

268. FBI memorandum of January 7, 1965 from Mr. Gale to Mr. Belmont, subject "La Cosa Nostra."

269. Individuals "made" in Sicily may have "sneaked" into American Mafia organizations. Such was reportedly the case of Cesare Bonventre into the Galante (formerly Bonanno) Family in 1977 (Lee Lamothe and Adrian Humphreys, *The Sixth Family* [Ontario: John Wiley and Sons, 2006], 67).

270. Paolo Violi in Montreal told Sicilian member Pietro Sciarra in 1974 that Sicilians in Canada were put on a five years probatory period before being considered ready for membership, so "that everyone can see what he's like" (Quebec Police Commission, *The Fight Against Organized Crime in Quebec,* 32, 90–1).

271. The President's Commission on Organized Crime observed, "It is now apparent that while Sicilian and American groups may cooperate in some crimes, there is, in fact, an independent Sicilian organization in the United States." (President's Commission on Organized Crime, *The Impact: Organized Crime Today* [April 1986] 51–7).

272. Francis A. J. Ianni, "Mafia and the Web of Kinship," in *An Inquiry into Organized Crime,* Luciano J. Iorizzo (ed.), The American Italian Historical Association, 1970, 11–12.

273. Francis A. J. Ianni with Elizabeth Reuss-Ianni, *A Family Business* (London: Routledge and Kegan Paul, 1972).

274. Vito Cascioferro mythically conspired to launch the Black Hand and other protection rackets in America, or created "an organizational structure for the Palermo-New York circuit" (Petacco, *Joe Petrosino*, 95).

275. Richey Papers, 81 (new pagination).

NOTES TO CHAPTER 4

1. New York Supreme Court (Criminal Branch) The People of the State of New York against Joseph Cohen, Jacob Cohen, David Jacobs and Abe Graff, John Jay College case no. 3244, 2, 4–6, (hereafter Cohen transcript).

2. Refer to John Hutchinson, *The Imperfect Union* (New York: E.P. Dutton, 1972); Jonathan Kwitny, *Vicious Circes* (New York: W.W. Norton, 1979). Illustrative of ignorance of the Baff case was a remark by the President's Commission on Organized Crime that the New York "meat industry" was first infiltrated in the 1920s by Jack "Legs" Diamond. (President's Commission on Organized Crime, *The Edge* (1986) 215.)

3. *New York Times (*hereafter *NYT)*, November 26, 1914.

4. New York Municipal Archives (hereafter NYMA), John P. Mitchel papers, box 218, "Interview with Mr. Joseph Cohen, generally known as King of the Chicken Pullers" (December 26, 1914).

5. NYMA, John P Mitchel papers, box 218, *The Baff Murder* (January, 1915).

6. *New York Tribune*, November 28, 1914.

7. *NYT*, December 16, 1914.

8. Mike Dash, *Satan's Circus* (New York: Crown Publishers, 2007), 335.

9. *NYT*, February 9, 1916.

10. *NYT*, December 27, 1914.

11. Marilynn Johnson, *Street Justice: A History of Police Violence in New York City* (Boston: Beacon Press, 2003), 109. The Wickersham Commission labeled New York "one of the worst spots where brutal methods have been used relentlessly" (*NYT*, August 11, 1931).

12. Denis Tilden Lynch, *Criminals and Politicians* (New York: The Macmillan Company, 1932), 173–182.

13. *NYT*, April 14, 1934.

14. *NYT*, September 9, 1934.

15. New York State Organized Crime Task Force, *Corruption and Racketeering in the New York City Construction Industry Final Report* (December 1989) Chapter 2.

16. NYMA, *The Baff Murder*.

17. *NYT*, April 5, 1910.

18. *NYT*, August 16, 1911; Annual Report of the Chief Clerk of the District Attorney's Office, County of New York, Year Ending December 31, 1911.

19. *NYT*, November 26, 1914.

20. NYMA, *The Baff Murder*.

21. *Cohen transcript*, 4.

22. *NYT*, November 26, 1914, November 28, 1914.

23. *New York Herald*, February 13, 1916.

24. *Cohen transcript*, 8.

25. Ibid., 2559.

26. NYMA, *The Baff Murder*.

27. NYMA, John P. Mitchell Papers, box 218, *In Re Poultry Situation The Rule of Gangsters.*
28. Philip B. Reister, *Report on the Live Poultry Industry in Greater New York* (1935) 123.
29. *NYT,* May 11, 1916; May 12, 1916.
30. Reister, *Live Poultry Industry,* 121.
31. *NYT,* March 23, 1917.
32. *NYT,* August 3, 1920.
33. *NYT,* August 6, 1920.
34. *NYT,* February 7, 1926.
35. *NYT,* August 3, 1928.
36. *NYT,* August 21, 1928.
37. *NYT,* November 22, 1929.
38. *NYT,* December 19, 1929.
39. New York State Organized Crime Task Force, *Corruption and Racketeering in the New York City Construction Industry Final Report* (December 1989); read also James B. Jacobs, *Mobsters, Unions, and Feds* (New York University Press, 2006).
40. Robert J. Kelly, *The Upperworld and the Underworld* (New York: Kluwer Academic, 1999), 6–7.
41. Jenna Weissman Joselit, *Our Gang* (Bloomington: Indiana University Press, 1983), 130.
42. New York State Organized Crime Task Force, *Corruption and Racketeering in the New York City Construction Industry: Interim Report* (June 1987), 44.
43. New York State Organized Crime Task Force, *Corruption and Racketeering in the New York City Construction Industry Final Report* (December 1989), 57.
44. Joselit, *Our Gang,* 130.
45. NYMA, *The Baff Murder.*
46. NYMA, "The Business of Chicken Pulling Intimidation," *In Re Poultry Situation: The Rule of Gangsters.*
47. NYMA, *The Baff Murder.*
48. NYMA, *In Re Poultry Situation: The Rule of Gangsters.*
49. Kelly, *The Upperworld and the Underworld,* 50.
50. Although Dewey said, "It was rumored, but could not be proven, that Tootsie Herbert was somehow an offshoot of Lepke and Gurrah" (Thomas E. Dewey, *Twenty Against the Underworld* [Garden City, NY: Doubleday, 1974], 315). Volkman wrongly asserted that Herbert was a partner of Gagliano *Famiglia* underboss Gaetano Lucchese in the 1930s (Ernest Volkman, *Gangbusters* [Boston: Faber and Faber, 1998], 36–7).
51. In a second recorded incident, among those seized in 1933 after wrecking the offices of the S.S. and B. Live Poultry Corporation was Nunzio Arra, a future Lucchese Family member. But Arra was working for Joseph Weiner, attempting to enforce another monopoly on the industry (*NYT,* April 7, 1933). Weiner was found guilty and jailed for up to 3 years in July 1933 for conspiracy to coerce.
52. Edwin Fenton, *Immigrants and Unions* (New York: Arno Press, 1975), 250.
53. Peter Reuter, *Racketeering in Legitimate Industries* (US Department of Justice, October 1987), 24; Rick Cowan and Douglas Century, *Takedown* (New York: G. P. Putnam's Sons, 2002).
54. New York State Crime Commission, *Interim Report of Evidence Adduced by the State Crime Commission Relating to Six Brooklyn Locals of the*

International Longshoremen's Association (September, 1952); New York State Crime Commission, *Public Hearings (No. 5)* 3, 1508–14.

55. Fenton, *Immigrants and Unions*, 259, 285, 586.
56. Proceedings First Constitutional Convention National Organizing Committee . . . April 11–12, 1943, 19, 43.
57. *NYT*, August 19, 1943. The McClellan Committee in 1958 also accused the union of operating "undemocratic" practices.
58. *NYT*, July 14, 1966.
59. *NYT*, April 14, 1966.
60. Joel Seidman, *The Needle Trades* (New York: Farrar and Rinehart, 1942 [1970 reprint]), 43.
61. Federal Writers' Project, *The Italians of New York* (New York: Arno Press, 1969), 191.
62. Rochester University, "Garment Trucking Racket and Marinelli" *Thomas Dewey Papers*, Series 1, box 90.
63. *NYT*, May 11, 1933, March 20, 1937, June 11, 1937. The Jewish Buchalter was the premier New York labor racketeer of the age.
64. Dewey, *Twenty Against the Underworld*, 305.
65. U.S. Congress, Select Committee on Improper Activities in the Labor or Management Field, *Investigation of Improper Activities in the Labor or Management Field*, hearings 85th Congress 2nd Session 1958, 12478.
66. Joseph F. O'Brien and Andris Kurins, *Boss of Bosses* (New York: Simon and Schuster, 1991), 208. U.S. Congress, Senate, *Organized Crime in America* hearings, 98th Congres, 1st Session, 1983, 260.
67. *Nation*, November 9, 1935.
68. Dewey, *Twenty Against the Underworld*, 314–5. In November 1928, Charles Herbert, a local 440 *schochtim* union agent and brother of "Tootsie" Herbert, was shot through the shoulder and head in an east side restaurant. His bodyguard, Irving Walker, was killed (*NYT*, November 17, 1928).
69. *NYT*, February 2, 1937.
70. *NYT*, August 18, 1937.
71. U.S. Congress, Senate Committee on Commerce, *Crime and Criminal Practices* 75th Congress 1st Session, Report No. 1189, 1937, 16–7.
72. Ralph Salerno, *The Crime Confederation* (Garden City: Doubleday and Co., 1969), 94–5.
73. State of California, *Third Interim Report* of the Special Crime Study Commission on Organized Crime (January 31, 1950), 23.
74. Patrick Downey, *Gangster City: The History of the New York Underworld 1900–1935* (New Jersey: Barricade Books, 2004), 142.
75. Domenico Nardone and Carmine diPaolo were indicted for the assault in November 1914 of a schoolboy in the Bronx by wounding him with gunfire (Bronx County Clerk Criminal Branch no. 849, 1914, People Against Domenico Nardone and Carmine diPaolo).
76. *NYT*, April 5, 1916.
77. *NYT*, April 6, 1916.
78. *NYT*, April 6, 1916.
79. *NYT*, April 10, 1916.
80. *New York Herald,* April 7, 1916.
81. New York Supreme Court (Criminal Branch), *The People of the State of New York against Frank Ferrara* (April 1916), John Jay College no. 3239, 502 (hereinafter Ferrara transcript).
82. *NYT*, April 8, 1916.
83. *Ferrara transcript, 105.*
84. Ibid., 9.

85. Ibid., 13–14.
86. Ibid., 10–17.
87. Ibid., 105–109.
88. Ibid., 177.
89. *NYT*, April 4, 1916.
90. Ibid., 19.
91. Ibid., 186.
92. Ibid., 237.
93. Ibid., 239.
94. Ibid., 240.
95. Ibid., 574.
96. Ibid., 580.
97. Ibid., 302.
98. Ibid., 306.
99. Ibid., 320.There were too many people around or the police were watching and Baff was wary.
100. *Ferrara transcript*, pp.324–330.
101. Ibid., 325.
102. Ibid., 329.
103. Ibid., p. 338.
104. Ibid., p. 331.
105. Ibid., p. 397.
106. Ibid., p. 455.
107. Ibid., 478–500.
108. Ibid., 380.
109. Ibid., 382–3, 408.
110. Ibid., 387–8, 412.
111. Ibid., 388, 409.
112. Ibid., 579, 582–3.
113. *NYT*, April 14, 1916.
114. *Cohen transcript*, 2343.
115. Ibid., 2337.
116. Ibid., 12–14.
117. Ibid. 285. Cardinale and defendant David Jacobs were slaughterhouse partners on 108th Street, financed by Joseph Cohen. But their venture failed in 1914 (*Cohen transcript*, 19).
118. *Cohen transcript*, 2573.
119. Ibid., 336.
120. Ibid., 2574.
121. Ibid., 2578.
122. Ibid., 20.
123. Ibid., 113.
124. Ibid., 128.
125. Ibid., 2614.
126. Ibid., 25.
127. *New York Herald*, July 7, 1917; *Cohen transcript*, 2615.
128. *Cohen transcript*, 147.
129. Ibid., 174–5. Arichiello was driving the wagon, while Joe Greco was inside with a rifle. But two boys played with the wagon, and Baff was absent from the Market.
130. Ibid., 132.
131. Ibid., 133.
132. Ibid., 2624.
133. Ibid., 24.

134. Ibid., 248.
135. Ibid., 380.
136. Ibid., 471.
137. Ibid., 381.
138. Ibid., 775.
139. Ibid., 776.
140. Ibid., 603.
141. Ibid., 604.
142. Ibid., 607.
143. Ibid., 236.
144. Ibid., 610.
145. Ibid., 662–3.
146. *NYT*, July 6, 1917; *Cohen transcript*, 2536.
147. Ibid., 692.
148. Ibid., 752.
149. Ibid., 691.
150. Ibid., 2532.
151. *Cohen transcript*, 593.
152. *Cohen transcript*, 730.
153. Ibid., 592.
154. Ibid., 593.
155. Ibid., 614–9.
156. Ibid., 620.
157. *NYT*, August 18,1917. Jacob Cohen and David Jacobs were acquitted.
158. Sorro was jailed for up to 20 years in August of 1921.
159. *NYT*, April 9, 1932.
160. *Cohen transcript*, 2336.
161. *NYT*, February 2, 1916.
162. *Cohen transcript*, 2533.
163. World War One draft card, 1917; US census return for 1910; 1925 New York State census for 225 and 227 East 107th Street.
164. *Cohen transcript*, 880–1.
165. Ibid., 877.
166. NYMA, New York Court of General Sessions Minutes.
167. *Cohen transcript*, 629.
168. Ibid., 795. "Tita" Rizzotto, born 1896 in Italy, was probably a brother of Jack Dragna's wife Frances Rizzotta. Tita vanished from sight after 1917.
169. Declaration of Intention no. 86096 (1914). "Tom" Dragna was born 1888 and died in 1977.
170. Ellis Island passenger arrivals, November 1, 1910.
171. *Los Angeles Times*, November 19, 1915.
172. *Los Angeles Daily Times*, November 20, 1915. See also In the Superior Court of the State of California, The People of the State of California vs. Jack Rizzotto, information (1915).
173. In order to resolve confusion caused between two men with the name of Angelo Gagliano and linked to the Gagliano-Greco saloon on East 107th Street, various documents were consulted. Angelo Gagliano, a self-described "janitor" in the saloon, was born 1870, eight years before the Gagliano figure in the Baff investigation, and had different parents and wife. The "janitor" Gagliano died in 1936, not in 1954, when the Baff identity died (Bronx death certificate no. 5187 (1936); *NYT*, February 6, 1936, New York State census, 1915).
174. *Ferrara transcript*, 103–5, 118.

175. NYT, May 18, 1961; *New York Tribune*, May 19, 1916; New York DA Record of Cases, cal. no. 19561, The People vs. Angelo Gagliano (1916).
176. Born 1878 in Corleone. Spelled as "Lippolito" Greco on his passenger arrival record.
177. Petition for Naturalization, November 1911; Declaration of Intention no. 2579 (1907); U.S. National Archives and Records Administration (hereafter NARA), RG 129, Inmate Case No. 2882, Giuseppe Morello; NARA, RG 87, daily reports of agents, New York, vol.34, March 13, 1912 (kindly supplied by Mike Dash).
178. Certificate of Naturalization no. 783470 (1912).
179. U.S. Circuit Court of Appeals for the Second Circuit, The United States of America vs. Giuseppe Calicchio et al., *Transcript of Record* (hereinafter 1910 trial transcript) 432.
180. Sylvester worked with Ciro Terranova as a plasterer, and around 1907 drove for his counterfeiting colleague Ignazio Lupo in respect to Lupo's wholesale grocery firm on Mott Street, delivering to co-conspirator Antonio Cecala's store at 9 Spring Street (1910 trial transcript, 380–388) Salvatore Valenti, Ciro Terranova's partner in mid 1910s plastering, lived in the 231 107th Street accommodation (Trow's Directory of the Boroughs of Manhattan and the Bronx, 1915, 1917–8 and 1915 New York State Census).
181. U.S. Congress, Senate, Committee on Government Operations, Permanent Subcommittee on Investigations, *Organized Crime and the Illicit Traffic in Narcotics*, hearings 88th Congress 1st Session 1963 (hereafter OCN), 1039; NARA, RG 170, DEA Records Subject Files of the Bureau of Narcotics and Dangerous Drugs 1916–1970, "International List of Persons Known to be Engaged in the Illicit Traffic in Narcotic Drugs," New York Major Violator No. 133. Born 1879 in Corleone, in July 1932, Marsalisi was arrested in Turkey on a narcotic charge but jumped bail and disappeared. In 1942, Marsalisi was fined in another narcotics conspiracy case (NARA, RG 170, Records of the DEA, Bureau of Narcotics and Dangerous Drugs, Subject Files of the Bureau of Narcotics and Dangerous Drugs, 1916–1970).
182. *Cohen transcript*, 841.
183. Ibid., 837.
184. Ibid., 338.
185. Gagliano was an uncle by marriage to Cardinale, and Gagliano was an uncle of Cardinale's wife. Cardinale married the daughter of Vincenzo Gagliano, Angelo's brother (*Cohen transcript*, 412–3).
186. To differentiate them from another Mafia connected Rao family, including Joey Rao, living around East 116th Street.
187. Joseph "Pip the Blind" Gagliano was known as one of the more important "uptown" heroin traffickers (NARA, RG 170, Entry 71A-3555, DEA Office of Enforcement Policy Classified Subject Files, 1932–1967, report of February 3, 1961; Pennsylvania State University, Anslinger Collection, box 4, folder 1 *Gagliano Narcotic Case*; OCN, 137). After his sentencing for selling Mexican heroin, on April 10, 1947, Joseph Gagliano committed suicide in Bronx County jail (*NYT*, April 11, 1947).
188. For Chicago, read John Landesco, *Organized Crime in Chicago* (Chicago:The University of Chicago Press, 1968); Robert M. Lombardo, *Organized Crime and the Concept of Community* (no date). Boston is covered in William Foote Whyte, *Street Corner Society* (The University of Chicago Press, 1955).
189. Gus Tyler, *Organized Crime in America* (Ann Arbor: The University of Michigan Press, 1962), 365.
190. Salerno, *The Crime Confederation*, 94.

191. Thomas A. Firestone, "Mafia Memoirs: What They Tell Us About Organized Crime," *Journal of Contemporary Criminal Justice* 9, (1993): 198–201. Upcomers such as the Gallo brothers—Joseph (born 1929) and Larry (born 1927)—had no experience or perhaps knowledge of the Mafia tradition in Italy. Their formative years were spent on the mean streets of Bensonhurst, Brooklyn.

192. Peter Maas, *Underboss* (New York: HarperCollins, 1997).

193. George Anastasia, *Blood and Honor* (New York: William Morrow, 1991).

194. Joseph D. Pistone with Richard Woodley, *Donnie Brasco* (London: Sidgwick and Jackson, 1988),131.

195. FBI, *La Causa Nostra*, New York Office January 31, 1963; FBI, *La Causa Nostra*, SAC, Philadelphia, May 14, 1963; FBI, *La Cosa Nostra*, Los Angeles Office, December 13, 1963; FBI, *Criminal "Commission"*, SAC, San Francisco, February 4, 1963.

196. Daniel Bell, "Crime as an American Way of Life," in *The End of Ideology* (New York: The Free Press, 1962), 146–7; Francis A. J. Ianni, *Ethnic Succession in Organized Crime Summary Report* (US Department of Justice, 1973), 1; Nelli, *The Business of Crime*, 255.

197. U.S. Congress, Senate, Committee on Government Operations, Permanent Subcommittee on Investigations, *Organized Crime and Illicit Traffic in Narcotics: Report* 1965, 13.

198. Francis A. J. Ianni with Elizabeth Reuss-Ianni, *A Family Business* (London: Routledge and Kegan Paul, 1972), 77.

199. FBI, *Mafia Monograph* (July 1958) section 1, 65.

200. Ianni, *A Family Business*, 69.

201. Joseph Bonanno with Sergio Lalli, *A Man of Honour* (London: Andre Deutsch, 1983), 63.

202. Celeste A. Morello, *Before Bruno Book 1—1880–1931* (1999), 88–9.

203. "DiLeonardo Testimony" http://www.onewal.com/nw-dileo.html.

204. FBI, *La Cosa Nostra*, New York Office July 1, 1963.

205. Bonanno, *A Man of Honour*, 76.

206. According to his book (p. 44), Gentile joined a U.S. Family in about 1905 in Philadelphia, a mere two years after first setting foot in America. Gentile never even hints at his year of initiation in Sicily.

207. Nick Gentile, *Vita di Capomafia* (Rome: Editori Riuniti, 1963), 41.

208. *Los Angeles Times*, May 26, 1917.

209. Refer also to the Cleveland situation in the mid 1970s (Ovid Demaris, *The Last Mafioso* [New York: Times Books, 1981], 333).

210. Again exemplified by the earlier career of Cleveland and Los Angeles figure Aladena "Jimmy" Fratianno, including stints as an union "organizer," that involved threatening parking lot owners and picket line mayhem (Demaris, *The Last Mafioso*, 9).

211. OCN, 136–9, 152.

212. *Organized Crime and Illicit Traffic in Narcotics: Report*, 11.

213. Valachi, *The Real Thing*, 4.

214. OCN, 134.

215. OCN, 142–3.

216. Probably born in Pescasseroli, Italy, in 1900, Petrelli came from the same streets as Valachi, and was widely acquainted with "all the mobs in New York City and then some." (Valachi, *The Real Thing*, 192). Between 1914 and 1929, Petrelli was arrested 25 times, including for juvenile delinquency, burglary, larceny, robbery and homicide. In 1926, he was locked up for 138 days, for receiving a stolen car. Petrelli's decision to thereafter abandon

robbery for the rackets may have been affected by this, his first substantial jail time (*NYT,* October 16, 1926). Petrelli was killed by gunfire in December 1953 in a bar on East 183rd Street. He was in the country illegally but had slipped back unnoticed (*New York Daily News,* December 10, 1953).
217. OCN, 158.
218. Bonanno, *A Man of Honour,* 124.
219. OCN, 165–6; Valachi, *The Real Thing,* 285.
220. FBI file on Shillitani, FOIPA Request no. 0988692.
221. OCN, 152.
222. Shillitani was jailed on May 25, 1932 for 20 years in Bronx County Court for the first-degree manslaughter of Benedetto Bellino. In December 1951, he was jailed for 15 further years on narcotics and counterfeiting charges that involved big-time traffickers Joseph Orsini and Francois Spirito (*NYT,* September 22, 1952). Shillitani apparently retired from criminal endeavors in the wake of a two years stretch imposed in August 1964 for contempt of court before a grand jury investigating organized crime (FBI report of July 25, 1963 from the New York office, file no. 92–2739). He died in a North Shore (Miami Beach) hospice in September 1990.
223. NYMA, DA Record of Cases, case no. 192657 (1932).
224. Manhattan death certificate no. 20894 (1921).
225. *World,* March 24, 1924.
226. *NYT,* February 8, 1924.
227. *NYT,* January 7, 1932.
228. New York DA Record of Cases no. 192657 (1932). Santuccio moved permanently from the Bronx to Hartford, Connecticut, in 1952, and died during surgery in Hartford Hospital on August 31, 1983, aged 83.
229. Bonanno, *A Man of Honour,* 46.
230. Bonanno, *A Man of Honour,* 49, 54.
231. OCN, exhibit 14E.
232. Brooklyn marriage certificate no. 15417 (1931).
233. FBI, New York Office, field office file no. 92–3603, March 29, 1965; *NYT,* June 13, 1970.
234. Bonanno, *A Man of Honour,* 105.
235. Detailed in Chapter 8.
236. Information on Domingo has previously appeared in David Critchley, "Buster, Maranzano and the Castellammare War, 1930–1931," *Global Crime* 7, no. 1 (2006) 46–51. Taylor and Francis, http://www.tandf.co.uk.
237. Downey, *Gangster City,* 159. May's was the most extensive effort to uncover the facts about Buster. But May's conclusion, that Buster's persona was invented to deflect attention from Valachi's misdeeds, is comprehensively refuted by the information collected here (Allan May, "Buster from Chicago—Revealed?" www.americanmafia.com, June 10, 2002).
238. Bonanno, *A Man of Honour,* 105.
239. Family History Library INTL Film 1962779. His grave headstone says that Domingo was born on March 29, 1910, while his birth certificate gives April 1910.
240. In Chicago they lived on Oak Street, nicknamed "Death Corner because of the large number of shootings, stabbings, and murders that were committed there." (Robert J. Kelly, *Handbook of Organized Crime in the United States* [Westport, Conn.: Greenwood Press, 1994], 181).
241. From 1915, Southern Italians were drawn increasingly to Benton Harbor from Chicago, so that by 1930 there were 450 Italians living in Berrien County, of which Benton Harbor was an administrative division (Lloyd T. Keenan,

A Civic and Industrial Survey of the City of Benton Harbor, Michigan [Benton Harbor Chamber of Commerce, 1925], 7; Russell M. Magnaghi, *Italians in Michigan* [East Lansing: Michigan State University Press, 2001], 20).

242. *News-Palladium*, July 18, 1931.
243. *News-Palladium*, September 10, 1928, September 11, 1928, September 13, 1928; *Chicago Tribune*, September 14, 1928.
244. *News-Palladium*, August 24, 1926, August 24, 1927, September 21, 1927, April 16, 1929.
245. *News-Palladium*, April 29, 1927; Berrien County Circuit Court Case no. 2162, criminal calendar page 602, box 602.
246. *News-Palladium*, January 1, 1926.
247. *St. Joseph Herald-Press*, October 22, 1927.
248. *News-Palladium,* October 24, 1927.
249. *St. Joseph Herald-Press*, October 22, 1927. The man reported as Louie Vieglo may have been Louis G. Veglia, born 1901 in Acerno, Italy, who died January 2000 in Port Charlotte, Florida.
250. *News-Palladium*, October 22, 1927.
251. Ibid., September 24, 1927.
252. Ibid., November 2, 1927.
253. *News-Palladium*, August 30, 1929.
254. State of Illinois County of Cook Inquest on the Body of Antonio Domingo (August 31, 1929) Inquest no. 95.
255. *News-Palladium*, August 30, 1929. Patsy Spilotro, the father of celebrity Chicago and Las Vegas crime figure Tony Spilotro, owned the restaurant in which Tony died, a hangout in 1929 for Circus Café Gang members (William F. Roemer, *The Enforcer* [New York: Donald I. Fine, 1994], 12).
256. 1930 US Census, New Castle Township, Westchester County, New York.
257. Office of the Chief Medical Examiner of the City of New York, Borough of Manhattan, case no. 2987 (1933).
258. *NYT*, May 31, 1933, June 1, 1933.
259. Gentile, *Vita di Capomafia*, 37.
260. Bonanno, *A Man of Honour*, 69–70.
261. Mark H. Haller, "Bureaucracy and the Mafia: An Alternative View," *Journal of Contemporary Criminal Justice* 8, no. 1 (1992).
262. Gaetano Lomonte and Rosa Portoghese witnessed Ciro Terranova's wedding (Manhattan marriage certificate no. 8192 [1909]).
263. *New York Herald*, January 7, 1917. The two Lomontes were also rumoured to have taken over leadership of the Morellos for a brief period after 1910 (*Washington Post*, February 5, 1922).
264. NARA, RG 87, daily reports of agents, vol. 41 reel 593, November 10–11, 1913.
265. NARA, RG 87, daily reports of agents, vol. 43, reel 594, May 26–7, 1914 (reference kindly supplied by Mike Dash).
266. *NYT*, May 24, 1914; Manhattan death certificate no. 16903 (1914).
267. Dimino came from Sciacca, born in about 1885.
268. Gentile, *Vita di Capomafia*, 69–70.The circumstances of Lomonte's fall as described by Gentile, in a barber's shop, does not accord with contemporaneous newspaper accounts.
269. Captain William A. Jones, "Murder for Sale," *True Detective Mysteries* IV, no. 4 (January 1926): 22+.
270. Manhattan death certificate no. 29667 (1915); *World*, October 14, 1915; *NYT,* October 14, 1915. Rosalia Lomonte may have been a sister of the Terranova brothers, born in 1892.

271. New York Supreme Court (Criminal Branch), The People of the State of New York against Antonio Impoluzzo, John Jay College case no. 3240.
272. *NYT*, February 11, 1916, February 15, 1916; Jones, "Murder for Sale."
273. *Fort Wayne Daily News*, March 10, 1917.
274. *NYT*, October 14, 1908.
275. *NYT*, October 31, 1909.
276. William J. Flynn, *The Barrel Mystery* (New York: The James A. McCann Co., 1920), 141.
277. Giuseppe Selvaggi, *The Rise of the Mafia in New York* (Indianapolis: Bobbs-Merrill, 1978), 25.
278. The whereabouts of the establishment varied between accounts, ranging from East 107th Street to East 125th Street (Tom Hunt, "Clutch Hand Confusion," http://www.onewal.com, 2002). Nash noted "the anguished screams of the victims" tortured and killed in the stable (Jay Robert Nash, *World Encyclopedia of Organized Crime* (London: Headline Books, 1992), 617). Thompson and Raymond noted "at least" 23 who were slaughtered there (Thompson and Raymond, *Gang Rule in New York*, 4). Asbury portrayed how the "infamous Murder Stable" (on East 125th Street) "became noted as the scene of more killings than any other spot in America" (Herbert Asbury, *The Gangs of New York* [New York: Paragon House, 1990], 267).
279. Downey, *Gangster City*, 82.
280. Manhattan death certificate no. 32570 (1911); *New York Herald*, October 30, 1911.
281. *NYT*, March 21, 1912.
282. Selvaggi, *The Rise of the Mafia*, 24.
283. Spinelli was known as "The Hetty Green" of Harlem's Little Italy. Valachi recalled how he used to sleep in the stable because of "bed bugs" in his 108th Street home situated nearby. Spinelli would hit Valachi when she caught him sleeping in the stable, "with a broom handle." (Valachi, *The Real Thing*, 10.)
284. *New York Herald*, March 21, 1912; Downey, *Gangster City*, 82–3.
285. *New York Herald*, February 20, 1914; *New York Tribune*, February 20, 1914.
286. In December 1912, two horses were stolen in Manhattan, worth $900. Andrew Rege and Louis Lazzara were seized, Lazzara for driving the wagon. The animals were found in their possession as they were about to be shipped to New Haven by boat (NYMA, DA Record of Cases 91763, The People vs. Andrew Rege and Luigi Lazzara [1912]).
287. New York Municipal Archives, DA Record of Cases no. 95249, The People vs. John Russomano.
288. *New York Herald*, October 8, 1915; Manhattan death certificate no. 29017 (1915).
289. *New York Tribune*, April 30, 1913; The People of the State of New York vs. Santa Barbara with Joseph Viserti, indictment filed June 13, 1913 for first degree murder.
290. *NYT*, October 9, 1915.
291. World War One draft card. Viserti became another bootlegging victim when, in 1921, he was shot down on Broome Street after a man broke into the restaurant he was in and opened fire from a doorway. Viserti had, police asserted, grown rich in the booze supplying business (*New York Daily News*, October 14, 1921; *New York Tribune,* October 14, 1921).
292. New York City property records, conveyances book (no. 91), *NYT*, August 2, 1924.
293. *NYT*, January 7, 1931.
294. *NYT*, May 16, 1915.

295. Albert Fried, *The Rise and Fall of the Jewish Gangster in America* (New York: Holt, Rinehart and Winston, 1980), 3–6.
296. *NYT*, May 12, 1915, May 13, 1915, May 14, 1915.
297. Joselit, *Our Gang*, Chapter 6.
298. *Cohen transcript*, 2532.
299. Charles Rappleye and Ed Becker, *All American Mafioso* (New York: Doubleday, 1991), 50–1.
300. *NYT*, February 27, 1930. Stefano LaSalle belonged to both the Morello and Reina groups and Reina operated in Morello's turf. Reina's links to the Morellos are outlined in this chapter.
301. FBI, SAC, San Diego to FBI Director, June 9, 1967; Demaris, *The Last Mafioso*, 68, 104.
302. New York State Crime Commission, *Proceedings Pursuant to the Governor's Executive Order of March 29, 1951*, 141.

NOTES TO CHAPTER 5

1. Sicilians "vastly outnumber" Calabrians in America. In 1912 New York City, according to Train, "you will find seven or eight Mafiosi." (*McClure's Magazine*, May 1912).
2. Within the Navy Street section of Brooklyn, Italians comprised about 70 percent of the population in 1907 (Janet Andrews, *The Italian Communities in South Brooklyn and Fort Greene: 1880–1917* (New York: Fordham University, 1974), 3, 6).
3. Humbert S Nelli, *From Immigrants to Ethnics* (New York: Oxford University Press, 1983), 65.
4. These are held by the New York State Archives as New York State Court of Appeals records: The People of the State of New York against Frank Fevrola, Case on Appeal (1921); The People of the State of New York against Angelo Giordano, 231 New York 633 pt. 1; The People of the State of New York against Pellegrino Marano: Case on Appeal, 232 New York 569 pt. 1; The People of the State of New York against Aniello Parretti: Cases and Points, 2939 (1921); The People of the State of New York against Tony Parretti, Case on Appeal, 244 N.Y. 527 pt. 1; The People of the State of New York against Alessandrio Vollero, Case on Appeal, 226 New York 587 pt. 1. The John Jay College, Lloyd Sealy Library, holds: New York City and County Court of General Sessions, The People vs. Ciro Terranova (1918). These trial records are referred to in the chapter by the surnames of the defendants, e.g. as the "Terranova transcript."
5. Virgil W. Peterson, *The Mob* (Ottowa, Illinois: Green Hill Publishers, 1983), 128.
6. Thomas Monroe Pitkin and Francesco Cordasco, *The Black Hand* (Totowa, NJ: Littlefield, Adams and Co., 1977), 209.
7. Ed Reid, *Mafia* (New York: Random House, 1952), 189–91.
8. David Leon Chandler, *The Criminal Brotherhoods* (London: Constable, 1976), 124–6.
9. Patrick Downey, *Gangster City: The History of the New York Underworld 1900–1935* (New Jersey: Barricade Books, 2004), 34–6.
10. Humbert S. Nelli, *The Business of Crime* (New York: Oxford University Press, 1976), 128–131.
11. Arrigo Petacco, *Joe Petrosino* (London: Hamish Hamilton, 1974), 72–3. Alfano was born in Naples in 1874.
12. *New York Times* (hereafter *NYT*) April 20, 1907.
13. *NYT*, September 11, 1910.
14. *NYT*, July 9, 1912.

15. Accounts of the Viterbo trial are contained in *Outlook* magazine, July 29, 1911, August 5, 1911; *Cosmopolitan Magazine*, August 1911; *Edinburgh Review*, October 1911; *McClure's Magazine*, November 1911; and in editions of the *New York Times*.
16. *NYT* May 5, 1911. Frank Denico's October 1912 death in Brooklyn was attributed to his appearance against the Camorra bosses at Viterbo (*NYT*, October 12, 1912).
17. Downey, *Gangster City*, 34–5. A similar type of assertion is made by Chandler in *The Criminal Brotherhoods*, 125.
18. *Terranova transcript*, 72. DeMaria was slain on May 9, 1916, on Navy Street (Brooklyn death certificate no. 10146 [1916]); *Nevada State Journal*, November 10, 1917. Alessandro Vollero "and his associates" were not indicted as Nelli claimed (*The Business of Crime*, 133). Daniello was caught by alert police action, and not by a Morello gang tip off (Chandler, *The Criminal Brotherhoods*, 124).
19. Felix DeMartini, "Blowing the Works in New York's Underworld" *True Detective Mysteries* X1 no. 1 (April 1929). Andrew Ricci was murdered in a President Street, Brooklyn, cigar store on November 14, 1917 (Brooklyn death certificate no. 22069 [1917]).
20. In a typical instance, Daniello said "We were talking amongst ourselves, and they would say, Now, that one and that one of the gang went over to Philadelphia to do this job, that one and the other one of the gang went over to Long Island to do some other job, this one and that one went up to Yonkers to do this job" (*Giordano transcript*, 231).
21. It stating that Pellegrino Morano "chief of the Navy St. Harlem and Coney Island gangs," ordered the deaths of Gallucci, Charles Lombardi, and Salvatore DeMarco, the last at the hands of Joseph Nazzaro. Morano "himself" slew Nick Morello and Eugene Ubriaco (Westchester County Archives, District Attorney files, box 349 folder 3).
22. *New York Herald*, October 20, 1914.
23. *Vollero transcript*, 472–3.
24. *New York Herald*, December 1, 1916.
25. DeMartini, "Blowing the Works," 95.
26. Pitkin, *The Black Hand*, 203–9.
27. *New York Herald*, September 3, 1912. Zaraca, nicknamed "Sharkey," preyed off pushcart peddlers in the locality.
28. *Fort Wayne Journal-Gazette*, December 12, 1915.
29. *NYT*, December 17, 1912.
30. *New York Herald*, December 16, 1912; *NYT*, December 17, 1912.
31. Court of General Sessions for New York County, The People of the State of New York against John Russomano (John Jay College case no. 1856) 216–7.
32. New York County Declaration of Intention no. 69824 (1913).
33. Court of General Sessions for New York County, The People of the State of New York against John Russomano (John Jay College case no. 1856) 278.
34. *Washington Post*, February 19, 1913; *New York Herald*, April 10, 1913; Downey, *Gangster City*, 85.
35. Arthur Woods, "The Problem of the Black Hand," *McClure's Magazine*, XXX111 (May 1909) 46. During the trial of John Russomano in 1914, Gallucci disputed a version of his police record in Naples proffered by the prosecution, claiming it was a case of mistaken identity (Court of General Sessions for New York County, The People of the State of New York against John Russomano [John Jay College case no. 1856] 237–242). In 1898, Gallucci was a suspect in the murder of Josephine Inselma on Elizabeth Street, portrayed by the police as her "lover" (*NYT*, April 19, 1898).

36. *NYT*, July 27, 1913; *New York Herald*, July 27, 1913. Gallucci blamed jealousy for the many allegations made against him. Local murders attributed to Gallucci were actually the result of "quarrels among the blackmailers themselves. They gamble, which leads to fighting, and they dispute the division of spoils." (*New York Herald*, January 7, 1917.)
37. New York Municipal Archives (hereafter NYMA), DA Record of Cases no. 95249, The People vs. John Russomano.
38. Although the newspapers claimed it was a new establishment, the place was known as the Café Degli in 1913.
39. *Washington Post*, May 18, 1915.
40. *New York Herald*, May 18, 1915; *NYT*, May 18, 1916.
41. *New York Herald*, May 18, 1915.
42. Surrogates' Court, New York County, In the Matter of Proving the Alleged Last Will and Testament of Giosue Gallucci (1917).
43. *Morano transcript*, 738.
44. *Morano transcript*, 246.
45. *Terranova transcript*, 97.
46. *Giordano transcript*, 169, people's exhibit No. 1, 195.
47. *Giordano transcript*, people's exhibit no. 1, 169.
48. *Giordano transcript*, people's exhibit no. 1, 186.
49. *Giordano transcript*, people's exhibit no. 1, 183.
50. *New York Herald*, July 1, 1917.
51. *Terranova transcript*, 92.
52. *Giordano transcript*, people's exhibit no. 1, 190.
53. *Morano transcript*, 296.
54. *Marano transcript*, 341–2.
55. *Giordano transcript*, people's exhibit no. 1, 178.
56. *Terranova transcript*, 125.
57. *Terranova transcript*, 5.
58. *Terranova transcript*, 196.
59. *New York Tribune*, July 21, 1916; *New York Herald*, July 21, 1916.
60. *Terranova transcript*, 148.
61. *Terranova transcript*, 9.
62. *Terranova transcript*, 140.
63. NYMA, Court of General Sessions, New York County, People of the State of New York against John Fetto, cal. no. 23837.
64. *Terranova transcript*, 147.
65. *New York Tribune*, October 14, 1916; *NYT*, October 14, 1916.
66. *Giordano transcript*, people's exhibit no. 1, 185.
67. *Morano transcript*, 692.
68. *Giordano transcript*, 187.
69. *Morano transcript*, 576.
70. *Morano transcript*, 486.
71. *Vollero transcript*, 423.
72. *Giordano transcript*, people's exhibit no. 1, 186.
73. *Vollero transcript*, 119.
74. *Morano transcript*, 269; *Vollero transcript*, 123, 472.
75. *Vollero transcript*, 123.
76. *Tony Parretti transcript*, 205.
77. *Morano transcript*, 196.
78. *Vollero transcript*, 127.
79. *Tony Parretti transcript*, 46.
80. *Tony Parretti transcript*, 539–544.
81. *Vollero transcript*, 60.

82. *NYT*, September 8, 1916.
83. *Vollero transcript*, 60.
84. *Giordano transcript*, 208; *Tony Parretti transcript*, 46.
85. *Vollero transcript*, 1000.
86. *Tony Parretti transcript*, 243–4, 505, 548.
87. *Giordano transcript*, 130.
88. *Giordano transcript*, 184; *Tony Parretti transcript*, 258.
89. *Morano transcript*, 144.
90. *Giordano transcript*, 18.
91. *Fevrola transcript*, 409.
92. *Giordano transcript*, 20.
93. *New York Herald*, October 6, 1916. Notaro stood trial in 1917 for the murder and was acquitted.
94. *New York Herald*, July 28, 1913.
95. "What they call Joe Chuck and Coney Island," it was whispered, "may be together with DeMarco." (*Terranova transcript,* 44; *Aniello Parretti transcript*, 121). Because of doubts over where their loyalty lay, Navy Street made sure that Nazzaro and Frank Clemente were absent when DeMarco was shot in July 1916 (*Terranova transcript*, 139).
96. *Fevrola transcript*, 445.
97. *Aniello Parretti transcript*, 58.
98. *Aniello Parretti transcript*, 60.
99. *Fevrola transcript*, 258.
100. *Aniello Parretti transcript*, 60.
101. Luigi DeMarco (May 17, 1916), Giuseppe Bellasana (October 6, 1916) and Antonio Lavelli (January 1917).
102. Brooklyn death certificate no. 10636 (1915).
103. *Morano transcript*, 249; *NYT*, September 10, 1915.
104. Daniello was reported as saying that "Nicholas Avrono" was a Navy Street victim on July 22, 1916 (DeMartini, "Blowing the "Works"). Salvatore Coppola and Alberto Altieri were accused of the homicide of "Michael Averno," and were due to stand trial in 1918. But the disposition of the case is unknown. "Michael Averna" is listed in the New York City death index and Ellis Island passenger records show a Michele Averna setting foot in New York in 1906, headed for his brother in law, interestingly to be found at the "Murder Stable" on East 108th Street.
105. Manhattan death certificate no. 31795 (1916).
106. Manhattan death certificate no. 5087 (1917).
107. Press coverage was dominated by the carnage of the Great War.
108. *Tony Parretti transcript*, 492, 518–9.
109. *Terranova transcript*, 172–3.
110. *Terranova transcript*, 74; Westchester County Archives, District Attorney files, box 349, folder 3.
111. Luigi Caruso was found shot in the head at Ninth and Fitzwater Streets on April 24, 1917. Frank Loscalzo was arrested (*Philadelphia Record*, April 25, 1917). Attempts to discover more about the others killed in Philadelphia were unproductive.
112. *Vollero transcript*, 192; *Giordano transcript*, 199; *Terranova transcript*, 82.
113. *Morano transcript*, 85.
114. *Morano transcript*, 239–240; *Vollero transcript*, 193–202.
115. *Terranova transcript*, 84.
116. *Morano transcript*, 537–9.
117. Sgroia recounted: "They say, we go up to Harlem and get a room, and somebody else say, "We are going to poison them.""(*Tony Parretti transcript*, 249).

118. *Vollero transcript*, 83–6.
119. Avellino, Benevento, Caserta, Naples and Salerno.
120. As Alfonso Pepe on the vessel Germania, though Daniello testified that he entered American illegally as a fugitive from Italian justice.
121. For the second time.
122. Date given on his 1930 census return.
123. But a Giacomo Notaro from Saviano landed in New York in 1903, aged 22.
124. *Giordano transcript*, Appellant's Brief, 399–400.
125. *Aniello Parretti transcript*, 80; *Giordano transcript*, 212.
126. *Morano transcript*, 254; *Terranova transcript*, 124.
127. *Giordano transcript*, 209.
128. *Morano transcript*, 256.
129. *Morano transcript*, 260.
130. *Terranova transcript*, 180.
131. *Morano transcript*, 270; *Aniello Parretti transcript*, 112; *Fevrola transcript*, 465.
132. *Vollero transcript*, 134.
133. Marano ran the Santa Lucia in 1906–9, and 1913–1916 (*Tony Parretti transcript*, 413).
134. *Vollero transcript*, 961–4.
135. *Morano transcript*, 51–3; *Vollero transcript*, 965–6.
136. *Morano transcript*, 52–3.
137. FBI, *La Causa Nostra,* New York Office, January 31, 1963, 19.
138. Westchester County Archives, District Attorney files, statement made by Salvatore Mara on March 20, 1913.
139. *Vollero transcript*, 534.
140. *Morano transcript*, 134.
141. Pitkin, *The Black Hand*, 209.
142. *Vollero transcript*, 659, 664, 692–3.
143. *Vollero transcript*, 206, 247; *Giordano transcript*, 204–5.
144. *Tony Parretti transcript*, 520.
145. *Morano transcript*, 104–5.
146. *Tony Parretti transcript*, 284–5.
147. *NYT*, January 11, 1914.
148. *NYT*, March 31, 1911; April 17, 1911.
149. *NYT*, April 17, 1911; "The Camorra in Modern Italy," *Edinburgh Review,* (October 1911), 379–396.
150. *Giordano transcript,* 182; *Terranova transcript*, 94, 101.
151. *Vollero transcript*, 80.
152. *Vollero transcript,* "A List of the Principal Persons Whose Names Appear in the Record," 51.
153. Ibid., 55.
154. *Terranova transcript*, 175.
155. *Vollero transcript*, 13.
156. *Vollero transcript*, 269–76.
157. *Vollero transcript*, 821.
158. *Giordano transcript*, people's exhibit no. 1, 170.
159. *Morano transcript*, 482.
160. *Vollero transcript*, 251, 820.
161. *Vollero transcript*, 558.
162. *Terranova transcript*, 4–5.
163. *Vollero transcript*, 82; *Vollero transcript*, 61.
164. *Vollero transcript*, 414–5; *Morano transcript*, 401.
165. *Vollero transcript*, 73.

166. *Vollero transcript*, 177.
167. *Vollero transcript*, 415–6, 418.
168. *Morano transcript*, 401.
169. *Vollero transcript*, 417.
170. Celentano was characterized by one reporter as "the biggest man in policy circles in the United States, "whose power was "greater even than that of Giosue Gallucci." (*Washington Post*, March 4, 1917).
171. *Vollero transcript*, 75.
172. *Morano transcript*, 303–4.
173. *Morano transcript*, 293.
174. *Vollero transcript*, 76–9, 167–172, 173–4, 437–449; *Morano transcript*, 434–5.
175. *Vollero transcript*, 81.
176. *Vollero transcript*, 502.
177. Alan A. Block, *East Side West Side* (Cardiff: University College Cardiff Press, 1982), 248.
178. Thomas C. Schelling, "What is the Business of Organized Crime?" *The Journal of Public Law* 20 (1971): 71–84.
179. Mark H. Haller, "Illegal Enterprise: A Theoretical and Historical Interpretation," *Criminology* 28 no. 2 (1980): 207—35; Dwight C. Smith, 'Organized Crime and Entrepreneurship', *International Journal of Criminology and Penology* 6 (1978): 161–77.
180. FBI, *La Cosa Nostra* Los Angeles Office , July 22, 1964.
181. *Vollero transcript*, 422–4; *Morano transcript*, 417.
182. *NYT*, December 1, 1916.
183. *Brooklyn Daily Eagle*, December 1, 1916. Early 20th century lower east side gangs' extortion activities were masked with a comparable veneer of acceptability. They would ask businesses for "voluntary" contributions to a picnic or ball, for instance—but refusals were not acceptable (Jacob A. Riis, *How the Other Half Lives* [New York: Dover Publications, 1971, reprint of 1901 ed.] 180).
184. *NYT*, February 26, 1913.
185. *NYT*, April 13, 1914.
186. Mealli was in the squad that investigated the Morello and Ubriaco homicides.
187. Who had arrested Angelo Giordano in October 1916.
188. *Morano transcript*, 282.
189. *Vollero transcript*, 69–70, 166.
190. *Vollero transcript*, 70.
191. *Morano transcript,* 286.
192. Born 1879 close to Nicosia, Sicily.
193. *Vollero transcript*, 189.
194. *Giordano transcript*, 194.
195. *Giordano transcript*, 218; *Vollero transcript*, 189, 192; *Morano transcript*, 436.
196. *Vollero transcript*, 189.
197. *Morano transcript*, 628.
198. *Morano transcript*, 625, 638.
199. *Morano transcript*, 633.
200. *Morano transcript,* 628.
201. No charges were brought against Ferrara, and like other allegations of bribery made during the trials, no arrests ensued.
202. *Morano transcript*, 205; *Vollero transcript*, 152—3.
203. *Vollero transcript*, 152.

204. For years, Carfano ran a Brooklyn tavern named "Jimmy Kelly's."
205. *Giordano transcript*, 311–2, 325–332.
206. *Giordano transcript*, 373.
207. *NYT*, September 15, 1915.
208. *NYT*, October 18, 1916.
209. *NYT*, January 25, 1917; *New York Tribune*, January 25, 1917.
210. Email from Thomas J. McDonald September 19, 2006.
211. *Edinburgh Review* October 1911, 388–9.
212. Frederic D. Homer, *Guns and Garlic: Myths and Realities of Organized Crime* (West Lafayette, Indiana: Purdue University Press, 1974), 120.
213. *Outlook* (New York) July 29, 1911; *Cosmopolitan Magazine*, August 1911.
214. *Giordano transcript*, 196.
215. *Tony Parretti transcript*, 24. Because 1930s Chicago crime syndicate head Francesco "Frank Nitti" Nitto was born in the same region of Italy as were many of the "Camorra" members identified, additional research was conducted. Nitto's sister Johanna was married to Vincenzo "Vollora" from Gragnano, a few miles from Nitto's hometown of Angri, and Gragnano was the birthplace of Vollero. Nitto's year of birth, 1886, approximated that of several of the Camorra members in Brooklyn. Nitti furthermore lived in the Navy Street section of Brooklyn. Notwithstanding these tantalizing clues of a potential connection, nothing definite could be established that tied Nitti to the figures noted in this chapter (Brooklyn marriage certificate no. 4691 [1894]; Petition for Naturalization no. 61355 [1924], Francesco Nitto; Kings County Surrogate's Court, July 1945, file no. 5212 of 1945; 1900 Brooklyn census; U.S. National Archives and Records Administration, RG 126, "Notorious Offenders," Frank Nitti). In his first years, Alphonse Capone lived in the same neighborhood (at 95 Navy Street, and 21, 38 and 46 Garfield Place). Whether Capone knew any of them is as unclear, though it was more a probability than a possibility that he did.
216. *Vollero transcript*, 726–7.
217. *Terranova transcript*, 73.
218. *Morano transcript*, 546.
219. *Morano transcript*, 550–551.
220. *Morano transcript*, 782.
221. *Vollero transcript*, 161.
222. *Vollero transcript*, 994.
223. *Vollero transcript*, 76.
224. *Morano transcript*, 253.
225. *NYT*, September 2, 1921.
226. NYMA, Court of General Sessions, New York County, People of the State of New York v. Giovanni Mancini, cal. no. 23860.
227. NYMA, Court of General Session, New York County, People of the State of New York, People of the State of New York v. Anthony Santulli, cal. no. 23860.
228. NYMA, Court of General Sessions, New York County, People of the State of New York v. John Esposito, cal. no. 23838.
229. NYMA, Court of General Sessions, New York County, cal. no. 23837, Memorandum, People v. Ciro Terranova (June 8, 1918).
230. *NYT*, May 14, 1937.
231. Manhattan death certificate no. 4180 (1938).
232. NYMA, Court of General Session, New York County, People of the State of New York v. Rocco Valente, cal. nos. 23837, 23838.
233. Email from Paolo Sgroia July 15, 2003.
234. *NYT* March 2, 1927.

235. *NYT* February 18, 1927.
236. *NYT*, July 2, 1926.
237. *NYT*, May 29, 1923.
238. Westchester County Archives District Attorney files box T-349 folder 2.
239. *NYT* September 26, 1923.
240. *Vollero transcript*, 51.
241. *Vollero transcript*, 63–4.
242. Pitkin, *The Black Hand*, 216. A Rhode Island gang, when he also refused to contribute to their defence fund, nominated Antonio Mancini to kill Altieri. But Mancini became impatient with shadowing Altieri, and decided to slay him in broad daylight on crowded Mulberry Street. Mancini was sentenced to 20 years to life imprisonment. Before he died, Altieri refused to reveal anything to the police (*Providence Journal*, December 21, 1921).
243. *NYT*, June 17, 1929.
244. *Daily Home News* (New Brunswick) January 1, 1925; New Jersey death certificate no. 375 (1925).
245. *Newark Star-Eagle*, August 17, 1925; New Jersey death certificate no. 3346 (1925).
246. *Morano transcript*, 701.
247. *Terranova transcript*, 178.
248. Compiled from information contained in Ellis Island passenger arrivals, the *New York Times*, and the 1920 Manhattan census.
249. According to his Corleone birth certificate, Stefano LaSala was born in November 1888. But LaSala's Declaration of Intention gave (November) 1889 as the right year of birth (Declaration of Intention Southern District of New York no. 385787). His New York State prison record noted August 1890, while LaSala's World War One draft card recorded 1892. The LaSala family came through Ellis Island in May 1897.
250. FBI, *Stephen LaSalla*, New York Office, May 28, 1963 .
251. NARA, RG 87, daily reports of agents, vol. 41, November 11, 1913 (kindly supplied by Mike Dash).
252. Read Rick Porrello, *To Kill the Irishman* (Cleveland, Ohio: Next Hat Press, 2001).
253. The standard work on the Gallo-Profaci war is Raymond V. Martin's, *Revolt in the Mafia* (New York: Duell, Sloan, 1963).
254. Moretti, a respected member of the Genovese family with parents from Calabria, was born in the East 109th Street building used as the Gallucci family's cigar store.
255. *FBI Criminal Intelligence Digest*, November 3, 1963.
256. Henry A. Zeiger, *The Jersey Mob* (New York: New American Library, 1975), 152.
257. *NYT*, November 18, 1926.
258. NYMA, Murder Inc. collection, box 8, "Misc. Documents."
259. www.ellisislandrecords.org/.
260. U.S. Congress, Senate, Committee on Government Operations, Permanent Subcommittee on Investigations, *Organized Crime and the Illicit Traffic in Narcotics* hearings 88th Congress 1st Session, 1963, 88.
261. He received a fracture of the skull and died in Rockaway Beach hospital (*Long Island Daily Press*, July 19, 1927; Queens death certificate no. 4024 [1927]).
262. *Morano transcript*, 381.
263. *Morano transcript*, 380.
264. *Morano transcript*, 380.
265. *Morano transcript*, 376–7.

266. *Morano transcript*, 381.
267. *Giordano transcript*, 150–153.
268. *Giordano transcript,* Appellant's Brief, 95–6.
269. Nicolo Gentile, *Translated Transcription of the Life of Nicolo (E) Gentile, Background and History of the Castellammare War and Early Decades of Organized Crime in America*, 121, 124.
270. Information on Francesco Amato came from his Petition for Naturalization Western District of Pennsylvania no. 41635 (1922).
271. *NYT*, August 18, 1932.
272. Nick Gentile, *Vita di Capomafia* (Rome: Editori Riuniti, 1963), 53–4.
273. NARA, RG 60, Joseph Valachi, *The Real Thing*, 146–8, 150. Originally from the village of Cervinara, Clemente entered New York in 1906.
274. Frank Clemente was gunned down in early February 1918. Clemente helped Vollero collect money for Ricci's funeral, which he also arranged (*Philadelphia Inquirer*, February 8, 1918; *Vollero transcript*, 636-7).
275. Peter Maas, *The Canary That Sang* (London: MacGibbon and Kee, 1969), 69; Valachi, *The Real Thing*, 145–6.
276. *NYT*, August 13, 1925, October 1, 1925, October 14, 1925.
277. Valachi, *The Real Thing*, 385–6.
278. Maas, *The Canary That Sang*, 110–1.
279. Manhattan marriage certificate, no. 15917 (1932).
280. Gentile, *Translated Transcription*, 115.
281. Mark H. Haller, "Bootleggers as Businessmen," in *Law, Alcohol, and Order*, David E. Kyvig (ed.) (Westport, CT.: Greenwood Press, 1985), 146.
282. Estes Kefauver, *Crime in America* (London: Victor Gollancz, 1952), 87–8.
283. U.S. Congress, Senate, Special Committee to Investigate Organized Crime in Interstate Commerce, *Third Interim Report* 82nd Congress 1st Session, 1951, 77–8.
284. NARA, RG 46 series 29, alphabetical name files, *Adonis, Joe;* Kefauver, *Crime in America*, 208.
285. *Gary Post Tribute*, April 5, 1935, April 6, 1935.
286. Humbert S. Nelli, *The Italians in Chicago, 1880–1930* (New York: Oxford University Press, 1970), 152–5.
287. *Vollero transcript*, 53–4.
288. *Morano transcript*, 76–7.
289. U.S. Congress, Senate, Committee on Government Operations, Permanent Subcommittee on Investigations, *Organized Crime and the Illicit Traffic in Narcotics*, hearings 88th Congress 1st Session, 1963, 156.
290. FBI, *La Causa Nostra*, New York Office, January 31, 1963.
291. Bonanno opined, "Many outsiders tried to copy the Sicilian ways, but since they didn't fully understand our Tradition, the result usually was a caricature."(Joseph Bonanno with Sergio Lalli, *A Man of Honour* [London: Andre Deutsch, 1983], 86–7).
292. Gentile, *Translated Transcription*, 134–7.
293. FBI, St. Louis Office, September 12, 1967.
294. FBI, *La Cosa Nostra*, Cleveland Office, June 15, 1964.
295. The Sicilians reported to Ignazio Denaro, with Giuseppe Rugnetta representing the Calabrians (FBI, *La Cosa Nostra Philadelphia Division*, Philadelphia Office, July 21, 1964; Celeste A. Morello, *Before Bruno and How He Became Boss* (book 3) (2005) 150–2).
296. Alan A. Block, "Organizing the Cocaine Trade," in *Organizing Crime*, Alan A. Block and William J. Chambliss (New York: Elsevier, 1981), 43–60.
297. One extract demonstrates the limitations of the Judah L. Magnes material that Block used: "Reddy McMahon, age 35 years, height 5 feet 4 inches,

red hair, came from prison about four months ago. He sells the stuff on his person. He can be found in the restaurant at 220 Ninth Avenue" (Judah Lieb Magnus Papers Central Archives for the History of the Jewish People, Schoenfeld Reports no. 1, film no. HM B/893, 58).

298. World War One draft registration card.

NOTES TO CHAPTER 6

1. Edward Behr, *Prohibition The 13 Years That Changed America* (London: BBC Books, 1997), 84.
2. Andrew Sinclair, *Prohibition The Era of Excess* (London: First Four Square, 1965), 198.
3. John Kobler, *Ardent Spirits* (London: Michael Joseph, 1974), 272–9.
4. Sinclair, *Prohibition*, 208.
5. World League Against Alcoholism, *Saloon Survey New York City* (1925) 13.
6. Peter A. Lupsha, "Organized Crime in the United States," in *Organized Crime A Global Perspective*, Robert J. Kelly (ed.) (Totowa, N.J.: Rowman and Littlefield, 1986), 44.
7. Gary Mormino, "A Still on the Hill," *Gateway Heritage* 7, no. 6 (1986): 3.
8. Stephen Fox, *Blood and Power* (New York: William Morrow, 1989), 66.
9. Francis A. J. Ianni with Elizabeth Reuss Ianni, *A Family Business* (London: Routledge and Kegan Paul, 1972), 55.
10. U.S. Congress, Select Committee on Improper Activities in the Labor or Management Field, *Investigation of Improper Activities in the Labor or Management Field*, hearings 85th Congress 2nd Session, 1958, 12221; Peter Reuter *Disorganized Crime* (Cambridge, MA: The MIT Press, 1983), 135–6.
11. James B. Jacobs, *Mobsters, Unions, and Feds* (New York: New York University Press, 2006), 4.
12. Fox, *Blood and Power*, 51.
13. Mark H. Haller, "Bootleggers as Businessmen," in *Law, Alcohol, and Order*, David E. Kyvig (ed.) (Westport, Conn.: Greenwood Press, 1985), 154.
14. Humbert S. Nelli, *The Italians in Chicago* (New York: Oxford University Press, 1970), 219; Humbert S. Nelli, "Italians and Crime in Chicago: The Formative Years, 1890–1920," *The American Journal of Sociology* 74 (1969): 391; Iannis, *A Family Business*, 55.
15. U.S. National Commission on Law Observance and Enforcement, *Enforcement of the Prohibition Laws of the United States*, 71st Congress 3rd Session, House document 722 (1931) 23; Sinclair, *Prohibition*, 213–4.
16. *New York Times* (hereafter *NYT*) February 26, 1922.
17. Doug Reed, *The Violation of Prohibition Laws in the Pacific Northwest* (Oregon Department of Justice, 1978); Behr, *Prohibition*, 139–142.
18. Mark H. Haller's paper presented at the 1980 meeting of the Organization of American Historians, *Bootlegging: The History of an Illegal Enterprise*.
19. Mark H. Haller, "Bootlegging: The Business and Politics of Violence," in *The History of Crime*, Ted Robert Gurr (ed.), vol. 1 (Westport, CT.: Sage Publications, 1989), 147.
20. Fox, *Blood and Power*, 25.
21. See for example the list in Mark H. Haller, *Bootleggers and American Gambling 1920–1950*, in Commission on the Review of the National Policy Toward Gambling, "Appendix 1" (1976) 110–111.

22. Leonard Katz, *Uncle Frank* (London: W.H. Allen, 1974), 65. Wolf and DiMona made a comparable comment (George Wolf with Joseph DiMona, *Frank Costello* [London: Hodder and Stoughton, 1974], 64). Discrepancies over Costello's date of birth are discussed in a FBI report of December 26, 1957 from the New York office.
23. Fox, *Blood and Power*, 42.
24. U.S. National Archives and Records Administration (hereafter NARA), RG 46 series 29, alphabetical name files, "Costello, Frank."
25. *NYT*, December 4, 1925.
26. *NYT*, November 19, 1926.
27. Nelli, *The Italians in Chicago*, 155.
28. Nelli's 1976 chapter on Prohibition was accordingly titled "Consolidation of the Syndicates."
29. Jay Robert Nash, *World Encyclopedia of Organized Crime* (London: Headline Books, 1992), 79.
30. Martin A. Gosch and Richard Hammer, *The Last Testament of Lucky Luciano* (London: Macmillan, 1975), 104–6.
31. Dennis Eisenberg, Uri Dan and Eli Landau, *Meyer Lansky: Mogul of the Mob* (London: Paddington Press, 1979), 145.
32. Graham Nown, *The English Godfather* (London: Ward Lock, 1987), 93–4.
33. Hickman Powell, *Ninety Times Guilty* (London: Robert Hale, 1939), 65.
34. Peterson, *The Mob*, 158.
35. Humbert S. Nelli, *The Business of Crime* (New York: Oxford University Press, 1976), 215.
36. Lupsha, *Organized Crime in the United States*, 46.
37. Joseph L. Albini, *The American Mafia* (New York: Appleton-Century-Crofts, 1971), 247.
38. Hank Messick and Burt Goldblatt, *The Mobs and the Mafia* (New York: Thomas Y. Crowell, 1972), 105; Hank Messick, *Lansky* (London: Robert Hale, 1973), 59; Nelli, *The Business of Crime*, 174.
39. *Atlantic City Press*, May 16, 1929, May 17, 1929.
40. Pasley, *Al Capone*, 292; Walter Noble Burns, *The One-Way Ride* (London: Stanley Paul, 1931), 280–1.
41. *Chicago Tribune*, September 9, 1929.
42. *Atlantic City Daily Press*, May 18, 1929; *Philadelphia Inquirer*, May 18, 1929; *New York Tribune*, May 18, 1929.
43. *Philadelphia Inquirer*, May 18, 1929.
44. *Atlantic City Daily Press*, May 18, 1929; *Philadelphia Inquirer*, May 18, 1929; *New York Tribune*, May 18, 1929.
45. *Philadelphia Inquirer*, May 18, 1929; *NYT*, May 18, 1929.
46. Fred D. Pasley, *Al Capone* (London: Faber and Faber, 1931 [1966 reprint]) 292.
47. Burns, *The One-Way Ride*, 281.
48. *Literary Digest*, May 15, 1929; *Atlantic City Press*, May 16, 1929, May 17, 1929, May 18, 1929; *New York Tribune*, May 18, 1929; *Los Angeles Times*, May 18, 1929.
49. *Chicago Tribune*, May 18, 1929. Named were Capone, Joseph Aiello, George "Bugs" Moran, Earl McErlane, Joe Saltis, and John Torrio.
50. *NYT*, April 1–2, 1939.
51. *NYT*, April 1, 1939; Elmer L. Irey, *The Tax Dodgers* (London: The Fireside Press, 1949), 151–2.
52. *NYT*, April 2, 1939, April 11, 1939.
53. NARA, RG 46, series 30, alphabetical geographical file, "NY Gambling."
54. George Wolf with Joseph DiMona, *Frank Costello* (London: Hodder and Stoughton, 1974), 38; Eisenberg, *Meyer Lansky*, 92.

55. NARA, RG 46 series 29, alphabetical name files, "Costello, Frank."
56. Mark H. Haller, "Philadelphia Bootlegging and the Report of the Special August Grand Jury," *Pennsylvania Magazine of History and Biography*, April 1985.
57. Sinclair, *Prohibition*, 214.
58. *NYT*, July 18, 1928.
59. U.S. National Commission on Law Observance and Enforcement, *Enforcement of the Prohibition Laws of the United States*, 71st Congress 3rd Session, House document 722 (1931) 29.
60. *NYT*, March 22, 1930.
61. *NYT*, July 18, 1923.
62. *NYT*, August 1, 1925, August 9, 1925; Brooklyn death certificate no. 15195 (1925); Joseph Bonanno with Sergio Lalli, *A Man of Honour* (London: Andre Deutsch, 1983), 66. Romano, of 117 Roebling Street, Brooklyn, died on August 4, 1925.
63. *NYT*, February 23, 1922.
64. *News-Palladium* (Benton Harbor), August 24, 1926.
65. Excerpts from this material previously appeared in my article, "Buster, Maranzano and the Castellammare War, 1930–1931," *Global Crime* 7 no. 1 (2006) 56–59.
66. *NYT*, December 17, 1930.
67. The date is confirmed by his birth certificate, his driving license, and in the statement of Joseph Palma.
68. Civil Registration Office, Comune of Castellammare marriage certificate. Elizabetta's brother was given as Calogero Minore on Ellis Island passenger manifests.
69. Bonanno, *A Man of Honour*, 70.
70. NARA, RG 46 series 29, alphabetical name files, "Adonis, Joe," and "Mafia (Suspects)."
71. Bonanno, *A Man of Honour*, 70.
72. NARA, RG 46 series 29, alphabetical name files, "Adonis, Joe," and "Mafia (Suspects)."
73. 1927 was favored by the U.S. immigration department (*NYT*, September 15, 1931).
74. Brooklyn 1925 census Elizabetta Maranzano and her family may have voyaged to New York to avoid being trapped in Sicily by the U.S. immigration quota system. The "Italian" quota for the year ending June 1924 was shortly to be exhausted and there was a rush of arrivals in the months preceding it (*NYT*, November 29, 1923).
75. *L'Ora*, January 23–4, 1962.
76. *Brooklyn Daily Eagle*, October 17, 1925; Bonanno, *A Man of Honour*, 70–1.
77. NARA, RG 46 series 29, alphabetical name files, "Adonis, Joe," and "Mafia (Suspects)."
78. After Maranzano was assassinated, Dutchess County officials said they had uncovered "a fair-sized account held in a Wappingers bank by the slain man for the past seven years," inferring 1924 as Maranzano's year of arrival (*Beacon News*, September 12, 1931).
79. National Archives of Canada, RG 76 C5 a, vol. 1, 146.
80. The Canadian Commissioner of Immigration in 1926 duly complained that aliens were gaining admission to America by way of Canada posing as agriculturalists "and gradually work their way down to the border." (*NYT*, September 2, 1926) Except for Britons, those males wishing to travel legally to Canada from Europe had to have an intended relationship with Canadian farming, either as a farm hand or a farm-owner.

81. "Maranzano, when things were right," Buffalo's Stefano Magaddino complained, "wanted to belong to New York, and when there was trouble he wanted to belong here." (FBI report of March 31, 1965 from SAC, Buffalo titled *Steve Magaddino AKA ar.*). In August 1925, Maranzano used the Jersey Street, Buffalo, address of Angelo Palmeri to obtain a pistol permit (Palmeri was a founder of the Mafia in Niagara Falls, and related to Magaddino). When Maranzano was arrested for revolver possession on Roebling Street, Brooklyn, he gave the house as his residence (*Brooklyn Daily Eagle*, October 17, 1925). Palmeri's address was also used to get pistol permits by Ciro Terranova, Salvatore Sabella (the Philadelphia boss) and Salvatore D'Aquila (Brooklyn boss and the Mafia's *capo di capi*) (communications with Mike Tona).
82. Sacco was arrested in Niagara Falls with Paul Palmeri, Angelo's brother, in 1914. The two Sacco brothers, Nino and Stefano, opened a restaurant in 1919 that was taken over by Buffalo leader Joseph Peter DiCarlo in 1920.
83. Bonanno, *A Man of Honour*, 75.
84. Maranzano's home in Wappingers Falls was situated in an isolated location at 86 Channingville Road (information supplied by Peter McGivney).
85. *Beacon News*, March 18–9, 1929.
86. *Beacon News*, December 27, 1929. Germano was born 1882 in Calabria (*Poughkeepsie Journal,* May 8, 1970).
87. *Beacon News*, March 19, 1929.
88. *Beacon News*, January 13, 1930.
89. *Sunday Courier*, January 12, 1930.
90. *Beacon News*, April 23, 1931. The charges against them were dropped. (*Poughkeepsie Eagle News*, April 21, 1931).
91. *Beacon News*, April 20, 1931; *Poughkeepsie Eagle News*, April 22, 1931.
92. *Beacon News*, September 11, 1931.
93. Communication from Mike Tona.
94. Sciortino was born in 1903 in New York to parents from Bagheria, Sicily.
95. When Maranzano's bank account was examined after his demise, a $400 check was found, payable to Mule (*Beacon News*, September 12, 1931). Mule was identified by the 1960s as a member of the Bonanno (formerly Maranzano) Family.
96. Vultaggio, Sciortino and Guastella were questioned over the Binnewater body find in 1931 (*Beacon News*, August 15, 1931, August 18, 1931). Vultaggio was reportedly a neighbor of Maranzano's in Wappingers Falls.
97. The Capaci, Sicily, born Nick Guastella introduced Maranzano to the bank in Wappingers where he opened an account. Prospero "Beau" Mule, son of Mule and his wife Caterina Vultaggio (a sister of Santo Vultaggio) married Guastella's daughter.
98. Run by the Lonardos and then the Porrellos.
99. FBI, *Joseph DiGiovanni*, Kansas City Office, March 17, 1953.
100. *The Bulletin* (Pomona, California) September 28, 1923, September 29, 1923, October 6, 1923.
101. For example, in Benton Harbor, Michigan, where a cluster of immigrants from Castellammare del Golfo, Sicily were linked to the manufacture and sale of illicit alky.
102. Two of the first analysts in this field were D.C. MacMichael, *The Behavior of Organized Crime Figures in Legitimate Business* (Menlo Park, CA.: SRI International, 1970); and Jean C. Jester, *An Analysis of Organized Crime's Infiltration of Legitimate Business* (Huntsville, TX.: Sam Houston State University, 1970).
103. New York County petition for naturalization, no. 124119 (1921). Vincent Gulotta, said to be a pioneer in bringing electricity to Corleone, fled to New

York after receiving death threats. He was assassinated April 1934 in his Second Avenue store; as Gulotta was preparing to close, two gunmen shot him at point blank range (*NYT*, April 11, 1934). According to Vincent Rao's descendants, the Gulotta death was avenged in Corleone by Rao's kin or by their allies in the town (email from Enid Ruzicka, July 19, 2003).

104. One of those arrested with Rao in 1919 was Frank Costello. Both were charged with grand larceny.

105. Millie Rao held the mortgage on the house owned by Gaetano "Tommy" Lucchese, a 1950s and 1960s New York City Family boss, in Lido Beach, Long Island. The Raos were part of his organization, as they had been of Gaetano Reina's and Tommaso Gagliano's.

106. *NYT*, May 2, 1931; FBI, *Vincent John Rao*, New York Office July 3, 1958.

107. *NYT*, August 6, 1938.

108. Bronx County Clerk, certificate of incorporation, Five Boro Hoisting Company.

109. *NYT*, January 14, 1931.

110. New York State Temporary Commission of Investigation, *Summary of the Activities During 1960*, 52–61; *NYT*, September 30, 1959, May 25, 1960.

111. New York State Temporary Commission of Investigation, *Summary of the Activities During 1960*, 54, 61.

112. May was incorrect in saying, "Hardly any information exists outside of the years 1930 and 1931" on Gagliano (Allan May, "Gaetano Gagliano A Mafia Short Story," www.americanmafia.com, June 19, 2000).

113. Refer to Chapter 7.

114. FBI, *Thomas Luchese*, New York Office, February 25, 1963.

115. No birth certificate for Tommaso Gagliano was found in Corleone, but the two years of his birth cited were indicated on his American records.

116. Manhattan marriage license no. 32130 (1921).

117. FBI, *Nunzio Pomilla*, New York Office, February 3, 1964. Among the witnesses to Pomilla's naturalization was Mariano Marsalisi of Chapter 4.

118. FBI, *Nunzio Pomilla*, New York Office, February 3, 1964. Lucchese claimed that he worked "in Gagliano's place" as a lathing operator in the 1920s. The name of the company he argued he could not remember, raising the possibility that it may have been United Lathing; Lucchese was a close associate of Gagliano by 1930 (New York State Crime Commission, *Proceedings Pursuant to the Governor's Executive Order of March 29, 1951*, 190).

119. *NYT*, March 18, 1925.

120. Bronx County Clerk, certificate of incorporation, United Lathing Company (1926).

121. Business certificate file no. 9307–31B (1931).

122. *NYT*, May 27, 1928; *New York Herald-Tribune*, May 27, 1928; Manhattan death certificate no. 15102 [1928]).

123. Names of the stockholders were supplied by Bronx County Clerk's office. In 1927, Thomas Milo was among 4 charged with conspiracy to rob the payroll of United Lathing. The son of one of the owners, Charles Rizzo, worked for the firm and gave the robbery team inside information. Milo was jailed for 25 years as a second offender, pardoned in 1928 by the New York State Governor and went on the control the private garbage collection service for the Genovese mob in Westchester County.

124. Bronx County Clerk, Oath of Inspectors and Certificate of Election of Directors of Williamsbridge Investing Corp. (1930); *NYT* April 12, 1935.

125. *NYT*, March 1, 1932.

126. Harold Seidman, *Labor Czars* (New York: Liveright Publishing, 1938), 148–9; *NYT*, March 1, 1932.

127. John McConaughy, *From Cain to Capone* (New York: Brentano's, 1931), 306.
128. *NYT*, August 24, 1929, January 11, 1929.
129. McConaughy, *From Cain to Capone*, 305–6.
130. *NYT*, January 24, 1930.
131. *NYT*, March 1, 1932.
132. United States District Court Southern District of New York, United States of America, Plaintiff vs. Antonino Montforte, C87–350.
133. *NYT*, May 22, 1932.
134. For selections, refer to *Wall Street Journal*, February 11, 1964; *NYT*, February 14, 1965; *U.S. News and World Report*, April 18, 1966.
135. New York State Organized Crime Task Force, *Corruption and Racketeering in the New York City Construction Industry: Final Report* (December 1989) 56.
136. *NYT*, March 1, 1932.
137. McConaughy, *From Cain to Capone*, 306.
138. *NYT*, February 27, 1930.
139. Explaining Valachi's comment that "Gagliano was more of a figurehead and Tommy Lucchese actually directed the operations of the Family" (FBI, *Thomas Luchese*, New York Office, February 25, 1963).
140. Valachi, *The Real Thing*, 338.
141. On this original 1915 Petition for Naturalization, Gagliano described himself as a "Lather," and one of Gagliano's witnesses, contractor Sebastiano DiPalermo, was a stockholder in United Lathing 14 years on (Petition for Naturalization, February 25, 1915, stockholders of the United Lathing Company as of January, 1929).
142. *NYT*, May 2, 1935.
143. Email from Enid Ruzicka October 2, 2006.
144. *NYT*, May 2, 1935.
145. When Gagliano died, his sole business asset consisted of an interest in the Central Lathing Company.
146. U.S. Circuit Court of Appeals for the Second Circuit, The United States of America vs. Giuseppe Calicchio, et al, *Transcript of Record* (1910), 456–460. Ciro Terranova officially worked as a plasterer contractor at 229 and 208 East 107th Street from at least 1910–1918, registered there as Morello & Company.
147. The majority of investors and shareholders in the United Lathing, had no identified links to the mob.
148. President's Commission on Organized Crime, *The Edge* (March 1986) 25.
149. Nelli, *The Business of Crime*, 243.
150. Jester, *An Analysis of Organized Crime's Infiltration of Legitimate Business*, 13; Jay Albanese (ed.) *Contemporary Issues in Organized Crime* (Monsey: Criminal Justice Press, 1995), 36.
151. For instance, that Masseria was "head of the Mafia in New York from 1920 to 1931," and in 1913 "decided to take over" the Morello group in Harlem. In that story, Masseria "personally led attacks on the headquarters of the Morello gang, shooting Charles Lamonti (sic) to death" (Nash, *World Encyclopedia*, 502).
152. Bonanno, *A Man of Honour*, 84.
153. No birth certificate was found for Giuseppe Masseria in 1886 or 1887 either in the Trapani provincial archives or in Family History Library microfilms. But Masseria's place of birth as Marsala is noted by Gentile and on his WW1 draft card, with 1887 as the year of birth on the card (Nick Gentile, *Vita di Capomafia* (Rome: Editori Riuniti, 1963), 96). His brothers were also recorded as Marsala born.

154. Office of the Chief Medical Examiner of the City of New York, Borough of Brooklyn, case no. 1457 (1931).
155. Some believed that he took a part in the abduction of 3 years old Michael Scimeca in June 1910. strangers "with promises of candy" luring Scimeca from his home. On September 9, the abductee mysteriously appeared at the home of his father Mariano's brother in law in Brooklyn but with (so it was reported) no ransom paid (*NYT* April 15, 1913, September 10, 1910; Pitkin, *The Black Hand*, 139–40).
156. John Jay College film no. 1736, People of the State of New York against Pietro Lagatutta and Giuseppe Masseria (1913); *NYT*, April 15, 1913.
157. New York State Prison receiving record, May 26, 1913.
158. Chandler, *The Criminal Brotherhoods*, 130–1.
159. New York Municipal Archives, DA Record of Cases no. 58645, The People vs. Giuseppe Lima and Joseph Masseria.
160. *NYT*, October 13, 1920.
161. Craig Thompson and Allen Raymond, *Gang Rule in New York* (New York: The Dial Press, 1940), 9–10.
162. Bonanno, *A Man of Honour*, 100.
163. NARA, RG 204, 230/40/1/3 box 956–Ignazio Lupo.
164. Born 1891 in Barcellona, Sicily.
165. "It was a question of power" (Gentile, *Vita di Capomafia*, 61). Ciro Terranova and John Pecoraro may have been among the unidentified others, leaving New York together on October 22, 1921. They returned on February 8, 1922.
166. Gentile, *Translated Transcription*, 27–8. When Lupo tried to re-enter America in mid 1922, he was detained and an attempt was made to return him to Italy as an "undesirable alien." Only an order from Washington led to Lupo's release (*NYT*, June 13, 1922).
167. Ellis Island passenger arrival records.
168. Gentile, *Vita di Capomafia*, 79.
169. New York Municipal Archives, DA Record of Cases, no. 35333, The People against Joseph Masseria.
170. *NYT*, May 9, 1922.
171. *World*, May 9, 1922; *NYT* May 9, 1922; *New York Tribune*, May 9, 1922, Manhattan death certificate no. 13893 (1922).
172. *New York Herald*, August 9, 1922; *NYT*, August 9, 1922; Downey, *Gangster City*, 140–2.
173. Manhattan death certificate no. 21067 (1922); *New York Herald*, August 12, 1922. On August 29, Charles Dongarro, to become a Gambino member, was arrested for the murder. Recounting the Valenti murder, newspapers referred to Valenti's supposed feud with Rosario Pellegrino that ended in Pellegrino's death on East 14th Street in 1914 (consult also *New York Herald*, August 12, 1922; *NYT*, June 15, 1914; March 21, 1915). "After being acquitted for the murder," Downey asserted, "Valenti was taken more seriously in the Italian underworld" (Downey, *Gangster City*, 138). The snag with the scenario is that it was one Giuseppe Valenti who was arrested and prosecuted in the matter, as the relevant closed case file shows (New York Municipal Archives, DA Record of Cases, no. 17087, The People vs. Giuseppe Valenti, Carmelo Allotta, Samuel Santore and Domenico Coniglaro).
174. Gentile, *Vita di Capomafia*, 90.
175. Gentile, *Translated Transcription*, 68–9; *Paese Sera*, September 28, 1963.
176. Gentile, *Vita di Capomafia*, 75.
177. In 1919, D'Aquila lived at 91 Elizabeth Street, where Nicolo Gentile stayed after his arrival in 1903 in New York. From there, Gentile was given a ticket

to Kansas City by the "trafficker of countrymen" Domenico Taormina (Gentile, *Vita di Capomafia*, 38). Accursio Dimino, a D'Aquila man, was shot in front of his store at that address in 1922 (*NYT*, May 20, 1922). He later died of his wounds.

178. Ellis Island passenger arrival records, Manhattan marriage certificate no. 27326 [1912]).

179. Gentile, *Translated Transcription*, 27.

180. NARA, RG 87, daily reports of agents, reel 591, New York, vol. 34, February 25, 1912, daily reports of agents, reel 591, New York, vol. 35, April 12, 1912. Information kindly supplied by Mike Dash. Vincenzo and Calogero Grisafi came from Caltabellotta, Sicily.

181. Gentile, *Translated Transcription*, 32, 39, 47.

182. *NYT*, October 11, 1928, Manhattan death certificate no. 2548 (1928). Immediately beforehand, Salvatore D'Aquila was seen in heated conversation with three men, raising the possibility that this was no cold-blooded gangland execution in which gunmen walked up to their victim and opened fire without warning.

183. *Parade magazine*, January 28, 1968. "Jim Carra" is believed to have been convicted narcotics trafficker and FBN informer Alfonso Attardi, born 1897 in Porto Empedocle, who died in 1972 in Suffolk County, New York. Vincent Mangano linked his "brother in law" D'Aquila lying dead in the city morgue with a residence at 81 Rapeleye Street in Brooklyn. But Mangano was not related to Salvatore D'Aquila, and 81 Rapeleye turned out to be a vacant lot. Of interest though was that one of the Mangano brothers did rent a garage on Rapeleye as a hangout, and that the Mangano family's mortician, Vincent Clemente, lived on Rapeleye (Chief Medical Examiner of the Borough of Manhattan, case no. 5765 [1928]; communications from Cathy Campbell).

184. Gentile, *Vita di Capomafia*, 80.

185. Bonanno, *A Man of Honour*, 84.

186. But perhaps leaving a lasting fissure in the group that was a feature of the rule of Paul Castellano in the 1970s and 1980s (NARA, RG 87, daily reports of agents, reel 590, July 1911). Carmelo Cordaro was acquitted of counterfeiting in November 1911, but the U.S. District Court in Trenton ordered him deported to face a murder charge in Italy (*Trenton Times*, November 3, 1911).

187. NARA, RG 87, daily reports of agents, vol. 41, reel 593, November 10–11, 27, 1913 (reference kindly supplied by Mike Dash).

188. DiLeonardo Testimony www.onewal.com/.

189. Born 1897 in Barcellona, Biondo became the underboss of the Gambino Family until his death in June of 1966. He was an apparent bootlegging confederate of Valenti, also from Barcellona.

190. Born in September 1898.

191. Philip Mangano was held in 1924 over the death of a witness against a local Mafia character, Joseph "Joe the Wolf" DiCarlo, son of former Buffalo boss Joseph Peter Di Carlo, and the owner of the house in which Mangano then lived (*Buffalo Commercial Advertiser*, January 3, 1924). In September 1925, Vincent Mangano and his wife Caroline acted as godparents to the daughter of Angelo Palmeri and his wife Laura Mistretta (information supplied by Mike Tona). The body of Philip Mangano was discovered in the Bergen Beach section of Brooklyn on April 19, 1951 with three shots to his head (*Times-Herald* [Washington DC], April 20, 1951). Vincent Mangano disappeared soon afterwards; his body was never found. Bonanno explained these events with reference to intrigues within the Mangano Family (Bonanno, *A Man of Honour*, 169).

192. In for example John Scarne, *The Mafia Conspiracy* (New Jersey: Scarne Enterprises, 1976), 109; and Nash, *World Encyclopedia of Organized Crime*, 54.
193. Cf. Appeals case, The People of the State of New York against Giuseppi Florina, Alias Giuseppe Speranza, Alberto Anastasio (1921).
194. *Brooklyn Eagle*, April 7, 1923; *New York Tribune*, April 29, 1923; *NYT* April 29, 1923.
195. *Cleveland Plain-Dealer*, December 6, 1928.
196. *Cleveland Magazine*, August 1978, 66.
197. Robert J. Schoenberg, *Mr Capone* (New York: William Morrow, 1992), 232.
198. Allan May, "Chicago's Unione Siciliana 1920–A Decade of Slaughter" (www.americanmafia.com/) 2000.
199. David Leon Chandler, *The Criminal Brotherhoods* (London: Constable, 1976), 138; Laurence Bergreen, *Capone: The Man and His Era* (New York: Simon and Schuster, 1994), 334.
200. Burns, *The One-Way Ride*, 252.
201. Bonanno, *A Man of Honour*, 124.
202. *NYT*, October 11, 1928.
203. Gentile, *Translated Transcription*, 27, 41, 58.
204. They were Profaci himself, Joseph Magliocco (born 1898 in Portella di Mare), Salvatore Lombardino and Emanuel Cammarata. While the last 2 individuals were New Jersey based, they became components of the Profaci Family, perhaps as former members of the Newark *Famiglia* disbanded about 1937 after its boss, Gaspare D'Amico, was wounded and his father killed. The D'Amicos, like Profaci, came from Villabate.
205. US Congress, Select Committee on Improper Activities in the Labor or Management Field, *Investigation of Improper Activities in the Labor or Management Field*, hearings, June–July 1958, 12345–9.
206. Raymond Martin, in an otherwise excellent study of the Gallo-Profaci war of the early 1960s, mistakenly gave September 1922 as the date of Profaci's disembarkation in New York (Raymond V. Martin, *Revolt in the Mafia* (New York: Duell, Sloan and Pearce, 1963), 18).
207. NARA, RG 46, series 29, alphabetical name files, "Mama Mia Importing Company." Profaci took out his first naturalization papers while living on Cambridge Avenue and Orleans Street in Chicago (Petition for Naturalization, Eastern District Court, Brooklyn, petition no. 77445 [1926]).
208. U.S. Congress, Senate, Special Committee to Investigate Organized Crime in Interstate Commerce, *Investigation of Organized Crime in Interstate Commerce*, hearings 82nd Congress 1st Session, 1951, part 7, p. 744; NARA, RG 46, series 29, alphabetical name files, "Mama Mia Importing Company."
209. Italiano, born 1860 in Santo Stefano Quisquina, Sicily, arrived in New York in 1903. He died in Tampa at the ripe old age of 70.
210. U.S. Congress, Senate, Special Committee to Investigate Organized Crime in Interstate Commerce, *Investigation of Organized Crime in Interstate Commerce*, hearings 82nd Congress 1st Session 1951, part 7, 743–50. Margaret "Mary" Italiano, Ignazio's daughter, was a witness to the wedding of Profaci to Ninfa Magliocco (Joseph Magliocco's sister) in 1928, and that of Ambrogio Magliocco (one of Joseph's brothers) in 1929 (Brooklyn marriage certificates 5145 [1928] and 18003 [1929]). Less explicable was an association uncovered through research between Profaci and the Italianos through Gaetano Mangano. Mangano came to America on the same vessel as Profaci but was Calabrian. His son Vincent, New York born in 1905, married Margaret Italiano in April 1930 in Tampa (New York State Archives, New York State prison admissions, no. 84813 [July 23, 1931], Manhattan birth

certificate no. 27972 [1905], Hillsborough County marriage certificate no. 4896 [1930]). When, in 1938, the Garcia Vega Cigar Factory in Tampa was robbed, this Vincent Mangano was tied to the case along with Salvatore "Red" Italiano, a local Mafia character, and reported nephew of Ignazio Italiano (NARA, RG 46 series 29, alphabetical name files, "Italiano, Salvatore"; *Tampa Morning Tribune*, December 2, 1938, December 3, 1938, November 8, 1938). Confusion between the New Yorker Vincent Mangano and the Sicilian born Brooklyn Mafia *capo* Vincent Mangano may have caused a mistaken link to be recorded between the Brooklyn Mafia and a subsequent faction of the Tampa Mafia. D'Aquila/Mangano member Domenico Arcuri, however, was godfather to Santo Trafficante Jr., later of the Tampa Mafia, the Trafficantes coming from the same Sicilian village.

211. FBI, *Giuseppe Traina*, New York Office, December 15, 1965; FBI, *Giuseppe Traina*, New York Office, April 5, 1966. Ignazio Italiano had five sons, Steve, Tony, Sam, Joseph and John.
212. NARA, RG 46, series 29, alphabetical name files, "Mama Mia Importing Co."
213. New York Municipal Archives, Albert Anastasia Collection, box 5, "Profaci, Joseph." Barbara Sr. attended the weddings of Profaci's daughters in 1949 and in 1954.
214. The Mama Mia Importing Company was incorporated in 1936 with Profaci and his wife as the directors and officers. Mama Mia was allegedly financed from his savings as an olive oil salesman and from a successful compensation claim for a knee injury Profaci suffered in 1928 whilst on honeymoon (NARA, RG 46, series 29, alphabetical name files, "Mama Mia Importing Co").
215. Gay Talese, *Honor Thy Father* (London: Souvenir Press, 1971), 14.
216. Email from Laura Castelli October, 2006.
217. Declaration of Intention, Kings County, no. 69469 (1917); World War One draft card (1917).
218. Bonanno, *A Man of Honour*, 87.
219. Oliver Pilat and Jo Ranson, *Sodom by the Sea* (New York: Doubleday Doran, 1941), 273, 282–3.
220. Downey, *Gangster City*, 118–9.
221. *NYT*, December 17, 1922.
222. *NYT*, February 7, 1921.
223. *NYT*, July 24, 1921.
224. Forte had been hired to drive Yale and his family home from a christening, but Yale had decided to walk (*NYT*, July 9, 1923).
225. Pilat and Ranson, *Sodom by the Sea*, 272.
226. *Chicago Daily Tribune*, December 17, 1920.
227. *Chicago Tribune*, November 14, 1924.
228. *NYT*, September 10, 1928; Burns, *The One-Way Ride*, 210–3.
229. Laurence Bergreen, *Capone: The Man and the Era* (New York: Simon and Schuster, 1994), 293.
230. *NYT*, July 8, 1928.
231. Edward D. Sullivan, *Look at Chicago* (London: Geoffrey Bles, 1930), 175–81; Downey, *Gangster City* 119, 122; Burns, *The One-Way Ride*, 207–9.
232. *New York Herald-Tribune*, July 2, 1928; Brooklyn death certificate no 14764 (1928). Schoenberg (*Mr. Capone*, 202–3) and Bergreen (*Capone*, 289) echoed a universally held sentiment that machine guns were used to execute Yale. For other examples, read Fred D. Pasley *Muscling In* (London: Faber and Faber, 1932), 150; Downey, *Gangster City*, 122. Eghigian is the latest author to repeat the gaffe (Mars Eghigian, Jr., *After Capone* (Nashville, TN: Cumberland House, 2006), 143). But eyewitness reports made no mention of machine gun fire; nor had the machine gun found in the abandoned car used by Yale's killers been fired. The coroner's report disclosed that Yale was hit twice on the

left side of his face by a shotgun blast; there was also a pistol wound over his left cheek, with the cause of death being ascribed to "gunshot wounds of head" (Office of the Chief Medical Examiner, case no. 2073 [1928]).

233. *Chicago Tribune*, May 24, 1959.
234. *NYT*, July 2, 1928, July 6, 1928, July 8, 1928.
235. *NYT*, January 8, 1928.
236. *Brooklyn Standard Union*, July 5, 1928.
237. Abbatemarco, born 1894 in New York City, was an integral part of the Yale alcohol-supplying ring. A witness to his killing saw a man at first talking to Abbatemarco, then firing at him. Abbatemarco's assassin disappeared before the police arrived.
238. Yale had formed a Bay Ridge-based employers' association to which Italian bakers in Brooklyn were persuaded "under threats of personal injury, sabotage," to join. The carrot for their cooperation was the promise that competitors would not be permitted to undercut association members. The association covered the area from 39th Street to Coney Island. Vittoria Sabatino recalled how in 1922, after he opened a bakery shop, his refusal to participate in the racket led to his store being attacked. When Sabatino proved stubborn, Yale offered to pay his association subscriptions. Hearing that, Sabatino reluctantly conceded to Yale's designs (NARA, RG 204, 230/40/1/3 box 956—Ignazio Lupo, 10–22).
239. Carfano and Yale were stopped together in 1922 carrying loaded pistols while in a car crossing the Manhattan Bridge (*NYT*, December 17, 1922). After Masseria was held over the death of "Broadway racketeer" and nightclub owner Frankie Marlow in 1929, he gave the police the address, 65 Second Avenue, used by Carfano (*NYT*, July 19, 1929). His FBI file and a Manhattan birth certificate show "Antonio Carfagno" as born in November 1895 on Oliver Street, the son of Giovanni Carfagno and Dongetta Visocchi from Naples.
240. Giovanni "Johnny Bath Beach" Oddo, Cassandro "The Chief" Bonasera, Salvatore "Sally the Sheik" Musacchio, and Joseph Magliocco.
241. *NYT*, July 10, 1928; *Brooklyn Daily Eagle*, March 30, 1930.
242. Alan Block, *East Side West Side* (Cardiff: Cardiff University Press, 1982), 249–51. In 1918, Piraino was acquitted of the stabbing murder of Gasparino Candello. Candello's body was discovered stuffed into a barrel. During 1920, Piraino was jailed for grand larceny (*NYT*, November 23, 1919, March 28, 1930; *Brooklyn Daily Eagle*, March 30, 1930).
243. Federal Bureau of Narcotics Memorandum Report, District No. 2, dated September 24, 1962.
244. U.S. Congress, Senate, Committee on Government Operations, Permanent Subcommittee on Investigations, *Organized Crime and the Illicit Traffic in Narcotics*, hearings 88th Congress 1st Session, 1963, 166.
245. Block, *East Side West Side*, 133–5.
246. NARA, RG 46 series 29, alphabetical name files, "Costello, Frank."
247. Block, *East Side West Side*, 135.
248. U.S. Congress, Senate, Special Committee to Investigate Organized Crime in Interstate Commerce, *Investigation of Organized Crime in Interstate Commerce*, hearings 82nd Congress 1st Session 1951, part 18, 765–8; NARA, RG 46 series 29, alphabetical name files, "Reinfeld, Joseph H."

NOTES TO CHAPTER 7

1. Part of this material has previously appeared in my article, "Buster, Maranzano and the Castellammare War, 1930–1931," kindly reproduced by

permission of *Global Crime,* 7, no. 1 (2006): 43–78. Taylor and Francis, http://www.tandf.co.uk.

2. U.S. Congress Senate, Committee on Government Operations, *Organized Crime and the Illicit Traffic in Narcotics: Report,* 89th Congress 1st Session, 1965, 12.

3. Donald R. Cressey, *Theft of the Nation* (New York: Harper and Row, 1969), 35.

4. Cressey, *Theft of the Nation*; Howard Abadinsky, *Organized Crime* (3rd ed.) (Chicago: Nelson-Hall, 1990), 138; Peter A. Lupsha, "Individual Choice, Material Culture, and Organized Crime," *Criminology* 19, no. 1 (1981).

5. Michael Woodiwiss, *Gangster Capitalism* (New York: Carroll and Graf, 2005), 3.

6. Read Joseph L. Albini, *The American Mafia* (New York: Appleton-Century-Crofts, 1971), Chapter 6; and Dwight C. Smith *The Mafia Mystique* (London: Hutchinson, 1975), Chapter 8. Albini devoted 3 pages to the War; there are five references to it in Smith. Albanese gave the War just 2 pages coverage (*Organized Crime in America* (2nd ed.) (Cincinnati, Ohio: Anderson Publishing, 1989), 44–5).

7. Refer to James B. Jacobs et al., *Busting the Mob* (New York: New York University Press, 1994), and his subsequent two books.

8. In Detroit, several homicides over that summer of 1930 were laid at the door of feuding within Italian organized crime, and in Chicago, Chief of Detectives John Stege told reporters of an "epidemic of the killing of Sicilians over the country." (*Detroit News*, July 13, 1930; *Chicago Examiner*, June 3, 1930).

9. Appearing in 1963 before the Senate, Detroit Police Commissioner George Edwards stated that his department "knew about the battles on the Detroit front but we did not know about the front which extended nationally." (U.S. Congress, Senate, Committee on Government Operations, Permanent Subcommittee on Investigations, *Organized Crime and the Illicit Traffic in Narcotics*, hearings 88th Congress 1st Session, 1963 [hereafter OCN], 426).

10. None of the passages related to the Castellammare War in the Martin Gosch and Richard Hammer and in the Eisenberg, Dan and Landau books has been used, because of their unreliability. (Martin A. Gosch and Richard Hammer, *The Last Testament of Lucky Luciano* [London: Macmillan, 1975]; Dennis Eisenberg, Uri Dan, Eli Landau, *Meyer Lansky: Mogul of the Mob* [London: Paddington Press, 1979]).

11. The major sources for Valachi are the OCN hearings part 1; Joseph Valachi's unpublished autobiography *The Real Thing* (U.S. National Archives and Records Administration [hereafter NARA], RG 60); and Peter Maas' treatment of Valachi's life story in *The Canary That Sang* (London: MacGibbon and Kee, 1969).

12. Michael Woodiwiss, *Crime, Crusades and Corruption* (London: Pinter, 1988), 147. The same criticism is made in Smith, *The Mafia Mystique*, 235, and by Albini in The *American Mafia*, 245. Morris and Hawkins also spoke of Valachi's reliance on "the loosest kind of hearsay," when recounting events (Norval Morris and Gordon Hawkins, *The Honest Politician's Guide to Crime Control* [Chicago: University of Chicago Press, 1969], 225).

13. Reuter contended that Valachi was "clearly coached, knew little, and was extremely inconsistent" (Peter Reuter, *Disorganized Crime* [Cambridge, MA: The MIT Press, 1983], 6). Yet law enforcement's contribution to the Senate hearings in which Valachi appeared was openly acknowledged. Moreover, the term Valachi utilized, "Cosa Nostra," was not invented by Valachi

to save FBI Director J. Edgar Hoover from embarrassment (Smith, *The Mafia Mystique*, 239–40). In truth, syndicate leaders had been overheard using the term since 1961, FBI agents at first wrongly spelling it "Causa Nostra" ("Our Cause") (information included in *FBI Criminal Intelligence Digest*, November 8, 1962; FBI, *La Causa Nostra*, New York Office January 31, 1963).

14. *Parade Magazine*, which reproduced a small section from *The Real Thing* in a "special report," stated that it took Valachi 8 months to write (issue March 21, 1965).

15. Woodiwiss, *Crime Crusades and Corruption*, 146.

16. Valachi "was always somewhere else when the gory aspects of the job were being done." (Phil Hirsch (ed.) *The Mafia* [New York, Pyramid 1971], 21.) But in "The Real Thing," Valachi did admit to being one of two men who shot at, and badly wounded, Newark organized crime figure Ruggerio "Ritchie the Boot" Boiardo on November 26, 1930 (Valachi, *The Real Thing*, 328; *New York Herald Tribune*, November 27, 1930).

17. Joseph Bonanno with Sergio Lalli, *A Man of Honour* (London: Andre Deutsch, 1983), 119.

18. *Times-Picayune* (New Orleans) October 6, 1937.

19. In October 1958, the Federal Narcotics Bureau intercepted a letter from Gentile to his old friend in New York, Joe Biondo. A narcotics agent posing as an emissary from Biondo saw Gentile, who, to prove his identity, gave the agent information. Once the narcotics agent revealed his true identity, Gentile "was so terrified he agreed to co-operate with the Bureau of Narcotics and the Italian police on the promise that the report of the incident would remain in confidential files" (*Saturday Evening Post*, July 16, 1960). The fact that Gentile was never extradited from Italy to answer narcotics charges in America may have owed more than a little to his cooperation with U.S. agents.

20. Antonino Calderone and Pino Arlacchi, *Men of Dishonor* (New York: Morrow, 1993), 156. Gentile may have first considered passing information in 1940 while in Naples, in exchange for a reconsideration of legal matters pending against him in America (FBI report of April 9, 1959 titled "Mafia").

21. *New York Times* (hereafter *NYT*), April 11, 1971.

22. John Dickie, *Cosa Nostra* (London: Coronet, 2004), 216, 224.

23. A manuscript covering Gentile's life to 1937 (Nicolo Gentile, *Translated Transcription of the Life of Nicolo (E) Gentile, Background and History of the Castellammarese War and Early Decades of Organized Crime in America*) came into the author's possession early in the research. In October 1963, a book appeared in Rome, *Vita di Capomafia*. There are several minor discrepancies between them, but the book otherwise reads like the manuscript. They are supplemented by interviews published in *Paese Sera* from September 14–October 1, 1963.

24. Dickie, *Cosa Nostra*, 223.

25. Not, as Gentile remembered it, in September 1930. The correct date is taken from Ellis Island passenger arrival records.

26. Patrick Downey, *Gangster City: The History of the New York Underworld 1900–1935* (New Jersey: Barricade Books, 2004), 142.

27. For a typical comment, read Maas, *The Canary That Sang*, 79.

28. Gentile, *Translated Transcription*, 71.

29. Bonanno, *A Man of Honour*, 85.

30. An account of Aiello's exploits before his years in Chicago is contained in Critchley, *Buster, Maranzano and the Castellammare War*, 61.

31. Gentile, *Translated Transcription*, 70.

32. Born in Galati Mamertino, Sicily, in 1891.

33. Illinois death certificate no. 27941 (1928); Declaration of Intention, Cook County, no. 160445 (1924); Petition for Naturalization, Northern District of Illinois, no.29007 (1926.) The history of the Unione is considered at length in Chapter 8.
34. *Chicago Tribune*, May 30, 1929.
35. *Chicago Tribune*, November 23, 1927. According to an FBI source, Aiello fled to Wisconsin. His brother Sam Aiello gained the protection of the Milwaukee Family until he was welcomed back to Chicago under *capo* Jim DiGeorge. Others who were part of the Aiello faction and who fled Chicago, were Carl Caputo, who went on to found the Madison, Wisconsin, Family, and Joe "Pizza Pie" Aiello, a distant cousin of Joseph Aiello, who joined Caputo in Wisconsin (NARA, Archives 11, FBI Headquarter Main Files 92–6054, box 6).
36. Nick Gentile, *Vita di Capomafia* (Rome: Editori Riuniti, 1963), 96.
37. Gentile, *Vita di Capomafia*, 96; Gentile, *Translated Transcription*, 72.
38. Lombardo was Capone's representative at two significant Chicago gangland bargaining sessions in 1926 (Laurence Bergreen, *Capone: The Man and His Era* [New York: Simon and Schuster, 1994] 207, 214; Robert J. Schoenberg, *Mr. Capone* [New York: William Morrow, 1992], 161, 166–7).
39. Masseria promised to give Aiello "everything west of Chicago" and on the West Side of Chicago as an inducement, offering to "check the ambitious Capone" in the process. In exchange, Masseria wanted "the rights to the east side of Chicago"(Bonanno, *A Man of Honour*, 87).
40. Ibid., 88.
41. Ibid., 165.
42. Ibid., 87.
43. Bonanno, *A Man of Honour*, 88. Aiello had connections to Rochester, New York, part of the Magaddino organization's sphere. Milazzo was believed by Bonanno to be the godfather to Aiello's son (Bonanno, *A Man of Honour*, 87).
44. Catalonotte's wife was Vincenza Perrone, the sister of Gaspare and Santo "Sam" Perrone, a later generation Detroit Mafioso. Catalonotte and Perrone were Alcamo, Sicily, born.
45. Bonanno, *A Man of Honour*, 88.
46. He was trailed to the home of Pasquale "Patsy Presto" Prestigiacomo, a partner in the Italo-American Importing Company, a front for sugar manufacturing on behalf of alcohol brewers (*Chicago Tribune*, October 28, 1930). Reports recovered in 1960 "in a battered, rusty safe in the vault of the chief investigator" for the State's Attorney recorded how Capone's men tracked Aiello in the weeks before his murder to Rochester, New York. However, Aiello returned to Chicago before the mission was fulfilled (*Chicago Tribune*, January 23, 1960).
47. Virgil W. Peterson, *The Mob* (Ottowa, Illinois: Green Hill Publications, 1983), 366.
48. Bonanno, *A Man of Honour*, 119–20; OCN, 166.
49. Valachi, *The Real Thing*, 286.
50. OCN, 166.
51. Bonanno, *A Man of Honour*, 88.
52. Danilo Dolci, *The Man Who Plays Alone* (London: Macgibbon and Kee, 1968), 213.
53. Gavin Maxwell, *The Ten Pains of Death* (London: Longmans, 1960), 65.
54. Salvatore Ruffino witnessed the marriage of Gaspare Milazzo to Rosaria Scibilia (Chapter 8), and Ruffino had strong links to 222 North Fifth Street, a locality used by the Schiro leader Vito Bonventre (Brooklyn marriage certificate no. 12669 (1914). Joseph Ruffino lived across from a bakery owned by Vito Bommetro at no. 222, used as a hangout by the Ruffinos. Bommetro,

like Philip Mazzara and Joseph DiBenedetto (Chapter 8), was an alibi witness for the Ruffinos at their 1913 trial (People of the State of New York against Pietro Lagattuta and Giuseppe Masseria, impleaded with Salvatore Ruffino and Giuseppe Ruffino, 1913 (John Jay College case no. 1736).

55. *NYT*, April 14, 1913, April 15, 1913; NARA, RG 87, daily reports of agents, roll 591, February, 28, 1912.
56. Gentile, *Translated Transcription*, 89–90.
57. Bonanno, *A Man of Honour*, 84.
58. Bonanno, *A Man of Honour*, 85. Valachi recounted how Profaci talked to Maranzano's gunmen during the War (OCN, 165–6; Valachi, *The Real Thing*, 285).
59. Jerry Capeci, *The Complete Idiot's Guide to the Mafia* (Indianapolis: Alpha, 2002), 271; David Leon Chandler, *The Criminal Brotherhoods* (London: Constable, 1976), 144; Peterson, *The Mob*, 363.
60. *NYT*, February 27, 1930.
61. "In private," Bonanno stated, "Tom Reina in the Bronx expressed admiration for Maranzano, the only one who had the guts to stand up to Joe the Boss." (Bonanno, *A Man of Honour*, 106).
62. Bonanno, *A Man of Honour*, 98.
63. *NYT*, March 2, 1930.
64. Chandler, *The Criminal Brotherhoods*, 145.
65. Pinzolo's brother in law was Joseph Riccobono, a prominent figure for the Gambino (former Mineo and Mangano) Family. Witnessing the marriage of Riccobono to Carmela Pinzolo was Marco LiMandri, another upcoming man of honor (Manhattan marriage certificate no. 17807 [1916]).
66. OCN, 163. Bonanno erroneously implied that once Pinzolo was shot, the whole of the Reina Family dedicated themselves to fight Masseria, a supposition echoed by Maas (Bonanno, *A Man of Honour*, 106; Maas, *The Canary That Sang*, 81).
67. Tony Scaduto, *Lucky Luciano* (London: Sphere Books, 1976), 82–3; Maas, *The Canary That Sang*, 78; Downey, *Gangster City*, 142.
68. Charles Grubert, "New York's Notorious "Ice Racket" Crime," *Master Detective* 4, no. 5 (July 1931).
69. *NYT*, February 27, 1930.
70. *NYT*, June 11, 1927.
71. Stoffenberg had failed to live up to an agreement to keep 15 blocks away from the operations conducted by a competitor and was severely beaten with a baseball bat, dying from his wounds. Five men were convicted of Stoffenberg's manslaughter, in January 1930. Among them was Joseph Panzarino, the wholesale ice dealer most affected by Stoffenberg's practices, who was jailed for 8–15 years in New York State prison (*NYT*, December 15, 1929, January 30, 1930).
72. Valachi, *The Real Thing*, 280.
73. Reina Family member Gaetano "Tommy" Lucchese, for instance, claimed in 1951 that he had only known Pinzolo "a matter of months" before Pinzolo was killed (New York State Crime Commission, *Proceedings Pursuant to the Governor's Executive Order of March 29, 1951*, 106–7).
74. Valachi, *The Real Thing*, 276; OCN, 163.
75. Born on April 25, 1887 in Castellammare del Golfo (Wayne County Certificate of Death no. 131460 [1930]), Milazzo often used his wife's maiden name of Scibilia.
76. Born October 1886 in Alcamo, Parrino had come to the United States in March 1910 (New York County Declaration of Intention, no. 155126; www.ellisislandrecords.org).

77. FBI file on Gaspare Milazzo. A magazine article of the day pictured Milazzo as "an educated hanger-on in the underworld with a knack of being able to straighten out misunderstandings." (Ralph Goll, "The Inside on the Jerry Buckley Mystery," *True Detective Mysteries* 15, no. 2 [May 1931]).
78. *Detroit News*, June 1, 1930; Wayne County death certificate no. 7449 (1930).
79. Larry Daniel Engelmann, Ph.D., *O Whisky: A History of Prohibition in Michigan* (Ann Arbor, MI.: University of Michigan, 1971), 446–9. LaMare's place and year of birth are unclear. His death certificate shows LaMare as born in 1884 in Italy to Nicholas and Rosa Sapio. Yet in 1920, he claimed to have been born about 1888. His year of arrival in America also differed between censuses. LaMare spent his formative years in Chicago, where he met and married. As of 1915, he was living in Detroit, where the first of his 13 arrests took place (1910 Chicago and 1920 Detroit censuses; Wayne County, Michigan, death certificate no. 1699 (1931); Chicago marriage certificate no. 447938 [1906]).
80. *Detroit News*, July 28, 1930.
81. Paul R. Kavieff, *The Violent Years* (New Jersey: Barricade Books, 2001), 58–60; Engelmann, *O Whisky*, 491–3.
82. Bonanno, *A Man of Honour*, 120.
83. Bonanno, *A Man of Honour*, 106–7.
84. According to witnesses, three men had been engaging Parrino in a "heated altercation" when one whipped out a gun and slew him. The killer and his two companions calmly walked out and disappeared (*NYT* January 20, 1931; Manhattan death certificate, no. 2435 [1931]); Downey, *Gangster City*, 158–9; Bonanno, *A Man of Honour*, 106–7).
85. Gentile, *Translated Transcription*, 73. After doing "his own investigation," Maranzano opined to the Schiro membership that Milazzo's slaying was "tantamount to a declaration of war against all Castellammarese." (Bonanno, *A Man of Honour*, 94).
86. *Detroit Free Press*, October 18, 1930, October 22, 1930, October 24, 1930; *Detroit News*, October 18, 1930, October 22, 1930, October 24, 1930. Regardless of the verdict, the police repeated their belief that Locano, Amico and a third Italian, Benny "The Ape" Sebastiano (whom the police had been unable to find until "he walked into the courtroom to help the defense"), were guilty of the Milazzo and Parrino slayings [*Detroit Free Press*, October 23, 1930]).
87. Friends of LaMare, the Weavers, were interviewed as part of the police investigation of his murder. LaMare had spoken to them immediately before he left for the Indianapolis Races on about May 26, 1930, some five days before Milazzo and Parrino were slain. LaMare even then told the Weavers that he "was going to be killed." (Detroit Police Department file on the LaMare case, statement of Mr and Mrs C.W. Weaver on February 8, 1931).
88. *Detroit News*, February 7, 1931, February 9, 1931, February 10, 1931. Joe Amico and Elmer Macklin were sought for questioning by the police, who considered that as friends of the dead man they were in a perfect position to double-cross him. An attempt was made to convict Amico, Macklin and Joe Girardi for the LaMare homicide in 1932. After a mistrial, Girardi was dropped from the case, and 8 days later, by a directed verdict, Macklin and Amico were also freed (State of Michigan in the Recorders' Court for the City of Detroit, no. A-3152, the People vs. Joe Amico, Elmer Macklin and Joe Girardi, March 1932; Kavieff, *The Violent Years*, 67).
89. Bonanno, *A Man of Honour*, 100. Though since Morello left Sicily in the 1890s and Maranzano was born in 1886, this claim would at first sight seem

far fetched. Morello briefly visited Sicily in 1921, as one of the "condemned 12" (Chapter 6), and may have then met Maranzano in Palermo.

90. Bonanno, *A Man of Honour*, 104.
91. Bonanno, *A Man of Honour*, 92–3.
92. American immigration authorities attempted in the summer of 1930 to trace Maranzano and his family for suspected fraud involving Maranzano's application for American citizenship (NARA, RG 59, General Records of the Department of State Visa Division Individual Case File 1933–1940, box 1360, same series 1924–32, box 70; RG 85 Entry 26, File 38/71, box 1012, letter of June 18, 1930.) Maranzano's family, if they were indeed living in Montreal, could not be unearthed.
93. Bonanno, *A Man of Honour*, 104.
94. Detectives watching the Hudson Sporting Goods Company store on Warren Street seized Bonanno and DiBenedetto, who were observed leaving the store carrying packages (*NYT* September 18, 1930; Bonanno, *A Man of Honour*, 108–9). Bonanno in his book related in graphic detail how the police beat him up after his arrest, but he never confessed. "This ordeal at the hands of the police was one of my proudest moments" (Bonanno, *A Man of Honour*, 108–113).
95. *Detroit News*, October 27, 1930, October 29, 1930. The *Detroit News* (October 27, 1930) suggested that Bonanno and DiBenedetto had represented themselves "as the coal company's agents" when they "appeared at the sporting goods house" in Brooklyn. Angelo Meli was born 1897 in San Cataldo, Sicily. Over a long career in organized crime, Meli was convicted only once, incurring a $100 fine for carrying a concealed weapon. His son Vincent was married to the daughter of Santo Perrone, while his two daughters wed Jack Tocco and the son of Sebastian Lucido, both prominent in the Detroit organization in coming years (OCN, Exhibit 51–14–4 [Meli, Angelo]; www.ellisislandrecords.org).
96. OCN, 193.
97. Chief Assistant U.S. Attorney Thomas E. Dewey argued that Gagliano's "actual income" in 1928 was $245,000 (*Bronx Home News*, March 1, 1932).
98. Maas, *The Canary That Sang*, 81.
99. Kings County Surrogate's Court, file no. 7873 year 1931, In the Matter of the Petition of Elizabetta Maranzano for Salvatore Maranzano.
100. OCN, 193–4; Valachi, *The Real Thing*, 338; FBI, *Thomas Luchese*, New York Office, February 25, 1963; Maas, *The Canary That Sang*, 81.
101. FBI, *Thomas Luchese*, New York Office, February 25, 1963.
102. Stefano Magaddino, "Charlie Buffalo" (Calogero DiBenedetto) and John Montana.
103. According to Valachi, Maranzano Family member Dominick "Mimi" Sabella was active in getting his brother Salvatore, also Castellammare born, into the War. Dominick Sabella was probably the "Mimi" that Bonanno referred to in his book as the "strong-arm blockhead" who tried to shake him down (*A Man of Honour*, 77–80).
104. For author Celeste Morello's consumption, Riccobene stated that went to New York with several other Philadelphia members. For the *Philadelphia Daily News*, Riccobene said he was asked but refused to join Sabella in New York (*Philadelphia Daily News*, December 27, 2000; Celeste A. Morello, *Before Bruno Book 1* [1999], 94).
105. Cressey, *Theft of the Nation*, 41.
106. Chandler, *The Criminal Brotherhoods*, 150. Similar comments appear in Stephen Fox, *Blood and Power* (New York: William Morrow, 1989), 67;

Cressey, *Theft of the Nation*, 40; Ralph Salerno and John S. Tompkins, *The Crime Confederation* (Garden City: Doubleday and Doubleday, 1969), 87.

107. Bonanno, *A Man of Honour*, 118.

108. OCN, 214.

109. Maas, *The Canary That Sang*, 90.

110. Bill Bonanno, *Bound by Honor* (New York: St. Martin's Paperbacks, 2000), 51.

111. Gay Talese, *Honor Thy Father* (London: Souvenir Press, 1971), 205.

112. An informant for the *Detroit News*, "in close touch" with the underworld, told it that Sicilian "townsmen" of Milazzo and Parrino in America were set on avenging their deaths. That event partially caused the Gaglio brothers and Sam Cifulco to be murdered (*Detroit News*, July 13, 1930). Sam and Joe Gaglio were ambushed on July 7, 1930 as they repaired a tire on their car at a Detroit gas station. Cifulco, "a Meli gunman," was slain July 12, 1930, by two men armed with shotguns, pistols and a machine gun, after they ran their car onto the curb (*Detroit Free Press*, July 8, 1930; *Detroit News*, July 12, 1930; Kavieff, *The Violent Years*, 63). The seizure of a .38 caliber gun used against the Gaglios inside the home of East Side leader Joe Catalonotte, appeared to corroborate the 1930 theory of why LaMare died (OCN, exhibit 23, 7). In the previously unreported New York cases, Sebastiano Domingo confided to Valachi that two unidentified men "that was supposed to be against the old man" (Maranzano) "walked into a trap" and were promptly slain by Domingo and a cohort despite their pleas for mercy (Valachi, *The Real Thing*, 333d).

113. Carl Sifakis, *The Mafia Encyclopedia* (New York: Facts of File, 1987), 215. Several executions Downey included were based on unsupported speculation, mixing shootings committed in other contexts with those caused by Castellammare War fighting (Downey, *Gangster City*, Chapters 14 and 15).

114. Bonanno, *A Man of Honour*, 102.

115. Bonventre left approximately $40,000 in his estate.

116. Office of the Chief Medical Examiner of the City of New York, Borough of Brooklyn, case no. 2448 (1930); *NYT*, July 16, 1930; *Brooklyn Daily Eagle*, July 16, 1930.

117. Bonanno, *A Man of Honour*, 102–3.

118. Gosch and Hammer, *The Last Testament of Lucky Luciano*, 128.

119. *NYT*, August 16, 1930; *World*, August 16, 1930; Maas, *The Canary That Sang*, 80.

120. Variously spelled as Perrano and Perranio. His death certificate gives Piranio, as does his passenger arrival record, an immigrant like Morello from Corleone.

121. *NYT*, August 16, 1930; *World*, August 16, 1930.

122. OCN, 167. In 1922, Stefano Rannelli was arrested in relation to the shooting of several bystanders on August 8 by gunmen aiming to remove Joe Masseria (see p. 156) (*New York Tribune*, August 16, 1922). During the War, Rannelli botched a contract, wounding Paul Gambino, the brother of Masseria member Carlo Gambino, and was demoted by Maranzano (OCN, 189; Valachi, *The Real Thing*, 319–320). Rannelli was born in the city of Palermo, Sicily. His date of birth was subsequently a matter of legal dispute, as was his year of arrival in America. After Maranzano was assassinated in September 1931, detectives found a letter addressed to the U.S. Custom House, informing interested parties that Rannelli had been in the employment of the Eagle Building Corporation, in whose offices Maranzano was killed (NARA, RG 60, File No. 40-9439). According to

Valachi, Rannelli later made the fatal mistake of plotting the overthrow of Vito Genovese and Lucky Luciano. Valachi and two others gunned down Rannelli on November 19, 1936 outside an apartment at 235 East 107th Street owned by the Vincent Rao family.

123. OCN, 168.
124. Maas, *The Canary That Sang*, 80.
125. *NYT* September 6, 1930; Manhattan death certificate no. 20943 (1930); Downey, *Gangster City*, 153–4.
126. Valachi, *The Real Thing*, 280–2.
127. Valachi, *The Real Thing*, 322.
128. The likeliest candidates were Ruggerio Consiglio and Giovanni Anselmo. A list of Italian gangland fatalities was compiled from *New York Times* articles published between September 6 and October 28, 1930. Four slayings fit the few facts known. In chronological order, they were:

    September 26, 1930. Joseph Bivone was found dead in a Monroe Street (Brooklyn) doorway with five bullets in his body. The police stated that he was probably "a victim of a gang dispute over territory."

    October 6, 1930. Carmine Piraino was shot dead on 85th Street, Brooklyn, "in much the same manner" as was his father Giuseppe Piraino that March. Peter Sardini, an acquaintance of Brooklyn *amici nostri*, insisted that Salvatore "Sally the Sheik" Musacchio was responsible for Carmine's demise, acting on the orders of "Manfredo" (probably Masseria ally Manfredi Mineo). The getaway driver was believed by Sardini to be Musacchio's close friend Tony "The Chief" Bonasera (New York Municipal Archives (NYMA), Murder Inc. Collection, "Statement No. 2512, Re: Statements of Peter Sardini," 18–24).

    October 8, 1930. Ruggiero Consiglio, a "wealthy building contractor," was ambushed in Brooklyn and two gunmen wounded his brother. Consiglio had been arrested several times before, including for playing a confidence game and for robbery. On his body was found a list of gang figures, among them Ciro Terranova and Anthony "Little Augie Pisano" Carfano of the Masseria setup.

    October 18, 1930. Giovanni Anselmo, a Brooklyn grape dealer, was shot down in front of his store at Avenue U and West 6th Street. Anselmo was acquitted with Joseph Piraino of the 1918 "barrel murder" of Gaspare Candello on Hicks Street, Brooklyn.

129. OCN, 167.
130. Chandler's contention that Pinzolo and Morello were unlucky enough to be targeted under the plan makes no sense, since the Gagliano led faction from Pinzolo's own Family killed him, and Maranzano's people had earlier murdered Morello (Chandler, *The Criminal Brotherhoods*, 146).
131. OCN, 180.
132. Milano became Cleveland boss upon the murder of Joseph Porrello in July, 1930.
133. Gentile, *Vita di Capomafia*, 101.
134. At least four of Masseria's brothers lived in Cleveland: Mercurio, John, Calogero and Salvatore "Sam." We cannot be sure which one Gentile was referring to. Salvatore was a convicted bootlegger, (*The Lima News*, March 2, 1930) and when the 1930 census was taken, his family and that of Rosario Porrello shared the same house on East 127th Street. John Masseria was "taken for a ride" and slain in New York in 1937 (*NYT*, June 23, 1937). Mercurio Masseria was also involved in organized crime.
135. Whose brother Bartolo (born 1904 in Palermo) was a listed member of the Lucchese Family in years to come.

136. *NYT, New York Herald Tribune, New York Daily News*, November 6, 1930. From Valachi we learn that the killers had originally hoped to use an apartment across the courtyard from the room they eventually utilized. Valachi, fearing that using the original apartment would lead to his arrest, vetoed the idea (Valachi, *The Real Thing*, 295; OCN, 171).

137. Plans to wait until Masseria showed up were abandoned for fear of discovery and of missing the opportunity to get the others. The feeling was, "Let us grab what we have" (*NYT, New York Herald Tribune*, November 6, 1930; OCN, 173).

138. *Bronx Home News*, November 6, 1930.

139. Frank "Chick 99" Callaci's sister supplied the furniture that the crew stalking Mineo and Ferrigno first used while they were waiting for their victims to appear on Pelham Parkway. It came from "106th and Third Avenue," where, Masseria knew, the Gaglianos met (OCN, 172 and 180; Valachi, *The Real Thing*, 299).

140. Bonanno, *A Man of Honour*, 116.

141. Gentile, *Vita di Capomafia*, 102–3.

142. Valachi, *The Real Thing*, 322.

143. Bonanno, *A Man of Honour*, 120.

144. Troia was born 1886 in San Giuseppe Iato, Sicily. At first active in Madison, Springfield and Rockford, Illinois, Troia met an abrupt end on August 22, 1935, when with his son Joseph and Frank Longo (a fellow Springfield transplant from San Giuseppe Iato), he was fired upon by 3 men who "raked" the Newark store in which they were meeting, a reputed lottery operation headquarters (New Jersey State Department of Health Certificate of Death no. 10603 (1935); *Newark Evening News* and *NYT*, August 23, 1935; *L'Ora*, January 24–25, 1962; Gentile, *Translated Transcription*, 168–70).

145. Born in Palermo in the 1890s, under the alias of Frank LaCort, Loverde was fined $5,000 in 1929 for operating a "still" in a large garage in Racine, Wisconsin (*Chicago Tribune*, May 1, 1930, June 12, 1930, October 9, 1930).

146. Gentile, *Vita di Capomafia*, 103. Yeast broker by trade, Siragusa was known as a "big shot" in the Pittsburgh bootlegging rackets. Born 1882 in Palermo, Siragusa entered America in September 1910, living in Brooklyn until moving on to Pittsburgh. There, he operated a bakery and later a sandwich shop before, in 1928, realizing the rich rewards from supplying illegal alcohol distillers with a vital raw ingredient (*Pittsburgh Press*, September 14, 1931, August 3, 1932; Pennsylvania Crime Commission 1990 Report, 115).

147. *Paese Sera*, September 23, 1963.

148. *Paese Sera*, September 23, 1963; Gentile, *Vita di Capomafia*, 107–111.

149. Gentile, *Translated Transcription*, 98.

150. Gentile, *Vita di Capomafia*, 111; *Paese Sera*, September 26, 1963.

151. Bonanno, *A Man of Honour*, 121–2; Valachi, *The Real Thing*, 329.

152. OCN, 198.

153. *NYT*, February 4, 1931.

154. Valachi, *The Real Thing*, 317; OCN, 188; Maas, *The Canary That Sang*, 92–3.

155. Catania had a lock on the Italian bread industry in the Bronx, in which Dutch Schultz had an interest. As a consequence of their "coercion and intimidation," the price of bread in the borough was "2 cents more, per loaf" than in Manhattan (New York Municipal Archives, WPA Italians in New York, MN # 21261 roll no. 262). As a test of his loyalty, Maranzano gave Frank Scalise, formerly with Masseria, the job of removing Catania. After nothing happened, a team composed of Domingo, Nick Capuzzi, Valachi, and Shillitani carried out the assignment (Valachi, *The Real Thing*, 322–3). Catania

was walking along Delmont and Crescent Avenue, The Bronx, to the Bank of Sicily on February 3, 1931 when he was felled by shotgun fire. Shillitani recited how "he saw the dust come out of Joe's coat as the bullets hit him in the back." Valachi drove them from the scene (*NY Herald Tribune*, *NYT*, February 4, 1931; Valachi, *The Real Thing*, 327; OCN, 191–2; Maas, *The Canary That Sang*, 93).

156. *New York Herald Tribune*, April 17, 1931.
157. *NYT*, April 16, 1931.
158. Gentile, *Vita di Capomafia*, 111. Since Gentile was a intimate of Masseria, this is probably a more accurate version than that given by Valachi, that the meeting was to decide how "to get Maranzano" (OCN, 199).
159. *New York Evening Post*, April 16, 1931.
160. *NYT*, April 16, 1931. Unsurprisingly given the amount of interest in the affair, several "suspects" in the Masseria murder case have been identified by pundits, though no prosecutions took place. Valachi named "those in attendance" with Masseria at the time of his demise as Lucky Luciano, Vito Genovese, Frank Livorsi (Ciro Terranova's chauffeur and aide) and Joseph Stracci (OCN, 211). While the ultimate decision to dispose of Masseria was no doubt taken by Luciano, the possible role of Vincent Mangano has not been considered. Mangano, as noted, had secretly moved across to Maranzano (NARA, RG 170, Records of DEA, BNDD "Subject Files of the Bureau of Narcotics and Dangerous Drugs," box 52, "Organized Crime Conference"; Bonanno, *A Man of Honour*, 121) while remaining close to Masseria—and was due to meet Masseria in the Coney Island restaurant on the day Masseria died. Maranzano had attempted to use Mangano to get Masseria before, "being that he has unlimited trust in him" (FBI report of July 1, 1963 from the New York Office titled *La Cosa Nostra*; NARA, RG 170, Records of DEA, BNDD "Subject Files of the Bureau of Narcotics and Dangerous Drugs," box 52; Gentile, *Vita di Capomafia*, 106). A New York Police Department report in 1940 named John "Johnny Silk Stockings" Giustra, who was with the Mangano crowd on the South Brooklyn piers, as their prime suspect in the Masseria case. Because Giustra was shot dead in July 1931, it was recommended, "the case be marked closed." (New York Municipal Archives, Murder Inc. collection, box 17, "Giuseppi Masseria"). This information points to Mangano as among those that set Masseria up for execution.
161. Albini, *The American Mafia*, 245.
162. Peter Lupsha, "Organized Crime in the United States," in *Organized Crime: A Global Perspective*, Robert J. Kelly (ed.) (Totowa, New Jersey: Rowman and Littlefield, 1986), 48.
163. FBI, *La Cosa Nostra*, New York Office, July 1, 1963; Gentile, *Vita di Capomafia*, 97.
164. Bonanno, *A Man of Honour*, 125.
165. Maas, *The Canary That Sang*, 97; Bonanno, *A Man of Honour*, 124. Which is why Maranzano could not "promote" Luciano as a reward for his help in getting rid of Masseria.
166. Valachi, *The Real Thing*, 342.
167. Attempts to identify the venue Valachi mentioned were stymied by the lack of detail in his description. But 1931 "Trow's General Directory" lists the Zion Palace and Bronx Winter Gardens on Washington Avenue.
168. Selwyn Raab, *Five Families* (New York: St. Martin's Press, 2005); Scaduto, *Lucky Luciano*, 89.
169. Maas, *The Canary That Sang*, 97.
170. Valachi, *The Real Thing*, 341–3; OCN, 215. Joseph Morello was also known as Peter Morello, probably from Piddu, the diminutive of Giuseppe in Sicilian.

171. Sean McWeeney, "The Sicilian Mafia and Its Impact on the United States," *FBI Law Enforcement Bulletin*, (February 1987): 4.
172. Bureau of Narcotics District No. 2, Memorandum Report of September 24, 1962 by Frank J. Selvaggi.
173. Gentile, *Translated Transcription*, 105; Bonanno, *A Man of Honour*, 127–8.
174. Chandler, *The Criminal Brotherhoods*, 155.
175. Ibid., 149.
176. OCN, 195.
177. OCN, 215; Valachi, *The Real Thing*, 342.
178. Bonanno, *A Man of Honour*, 125.
179. Ibid., 128–9.
180. Cressey, *Theft of the Nation*, 38.
181. Gentile, *Translated Transcription*, 39, 41. Masseria was "stained with the most horrible vileness."
182. Refer to *Paese Sera*, September 19, 1963. Which was why Vito Cascioferro could not send Maranzano to America as his "direct representative" (Chandler, *The Criminal Brotherhoods*, 136) or as a "bridge-head for the eventual and triumphant return of Don Vito back into the New York underworld" (Thom L. Jones, "The Sun King of the Mafia" http://realdealmafia.com/mobcorner_intro.html).
183. Henner Hess, *Mafia and Mafiosi: The Structure of Power* (Farnborough, Hants.: Saxon House, 1973), 92.
184. Dickie, *Cosa Nostra*, 298.
185. Anton Blok, *The Mafia of a Sicilian Village 1860–1960* (Cambridge: Polity Press, 1988), 145.
186. Bonanno, *A Man of Honour*, 123. Valachi's knowledge of the boss of bosses was limited to his just hearing of the term (OCN, 80–1).
187. The fourth *capo di capi*, Gaspare Messina of Boston, only occupied the "post" as a stop-gap between Masseria and Maranzano.
188. Gentile, *Vita di Capomafia*, 90.
189. *L'Ora*, September 26, 1963.
190. An excellent example is found in the article "Where the Mafia Goes to Die," by Pietro Donato (*Oui*, August 1974).
191. Lucchese explained that his appearance with Biondo and Luciano was purely accidental. "I wanted to see a fight, and we wasn't together at all. In the morning I'm taking the train and these people are going into town to use the station, and we met in the lobby." He never again saw them (New York State Crime Commission, *Proceedings Pursuant to the Governor's Executive Order of March 29, 1951*, 77–9; New York State Crime Commission, *Public Hearings No. 4*, 1952, 313–5).
192. Not in June 1931 as Capeci and even Bonanno stated.
193. According to the *New York World-Telegram*, Maranzano "sat on a dais placed over the spot where "Joe the Boss" had been killed." (September 11, 1931).
194. *New York Herald Tribune*, August 2, 1931.
195. *New York Herald-Tribune*, August 2, 1931; *New York Sun*, August 3, 1931. Marty Salvatore, president of the Society, saw it as the ideal venue to "create peace and harmony among the factions of Italians and Sicilians of New York" and to end the "feuds and vendettas which have caused so much bloodshed among his countrymen in this city" (*New York Herald Tribune*, August 2, 1931). Former Secret Service agent Joe Palma told Kefauver's investigators in 1951 of the existence and basic function of the celebration (NARA, RG 46, series 29, alphabetical name files, "Mafia (Suspects)") Until Valachi spoke, the police wrongly believed that Maranzano was killed for not handing over the proceeds from the sale of tickets to the bash.

196. FBI report. Albany office, December 1957, "Joseph Barbara, Sr."; *NYT*, September 17, 1935; Manhattan death certificate no. 19919 (1935).
197. *NYT*, August 18, 1930. The festival ended in Manhattan in the late 1940s or early 1950s (email from Raymond Bono Geany, July 26, 2006).
198. Certificate of incorporation of the Sciacca Maritime Association, July 1899.
199. John C. Sabetta, *Report to the Mayor Concerning the Matter of San Gennaro and the 1995 San Gennaro Feast* (December 1995).
200. Gentile, *Translated Transcription*, 107.
201. Bonanno, *A Man of Honour*, 124.
202. Maas, *The Canary That Sang*, 98.
203. OCN, 217–8.
204. Gentile, *Vita di Capomafia*, 115.
205. Valachi, *The Real Thing*, 355. Gentile says that $150,000 was raised (*Paese Sera*, September 28, 1963). In excess of $200,000 was spent on the banquet, according to Stefano Magaddino (FBI report of March 31, 1965 from SAC, Buffalo titled *Steve Magaddino AKA ar.*).
206. Bonanno, *A Man of Honour*, 137.
207. FBI, *Steve Magaddino AKA ar*, SAC, Buffalo, March 31, 1965.
208. FBI, *Steve Magaddino AKA ar*, SAC, Buffalo, March 31, 1965.
209. OCN, 216–8; Valachi, *The Real Thing*, 355; Gentile, *Vita di Capomafia*, 115–6; and in Gentile's September 1963 *Paese Sera* magazine interviews.
210. OCN, 221; Valachi, *The Real Thing*, 355–6. Bonanno recalled how Maranzano gave $80,000 for him to hold onto, with no questions to be asked as to its use (*A Man of Honour*, 130).
211. Valachi, *The Real Thing*, 361.
212. OCN, 221; Valachi, *The Real Thing*, 362. Bonanno alleged that he only knew of the "hit list" after Maranzano died (Bonanno, *A Man of Honour*, 139).
213. Maas, *The Canary That Sang*, 100.
214. Valachi, *The Real Thing*, 350–1.
215. Valachi, *The Real Thing*, 352. Daniel Iamascia was killed in June 1931 while he was with Schultz, when he whipped out his revolver in the mistaken belief that detectives trailing them were elements of the Vincent Coll gang fighting Schultz (*NYT*, June 18, 1931).
216. Gentile, *Translated Transcription*, 110.
217. FBI, *La Cosa Nostra*, New York Office, Field Office File No. 92–2300, July 1, 1963; Gentile, *Vita di Capomafia*, 117; Gentile, *Translated Transcription*, 110.
218. Gentile, *Vita di Capomafia*, 116.
219. Bonanno, *A Man of Honour*, 140.
220. Hickman Powell, *Ninety Times Guilty* (London: Robert Hale, 1939), 81; Burton B. Turkus and Sid Feder *Murder Inc.* (New York: Manor Books, 1974), 71–3.
221. Scaduto, *Lucky Luciano*, 74.
222. Sid Feder and Joachim Joesten, *The Luciano Story* (New York: DaCapo Press, 1994), 82. Insights into Luciano's role in the industry are recorded in Court of Appeals of the State of New York, The People of the State of New York against Louis Buchalter, Emanuel Weiss and Louis Capone (1942), testimony of Max Rubin.
223. Block, *East Side West Side*, 172.
224. Paul R. Kavieff, *The Life and Times of Lepke Buchalter* (New Jersey: Barricade Books, 2006), 53.
225. *NYT*, July 1, 1931.

226. Matthew Josephson, *Sidney Hillman: Statesman of American Labor* (Garden City, NY: Doubleday, 1952), 334.
227. *NYT*, August 1, 1931; John Jay College, Burton Turkus Papers, Re: Death of Guiseppe Masseria.
228. Shortly before the killing, John Ferreri had been acquitted of a charge of assaulting a union official (*NYT*, September 12, 1940). The Ferreri case was resurrected periodically by prosecutors. It was linked to the "Murder Inc." probe, for example, and to police corruption in Brooklyn (*Brooklyn Eagle*, September 12, 1940, September 19, 1940, November 25, 1940, December 4, 1941).
229. Scaduto, *Lucky Luciano*, 90.
230. Harry "Dutch" Goldberg was a leading but less known New York and California racketeer of the period.
231. Turkus and Feder, *Murder Inc.* 71–3.
232. Bonanno, *A Man of Honour*, 151.
233. Scaduto, *Lucky Luciano*, 91.
234. Two hats were found after Maranzano was killed, according to the *Sun*. "Chicago-sold," one had written on it "an address adjoining" Maranzano's Brooklyn residence (*Sun*, September 11, 1931).
235. Appearing in Powell, *Ninety Times Guilty*, 81–2.
236. Levine, Luciano, the Lansky brothers Jake and Meyer, and Benjamin "Bugsy" Siegel had been confederates in a bootlegging ring (NARA, RG 46 series 29, alphabetical name files, "Costello, Frank").
237. Feder and Joesten, *The Luciano Story*, 83.
238. Gagliano underboss Lucchese recalled to the State Crime Commission how, with Gagliano, he was waiting to see Maranzano. They were "not there a few minutes when some people with badges come in and they lined us all up." "The first thing we knew we heard shuffling inside" It was planned to kill the *capo di capi* quietly using stiletto knives. But the ferocity of Maranzano's resistance necessitated the use of guns. Nonetheless, the fatal wound was made by a stiletto; Maranzano was found dead by his secretary slumped in his chair (*Sun*, September 11, 1931; New York State Crime Commission, *Vol. 1 Public Hearing No. 4 New York County*, 309; New York State Crime Commission, *Proceedings Pursuant to the Governor's Executive Order of March 29, 1951*, 111; Office of the Chief Medical Examiner, Borough of Manhattan, case no. 5431 [1931]).
239. Valachi reported how the Italians "helped (the Jews) when they had trouble among themselves." (OCN, 229.) Maas confused the timeline, wrongly stating that the "Jew War" came before the murder of Maranzano (*The Canary That Sang*, 104).
240. Valachi, *The Real Thing*, 423.
241. *NYT*, July 3, 1933.
242. In February 1932, Coll met a fitting end for a Prohibition gangster, machine-gunned to death in a West 23rd Street drugstore. Weinberg was reputed to be the lookout man in the slaying (*NYT*, *NY Herald-Tribune*, February 8, 1932). Weinberg "disappeared" in 1935 after being instrumental in the take-over by Schultz of the Harlem policy game (Paul Sann, *Kill the Dutchman!* (New York: Popular Library, 1971), 67, 152–3).
243. OCN, 231.
244. Chandler added that Coll was enlisted by Maranzano because he "could approach" Luciano and Genovese "without arousing suspicion." Questions remain. If the murders of Luciano and Genovese were to be carried out on or near the Maranzano office, they would have pointed to Maranzano's involvement even though he did not pull the trigger. And how Coll, whose face was known to most New Yorkers, envisaged pulling off the Luciano

and Genovese hits without being recognized is unexplained. Luciano moreover was known to travel with bodyguards, who would be expected to drop Coll if he attempted to kill their boss (Maas, *The Canary That Sang*, 106; Chandler, *The Criminal Brotherhoods*, 160; OCN, 230). Weinberg told basics of the story to Dixie Davis, but in his account, there was no mention of Coll's role (*Collier's*, August 5, 1939).
245. OCN, 222.
246. "That day, the Gap came around and he decided we would go to Brooklyn." Petrelli correctly thought that anyone looking for Valachi to do him harm would give Valachi "the benefit of the doubt" if Petrelli, who was not wanted, was in his company (OCN, 222; Valachi, *The Real Thing*, 368–9).
247. Valachi, *The Real Thing*, 366. Rumors had long circulated that "Tommy" Lucchese, the Gagliano underboss, betrayed Maranzano (e.g. in Feder, *The Luciano Story*, 85).
248. Gentile, who supplied the least number of murders, was in Sicily over the first months of the War. Valachi omitted the fatalities occurring in Detroit, and those of Vito Bonventre and Joseph Parrino. Bonanno only skipped the two "pact" fatalities and that of Catania.
249. Against the case that, "The background of the Commission case is the history of Cosa Nostra itself" (Jacobs, *Busting the Mob*, 79).
250. Following the passage of interstate laws against racketeering in 1961, Kennedy was anxious to promote at the federal level legal wiretap laws and ones related to the granting of immunity from prosecution to key informers. A draft wiretap bill had been presented in 1962 to Congress, where it was in limbo.
251. Robert F. Kennedy, *The Enemy Within* (New York: Da Capo Press, 1994 [1st ed. in 1960]).
252. *NYT*, October 13, 1963, April 3, 1965.
253. "Where once there had been small and isolated neighborhood gangs, now the major interests of the underworld were really all one mob" (Powell, *Ninety Times Guilty*, 80).
254. FBI, *Wanted by the FBI: The Mob. FBI Organized Crime Report–25 Years After Valachi*, 9.

NOTES TO CHAPTER 8

1. Humbert S. Nelli, *The Business of Crime* (New York: Oxford University Press, 1976), 207.
2. *New York Times* (hereafter *NYT*) November 10, 1935; Dwight C. Smith, *The Mafia Mystique* (London: Hutchinson, 1975), 65.
3. *NYT* July 8, 1928.
4. *NYT*, May 27, 1929.
5. "Crime as an American Way of Life," in Daniel Bell, *The End of Ideology* (New York: The Free Press, 1962), 129.
6. Craig Thompson and Allen Raymond, *Gang Rule in New York* (New York: The Dial Press, 1940), 354–5.
7. Mark H. Haller, "Bureaucracy and the Mafia: An Alternative View," *Journal of Contemporary Criminal Justice* 8, no. 1 (1992): 18.
8. Ralph Salerno and John S. Tompkins, *The Crime Confederation* (Garden City: Doubleday and Doubleday, 1969), 87.
9. U.S. Congress Senate, Committee on Government Operations, *Organized Crime and the Illicit Traffic in Narcotics: Report*, 89th Congress 1st Session, 1965, 13.
10. Francis A. J. Ianni with Elizabeth Reuss-Ianni, *A Family Business* (London: Routledge and Kegan Paul, 1972), 72–3.

11. Ianni, *A Family Business*, 56, 59.
12. Peter A. Lupsha, "Organized Crime in the United States," in *Organized Crime A Global Perspective*, Robert J. Kelly (ed.) (Totowa, N.J.: Rowman and Littlefield, 1986), 47–8.
13. Nelli, *The Business of Crime*, 179–80.
14. U.S. Congress, Senate, Committee on Government Operations, Permanent Subcommittee on Investigations, *Organized Crime and the Illicit Traffic in Narcotics*, hearings 88th Congress 1st Session, 1963 (hereafter OCN), 96.
15. FBI, *Charles LoCicero*, New York Office August 16, 1960.
16. Bill Bonanno, *Bound by Honor* (New York: St. Martin's Paperbacks, 1999), 16.
17. FBI, *La Cosa Nostra*, New York Office July 1, 1963.
18. FBI, *La Cosa Nostra*, Buffalo Office, July 27, 1962.
19. Joseph Bonanno with Sergio Lalli, *A Man of Honour* (London: Andre Deutsch, 1983), 162–4.
20. U.S. National Archives and Records Administration (hereafter NARA) RG 60, Joseph Valachi, *The Real Thing*, 6n.
21. Bonanno, *A Man of Honour*, 163.
22. Burton B. Turkus and Sid Feder, *Murder Inc.* (New York: Manor Books, 1974), 70; Giuseppe Selvaggi, *The Rise of the Mafia in New York* (Indianapolis: The Bobbs-Merrill Co., 1978), 74.
23. *FBI Criminal Intelligence Digest*, March 11, 1963; FBI, *La Cosa Nostra Chicago Division*, Chicago Office, July 16, 1964.
24. Nelli, *The Business of Crime*, 140.
25. Stephen Fox, *Blood and Power* (New York: William Morrow, 1989), 44.
26. Nelli, *The Business of Crime*, 180.
27. Bonanno, *A Man of Honour*, 163–4.
28. *New York Herald*, June 19, 1936.
29. James B. Jacobs, *Mobsters, Unions, and Feds* (New York: New York University Press, 2006), 4; Peter A. Lupsha, "Individual Choice, Material Culture, and Organized Crime," *Criminology* 19 no.1 (1981): 10–1; Donald R. Cressey, *The Functions and Structure of Criminal Syndicates* Task Force Report: Organized Crime, (U.S. Government Printing Office 1967), 37–8; Robert J. Kelly, *The Upperworld and the Underworld* (New York: Kluwer Academic Press, 1999), 52–3.
30. Selwyn Raab, *Five Families* (New York: St. Martin's Press, 2005).
31. Nelli, *The Business of Crime*, 207.
32. Feder, *The Luciano Story*, 78.
33. Mark H. Haller, "Bootleggers and American Gambling 1920–1950" in Commission on the Review of the National Policy Toward Gambling, *Gambling in America Appendix 1* (October 1976), 102–43; Mark H. Haller, "The Changing Structure of American Gambling in the Twentieth Century," *Journal of Social Issues* 35, no.3 (1979): 89–90.
34. Lupsha, *Individual Choice*, 9.
35. Nelli, *The Business of Crime*, 202–3.
36. Nelli, *The Business of Crime*, 207.
37. John Dickie, *Cosa Nostra* (London: Coronet, 2004), 221, 228–9.
38. *Paese Sera*, September 24, 1963.
39. Detailed biographies were collected on most of those specified, but space limitations prevented their inclusion.
40. Thomas A. Firestone, "Mafia Memoirs: What They Tell Us About Organized Crime," *Journal of Contemporary Criminal Justice* 9 (1993): 198–201.
41. Especially revealing in the narcotics traffic where the Bonannos were strong despite the leaderships' distaste for it ("My Tradition outlaws narcotics," Bonanno opined [*A Man of Honour*, 209]).
42. *NYT*, March 2, 1930.

43. *Paese Sera*, September 24, 1963.
44. Gentile, *Translated Transcription*, 104, 114.
45. Michael Woodiwiss, "Making Mr. Big," *BBC History* 3, no. 4 (2002): 25–8; Bonanno, *Bound by Honor*, 52.
46. Joseph L. Albini, "The Mafia and the Devil: What They have in Common," *Journal of Contemporary Criminal Justice* 9, no. 3 (1993): 243.
47. Donald R. Cressey, *Theft of the Nation* (New York: Harper and Row 1969), 44.
48. Hickman Powell, *Ninety Times Guilty* (London: Robert Hale, 1939), 83.
49. Turkus and Feder, *Murder Inc.*, 74.
50. For salient examples, read The President's Commission on Law Enforcement and Administration of Justice, Task Force on Organized Crime, *Task Force Report: Organized Crime* (1967) 38; Tony Scaduto, *Lucky Luciano* (London: Sphere Books, 1976), 93–4; David Leon Chandler, *The Criminal Brotherhoods* (London: Constable, 1976), 160.
51. Correcting Nelli's view that "The story was later repeated, and embellished, by Joe Valachi in testimonies before the McClelland Committee in 1963" (Robert J. Kelly (ed.) *Organized Crime: A Global Perspective* [Totowa, N.J.: Rowman and Littlefield, 1986], 2).
52. Joseph L. Albini, *The American Mafia: Genesis of a Legend* (New York: Appleton-Century-Crofts, 1971), 245.
53. Albini, *The American Mafia*, 244–5.
54. Gay Talese, *Honor Thy Father* (London: Souvenir Press, 1971), 207.
55. Nelli, *The Business of Crime*, 181–5.
56. Alan A. Block, "History and the Study of Organized Crime," *Urban Life* 6, no. 4 (1978), 460.
57. There were at least two other Italian organized crime homicides that took place in New York City within a week of the Maranzano killing, those of small-time alcohol dealer Frank Plescia on September 14, and Joseph Mannino. Felled on September 13, Mannino had been arrested with Joe Piraino in 1920, and had remained on friendly terms with Piraino (*NYT*, September 14, 1931). Mannino was found lying on Union Street with gunshot wounds to his body and head (*New York Herald Tribune*, September 15, 1931; *NYT*, September 13, 1931; New York Municipal Archives, Murder Inc. collection, box 8, "Misc. News Clippings").
58. Bonanno, *A Man of Honour*, 150.
59. *Newark Star-Ledger*, November 15, 1931; Patrick Downey, *Gangster City: The History of the New York Underworld 1900–1935* (New Jersey: Barricade Books, 2004), 166.
60. *Newark Star-Ledger*, September 14, 1931; *Jersey Observer*, September 14, 1931.
61. Maas, *The Canary That Sang*, 106; OCN, 232; Valachi, *The Real Thing*, 365–6. How Valachi learned of their murders is unclear; his 1963 testimony and autobiography are inconsistent on this point. He presumed a link, and was not told of one. In another telling, Valachi claimed that one of Ciro Terranova's "nephews" killed LePore, in the mistaken assumption that LePore had killed Terranova kinsman Joe Catania earlier in 1931 (NARA, memorandum to New York County District Attorney dated July 22, 1963). If Valachi is believed, evidence points to Ciro Catania, one of Joe Catania's brothers, as the guilty party.
62. OCN, 223–6; Valachi, *The Real Thing*, 368–9.
63. Stephen Casertano was born in Caserta, Italy, in 1902 (Declaration of Intention, Southern District of New York, no. 178250 [1925]).
64. Block, *History and the Study of Organized Crime*, 460.

65. Nicolo Gentile, *Translated Transcription of the Life of Nicolo (E) Gentile, Background and History of the Castellammarese War and Early Decades of Organized Crime in America* (no date), 113.
66. *Pittsburgh Press*, September 14, 1931, August 3, 1932.
67. Nelli, *The Business of Crime*, 200. The 1924 Immigration Act had limited the number of immigrants to America who could be admitted from any country to 2 percent of the number of people from there who were living in the United States in 1890. With the imposition of the quota, only 4,000 Italians per year were allowed in.
68. Chandler, *The Criminal Brotherhoods*, 57–8, 136.
69. *New York Sun*, September 11, 1931; *NYT*, September 11, 1931; *New York America*, August 12, 1931.
70. Dickie claimed, "Official American sources estimate that 500 of them escaped Mori's clutches by emigrating to the USA" (*Cosa Nostra*, 189). Refer also to Block, *East Side West Side*, Chapter 1; Nelli, *The Business of Crime*, 200.
71. NARA, RG 60, File No. 40–9439. An imitation, leather covered memorandum book, found on the sidewalk that included the names of Italian crime figures belonged to James F. Alescia, to whom the office used by Maranzano had been rented. Presuming that it was Maranzano's, the contents were splashed over the newspapers on September 11 (*NYT*, September 12, 1931). Alescia was slain in May 1932.
72. J. Richard Davis, "Things I Couldn't Tell Till Now," *Colliers*, August 5, 1939; Turkus and Feder, *Murder, Inc.*, 62–3; Thompson and Raymond, *Gang Rule in New York*, 4; Cressey, *Theft of the Nation*, 44; Nelli, *The Business of Crime*, 210; Scaduto, *Lucky Luciano*, 28.
73. Feder and Joesten, *The Luciano Story*, 85.
74. Powell, *Ninety Times Guilty*, 62.
75. Examples of this contention are found in Jay Robert Nash's *World Encyclopedia of Organized Crime* (London: Headline Books, 1992), 207, 706; John Kobler, *Capone* (New York: G.P. Putnam's Sons, 1971), 34–5; Downey's, *Gangster City*, and in Thompson and Raymond, *Gang Rule in New York*, 4.
76. Cressey, *Theft of the Nation*, 44.
77. Ianni, *A Family Business*, 58.
78. John Landesco, *Organized Crime in Chicago* (Chicago: University of Chicago Press, 1968), 195, 199, 200.
79. Giovanni Schiavo, *The Truth About the Mafia* (New York: The Vigo Press, 1962), 133.
80. Albini, *The American Mafia*, 207.
81. Smith, *The Mafia Mystique*, 83.
82. Schiavo, *The Truth About the Mafia*, 133.
83. Edwin Fenton, *Immigrants and Unions* (New York: Arno Press, 1975), 52.
84. Nelli, *From Immigrants to Ethnics*, 115–7.
85. New York City's archives, together with a comprehensive search of directories of clubs and association in New York City yielded nothing to suggest the existence of the Unione there. Annual editions of *The Brooklyn Daily Eagle Almanac* contained no such organization. Talks with those who knew about Italian-American organizations came up with the same negative result (communication with Rick Warner).
86. Schiavo, *The Truth About the Mafia*, 133–4. Schiavo made the point that a few non-Sicilians were admitted as members, including Barasa.
87. Walter Noble Burns, *The One-Way Ride* (London: Stanley Paul, 1931), 206.
88. Kobler, *Capone*, 162–3: "As a non-Sicilian Capone could not qualify for even rank-and-file membership." Downey's *Gangster City* (122) states: "Unione

heads were traditionally always Sicilian." Eghigian and Porrello make the
same mistake (Mars Eghigian, Jr., *After Capone* [Nashville, TN: Cumberland House, 2006], 108; Rick Porrello, *The Rise and Fall of the Cleveland
Mafia* [New Jersey: Barricade Books, 1995], 80). According to May, "The
Unione Siciliana's leadership exclusivity would be a stone in the shoe of the
most infamous gangster of all time—Al Capone, who was of Neapolitan heritage" (Allan May "Chicago's Unione Siciliana, 1920—A Decade of Slaughter," http://crimemagazine.com/unioneII.htm).

89. NARA, RG 46, folder title list for series 29, alphabetical name index, "Mafia
and Union Sicilione," condensed in the *Washington Post,* September 11, 1955.
90. Ellis Island passenger arrivals; FBI, *Joseph Rosato*, New York Office, January 8, 1960.
91. LaPorta's story was first made public in the *Washington Post*, September 11,
1955.
92. Fenton, *Immigrants and Unions*, 52.
93. Turkus and Feder, *Murder, Inc.* 63.
94. FBI report of March 31, 1965 from SAC Buffalo to the FBI Director, subject
Steve Magaddino AKA ar., 10.
95. Maas, *The Canary That Sang*, 108; OCN, 236; FBI, *La Causa Nostra*,
New York Office, January 31, 1963. Among the council members, Valachi
recalled, was Joseph Biondo and Vincent Rao (FBI, *The Criminal "Commission"* from SAC, New York September 26, 1962).
96. Block, *History and the Study of Organized Crime*, 463.
97. A lack of family ties within the Chicago "outfit's" membership is illustrated
by genealogical charts contained in NARA, RG 170, accession number
170–74–4, BNDD "Subject Files of the Bureau of Narcotics and Dangerous
Drugs," box 52.
98. Landesco, *Organized Crime in Chicago*, 180.
99. E.g. in Andrew Sinclair, *Prohibition* (London: Four Square Books, 1965),
234–242; Kenneth Allsop, *The Bootleggers* (London: Four Square Books,
1966), Chapter 13; and Edward Behr, *Prohibition The 13 Years That
Changed America* (London: BBC Books, 1997).
100. *Times* [London], July 3, 1928.
101. *Bronx Home News*, November 6, 1930.
102. California Assembly Interim Committee Reports 1957–1959, volume 20 no.
10, Report of the Subcommittee on Rackets, 19.
103. Antonio "Tony Bender" Strollo had Neapolitan roots. Michele "Mike"
Miranda, another member close to Genovese, was born 1896 in San Giuseppe
Vesuviano near Naples. Among Masseria *caporegimes*, Vincent Alo's (born
1904) parents were from Cosenza; Gaetano Ricci (1893) was born in Vieste
(Foggia province); Michael Coppola (1900) was a product of Campagna, as
were the Eboli brothers and Anthony Carfano. Joe Adonis was born in Mon-
temarano, Avellino.
104. www.ellisislandrecords.org.
105. *NYT*, November 19, 1924; information supplied by Tom Hunt.
106. *Chicago Tribune*, February 17, 1926.
107. *NYT*, November 11, 1930; *Brooklyn Daily Eagle*, November 11, 1930.
108. *NYT*, April 20, 1931.
109. Gentile, *Translated Transcription*, 116.
110. *NYT*, September 12, 1932.
111. Gentile, *Translated Transcription*, 116.
112. Registri dello Stato Civile 1820–1920, FHL INTL Film 1965253, Nascite
1886–1899 Lercara Friddi no. 524; World War One draft registration card
(1918).

113. www.ellisisland.org.
114. Scaduto, *Lucky Luciano*, 19.
115. Scaduto, *Lucky Luciano*, 20; Feder and Joesten, *The Luciano Story*, 45.
116. *NYT*, June 19, 1936; Powell, *Ninety Times Guilty*, 71; Scaduto, *Lucky Luciano*, 43. Luciano justified it as the act of an immature adolescent; "As you get older, you get educated" (*Washington Post*, August 14, 1951).
117. NARA, RG 170, DEA Office of Enforcement Policy Classified Subject Files 1932–1967, Entry 71A-3555, report of January 5, 1954 to Harry Anslinger from Charles Siragusa; NARA, RG 170, DEA Office of Enforcement Policy Classified Subject Files, 1932–1967, box 03, folder "Siragusa's Testimony on Luciano October 26, 1951".
118. Thomas E. Dewey, *Twenty Against the Underworld* (Garden City, New York: Doubleday, 1974), 242; Powell, *Ninety Times Guilty*, 71; Scaduto, *Lucky Luciano*, 44; Feder and Joesten, *The Luciano Story*, 58.
119. *New York Herald Tribune*, June 19, 1936.
120. New York Municipal Archives, Luciano collection, location 11, "Digest of Grand Jury Testimony of Lucky Luciano".
121. New York Municipal Archives, Luciano collection, location 11, "Re: Lucky 1929 Ride" (May 27, 1936).
122. *NYT*, June 19, 1936.
123. NARA, RG 170 entry 71A-3555, DEA Office of Enforcement Policy Classified Subject Files 1932–1967.
124. Moretti's parents were from Spezia.
125. *Newark Star-Ledger*, October 5, 1951.
126. Bonanno tells us that all those at his initiation into the Schiro Family were Sicilian (*A Man of Honour*, 80).
127. The Schiro surname was unknown in Castellammare del Golfo, and no Schiros appeared on passenger arrival records as originating from Castellammare. Research uncovered four men named Nicolo Schiro living in New York at around the "right" period. The 1872 born Schiro was marginally the oldest of the group, matching Bonanno's description of the Schiro he knew, "getting on in years" (*A Man of Honour*, 93). His stated occupation and place of residence better matched that expected of a Mafioso of that era. Crucially, his movements accorded with information given to the Secret Service, that the Family leader Schiro returned to New York from Italy in 1913 (NARA, RG 87, daily reports of agents, vol. 41, reel 593, November 11, 1913). After living in Bloomfield, New Jersey, Schiro returned to Italy after the outbreak of war in September 1939, and in 1950, his Italian citizenship was re-acquired after it was noted by U.S. authorities that he had failed "to establish permanent residence in the United States" before 1944 (U.S. Immigration and Naturalization Service, certificate of the loss of the nationality of the United States, letter from General Consulate Palermo, October 14, 1949). His Bloomfield house was not sold, however.
128. Passenger arrivals in New York showed the key Bonventre and Magaddino Mafiosi exodus from Sicily to Brooklyn occurring from 1903.
129. Bonanno, *A Man of Honour*, 124.
130. Not to be confused with the man of the same name born in 1891, and detailed later.
131. 1915 Brooklyn census, Kings County Petition for Naturalization no. 23703 (1915).
132. A witness at the trial of the Ruffino brothers in 1913 for burglary was named in the transcript as Vito Bommetro, self-described as the owner of a "bake shop" at 222 North Fifth Street. Whether this was, in reality, Vito Bonventre is not known.

133. According to the *New York Herald*, the fatalities grew out of personal feuds, women, and rows over card games, an assessment echoed by a Buffalo police spokesman. The *Brooklyn Daily Eagle* informed its readers that the deaths mostly grew from feuds or were committed against informers. The Detroit police department was convinced though that they were the work of the "Camorra," while acknowledging that they were as attributable to "private or gang feuds entirely local."

134. *Brooklyn Standard Union*, August 17, 1921.

135. Bonanno, *A Man of Honour*, 63.

136. *Asbury Park Evening Press*, August 9, 1921, August 10, 1921, August 12, 1921. Fontano was born in March 1891, disembarking in New York in 1912. Although born as Bartolomeo Fontana, he was more often reported in the New York newspapers under the surname of Fontano.

137. Michael Fiaschetti, *You Gotta Be Rough* (New York: A. L. Burt, 1930), 77.

138. Noted by Fiaschetti (*You Gotta be Rough*, 76). Fontano had told his captors that he had been forced to take care of Caiozzo; otherwise he would be "burned" (murdered) by the gang he belonged to. A friend confided to Fontano, so the story went, that he was scheduled to disappear permanently and "Fontano had seen enough of the Good Killers' actions in Detroit to know the grave position he was in" (Thomas Hunt and Michael A. Tona, "The Good Killers: 1921's Glimpse of the Mafia," *On the Spot Journal*, (Spring 2007): 13). Whether this bizarre gang practice, which seemed calculated to drive members into the hands of the law for protection and was unknown anywhere else in the Mafia, was the actual reason for Fontano's cooperation with law enforcement is open to question.

139. FBI, *Steve Magaddino AKA AR*, SAC, Buffalo, March 31, 1965.

140. Comune of Castellammare del Golfo, Civil Registration Office, death certificate. Antonio Magaddino, another of Stefano's brothers, was arrested on August 14, 1916 in Castellammare for a homicide and freed in July 1917. An enquiry in Sicily failed to elucidate who Magaddino's alleged victim was (Immigration and Naturalization Service, File on Antonino Magaddino, Statement of Antonino Magaddino [1954]); Bonanno *A Man of Honour*, 41.

141. Annual Report of the Police Department City of New York for the Year 1921, 248.

142. *Freehold Transcript*, August 19, 1921; *Brooklyn Standard Union*, August 17, 1921.

143. DiGregorio was a cousin of Gaspare DiGregorio, the brother of Matteo DiGregorio. Gaspare DiGregorio was a Bonanno Mafia figure with links to the Magaddinos in Buffalo. Bartolomeo was married to Stefano Magaddino's wife's sister, and his son married the daughter of Magaddino's sister.

144. *NYT*, May 23, 1913.

145. Hunt and Tona, "The Good Killers," 18.

146. Claiming that, "two innocent people were killed" in Brooklyn. "Police suspicion fell on Stefano and Gaspar, who removed themselves from Brooklyn" (*A Man of Honour*, 63).

147. *World*, August 20, 1921.

148. *Detroit News*, August 24, 1921. Licato was gunned down and expired while walking along Clinton Street on October 15, 1920. He had been acquitted of the slaying of Roggers (*Detroit Times, Detroit News*, October 16, 1920; *Detroit Free Press*, October 16, 1920). The Roggers case was believed linked to a raid made in the "Italian" district by 3 detectives including Roggers, in which a stolen car was recovered in Tony Giannola's Wyandotte barn. Licato was seen fleeing the area after the Roggers shooting with a gun in his hand, and the seriously wounded Detective Sergeant

Joseph Kolb identified Licato as one of Roggers' assassins (*Detroit News*, July 25, 1917, July 26, 1917, August 29, 1917).

149. *NYT*, August 17, 1921.
150. Hunt and Tona, "The Good Killers," 16–7.
151. *NYT*, August 19, 1921.
152. "Print journalists accepted and printed as fact the speculations of law enforcement officials, grossly exaggerating the gang-related death toll and expanded the gang's stomping grounds without any apparent cause aside from a motivation to sell papers." (Hunt and Tona, "The Good Killers," 17).
153. Fiaschetti, *You Gotta Be Rough*, 77.
154. *Detroit News*, August 25, 1921.
155. It was unknown if the killers of Puma were friends of the fallen Caiozzo, or whether they were dispatched to silence Puma because of concerns he might confess under the pressure (*NYT*, November 5, 1922).
156. Hunt and Tona, "The Good Killers," 21.
157. *Asbury Park Evening Press*, March 21–2, 1922.
158. FBI, *Steve Magaddino Was*, Buffalo Office, February 28, 1958.
159. *Asbury Park Evening Press*, March 23, 1922.
160. *Brooklyn Standard Union*, August 17, 1921.
161. *Asbury Park Evening Press*, August 17, 1921; *Brooklyn Standard Union*, August 17, 1921; *NYT*, August 17, 1921; *World*, August 18, 1921.
162. *NYT*, August 17, 1921; *New York Herald*, August 17, 1921.
163. *New York Tribune*, August 18, 1921.
164. No New York City death certificate for a Vito Bonventre in this time frame (1900–1910) exists, and none of the New York dailies reported the slaying then of a Vito Bonventre.
165. In one report, in about 1913 (*Brooklyn Standard Union*, August 17, 1921).
166. *New York Herald*, April 15, 1908.
167. *Brooklyn Daily Eagle*, April 16, 1908; *New York Herald*, April 15, 1908.
168. The accused were scheduled to appear in court on April 23, 1908, the last known record of the matter.
169. Ellis Island passenger arrival records, birth certificates from Castellammare del Golfo. Vito Bonventre was related to Bonanno Family member John Morales through Morales' marriage to Bonventre's daughter.
170. The "Neapolitan Prince," arriving in New York port on April 23, 1906.
171. To differentiate him from the other Bonanno relative of the name born in 1875, arrested in 1921 on Fontano's information, and slain at the start of the Castellammare War in 1930 (Chapter 7).
172. Bonanno, *A Man of Honour*, 67.
173. Bonanno, *A Man of Honour*, 282. Vito Bonventre was subsequently identified as an inducted member of the Sciacca (formerly Bonanno) Family (FBI report, October 20, 1967 from New York office on LCN).
174. *NYT*, April 21, 1913. The victim's name was incorrectly spelled across newspapers as "Pucilaco," "Pucilato" and "Puccilato."
175. *NYT*, September 15, 1921. The *New York Times* in 1921 wrongly contended that Buccellato was killed in 1914, and at a different address on Chrystie Street. His death certificate also got the place of his death wrong, listing it at 192 Chrystie.
176. *NYT*, June 23, 1920.
177. *New York Tribune*, December 30, 1920; *NYT*, December 30, 1920.
178. *NYT*, March 1, 1921.
179. *New York Herald*, April 24, 1921.
180. *NYT*, June 17, 1921.

181. Court of General Sessions of the Peace City and County of New York "The People Against Joseph Ales" indictment filed September 13, 1921 for first degree murder.
182. *NYT*, September 18, 1921.
183. Since Carlo Barbara went to considerable lengths to disguise his real identity, proof of his relationship to Joseph Barbara Sr. involved an examination of the obituary of Joseph Barbara, Carlo's 1966 obituary, his naturalization papers, Ellis Island passenger immigration arrival records, Carlo's World War One draft card, his 1928 marriage certificate, and his birth certificate in Castellammare.
184. *NYT* October 20, 1954, October 31, 1954.
185. *New York Herald*, November 12, 1917; *Brooklyn Daily Eagle*, November 12, 1917; *NYT*, November 12, 1917.
186. *Buffalo Times,* December 23, 1927.
187. *Buffalo Daily Courier*, February 28, 1929; Erie County death certificate no. 1693 (1929).
188. *New York Tribune*, December 11, 1917; Brooklyn death certificate no. 23865 (1917).
189. Brooklyn death certificate no. 1341 (1918).
190. *Detroit News*, February 2, 1912.
191. *Detroit News*, July 26, 1917. There is no support for Kavieff's assertion that the Giannolas was involved in the Black Hand (Paul R. Kavieff, *The Violent Years* [New Jersey: Barricade Books, 2001], 6).
192. *Detroit News*, January 4, 1919.
193. *Detroit Free Press*, September 29, 1920.
194. *Detroit Free Press*, October 9, 1918.
195. Swept along in a wave of immigrants from Terrasini to Detroit, as the original "Sicilians" in the city (John C. Vismara, "Coming of the Italians to Detroit," *Michigan History* 2, no.1 [1918]: 119).
196. Born 1876 (Wayne County death certificate no. 12186 [1920]).
197. Born 1887 (Wayne County death certificate no. 9337 [1918]).
198. St. Patrick Church baptisms, Wyandotte, Michigan, May 23, 1915.
199. *Wyandotte Herald*, August 27, 1915.
200. *Detroit Free Press*, September 29, 1920.
201. *Detroit Free Press*, January 4–5, 1919, October 3, 1919.
202. *Detroit News*, August 29, 1917; *Detroit Free Press*, February 7, 1919, October 3, 1919, September 29, 1920.
203. *Detroit News*, January 29, 1920; *Detroit Free Press*, January 30, 1920.
204. *Detroit Free Press*, August 7, 1913; *Detroit News*, August 9, 1913.
205. *Detroit Free Press*, November 25, 1913; *Detroit News*, November 25, 1913, November 26, 1913.
206. *Detroit News*, August 7, 1913.
207. *Detroit News*, November 25, 1913; *Detroit Free Press*, November 25, 1913.
208. *Detroit News*, April 7, 1914.
209. *Detroit News*, April 8, 1914, April 13, 1914.
210. *Detroit News*, April 13, 1914.
211. *Detroit News*, April 15, 1914.
212. *Detroit News*, March 18, 1917.
213. *Detroit Free Press*, March 18, 1917.
214. *Detroit Free Press*, February 5, 1919.
215. *Detroit News*, December 23, 1917.
216. Buccellato's wife's brother was married to Ilado's sister. Brucia stayed at 215 North 5th Street, Williamsburg, where Frank Finazzo lived until his

murder (above). Finazzo's sister married the deceased Felice Buccellato, Pietro's brother. Furthermore, Pietro Buccellato had lived at the same place (230 North 5th) as Antonio Mazzara before Mazzara was shot to death in November, 1917 (above) (New York Police Department report of January 24, 1918 to the Detroit Supt. of Police, in the Pietro Buccellato closed case file).

217. *Detroit News*, March 27, 1918.
218. *Detroit News*, March 18, 1918; *Detroit Free Press*, March 19, 1918. No evidence exists that "Angelo (Angel Face) Torres" was responsible for the murder of John Vitale or that of his allies (Kavieff, *The Violent Years*, 18).
219. See Chapter 5.
220. City of Detroit Recorder's Court, The People vs. Giovanni Torres for murder (1918), Detroit Police Department closed case file on the Pietro Buccellato murder.
221. Wayne County death certificates 2965 (1917), 5471 (1919), 12665 (1917).
222. *Detroit News*, June 7, 1918, June 9, 1918, June 11, 1918. In the view of the trial judge, the acquittal went against the weight of the evidence. The jurors were discharged only after Judge Wilkins gave them a stern lecture on citizenship.
223. *Detroit News*, June 10, 1918.
224. Brooklyn death certificate no. 7220 (1930); *NYT* March 28, 1930; *Brooklyn Daily Eagle*, March 29, 1930.
225. *Detroit News*, August 11, 1920, August 12, 1920. Meli was standing with two former Giannola men, Giuseppe Manzello and Angelo Polizzi, when they were shot and wounded. Zerilli was a roommate of both men and, with William Tocco, was initially charged with the murder of Antonio Badalamenti prior to the attack on Manzello and Polizzi.
226. Martinico, Bonventre, Fontano, Barbara, Giallo, Puma, Cruciato, and Magaddino.
227. *NYT*, August 17, 1921.
228. Letizia Paoli, *Mafia Brotherhoods* (New York: Oxford University Press, 2003), 220; R. Thomas Naylor, "Mafias, Myths, and Markets," *Transnational Organized Crime*, vol. 3 no. 3 (1997), 18.
229. Bonanno, *Bound by Honor*, xx. One of Gaspare Milazzo's daughters, for example, married Detroit's Dominic "Sparky" Corrado.
230. Cressey, *The Functions and Structure of Criminal Syndicates*, 39.
231. *Psychology Today*, December 1975.
232. Donald Goddard, *Joey* (London: Harper and Row, 1974), 75.
233. In 1950s Los Angeles, Louis Tom Dragna, who had "never proved himself," was considered for promotion according to his critics solely because he was the son of Tom Dragna, *consiglieri* of the local Mafia organization. An angry rank and file imposed a "death sentence" on Louis and Tom Dragna, which was "withdrawn" only after Gaetano Lucchese in New York intervened (FBI, Los Angeles Office, July 22, 1964).
234. Bonanno, *A Man of Honour*, 141.
235. *Boston Sunday Globe*, June 16, 1957; information supplied by Frances Messina; Boston city directories, 1925, 1927, 1928.
236. Annual reports of the Pennsylvania Crime Commission; Giovanni Schiavo, *Four Centuries of Italian-American History* (New York: Vigo Press, 1952), 464–5; FBI, *La Cosa Nostra Philadelphia Division*, Philadelphia Office, May 14, 1965.
237. Joseph Traina (Brooklyn), Joseph Profaci (Brooklyn), Joseph Bonanno (Brooklyn), Vincent and Philip Mangano (Brooklyn), Stefano Magaddino (Buffalo), Paul Ricca (Chicago), Alfred Polizzi (Cleveland), and Frank Milano (Cleveland). Block asserted that the FBI "missed" this report (Robert

J. Kelly, et al., *Handbook of Organized Crime in the United States* [Westport, CN.: Greenwood Press, 1994], 44). But it appears in the FBI files on Stefano Magaddino and Frank Milano.

238. U.S. Congress, Select Committee on Improper Activities in the Labor or Management Field, *Investigation of Improper Activities in the Labor or Management Field*, hearings 85ᵗʰ Congress 2ⁿᵈ Session, 1958, 12226–7.

239. FBI report of September 12, 1960 from Chicago office titled *Samuel M. Giancana*.

240. Valachi barely mentioned the Commission during his open testimony even though his compatriot Girolomo "Bobby Doyle" Santuccio was in Chicago at its inception (OCN, 371). What follows therefore comes from Bonanno and Gentile.

241. Examples of a misinterpretation of the Commission's functions and powers are found in President's Commission on Organized Crime, *The Impact: Organized Crime Today* (April 1986) 42; U.S. Congress, Senate, Committee on Governmental Affairs, Permanent Subcommittee on Investigations, *Organized Crime: 25 Years After Valachi*, hearings 100ᵗʰ Congress 2ⁿᵈ Session 1988, 14.

242. FBI, *Angelo Bruno Special Summary Report*, July 28, 1962; Bonanno, *Bound by Honor*, 52.

243. Bonanno, *A Man of Honour*, 225.

244. Though Valachi and Cressey said that recruitment stopped from 1931 to "around 1954," (OCN, 297; Cressey, *Theft of the Nation* 45–6) a few members were admitted in the 1940s, including Sam DeCavalcante and Nick Delmore of the Elizabeth (New Jersey) Family, Angelo Lonardo (Cleveland), Aladena "Jimmy" Fratianno and 4 others in Los Angeles, and Ruggerio "Ritchie the Boot" Boiardo, Gerardo Catena, and Angelo "Gyp" DeCarlo in New Jersey.

245. The establishment of the Commission for example, did not prevent the summary execution of Pittsburgh boss John Bazzano Sr. in 1932, when Bazzano traveled to Brooklyn to justify his ordering the deaths of three of his *amici* in Pittsburgh. According to Gentile, those listening lost patience with Bazzano's explanation, and mercilessly fell on him without using any of the mechanisms then available to resolve the matter peacefully.

246. James B. Jacobs et al., *Busting the Mob* (New York: New York University Press, 1994), 90.

247. Bonanno says that every five years, a "national convention" was held. But if the "Commission" assembly that Bonanno claims happened in 1956 (Bonanno, *A Man of Honour*, 160) was that discovered near the Joseph Barbara Sr. place in Binghampton, it was anything but "national" in scope. And cooperating witness Vincent Cafaro testified to taking Anthony "Fat Tony" Salerno of the Genovese *borgata* to a number of believed "Commission" meetings, that turned out to be gatherings of the New York City "concrete club" that controlled a segment of the city's building industry.

248. Giovanni Falcone, *Men of Honour* (London: Warner Books, 1992), 115; FBI, *La Causa Nostra*, January 31, 1963.

249. Lupsha, *Organized Crime in the United States*, 35.

250. Nelli, *The Business of Crime*, 219.

251. Bonanno, *A Man of Honour*, 86–7.

252. Bonanno, A *Man of Honour*, 87.

NOTES TO CHAPTER 9

1. The New Jersey State Commission of Investigation declared that the state's "armed" drug trafficking gangs were alike to the 1920s Mafia, in that they

"consolidated power through organization and violence." This segment of organized crime was "in a stage similar to that of La Cosa Nostra around the beginning of this century," exhibited in a "propensity for violence" and in a "crude" approach to organization." (New Jersey State Commission of Investigation, *The Changing Face of Organized Crime in New Jersey A Status Report* (May 2004) 21; President's Commission on Organized Crime, *The Impact* [April 1986] 116).

2. Joseph L. Albini, *The American Mafia* (New York: Appleton-Century-Crofts, 1971), 324.
3. John Landesco, *Organized Crime in Chicago* (Chicago: University of Chicago Press, 1968), 180.
4. Letizia Paoli, "The Paradoxes of Organized Crime," *Crime, Law and Social Change* 37 (2002) 51–97; Letizia Paoli, *Mafia Brotherhoods* (New York: Oxford University Press, 2003), 12.
5. Mark H. Haller, "Illegal Enterprise: A Theoretical and Historical Interpretation," *Criminology* 28, no. 2 (1990): 222.
6. Mark H. Haller, "Bureaucracy and the Mafia: An Alternative View," *Journal of Contemporary Criminal Justice* 8, no. 1 (1992): 1–10.
7. Peter Reuter and Jonathan Rubinstein, "Fact, Fancy, and Organized Crime," *The Public Interest*, no. 53 (1978): 49.
8. Joseph Bonanno with Sergio Lalli, *A Man of Honour* (London: Andre Deutsch, 1983), 152. Valachi testified that he "never earned anything from the family," and "I myself earned my own money" (U.S. Congress, Senate, Committee on Government Operations, Permanent Subcommittee on Investigations, *Organized Crime and the Illicit Traffic in Narcotics*, hearings 88th Congress 1st Session 1963, 83). "You get nothing," he maintained, "only what you earn yourself" (Ibid., 109).
9. Pino Arlacchi, *Men of Dishonor* (New York: William Morrow and Co., 1992), 8, 145; Paoli, *Mafia Brotherhoods*, 147.
10. Herbert Edelhertz and Thomas D. Overcast, *The Business of Organized Crime* (Loomis, CA.: The Palmer Press, 1993), 135.
11. President's Commission on Organized Crime, *Organized Crime and Money Laundering* (March 1984) 27.
12. R. Thomas Naylor, "Mafias, Myths, and Markets: On the Theory and Practice of Enterprise Crime," *Transnational Organized Crime* 3, no. 3 (1997), 18.
13. FBI, *La Causa Nostra*, New York Office, January 31, 1963.
14. Haller, *Bureaucracy and the Mafia*, 2–3.
15. Reuter and Rubinstein, "Fact, Fancy, and Organized Crime," 45–67.
16. U.S. Treasury Department, Bureau of Narcotics, *Traffic in Opium and Other Dangerous Drugs for the Year Ended December 31, 1937*, 35–6; U.S. National Archives and Records Administration (hereafter NARA), New York office, SDNY C101–276 (1938).
17. Consult the FBI reports in the John F. Kennedy Assassination Records Collection. Refer also to *The Mafia Talks*, by Joseph Voltz and Peter J. Bridge (Greenwich, Conn.: Fawcett Publications, 1969); and *The Jersey Mob*, by Henry A. Zeiger (New York: New American Library, 1975).
18. NARA, RG 170, DEA Office of Enforcement and Policy Classified Subject Files, 1932–1967 folder "Luciano, Charles (Lucky)," RG 46 series 29, alphabetical name files, "Mafia (Suspects)."
19. Read for example the excellent study on rural Kentucky by Gary W. Potter and Larry K. Gaines, "Country Comfort," in *Journal of Contemporary Criminal Justice* 8, no. 1 (1992): 36–61; and of Scranton, Pennsylvania in Gary W. Potter's, *Criminal Organizations* (Prospect Heights, Illinois: Waveland Press, 1994).

20. U.S. Congress Committee on the Judiciary, *Organized Crime in America*, hearings 98th Congress 1st Session 1983, 251–265.
21. Donald R. Cressey, *Theft of the Nation* (New York: Harper and Row, 1969), xi.
22. U.S. Commission on the Review of the National Policy Toward Gambling, *First Interim Report* (1975) 29.
23. Reporting, "There is no uniformity of traditional organized crime control over illegal gambling throughout the country; in some cities such control exists, but not in others. Even where organized crime is a factor, the extent of its involvement varies." (Commission on the Review of the National Policy Toward Gambling, *Gambling in America: Final Report* [1976] 171).
24. David A. Caputo, *Organized Crime and American Politics* (University Programs Modular Studies, 1974), 1–2.
25. *Forbes*, September 29, 1980.
26. Cleveland underboss Angelo Lonardo gave any money he made to Maishe Rockman, a Jewish associate, for safekeeping and for doling out on "official" Family business when and where required (U.S. Congress, Senate, Committee on Governmental Affairs, *Organized Crime: 25 Years After Valachi*, hearings 100th Congress 2nd Session, 1988 104–5). Neither did Aladena Fratianno, a ranking Chicago, Cleveland and West Coast figure hear of "them laundering the money through banks" (President's Commission on Organized Crime, *Organized Crime and Money Laundering* (March 1984) 44–5).
27. *Forbes*, October 21, 1991.
28. *Red Bank Register,* December 23, 1952, March 3, 1953, March 5, 1953, August 20, 1953; Hank Messick, *The Private Lives of Public Enemies* (New York: Peter H. Wyden, 1973), 132.
29. M. Libonati and H. Edelhertz, *Study of Property Ownership and Devolution in the Organized Crime Environment* (1983).
30. President's Commission on Organized Crime, *The Impact* (April 1986) 439.
31. Ibid. 460.
32. Peter Reuter, *Disorganized Crime* (Cambridge, MA.: The MIT Press, 1983), 2–3.
33. Reuter, *Disorganized Crime*, xi; Reuter and Rubinstein, *Fact, Fancy, and Organized Crime*, 54; Peter Reuter and Jonathan Rubinstein, *Final Report Illegal Gambling in New York: Operation and Regulation* (New York: Center for Research on Institutions, 1981).
34. John Cummings and Ernest Volkman, *Goombata* (Boston: Little, Brown and Co., 1990), 101–2.
35. Murray Kempton, "Crime Does Not Pay," *The New York Review*, November 9, 1969, 5–6+.
36. Jay Albanese, *Organized Crime in America* (2nd ed.) (Cincinnati, Ohio: Anderson Publishing, 1989), 3.
37. Stier and Richards thus perceived organized crime as "progressing through three stages . . . in an evolving relationship with the social organism." (Edwin H. Stier and Peter R. Richards, "Strategic Decision Making in Organized Crime Control," in *Major Issues in Organized Crime Control*, Herbert Edelhertz (ed.) U.S. Department of Justice [1987] 66).
38. Alan A. Block, "History and Historiography," in *Handbook of Organized Crime in the United States*, Robert J. Kelly et al. (eds.) (Westport, CT.: Greenwood Press, 1994), 40.

Selected Bibliography

PRIMARY SOURCES

Government Hearings and Reports (Chronologically)

U.S. Congress, Senate, Special Committee to Investigate Organized Crime in Interstate Commerce, *Investigation of Organized Crime in Interstate Commerce*, hearings 82nd Congress 1st Session, 1951.

U.S. Congress, Senate, Special Committee to Investigate Organized Crime in Interstate Commerce, *Third Interim Report*, 82nd Congress 1st Session, 1951.

U.S. Congress, Senate, Committee on Government Operations, Permanent Subcommittee on Investigations, *Organized Crime and the Illicit Traffic in Narcotics*, hearings 88th Congress 1st Session, 1963.

U.S. Congress Senate, Committee on Government Operations, *Organized Crime and the Illicit Traffic in Narcotics: Report*, 89th Congress 1st Session, 1965.

The President's Commission on Law Enforcement and Administration of Justice, Task Force on Organized Crime, *Task Force Report: Organized Crime*, Washington, DC, 1967.

U.S. President's Commission on Organized Crime, *The Edge: Organized Crime, Business, and Labor Unions*, Washington, D.C., March 1986.

U.S. President's Commission on Organized Crime, *The Impact: Organized Crime Today*, Washington, D.C., April 1986.

U.S. Congress, Senate, Committee on Governmental Affairs, Permanent Subcommittee on Investigations, *Organized Crime: 25 Years After Valachi*, hearings 100th Congress 2nd Session, 1988.

Newspapers (published in New York City unless otherwise stated)

Asbury Park Evening Press (Asbury Park, New Jersey)
Atlanta Constitution (Atlanta, Georgia)
Brooklyn Daily Eagle
Buffalo Daily Courier (Buffalo, New York)
Chicago Tribune (Chicago)
Detroit Free Press (Detroit)
Detroit News (Detroit)
Freehold Transcript (Freehold, New Jersey)
New York Daily News
New York Herald
New York Times
New York Tribune

News-Palladium (Benton Harbor, Michigan)
Newark Evening News (Newark, N.J.)
Poughkeepsie Eagle News (Poughkeepsie, N.Y.)
Red Bank Register (Monmouth County, N.J.)
Sun
Sunday Courier (Poughkeepsie, N.Y.)
Washington Post (Washington, D.C.)
The Wilkes-Barre Record (Wilkes-Barre, Pennsylvania)
World

Trial Transcripts (by name of defendant)

New York City and County Court of General Sessions, The People against Joseph
    Ales (1921).
U.S. Circuit Court of Appeals for the Second Circuit, The United States of America
    vs. Giuseppe Calicchio, et al. Transcript of Record (1910).
New York Supreme Court (Criminal Branch), The People of the State of New York
    against Joseph Cohen, Jacob Cohen, David Jacobs and Abe Graff (1917).
New York Supreme Court (Criminal Branch), The People of the State of New York
    against Frank Ferrara (1916).
New York State Court of Appeals, The People of the State of New York against
    Frank Fevrola, Case on Appeal (1921).
New York State Court of Appeals, The People of the State of New York against
    Angelo Giordano, 231 New York 633 pt. 1.
New York Supreme Court (Criminal Branch), The People of the State of New York
    against Antonio Impoluzzo (1916).
New York State Court of Appeals, The People of the State of New York against
    Pellegrino Marano: Case on Appeal, 232 New York 569 pt. 1.
New York State Court of Appeals, The People of the State of New York against
    Aniello Parretti: Cases and Points, vol. 2939 (1921).
New York State Court of Appeals, The People of the State of New York against
    Tony Parretti, Case on Appeal, 244 N.Y. 527 pt. 1.
New York State, The People of against Salvatore Rufino and Giuseppe Rufino,
    impleaded with Pietro Lagatutta and Giuseppe Masseria, 1913 (John Jay Col-
    lege case no. 1736).
New York City and County Court of General Sessions, The People of the State of
    New York against John Russomano, John Jay College Case no. 1856.
New York City and County Court of General Sessions, The People vs. Ciro Ter-
    ranova (1918).
New York State Court of Appeals, The People of the State of New York against
    Alessandrio Vollero, Case on Appeal, 226 New York 587 pt. 1.

Miscellaneous records

Federal Bureau of Investigation files on:
"Joseph Barbara, Sr."
"Anthony Carfano"
"Jack Ignazio Dragna"
"Stefano LaSalle"
"Stefano Magaddino"
"Vincent Mangano"
"Salvatore Maranzano"
"Vincent Rao"

"Dominick Sabella"
"Girolamo (James) Santuccio"
"Salvatore Shillitani"
"Giuseppe Traina"
Federal Bureau of Investigation report of January 31, 1963, from the New York office titled *La Causa Nostra* (John F. Kennedy Assassination Records Collection, U.S. National Archives and Records Administration, College Park, Maryland).
Gentile, Nicolo, *Translated Transcription of the Life of Nicolo (E) Gentile, Background and History of the Castellammarese War and Early Decades of Organized Crime in America* (no date).
Richey, Lawrence Papers, *Black Hand Confessions 1910*, Herbert Hoover Presidential Library, Box 1.
U.S. National Archives and Records Administration, Record Group 129 (Bureau of Prisons) inmate case numbers 2882 (Giuseppe Morello), 2883 (Ignazio Lupo).
U.S. National Archives and Records Administration, Record Group 204 (pardon case files), 230/39/box 663 (Giuseppe Morello), 230/40/1/3 box 956 (Ignazio Lupo).
Valachi, Joseph, *The Real Thing* (1965) Record Group 60, MLR Entry no. 306H 60.10.3, U.S. National Archives, College Park, Maryland.

SECONDARY SOURCES

Albini, Joseph L. *The American Mafia*: New York: Appleton-Century-Crofts, 1971.
Block, Alan A. "History and the Study of Organized Crime," *Urban Life* 6, no. 4 (1978).
———. *East Side West Side*: Cardiff: University College Cardiff Press, 1982.
———. "History and Historiography," in Robert J. Kelly et al. (eds.) *Handbook of Organized Crime in the United States*: Westport, CT: Greenwood Press, 1994.
Bonanno, Bill. *Bound by Honor,* New York: St. Martin's Paperbacks, 1999.
Bonanno, Joseph with Sergio Lalli. *A Man of Honour*: London: Andre Deutsch, 1983.
Chandler, David Leon. *The Criminal Brotherhoods*, London: Constable, 1976.
Chilanti, Felice. Series of articles in *Paese Sera*, September 14, 1963–October 1, 1963.
Cressey, Donald R. *Theft of the Nation*: New York: Harper and Row, 1969.
Critchley, David. "Buster, Maranzano and the Castellammare War, 1930–1931," *Global Crime* 7, no. 1 (2006).
Dickie, John. *Cosa Nostra*: London: Coronet, 2004.
Downey, Patrick. *Gangster City: The History of the New York Underworld 1900–1935*: New Jersey: Barricade Books, 2004.
Feder, Sid and Joachim Joesten. *The Luciano Story*: New York: Da Capo Press, 1994.
Fijnaut, Cyrille. "Organized Crime: A Comparison Between the United States of America and Western Europe," *British Journal of Criminology* 30, no. 3 (1990).
Firestone, Thomas A. "Mafia Memoirs: What They Tell Us About Organized Crime," *Journal of Contemporary Criminal Justice* 9 (1993).
Flynn, William J. *The Barrel Mystery*: New York: The James A. McCann Co., 1920.
Fox, Stephen. *Blood and Power*: New York: William Morrow, 1989.
Gentile, Nick. *Vita di Capomafia*: Rome: Editori Riuniti, 1963.

Haller, Mark H. "Bootleggers and American Gambling 1920–1950," in Commission on the Review of the National Policy Towards Gambling, *Gambling in America Appendix 1*, Washington, D.C. October 1976.

———. "Bootleggers as Businessmen," in David E. Kyvig (ed.) *Law, Alcohol, and Order*: Westport, CT.: Greenwood Press, 1985.

———. "Illegal Enterprise: A Theoretical and Historical Interpretation," *Criminology* 28, no. 2 (1990).

———. "Bureaucracy and the Mafia: An Alternative View," *Journal of Contemporary Criminal Justice* 8, no. 1 (1992).

Homer, Frederic D. *Guns and Garlic: Myths and Realities of Organized Crime*: West Lafayette, Indiana: Purdue University Press, 1974.

Hunt, Thomas and Michael A. Tona. "The Good Killers: 1921's Glimpse of the Mafia" *On the Spot Journal*, Spring 2007.

Ianni, Francis A. J. with Elizabeth Reuss-Ianni. *A Family Business*: London: Routledge and Kegan Paul, 1972.

Iorizzo, Luciano J. (ed.) *An Enquiry into Organized Crime*: Staten Island, N.Y.: The American Italian Historical Association, 1970.

Jacobs, James B. et al. *Busting the Mob*: New York University Press, 1994.

Kelly, Robert J. (ed.) *Organized Crime A Global Perspective*, Totowa, N.J.: Rowman and Littlefield, 1986.

———. *The Upperworld and the Underworld*: New York: Kluwer Academic, 1999.

Kendall, John S. "Blood on the Banquet," *Louisiana Historical Quarterly*, XX11 (1939).

Lupsha, Peter A. "Individual Choice, Material Culture, and Organized Crime," *Criminology* 19 no. 1 (1981).

———. "Organized Crime in the United States," in Robert J. Kelly (ed.) *Organized Crime A Global Perspective*: Totowa, N.J.: Rowman and Littlefield, 1986, 32–57.

Maas, Peter. *The Canary That Sang*: London: MacGibbon and Kee, 1969.

Morello, Celeste A. *Before Bruno Book 2–1931–1946* (2001).

Nelli, Humbert S. *The Business of Crime*: New York: Oxford University Press, 1976.

New York State Organized Crime Task Force. *Corruption and Racketeering in the New York City Construction Industry: Final Report* (December 1989).

Paoli, Letizia. *Mafia Brotherhoods*: New York: Oxford University Press, 2003.

Petacco, Arrigo. *Joe Petrosino*: London: Hamish Hamilton, 1974.

Peterson, Virgil W. *The Mob*: Ottowa, Illinois: Green Hill Publishers, 1983.

Pitkin, Thomas Monroe and Francesco Cordasco. *The Black Hand*: Totowa, NJ: Littlefield, Adams and Co., 1977.

Reuter, Peter and Jonathan B. Rubinstein. "Fact, Fancy and Organized Crime," *The Public Interest*, no. 53 (1978).

———. *Illegal Gambling in New York: Operation and Regulation Final Report*: New York: Center for Research on Institutions, 1981.

Salerno, Ralph and John S. Tompkins. *The Crime Confederation*: Garden City: Doubleday and Doubleday, 1969.

Smith, Dwight C. *The Mafia Mystique*: London: Hutchinson and Co., 1975.

Thompson, Craig and Allen Raymond. *Gang Rule in New York*: New York: The Dial Press, 1940.

Turkus, Burton B. and Sid Feder. *Murder Inc.* New York: Manor Books, 1974.

Woodiwiss, Michael. *Crime, Crusades and Corruption*: London: Pinter, 1988.

———. *Organized Crime and American Power: A History*: Toronto: University of Toronto Press, 2001.

About the Author

A former public sector employee, David Critchley received his doctorate from Liverpool John Moores University, and is the author of the 1984 bibliography *International Perspectives on Organized Crime* and of articles in *Global Crime* and *Chronicle*, the magazine of the Historical Society of Michigan. This book is the product of 10 years of research in both the United States and the United Kingdom.

Index

Note: Both Anglicized and Italian versions of forenames of the individuals referred to are used throughout the book. Furthermore, where a conflict arises over the spelling of a surname, the most common usage is applied.

A

Abadinsky, Howard, 15
Abbate, Frank, 135
Abbatemarco, Frank "Frankie Shots," 163
Abbatemarco, Michael, 163, 292n237
Abbatemarco, Tony "Tony Shots," 163
Accardo, Tony, 231
Ace Lathing Company, 148. *See also* Arra, Nunzio; Mafia, New York City
Adamo, Salvatore, 226
Adamo, Vito, 226
Adonis, Joe (real name Giuseppe Doto): investments, 135; in Masseria Family, 163, 231; on Maranzano's hit list, 191; bootlegging, 142, 192; age of, 205; and Willie Moretti, 213; as Neapolitan, 310n103
Aiello, Joseph "Pizza Pie," 295n35
Aiello, Joseph: Atlantic City conference, 142, 283n49; origins of Castellammare War, 171–172; financing the War, 179; murder of, 172, 295n46; age of, 204. *See also* Castellammare War; Magaddino, Stefano; Milazzo, Gaspare
Aiello, Sam, 295n35
Albanese, Jay, 5, 8, 293n6
Alberti, Joseph, 151–152
Albini, Joseph L.: contradictions in accounts of syndicated crime, 5; irrelevance of Mafia, 7; view of the Mafia, 11, 234; Black Hand, 61; 1928 Atlantic City meeting, 141; Castellammare War, 186, 293n6; Mafia "Purge," 207; Unione Siciliana and the Mob, 209
Ales, Joseph, 224, 229
Alescio, Tony, 226
Alfano, Enrico, 106, 120, 126, 273n11
Alfano, Vincenzo, 224
Allegra, Melchiorre: Sicilian Mafia structure, 62; Sicilian Mafia initiation, 63; Salvatore Maranzano, 144; and Sicilian Mafia "boss of bosses," 189. *See also* Mafia, Sicily
Alo, Vincent "Jimmy Blue Eyes," 135, 310n103
Altieri, Alberto, 117, 120, 129, 276n104, 280n242
Amato, Frank, 132, 134
Ambrosino, Pasquale, 132
"Americanization": overview, 4, 210, 233, 236; Castellammare War and, 12, 197–200; post-Castellammare War settlement and Sicily, 71; recruitment modes, 91; "Purge" hypothesis, 199, 207–208, 210; depiction of Mafiosi types, 200–202; Masseria Family as Americanized, 211; Schiro group as orthodox, 214; importance of kinship, 229–230; leaders after the Castellammare

War, 230–231. *See also* Castel-
lammare War; Cleveland 1928
gathering; "Commission;" La
Cosa Nostra; Mafia, America;
Mafia, Sicily; "Purge;" Unione
Siciliana; *names of individuals*
Amico, Joe, 177, 297nn.86, 88
Anastasia, Albert (real name Umberto
Anastasio): Atlantic City 1929
conference, 141; birth, 158;
1920 conviction, 158; 1923
wounding, 158; Morello murder,
180; age, 205; on the "Commis-
sion," 233
Anselmo, Giovanni, 300n128
Antona, Angelo, 182
Apalachin, Mafia summit at, 3, 141, 224
Arcara, Epifanio, 260n232
Arcuri, Domenico, 157, 291n210
Arena, Calogero, 226
Arichiello, Giuseppe, 16, 81–83, 85–86,
89
Arra, Nunzio, 148, 264n51
Atlantic City 1929 conference, 139–
142, 160. *See also* "Big Seven;"
Prohibition (Volstead Act);
names of individuals
Attanasio, Andrea, 107
Attardi, Alfonso, 1289n183
Automint Vent Company, 148. *See also*
Rao, Vincent John
Averna, Michael, 276n104

B

Badalamenti, Antonio, 315n225
Baff, Barnet: questions raised by case,
12, 235; conspirators' addresses,
16; murder of Baff, 72; importance of case, 72; political
background, 72–73; poultry
racketeering, 73–76, 79; Baff's
activities as reason for his murder, 74; trial of alleged slayers,
79–85; Baff killing and Harlem
Mafia, 85–86, 100–101; ignorance of case, 263n2. *See also*
Mafia, New York City; *names of
individuals*
Baff, Harry, 75, 82
Bagnano, Joe, 24
Barasa, Bernard, 209, 309n86
Barbara, Carlo, 183, 224, 314n183
Barbara, Joseph, Sr., 3, 162, 190, 214,
224, 291n213, 316n247

Barlo, Charles "Kid Baker," 256n123
Barone, George, 91
Battaglia, Giuseppe, 37
Bazzano, John, Sr., 134, 208, 316n245
Beare, Margaret, 5, 7
Behan, Tom, 10
Belea, Bruno, 193
Bell, Daniel, 199
Bellasana, Giuseppe, 276n101
Bellino, Benedetto, 270n222
"Big Seven," 141–142. *See also* Atlantic
City 1929 conference; Prohibi-
tion (Volstead Act)
Biondo, Joseph: element in D'Aquila
Family, 157, 231; 1931 Cleve-
land arrest, 190, 303n191; plot
against Salvatore Maranzano,
192; friend of Lucky Luciano,
213; death, 289n189; friend
of Nicolo Gentile, 294n19; as
"council" member, 310n95
Bivone, Joseph, 300n128
Bizzaro, Eugene, 113, 117, 121–122
Black Hand: relationship to Mafia, 11,
20, 26–32, 34–35; public impact
of, 20; districts terrorized by,
20; categorization of, 20–21;
labeling of crimes as Black
Hand, 20–21; cases and numbers, 22; motives for, 22–23;
organization of, 23–25; rituals,
25–26; territorial dimension,
32–33; in Sicily, 32, 250n148;
decline of, 33–34; causes of, 34.
See also Mafia, Sicily; *names of
individuals*
Block, Alan A: Mafia imagery, 2; need
for more research, 5, 7; and
the Mafia, 6; power syndicates,
123; 1910s cocaine traffic,
137, 281n297; Prohibition era
organized crime, 164; Lepke
Buchalter, 193; Mafia "Purge,"
207–208, 210; Mafia immigrants
imported in 1920s, 208
Blok, Anton, 62, 189
Boiardo, Ruggerio "Ritchie the Boot,"
132, 294n16
Bommetro, Vito, 295n54, 311n132
Bonaguar, Tessie, 129
Bonanno, Bill: role of Mafiosi, 31; number of original New York City
Families, 36; Castellammare War
death toll, 180; traditionalists in

Mafia, 200; Lucky Luciano and Commission, 206

Bonanno, Joseph: territory in Mafia, 9; immigrant institutions, 16; role of U.S. Mafiosi, 31; Mafia initiation ritual, 63; life in Sicily and how joined Mafia, 92, 96; why fought Joe Masseria, 95, 171; police record, 96; why joined the Mafia, 99; on non-Sicilians in Families, 136, 281n291; bootlegging, 143, 146; Buccellato family rivalry, 144, 219; limitations of account, 168, 170; Americanization discourse, 204, 206; kinship in Mafia, 229; as head of Maranzano group, 230; on the Commission, 232; leverage gained from Mafia membership, 236; on "Grand Council," 315n237. *See also* Americanization; "boss of bosses;" Castellammare War; "Commission;" "Good Killers;" La Cosa Nostra; Mafia, New York City

Bonanno, Salvatore, 219, 223

Bonasera, Cassandro "The Chief," 292n240, 300n128

Bonventre, Antonino, 216

Bonventre, Cesare, 262n269

Bonventre, Giovanni, 223, 230

Bonventre, Giuseppe, 222

Bonventre, Pietro, 222

Bonventre, Vito (born 1875): related to Domingos, 99; Brooklyn residences of, 216, 295n54; one of "Good Killers," 219–220, 222; murder of, 178, 180, 306n248; age, 205; estate, 299n115. *See also* Castellammare War; "Good Killers"

Bonventre, Vito (born 1891), 222–223, 313nn.164, 169, 173

Bordonaro, Natale, 117

Boscarino, Giuseppe, 48

Bosco, Anthony, 225

Bosco, Mary, 225

Bosco, Pietro, 225–226

"boss of bosses" (*capo di capi*): Joe Morello as, 46, 50–51, 60, 149; Salvatore D'Aquila as, 49, 99, 155; role of "boss of bosses," 160, 188–189; Castellammare War and, 184; in Sicily, 189;

abolition of, 187; Salvatore Maranzano as, 190; Valachi on, 303n186. *See also* Castellammare War; La Cosa Nostra; Morello, Giuseppe

Bova, Rafael, 24

Bozzuffi, Antonio, 31

Bozzuffi, John, 31, 250n134

Brancaccio, Salvatore, 68, 261n248

Briganti, Rosario, 223–224

Bronfman brothers, 140

Brown, Harry, 206

Browne-Vinters, 164

Brucia, Joseph, 228, 314n216

Buccellato family, 144, 217, 219, 226

Buccellato, Felice, 226–228, 314n216

Buccellato, Joseph, 227–228

Buccellato, Pietro "Peter," 228, 314n216

Buccellato, Vito, 223–224, 313n175

Buccoza, Angelo, 30

Buchalter, Louis "Lepke": Atlantic City 1929 conference, 141; garment rackets, 77, 79, 194–195; role in Maranzano murder, 194; Tootsie Herbert connection, 264n50

Buendo, Salvatore, 225

Bueta, Edwardo, 24

Bufalino, Charles, 29

Buonomo, Amadeo, 102, 110–111, 113, 256n123

Burke, Frank, 84

Burns, Walter Noble, 142

Busardo, Joseph, 158

Buscetta, Tommaso, 3

Byrnes, Thomas, 39

C

Cafaro, Vincent, 316n247

Caiozzo, Camillo, 173, 218–222, 229

Calamia, Santo "Joseph," 52, 54–56, 59

Calderone, Antonino, 27, 63

Calicchio, Giuseppe, 46–49, 69–70

Callaci, Frank "Chick 99," 205, 301n139

Callahan, Mollie, 252n22

Callego, Carlo, 226

Cambria, Angelo, 27

Cammarata, Emanuel, 203, 290n204

Camorra (Brooklyn): security practices and recruitment process, 25, 125–126; and East Harlem deaths, 102; links to

Naples, 105; historiography on, 105–106; leaders, 108, 118; murders committed by, 108–117, 276n111; merger of the two organizations, 114, 118; membership, 117–120; initiation ritual, 119; market-driven enterprises, 121; predatory activities, 121–123; official corruption and, 124–125; members sentenced, 127–129; and murdered, 129–130. *See also* "Americanization;" Camorra (Naples); Mafia, New York City; Santa Lucia hotel-restaurant; *names of individuals*

Camorra (Naples), 119–121, 125–126. *See also* Camorra (Brooklyn), *names of individuals*

Canale, Giuseppe/Salvatore, 50, 255n106

Canarelli, Nicholas "Nick the Fixer," 112, 124

Candello, Gaspare, 292n242, 300n128

Candillo, Vincenzo, 125

Capalongo, Tony (real last name Vivola), 108

Capeci, Jerry, 174, 303n192

Capitol Coal Company, 178. *See also* Castellemmare War; Meli, Angelo

Capone, Alphonse: links to Benton Harbor, Michigan, 97; 1929 Atlantic City meeting, 141–142; and Frankie Yale, 162–163; age, 205; in 1910s Brooklyn, 279n215; origins of Castellammare War, 171–172, 295n38; effect of Castellammare War on fortunes of, 186, 188; and Maranzano's coronation, 191; role in Salvatore Maranzano murder, 192; on Maranzano's hit list, 191; Unione Siciliana, 209, 309n88. *See also* Atlantic City 1929 conference; Castellammare War; Chicago "outfit" (syndicate)

Cappiello, Nicolo, 22

Capuano, Damien, 21

Caputo, Carl, 295n35

Caputo, John, 26

Capuzzi, Nick, 94, 301n155

Caradonna, Vito, 223

Caramandi, Nicholas, 91

Carbone, Stanislao, 28

Cardinale, Antonio, 16, 81–84, 89, 266n117, 268n185

Cardinale, Joseph, 83

Cardinali, Bartholdi, 21

Carfano, Anthony "Little Augie Pisano": James DeSalvo related to, 125, 279n204; Bronx lathing sector, 148; murder of Mike Abbatemarco, 163; policy game, 163; as Masseria Family member, 163, 292n239; age, 205; birth, 292n239, 310n103. *See also* Yale, Frankie

Carfano, August, 148

Carido, Filipo, 24

Carollo, Giovanni, 222–223

"Carra, Jim." *See* Attardi, Alfonso

Carrao, Charles, 124

Carriera, Vincent, 237

Caruso, Angelo, 214

Casano, Antonio, 42

Cascio, James, 58

Cascioferro, Vito: 1902 arrest, 40–41; life in Sicily, 40; Morello ally, 51, 261n248; origin, 55; Joseph Petrosino murder suspect, 68–69; compared to Enrico Alfano, 106; extent of power, 263n274, 303n182. *See also* Frauto, Stella; Morello, Giuseppe; Pecoraro, Giovanni; Petrosino, Joseph

Casella, Frank, 152

Casertano, Steve "Buck Jones," 208

Castellammare War: overview, 12–13, 164–165, 186–187, 195–196, 236; effect on relations with Sicily, 70; recruitment for War, 93–96; Salvatore D'Aquila murder and, 157; historiography, 166, 180; sources utilized, 166–168, 170, 293nn.10–11, 294nn. 19, 23; origins, 170–173; Gaetano Reina slaying, 174–176; rebellion of Gagliano faction, 176, 181–182; Gaspare Milazzo slaying, 176–178; Salvatore Maranzano assumed command, 178; financing the War, 179; in other cities, 179, 182; murders, 179–183, 293nn8–9, 299n113; moves to end, 183–185; end of the War, 185–186; effects of the War, 186–188,

196–197; Mafia organization during the War, 188; supremacy of Maranzano, 190–191; removal of Maranzano, 191–195; political uses made of War's narrative, 196–197; post-War New York City heads, 230. *See also* "Americanization;" "boss of bosses;" "Commission;" La Cosa Nostra; Mafia, America; *names of individuals*

Castellano, Paul, 289n186

Catalonotte, Joseph, 299n112

Catalonotte, Salvatore "Sam Sings in the Night," 172, 177, 295n44

Catania, Antonio, 52

Catania, Ciro, 308n61

Catania, James "Jimmy the Baker," 52, 257nn129–130

Catania, Giuseppe (died 1902), 42

Catania, Giuseppe "Joe the Baker" (died 1931): as related to Joseph Catania (1902), 42; related to Ciro Terranova, 52, 257n129; interest in bread industry, 301n155; hijacking operations, 191; murder of, 94, 185–186, 301n155, 308n61

Catena, Gerardo "Jerry," 142, 316n244

Cecala, Anthony: role in counterfeiting scheme, 46; how became a counterfeiter and sentenced, 48–49; paroled, 49; police corruption, 50; relationship to Joe Morello, 51; birthplace, 55; murder of Joseph Petrosino, 65; John Pecoraro and, 67–68; crimes before counterfeiting, 69; United Lathing interest, 149; murder of, 151; Spring Street store, 268n180

Celentano, Antonio, 113, 122, 278n170

Central Lathing Company, 149, 287n145. *See also* Gagliano, Josephine

Ceola, Baldassare, 66, 68, 261n246

Chandler, David Leon: importance of Morello Family, 36; New Orleans Family, 60; Brooklyn Camorra, 106; Giuseppe Masseria, 154; Gaetano Reina murder, 174–175; Castellammare War, 180, 188; immigrants

imported by Salvatore Maranzano, 208; Castellammare War deaths, 300n130; Maranzano murder, 305n244. *See also* Morello, Antonio

Chiarella, Giuseppe, 116

Chicago "outfit"(syndicate): imagery about, 12, 140, 196, 210–211 236–237, 242n20; initiation ritual, 64; links between members, 63–64, 260n218, 310n97. *See also* Atlantic City 1929 conference; Castellammare War; Cleveland 1928 gathering; Unione Siciliana; *names of individuals*

Cieravo, Salvatore "Rose," 219, 222

Cifulco, Sam, 299n112

Cina, Salvatore: role in counterfeiting, 46; arrest and incarceration, 48; released, 49; birthplace, 55; crimes before counterfeiting, 69; Highland farm, 254n67; related to Vincenzo Giglio, 262n258

Cipolla, Leonardo, 58

Cipriano, Salvatore, 226

Ciurleo, Nicolo, 25

Clemente, Carmine "Dolly Dimples," 134, 281n273

Clemente, Frank "Coney Island," 108, 112, 116–117, 134, 276n95, 281n274

Clemente, Giuseppe, 40

Clemente, Salvatore "The Dude," 39–42, 89, 157

Clemente, Vincent, 289n183

Cleveland 1928 gathering: Paolo Palazzolo at, 135; events, 158, 160; Joe Profaci and, 160–161; in the Americanization discourse, 202–204. *See also names of individuals*

Cohen, Jacob, 83, 267n157

Cohen, Joseph "Big Joe": role in poultry industry, 74; and Baff murder, 74, 266n117; and Dopey Fein, 76; trial of, 83–5; sentenced, 85; murdered, 85. *See also* Baff, Barnet

Coll, Vincent "Mad Dog," 195, 304n215, 305nn.242, 244

Colonial Trading Company, 238. *See also* Genovese, Vito

Colosimo, James, 33, 162, 209, 251nn158–159

Columbus Wet Wash Laundry, 85–86, 88, 103, 260n232. *See also names of individuals*
Comito, Antonio: role in counterfeiting, 46–47; arrest and confession, 48; trial testimony, 48; trial of Joe Boscarino, 48; relationship to Joe Morello, 51; birthplace, 55; Joseph Petrosino murder, 64; and John Pecoraro, 68; told of a secret order, 70; Salvatore Manzella and, 250n138; motives as informer, 255n91
"Commission": exposed, 3, 231–232; Los Angeles Family and, 103; constitutional powers, 131, 232; membership of, 135, 186, 232–233; as La Cosa Nostra command center, 164, 232; replaced the "boss of bosses," 187, 201; Luciano role, 201–202, 206. *See also* "Americanization;" "boss of bosses;" Castellammare War; La Cosa Nostra; Mafia, America
Coniglio, Michele, 38, 54
Consiglio, Ruggerio, 300n128
Constantine, Joe, 228
Conti, Gregorio, 93
Conti, Joe, 122
Cook, Fred, 51, 237
Coppola, Michael "Trigger Mike," 310n103
Coppola, Salvatore, 276n104
Coppola, Vincenzo "Jim," 190
Corbi, Frank, 27, 248n90
Corbi, Pasquale, 27
Corbi, Tony, 248n90
Cordaro, Carmelo, 157, 289n186
Cosmano, Vincenzo, 34
Costa, Salvatore, 108, 117, 136–137
Costabile, Giuseppe, 29, 176, 250n123
Costantino, Calogero, 54–55, 68–69, 261nn.241, 248
Costello, Edward, 140
Costello, Frank (real name Francesco Castiglia): published accounts on, 1; in Louisiana, 60; other investments, 135; illicit liquor trafficking, 140, 142–143; 1929 Atlantic City event, 141; on Salvatore Maranzano's execution list, 191; decision to kill Maranzano, 194; Americanization and,

202; Willie Moretti and, 213; birth, 205, 283n22
Cressey, Donald R.: power of Mafia, 2; view of U.S. Mafia origin, 61; U.S. Mafia and kinship, 62, 230, 245n71; Castellammare War, 166; "boss of bosses," 188; Americanization, 199; Unione Siciliana, 209; Mafia control over illicit gambling, 237
Crocervera, Isadore, 42–43
Cruciato, Mariano "Mimi," 220, 315n226
Cucchiara, Frank, 231
Cummings, John and Ernest Volkman, 238
Cuocolo, Gennaro, 106–107, 126
Cuocolo, Maria, 106–107, 126
Curatolo, Antonio, 223–224
Cusmano, Vitorio, 226

D

D'Agati, Frank, 16, 19
D'Agati, Giulio, 162
D'Amico, Gaspare, 290n204
D'Andrea, Tony, 41–42, 209
Daniello, Raffaele "Ralph the Barber" (real name Alphonso Pepe): arrest and confession, 107–108; Joe DeMarco murder, 112; Eugene Ubriaco and Nick Morello murders, 112–113; Joe Verrazano murder, 115; other murders, 116–117; wounded, 117; date and place of birth, 117; Navy Street organization, 118; initiation ritual, 119; police record, 120; enterprises, 121, 137; corruption, 124–5; relations with other gang members, 126; jailing and murder, 130; journey to America, 277n120. *See also* Camorra (Brooklyn); Mafia, America; "Murder Stable"
Danna, Vincent, 97
D'Aquila Family: territorial bases, 32, 154; extension of power, 36, 99–100, 157; from the Morello *borgata*, 36, 156; membership of, 156–158; Manfredi Mineo in conflict with, 100; influence in Cleveland, 156, 182; kinship within, 156; Buffalo

link, 285n81. *See also names of individuals*

D'Aquila, Salvatore "Toto": early New York residence, 10; as "boss of bosses," 49, 155–156, 160, 189; rivalry with Joe Masseria, 155–156; origin, 156; murder of, 157, 289n182; effect of his murder, 161–164, 177, 186; alleged tie to Vincent Mangano, 289n183. *See also* "boss of bosses;" Castellammare War; Cleveland 1928 gathering; *names of individuals*

DeBellis, John "Johnny Dee," 208

DeCarlo, Angelo "Gyp" or "Ray": kinship in Mafia, 62; and "combination,"132; bootlegging, 142; boasting, 243n32; secrecy in Mafia, 249n105; initiation into Mafia, 316n244

DeCavalcante, Sam, 238, 316n244

DeLeo, Calogero, 157

DelGaudio, Gaetano, 109

DelGaudio, Nicolo, 108–109, 113, 123

DelGiorno, Thomas, 91

Delmore, Nick, 316n244

DeMarco, Joseph: and the Morellos, 111; "Murder Stable," 111; plot to kill, 111–113, 274n21; Generoso Nazzaro and, 116; murder of, 105, 108, 112; sentences given his killers, 127. *See also* Camorra (Brooklyn); *names of individuals*

DeMarco, Luigi, 276n101

DeMarco, Salvatore, 112, 116, 274n21

DeMaria, Louis, 107, 121, 274n18

DeMartini, Felix, 108

Denico, Frank, 274n16

Deodati, Antonio, 39

DePeche, Angelo, 57, 257n150

DePriema, Giuseppe, 42–44, 55, 253n45, 254n59

Desiderio, Ernesto, 117, 120–121

DeSimone, Frank, 123

DeSimone, Rosario, 257n151

Dewey, Thomas E., 78–79, 206, 264n50

Diamond, Jack "Legs," 263n2

DiBenedetto family, 145

DiBenedetto, Antonio, 224–225, 228

DiBenedetto, Calogero "Charlie Buffalo," 96, 178, 298nn.94, 102

DiBenedetto, Joseph, 225, 295n54

DiCarlo, Joseph "The Wolf," 289n191

DiCarlo, Joseph Peter, 27, 285n82

DiCarlo, Samuel, 203

DiChristina, Charles, 56, 58

DiChristina, Paolo. *See* Marchese, Francesco Paolo

Dickie, John: importance of territory, 9; Mafia and extortion, 34; Morello group's success, 50; importation of Sicilian structures to America, 61; Corleone initiation ritual, 63; importance of Nicolo Gentile, 168; "Purge" and Americanization proposals, 199–200, 202; Sicilians imported by Salvatore Maranzano, 208, 309n70

Didato, Dominick, 77

DiGeorge, Jim, 295n35

DiGiorgio, Joseph, 22, 30

DiGiorgio, Vito, 57–58, 257nn.148

DiGiovanni, Joseph, 27, 34, 249n109

DiGitano, Sebastiano, 51

DiGregorio, Bartolomeo, 219, 312n143

DiGregorio, Gaspare: wedding of, 77; witness at Joseph Bonanno's wedding, 96; related to Stefano Magaddino, 96; criminal record, 96; in Castellammare War, 97; age, 205

DiGregorio, Maria, 216

DiGregorio, Matteo, 216, 312n143

DiLeonardo, Jimmy, 93, 157

DiLeonardo, Michael "Mikey Scars," 92–93, 157

DiMaggio, Vincent, 237

DiMartini, George, 59–60

Dimino, Accursio, 100, 271n267, 289n177

Dioguardi, Dominick, 151

Dioguardi, John "Johnny Dio," 151

DiPaolo, Carmine, 80, 82–83, 88, 265n75

DiPuma, Anna, 38

DiSalvo, James "Jimmy Kelly," 125, 279n204

Dispenza, Rosario, 56, 60, 257n140

Distillers-Seagram Corporation, 164. *See also* Prohibition (Volstead Act)

Dolci, Danilo, 173

Domingo, Sebastiano "Buster from Chicago": killer in Castellammare War, 94, 97; identity of, 96–97, 270n237; life in Michigan, 97–98; murder of Tony Domingo, 98; murder of, 99; ties to Vito Bonventre, 99; birth, 270n239. *See also* "Americanization;" Castellammare War
Dongarro, Charles, 288n173
Doran, James H., 143
Downey, Patrick: book, 7, 243n43; Black Hand and Mafia, 20; "Murder Stable," 101; Brooklyn Camorra, 106–107; Gaetano Reina murder, 175; Charles Morello murder, 256n123; Rosario Pellegrino murder, 288n173
Dragna family, 147
Dragna, Gaetano "Tom," 86–87, 267n169, 315n233
Dragna, Jack: Black Hand conviction, 27; role in slaying of Barnet Baff, 80, 84–86, 103; 1917 arrest, 86, 93; early life, 86–87; connections to Angelo Gagliano and Morellos, 88–89; tie to Corleone Mafia, 87; death of, 103; link to Lucchese Family, 103. *See also* Black Hand; *names of individuals*
Dragna, Louis Tom, 315n233

E

Eagle Building Corporation, 299n122. *See also* Maranzano, Salvatore; Rannelli, Stefano
Eastman, Monk, 19
Eboli brothers, 310n103
Eisenberg, Dennis et al., 141, 293n10
Empire Yeast Company, 151. *See also* Cecala, Anthony; Traina, Joseph
Enea, Pasquale, 55, 66, 260n233
Erickson, Frank, 135
Esposito, George, 109, 116
Esposito, John "Lefty": arrest, 108; murder of Joe DeMarco, 112; murders of Joe Morello and Eugene Ubriaco, 114; as Navy Street member, 117, 126; earlier criminal career, 120–121, 126; helped the prosecution, 127; murder, 130
Evola, Natale "Joe Diamond," 78, 190

F

Fanaro, Giuseppe, 43–44, 157
Fazia, Antonio, 23
Feder, Sid and Joachim Joesten, 7, 209
Federal Bureau of Investigation (FBI): Apalachin and later, 3; term *Cosa Nostra*, 8, 293n13; New Orleans Mafia, 60; ban on Sicilian members, 71; Mafia recruitment, 91; Valachi and, 167; fight against organized crime, 168; types of informers, 241n12; records on Mafia, 243n47. *See also* "Commission"
Federal Bureau of Narcotics (FBN), 3, 61, 231, 242n13
Fein, Benjamin "Dopey," 76, 103, 120
Fendi, Andrea, 50
Ferrantelli, Michele, 68
Ferrara, Antonio, 125, 134, 278n201
Ferrara, Frank, 80–86
Ferraro, Joseph, 162
Ferreri, Guido, 193
Ferreri, John, 193, 305n228
Ferrigno, Bartolo, 300n135
Ferrigno, Stefano, 94, 182–183, 185, 211
Fetto, John, 108, 112, 117, 127
Fevrola, Frank "Don Chichi," 116–117, 120, 129
Fiaschetti, Michael, 218, 221
Filastro, Ciccio, 24
Finazzo, Frank, 216, 225, 314n216
Finazzo, Giovanni Battista, 66, 260n232
Firestone, Thomas A., 5
Five Boro Hoisting Company, 148. *See also* Gagliano, Joseph; Rao, Vincent John
Five Boroughs Truckmens' Association, 77–78. *See also names of individuals*
Flaccomio, Antonino, 39
Florina, Joseph, 158
Florio, Vincenzo, 254n61
Flynn, William J.: Mafia and Black Hand, 20; Black Hand, 23, 29; Flaccomio murder, 39; murder of Benedetto Madonia, 43; the Morello ring, 46, 54, 59; Antonio Comito, 48; Joseph Petrosino murder, 64; Ignazio Lupo's murders, 255n104

Foley, Thomas F., 125

Fontana, Giuseppe: Sicilian arrests, 38, 66–67, 261n235; murders linked to in New York, 50; Morello ally, 50, 261n248; origin, 55; Joseph Petrosino murder suspect, 66; murder of, 99–100, 157. *See also* D'Aquila, Salvatore; Morello, Giuseppe

Fontano, Bartolomeo (real last name Fontana): role in Camillo Caiozzo murder, 218–219; confession of, 218–219; death of, 222; limitations of evidence, 222, 229, 312n138; birth, 312n136. *See also* "Good Killers;" Schiro Family; *names of individuals*

Forte, Frank, 162, 291n224

Fox, Stephen, 139

Fratianno, Aladena "Jimmy," 91, 236, 269n210, 316n244, 318n26

Frauto, Antonio, 40–41

Frauto, Stella, 39–41, 252n23

Froise, Anthony, 193

G

Gagliano, Angelo: testified for Joe Morello, 52; saloon owner, 81; ties to Morellos, 86, 88–89, 99; Barnet Baff case, 88–89; related to Gaglianos and Raos, 89, 148; as "Murder Stable" owner, 103; the "other" Angelo Gagliano, 267n173; related to Tony Cardinale, 268n185. *See also* Columbus Wet Wash Laundry; *names of individuals*

Gagliano, Joseph "Pip the Blind," 148, 268n187

Gagliano, Josephine, 149

Gagliano, Tommaso "Tommy": associates among Angelo Gagliano contacts, 89; Castellammare War, 94–95, 176, 179, 181–182, 188; Bronx lathing sector involvement, 148–153; origin, 148–149, 205, 286n115; murder of Murray Marks, 195; in plot against Salvatore Maranzano, 195; head of Family, 230, 287n139; as a traditionalist, 233; information on, 286n112; Tommy Lucchese worked for, 286n118; Salvatore Maranzano killing, 305n238.

See also Castellammare War; Plasterers' Information Bureau; United Lathing Company; *names of individuals*

Gagliano, Vincenzo, 89

Gaglio, Joe, 299n112

Gaglio, Sam, 299n112

Galante, Gaspare, 222–223

Galante, Mariano, 219, 222, 224

Galinto, Anton, 33

Gallo brothers, 131, 230, 269n191

Gallucci, Gennaro, 109

Gallucci, Giosue: Lomontes and, 99; Pasquarella Spinelli murder and, 102; and Morello-Lupo territory, 106; origin, 108, 110, 274n35; attacks on, 108–110; murder of Nicolo DelGaudio, 109; murder of, 111, 116, 118, 274n21; assets, 111; underworld power, 110–111, 275n36. *See also* Camorra (Brooklyn); "Murder Stable;" *names of individuals*

Gallucci, Luca, 111

Gambetta, Diego, 32, 34, 63

Gambino, Andrea, 254n55

Gambino, Carlo, 92, 205, 299n122

Gambino, Paul, 299n122

Garofalo, Frank, 230

Genna family, 34, 209

Gennaro, Joseph "Blackie," 248n92

Genova, Antonio, 43, 58

Genova, Francesco, 55–56, 58–60

Genovese, Anna, 238

Genovese, Vito: and George Barone, 91; in "combination," 132; 1924 arrest, 132; spoke to Tony Parretti, 132–134; and Alessandrio Vollero, 134–135; Joe Valachi and, 134–135; illicit liquor enterprises, 142; role in Masseria Family, 155; on Maranzano's execution list, 191, 305n244; Salvatore Maranzano murder, 195, 305n244; age, 205; as "Americanized," 206, 233; Saverio Pollaccia murder, 212; Italian lottery, 213; police record, 213; wealth of, 238; as plotter against Joe Masseria, 302n160

Gentile, Nicolo: Mafia Purge myth, 6; informal power in Mafia, 11; Mafia structure, 62; Mafia initiation ceremony, 63; recruitment into Mafia, 93, 269n206; first jobs in America, 93; Pittsburgh Camorra, 134; member of Mangano *borgata*, 136; as arbitrator, 155; on D'Aquila membership, 156–157; recollections on Castellammare War, 167–168; cooperation with FBN, 168, 294n19; birth, 168; limitations of statements, 168, 170; in Schiro Family, 214; Pueblo Family, 247n49; sources on life of, 294n23. *See also* "Americanization;" Castellammare War; Mafia, America; Mafia, Sicily

Geraci, Joseph, 56
Geraci, Rocco, 258n168
Germano, Rocco, 146–147, 285n86
Giaconas, 59
Giallo, Vito, 224
Giamari, Alfred, 125
Giamari, John, 125
Giamari, Michael, 125, 134
Giancana, Sam, 231
Giannola, Sam, 225–226
Giannola, Tony, 220, 225–226, 312n148
Giglio, Angelo S., 262n258
Giglio, Ignazio, 262n258
Giglio, Vincenzo, 46, 48–49, 55, 69, 254n67, 262n258
Gilardo, Jake, 57
Giordano, Angelo, 112, 115, 117–118, 125–127, 134
Giordano, Biaggio, 22, 158, 247n54
Giordano, James, 122, 126
Giorga, Gaetana, 95
Girardi, Joe, 297n88
Giustra, John "Johnny Silk Stockings," 302n160
Gleason, John, 252n22
Goldberg, Harry "Dutch," 193, 305n230
"Good Killers": Detroit fatalities attributed to, 220, 222, 225–229; Camillo Caiozzo murder, 218–219; arrests, 219, 221; Sicilian aspect to murders, 219, 226, 228–229; named by Bartolomeo Fontano, 220; number of victims, 222; prosecutions, 222; New York City victims of, 222–225, 312n133. *See also* "Americanization";

Schiro Family; *names of individuals*
Gordon, Waxey (real name Irving Wexler), 142, 164, 195
Gosch, Martin A. and Richard Hammer, 140, 180, 293n10
Goss, Frank, 140
Gotti, John, 238
Graff, Abe, 83–85
Grantello, Joseph, 223
Gravano, Salvatore "Sammy the Bull," 91
Greco, Ippolito: residence in Harlem, 16; role in Barnet Baff murder, 80–85; links to Harlem underworld, 86, 88; saloon, 80–81; rivalry with Tommaso Lomonte, 100; murdered, 102; birth, 268n176. *See also* Baff, Barnet; "Murder Stable;" *names of individuals*
Greco, Joseph, 81, 266n129
Greene, Danny, 131
Grimaldi, Fiore, 121
Grimaldi, Frank, 121
Grimaldi, John, 121
Grimaldi, Mike, 121, 125
Grimaldi, Ralph, 121
Grisafi, Calogero, 157, 289n180
Grisafi, Vincenzo, 157, 289n180
Grottano, Bennie, 124
Gruppuso/Gruppose, Nicolo, 190
Guardalabene, Vito, 27, 249n106
Guastella, Nick, 147, 285nn96–97
Guastello, Philip, 177
Guinta, Joseph, 135, 160
Gulotta, Calogero, 58
Gulotta, Gaspare, 58
Gulotta, Pietro "Pete Herman," 58
Gulotta, Vincent, 285n103

H
Haller, Mark H.: lack of work by on Mafia, 7; benefits from Mafia membership, 13, 237; New Orleans bootleggers, 60; attitude of Mafiosi, 99; victimless crimes, 123; alcohol traffic, 139, 143; Prohibition and Americanization, 202; fragmentation of illicit enterprises, 236
Harrigan, John, 146
Harrigan, Thomas, 146
Henderson, Parker, 163

Herbert, Arthur "Tootsie," 79, 264n50
Herbert, Charles, 265n68
Hess, Henner, 62, 189, 250n141
Hickson, William, 199
Hillman, Sidney, 193
Hoover, J. Edgar, 293n13
Hunt, Thomas, 46, 52, 220, 272n278, 312n138, 313n152
Hybel, Judith, 244n52

I

Iamascia, Anthony, 191
Iamascia, Daniel, 191, 304n215
Ianni, Francis A.J. and Elizabeth Reuss: work on the Mafia, 7; Black Hand, 32, 35; Sicilian Mafia impact in America, 71; importance of kin in Mafia, 92, 230; Americanization in Mafia, 199; Unione Siciliana, 209
Ignatz Florio Co-Operative Association Among Corleonesi: incorporated, 31; links to Morellos, 45–46, 51–52, 55–56; name, 254n61. *See also names of individuals*
Ilado, Vincenzo, 228, 314n216
Impoluzzo, Antonio, 101. *See also* Lomonte, Tommaso
Inzerillo, Pietro, 43–44, 51, 55, 66, 253nn.42, 51
Italiano, Ignazio: 1928 Cleveland meeting, 160–161, 204; birth, 203, 262n258; death, 290n209; Italiano sons, 290nn211. *See also* Mangano, Vincent; Profaci, Joseph
Italiano, Margaret, 290n210
Italiano, Salvatore "Red," 290n210

J

Jacko, Giuseppe, 109
Jacobs, David, 83, 266n117, 267n157
Jacobs, James B., 1, 6, 139, 166, 232
Jatti, John, 24
Jenkins, Philip and Gary Potter, 8, 244n50
"Jew War," 195, 305n239
"John the Painter," 146
Jones, Daniel, 84
Jones, William, 100
Joselit, Jenna Weissman, 20, 75

Journeymen Barbers' International Union, 77. *See also* Mafia, New York City; Tartamella, Giovanni

K

Kastel, Phil, 60, 135
Katzenberg, Yasha, 142
Kefauver Committee, 3, 61, 103, 135, 161, 209
Kelly, Robert J., 9
Kempton, Murray, 238
Kendall, John S., 58–59
Kennedy, Robert F., 168, 196, 306n250
Kolb, Joseph, 312n148
Kolosov, Leonid, 63

L

La Cosa Nostra (LCN): legend of, 1–2, 4, 196, 316n1; criticisms of LCN model, 7–8; Salvatore Maranzano and, 144; Castellammare War and, 165–166, 196; reality of LCN, 165, 187, 236; current views on, 166; Bronx meeting to unveil LCN, 187–188; influence of Prohibition era descriptions, 196, 199; and Americanization, 197–198. *See also* "boss of bosses;" Castellammare War; "Commission;" Mafia, America; Mafia, Sicily; Maranzano, Salvatore; Valachi, Joseph
Labruzzo, Calogero, 178
Labruzzo, Fay, 178
Lacolla, Felicio, 116
LaDuca, Vito, 30–31, 43–44, 55
Lalamia, Giuseppe, 43
LaMare, Chester, 177–178, 297n79, 297nn87–88, 299n112
Lamole, Louis, 96
Lanasa, Antonio, 22, 30
Landesco, John, 21, 210, 236
Lansky, Meyer, 60, 135, 141–142, 193, 195, 305n236
LaPlaca, Dominick, 214
LaPorta, Joseph, 209–210, 310n91
Larasso, Lou, 64, 260n223
LaSalle, Stefano (real last name LaSala): and Morellos, 47, 89; Harlem lottery game, 111, 113; Joe DeMarco murder, 111–112; targeted for murder, 130; early life, 130; later career in Mafia, 130; member of Gagliano Family,

230; birth, 280n249. *See also* Camorra (Brooklyn); Morello, Giuseppe

LaTorre, Stefano "Steve," 29

Lauricella, Dominick, 27

Lauritano, Leopoldo: leader of Navy Street, 108, 118; Giosue Gallucci murder, 111; Joe DeMarco murder, 112; war with Morellos, 117; birthplace, 118; initiation ceremony, 119; previous record, 120; ventures, 121; municipal corruption, 124; not called to testify, 127; conviction, 127–128; Davide Prevete and, 134

Lavelli, Antonio, 276n101

Lazzara, Luigi, 102, 272n286

Lenere, Nicolina "Nellie," 101

Leone, Matteo, 116

LePore, James, 207, 308n61

Levine, Sam "Red," 195, 305n236

Licato, Andrea, 220, 226, 312n148

Licato, James, 125

Licavoli, James, 91

Licavoli, Thomas "Yonnie," 91

Lima, Gioacchino: residence in New York, 52; as Morello associate, 54, 87; Joseph Petrosino murder suspect, 66; life in Corleone, 67; Angelo Gagliano, 88; Salvatore Romano and, 250n144; death, 256n125

LiMandri, Marco, 296n65

"Lisante, Stadler," 222

Livorsi, Frank, 205, 302n160

Locano, Joe, 177, 297n86

LoCicero, Charles "Charlie Sits," 200

LoCicero, Vincenzo, 157

Lolordo, Pasqualino, 160, 203

Lombardi, Charles "Three-Fingered Charlie," 112, 127, 274n21

Lombardi, Giuseppe, 219, 222

Lombardino, Salvatore, 203, 290n204

Lombardo, Antonio: and body in Hagar Township, Michigan, 97; and 1928 Cleveland meeting, 160; murder, 162; origins of Castellammare War, 171; Unione Siciliana, 171, 209; and Al Capone, 295n38

Lombardo, Robert M., 21, 32, 34

Lomonte family: and murder of Giuseppe Fanaro, 44; members of Morello gang, 54, 89, 99; Harlem saloon, 154, 173. *See also* Greco, Ippolito; Morello, Giuseppe; "Murder Stable"

Lomonte, Fortunato, 54, 100, 271n268

Lomonte, Gaetano, 54, 271n262

Lomonte, Rosalia, 100

Lomonte, Tommaso, 100–101, 111, 113, 256n123

Lonardo, Angelo, 92, 156, 316n244, 318n26

Lonardo, John, 156

Lonardo, Joseph, 156

Longo, Frank, 301n144

LoPiccolo, Stefano, 157

Loverde, Salvatore "Toto," 184, 301n145

Lucchese, Gaetano "Tommy": initiation ceremony in Family of, 63; garment district, 78–79; point of contact for Los Angeles on Commission, 103, 315n233; took Family over, 149; Joe Pinzolo murder, 181, 296n73; with Joe Biondo, Lucky Luciano, 190, 303n191; age at immigration, 205; Joe LaPorta, 210; on Commission, 233; and poultry racket, 264n50; Lucchese house, 286n106; worked for Gagliano, 286n118; as less of a figurehead, 287n139; Salvatore Maranzano murder, 305n238, 306n247

Luciano, Antonio, 56

Luciano, Salvatore (died 1902), 56

Luciano, Salvatore "Charlie Lucky" (real last name Lucania) (died 1962): popular image of, 1; and Aladena Fratianno, 91; liquor trafficking, 140, 142, 305n236; Atlantic City 1929 meeting, 141; in Masseria Family, 155, 212; arrests, 190, 213, 303n191; Salvatore Maranzano's hit list, 191; Maranzano's murder, 192–195, 305n244; New York clothing industry, 193–194; position in Americanization debate, 196, 199–204, 206–207, 209–210, 236; as inventor of Commission, 206; creator of "council of six;" 210; origin, 212–213; assault on, 213; 1936 conviction, 213; enhanced status after Castellammare War, 187, 230; fall of Masseria, 302n160

Lucido, Sebastiano, 298n95

Lupo, Ignazio "The Wolf": Bozzuffi kidnapping, 31; as Black Hand predator, 31; Black Hand victim, 33; member of Morello gang, 42; Giuseppe Catania murder, 42; Benedetto Madonia murder, 43; role in counterfeiting, 46–48, 51; relationship to Joe Morello in gang, 46, 254n71; origin, 47, 55, 254n77; sentenced, 48; paroled, 50; re-incarcerated, 50; related to Morellos, 52; New Orleans connection, 58–59; Joseph Petrosino assassination, 65–66; 1921 trip to Italy, 155; as Unione Siciliana head, 209; murders attributed to, 255n104; Nicolo Sylvester and, 268n180. *See also* Black Hand; Genova, Francesco; Morello, Giuseppe; Unione Siciliana

Lupo, Salvatrice, 50, 52, 256n122

"Lupollo," Giuseppe, 32, 92, 199. *See also* Ianni, Francis A.J.

Lupsha, Peter A.: poor quality of extant research, 5; and Castellammare War, 12; Prohibition and organized crime, 138; 1929 Atlantic City conference, 141; Americanization of Mafia, 202, 233

Lynch, Denis Tilden, 73

Lyons, Bernard, 152

M

Maas, Peter, 175, 179–180, 182, 187, 191, 305n239

Macaluso, Marco, 45, 55, 88

Macaluso, Mariano, 45

Maceo, Sam, 237

Macklin, Elmer, 297n88

Madonia, Benedetto, 42–45, 59, 253n45, 254n59, 255n107, 256n123. *See also* Morello, Giuseppe

Mafia, America: profits from Mafia crime, 1, 238, 318n26; inadequacy of literature on, 1, 5; existence of, 8, 243n47, 244n50; alien conspiracy paradigm, 2–3, 242n13; critique of paradigm, 3–4; importance of 1931, 4; territorial control, 9–10, 32–33; organizational hierarchy, 10–11; recruitment, 89, 91–96, 99, 104, 235; policy of non-interference in other Families' affairs, 130–131, 185; ethnic divisions

within Families, 136, 281nn. 291, 295; Volstead Act and, 139, 144–147, 164; racial exclusivity in, 147, 235, 237; penetration of legitimate businesses, 75–79, 149, 151–154; alleged centralization, 164–165, 187, 196–197 236; Sicilian domination in, 203; significance of kinship, 229–230; advantages gained from membership, 236–237; fragmentation of operations, 236, 245n65, 317n8; control over illegal gambling, 237–238, 318n23; 1940s recruitment, 316n244. *See also* "Americanization;" Black Hand; "boss of bosses;" Castellammare War; "Commission;" Kefauver Committee; La Cosa Nostra; Mafia, New York City; Mafia, Sicily; Prohibition (Volstead Act); Unione Siciliana

Mafia, Newark (N.J.), 187, 290n204

Mafia, New York City: need for fresh materials on, 1–2, 4; effect of misleading accounts, 2, 165, 234; diffuseness of the local Mafia, 2, 165, 234; importance of New York City, 4–5, 242n21; literature on, 6–7; exceptionality of Mafia in, 7–9, 244nn. 52, 54–55; poverty and, 14–16, 19; pre-Mafia organized crime, 19–20; Black Hand in New York, 26–32; territorial difficulties, 32–33, 99–103, 164; New York City Mafias, ca. 1910, 36; Morello Family, 36–52, 54–56, 64–70; industrial racketeering, 76–79; mainland Italians in, 104, 132,135, 235; emergence of Masseria Family, 154–156, 211; D'Aquila Family, 156–158; Profaci Family, 161–162; local Mafia after 1931, 210, 230–231; Schiro Family, 214, 216; overview, 234; membership of a Family, 317n8. *See also* Black Hand; Camorra (Brooklyn); Mafia, America; Mafia, Sicily

Mafia, Philadelphia, 2, 8, 136, 179, 216, 244n50, 269n206, 298n104. *See also* Sabella, Salvatore

Mafia, Sicily, and U.S. Mafia: overview, 2, 11, 14, 36, 61, 71, 235; Mafia

as a state of mind, 3, 241n11;
organizational similarities with
New York City Families, 3, 11,
61–62, 242n13, 259n201; role of
Mafiosi in Sicily and America, 31,
61; Sicilian counterfeiting, 38; size
of New York and Sicilian groups,
51; significance of kinship, 61–62,
92–93; letters of consent, 62–63;
entry rituals, 63–64; recognition
passwords, 64; Joseph Petrosino
murder, 64–69; Morello counterfeiters and Sicily, 69–70; U.S.-
Sicily relations after 1931, 70–71,
196, 262nn270–271; shared
recruitment patterns, 89, 92;
Salvatore Maranzano's alleged use
of imported Mafiosi, 208; Sicilian sourced *vendetta*, 216–229.
See also Allegra, Melchiorre;
"boss of bosses;" Dragna, Jack;
Gentile, Nicolo; Mafia, America;
Maranzano, Salvatore; Morello,
Giuseppe; Terranova, Ciro
Mafia, St. Louis, 21, 35, 136
Magaddino, Antonio, 312n140
Magaddino, Pietro, 219
Magaddino, Stefano (Joseph Bonanno's
uncle), 144
Magaddino, Stefano "Steve" (Joseph
Bonanno's cousin): related to
Gaspare DiGregorio, 96; and
origins of Castellammare War,
172; in financing the War, 179;
link to Salvatore Sabella, 179;
distrust of Salvatore Maran-
zano, 191, 285n81; outbreak
of another War, 191; age, 205;
1931 "Purge," 210; residence in
Brooklyn, 216; feud with Buc-
cellato family, 217; 1921 arrest,
219, 222; gained from Castellammare War, 231; related to Aiellos,
295n43; Coney Island banquet,
304n205; related to Bartolomeo
DiGregorio, 312n143; member
of "Grand Council," 315n237.
See also Castellammare War;
"Good Killers;" "Purge"
Maggiore, Calogero, 39
Magliocco, Ambrogio, 290n210
Magliocco, Giovanni, 16, 19
Magliocco, Joseph, 160–161, 203, 231,
290n204, 292n240. *See also*

Cammarata, Emanuel; Profaci,
Joseph
Magliocco, Ninfa, 290n210
Maida, Jerry, 102
Mallamo, Dominico, 25, 248nn.90, 92
Maltisi, Mike, 227
Mama Mia Importing Company,
290n208, 291n214. *See also*
Profaci, Giuseppe
Mancini, Antonio, 280n242
Mancini, John, 108, 119, 121, 126–127
Mangano Family, 77, 136
Mangano, Gaetano, 290n210
Mangano, Philip, 68, 157, 289n191
Mangano, Vincent (born 1888): reputa-
tion, 19; murder of Giovanni
Pecoraro, 68; origin, 157, 203,
205; and Buffalo Family, 157,
289n191; 1928 Cleveland arrest,
160; joined Salvatore Maran-
zano, 183; Maranzano ordered
the death of, 191–192; role in
Maranzano death, 192; as boss
after Maranzano, 230–231; and
"Americanization," 233; Sal-
vatore D'Aquila, 289n183;
murder of, 289n191; identity,
290n210; possible role in Mas-
seria murder, 302n160; member
of "Grand Council," 315n237
Mangano, Vincent (born 1905),
290n210
Mannino, Anthony, 30
Mannino, John, 30–31
Mannino, Joseph, 308n57
Manzella, Salvatore, 31, 250n138
Manzello, Giuseppe, 315n225
Mara, Salvatore, 24
Maranzano, Domenico, 144
Maranzano, Giuseppe, 178
Maranzano, Nicolo, 144
Maranzano, Salvatore: initiation into
Family of, 63; transatlantic
Mafia links, 70–71; recruitment
into Maranzano Family, 93, 96;
upstate liquor enterprises, 144,
146; origin, 144; family arrives
in New York, 144, 284n74;
Maranzano's own entry into
America, 144, 284n78; in
Canada, 145, 284n80; links to
Buffalo Family, 145, 285n81;
upstate associates, 147; and
Castellammare War, Chapter

7; murder, 195, 305nn.238, 244; in Americanization debate, 198–200, 204–206; establishment of Commission, 206; and "Purge," 207–208, 308n57; alleged army of imported Sicilian members and, 208, 210; Joe Bonanno took over his Family, 230; *names of individuals*
Marcello, Carlos, 58, 60
Marchese, Francesco Paolo, 42, 58–59
Marchese, Rosalie, 258n163
Marinelli, Albert, 155
Maritime Society of Sciacca, 190. *See also* Maranzano, Salvatore
Marks, Murray, 195
Marlow, Frankie, 292n239
Marrone, Charles "Charlie Baker," 256n123
Marsalisi, Mariano, 89, 268n181, 286n 117
Marthera, Vita, 154
Martin, Samuel, 124
Martinico, Antonio, 224
Marvalesi, Maria, 52
Marziano, Antonino, 152
Masseria, Calogero, 300n134
Masseria, Giuseppe "Joe the Boss": and Joe Morello, 50, 155; and Castellammare War, 95, 97, 165, 170–178, 180–186; non-Sicilians in Family of, 135, 206, 211–213, 231, 310n103; origin, 154, 287n153; emergence of his Family, 154–155; rivalry with Salvatore D'Aquila, 155–156; Cleveland contacts, 156, 300n134; 1913 conviction, 154, 173; murder of, 185–186, 302nn.158, 160; Luciano Family the successor to, 187, 230; as "boss of bosses;" 188–189; Americanization and, 198–202, 204–206; lack of kinship ties in Family of, 211, 213; myths around, 287n151. *See also* "Americanization;" "boss of bosses;" Castellammare War; La Cosa Nostra; Mafia, New York City; *names of individuals*
Masseria, John, 300n134
Masseria, Mercurio, 300n134
Masseria, Salvatore, 300n134

Matesi, Francesco. *See* Genova, Francesco
Matranga, Charles, 59, 258n168
Mauro, Al, 237
Mauro, Salvatore, 223
Maxwell, Gavin, 173
May, Allan, 270n237, 286n112, 310n88
Mazzara family, 145
Mazzara, Antonio, 216, 224, 228, 314n216
Mazzara, Philip, 216, 225, 295n54
Mazzola, Patrina, 226
McAdoo, William, 22
McCluskey, Mike, 151
McCoy, William, 139
Mealli, Mike, 124, 278n186
Medaglia, Tony, 112
Meli, Angelo, 177–178, 205, 229, 298n95, 315n225
Meli, Francesco, 256n118
Meli, Vincent, 298n95
Melita, Mariano, 226
Mendolia, Marianna, 257n129
Merlo, Mike, 211
Messina, Gaspare, 184, 231, 303n187
Messina, Salvatore, 223
Methodology utilized, 5–6, 243n32
Migliaccio, Gaetano, 122
Milano, Frank, 135, 162, 182, 300n132, 315n237
Milazzo, Gaspare: and origins of Castellammare War, 172; murder of, 176–177, 299n112; use of his murder by Salvatore Maranzano, 177–178, 186, 297n85; links to Bonventre family, 179, 216, 295n54; age, 205; related to Aiellos, 295n43; birth, 296n75; related to Dominic Corrado, 315n229. *See also* Castellammare War; *names of individuals*
Milo, Thomas, 286n123
Milone, Antonio B., 46, 51, 55
Milone, Biaggia, 38
Milone, Domenico, 38, 46–47
Milone, Ignazio, 50, 55, 66–67, 149
Mineo, Manfredi: 1910s group, 36, 44, 100; murder of, 94, 182–183; betrayer of Salvatore D'Aquila, 157; took over D'Aquila Family, 157; ally of Joe Masseria, 174; disintegration of former Mineo Family, 183, 187; age,

205; Carmine Piraino murder, 300n128. *See also* Castellammare War; Cordaro, Carmelo; D'Aquila, Salvatore

Minore family, 262n261

Minore, Elizabetta, 144

Mione, Peter "Petey Muggins," 208

Miranda, Michele "Mike," 155, 231, 310n103

Mistretta, Laura, 289n191

Mitchel, John Purroy, 72–73

Monaco, Frank "Chick," 101–102

Monaco, Samuel, 207–208

Montana, John, 298n102

Monforte, Antonio, 149, 151–152

Monforte, Nunziata "Nancy," 151

Montimagno, Gaetano, 125

Morales, John, 313n169

Moran, George "Bugs," 141–142, 171, 283n49

Morano, Pellegrino: head of Coney Island syndicate, 106, 108, 118; and murder of Giosue Gallucci, 111, 118, 274n21; and murder of Joe DeMarco, 112; murders of Joe Morello and Eugene Ubriaco, 112–113, 123, 274n21; interest in policy game, 113, 123; murder of Joe Verrazano, 114–115; age, 118; ritual, 119; police record, 120; Santa Lucia interest, 121; birth, 125; how long knew the others, 126; sentenced, 128; and the Morellos, 130

Moreci, Vincenzo, 55, 57, 59–60, 258n168

Morello, Antonio, 256n118

Morello, Calogero "Charles," 256n123

Morello, Celeste A., 8, 27, 179

Morello, Giuseppe "Peter": Black Hand and, 25, 29, 30–32; importance of in the early history, 11–12, 36; his organization as an offshoot of the Sicilian Mafia, 36, 60–63, 71; early life, 37–38; Sicilian counterfeiting, 38; (1900) counterfeiting arrest, 39; (1908–1909) counterfeiting, 46–48, 69–70; jailed, 48–49; released, 50; power of the Morello syndicate, 50–51; other murders allegedly by, 50; cohesiveness of Morello group, 51; the Morello organization, 51–52, 54–56, 229; Morello-

Terranova family, 52–54; contacts in Louisiana, 56–60; East Harlem interest, 87–88; lathing/plastering interests, 149, 151–153; Joe Masseria and, 154–155, 175–176; condemned by D'Aquila, 155; murder, 94, 180–181, 300n130; age, 204–205, 251n6; year of emigration, 252n14; 1911 confession, 261n252. *See also* "boss of bosses;" Callahan, Mollie; Ignatz Florio Co-Operative Association Among Corleonesi; Mafia, America; Mafia, New York City; Mafia, Sicily; United Lathing Company; *names of individuals*

Morello, Nicholas: knew Salvatore Clemente, 39; seized in 1909, 47; takes over gang, 49; gang organization, 88, 99, 130; struggle against Salvatore D'Aquila, 99–100, 157; Gaetano Reina takes over from, 103, 273n300; cooperation with Brooklyn Camorra, 109–112; Morellos regroup, 117; Morello enterprises, 121; choice of non-Sicilians as associates, 137. *See also* Camorra (Brooklyn); *names of individuals*

Morello, Nicolina "Lena," 52, 54, 87, 152, 256n124

Morello, Salvatore, 47, 254n78

Moretti, Guarino "Willie Moore": in "combination," 132; bootlegging enterprises, 142; relatives, 213–214; in Masseria Family, 231; birth, 280n254, 311n124

Mori, Cesare, 208

Mormino, Gary, 139

Morone, Joe, 124

Mule, Prospero, 285n97

Mule, Vito, 147, 216, 285n95

"Murder Stable": link to Angelo Gagliano, 89, 103; Lomontes and, 99; horse stealing and, 101; location, 272n278; murders connected to, 101–102, 106; decline in number of murders, 102–103. *See also names of individuals*

Musacchio, Salvatore "Sally the Sheik," 231, 292n240, 300n128

Musolino, Giuseppe, 24, 248n74

Mutoc, Paul, 228

N

Nardone, Domenico, 265n75
Nash, Jay Robert, 140, 246n23, 272n278, 287n151
Naylor, R. Thomas, 229, 236
Nazzaro, Generoso "Joe Chuck": ethnicity, 108, 116; Giosue Gallucci murder, 111, 116; Joe DeMarco murder, 112; Salvatore DeMarco murder, 112, 116, 274n21; murder of, 116; Frank Fevrola jailed for murder of, 129
Nelli, Humbert S.: Italian immigration, 4; existing accounts as inaccurate, 5; and Black Hand, 20, 22; Black Hand and Prohibition, 34; initiation ceremonies, 64; Brooklyn Camorra, 106; regionalism in Mafia, 136; effect of Prohibition on Mafia, 140; Atlantic City 1928 gathering, 141; racketeering, 153; Americanization," 199, 202, 233; "Purge," 199, 207, 308n51; Maranzano's imported soldiers, 208
Newmark, Aaron, 84
Nicolosi, Ben, 149
Nitti, Frank (real name Francesco Raffaele Nitto), 279n215
Nizzarri, Serrino, 23
Notarbartolo, Emmanuele, 66, 261n235
Notaro, Tony: testified for state, 108; murder of Joe Verrazano, 115; origin, 118; made a Camorrista, 119; criminal background, 120; arrested, 122, 126; Davide Previte and, 134; acquitted of Verrazano murder, 276n93

O

O'Banion, Dion, 162, 209, 211
Oddo, Giovanni "Johnny Bath Beach," 292n240
Oldani, Louis, 228
Olmstead, Roy, 139
Orlofsky, Philip, 193
Orsini, Joseph, 270n222
Ortoleva, Francesco, 38
Osowski, Frank, 160

P

Pagano, Bartolomeo, 112, 114, 124, 126–127
Palazzolo, Paolo "Big Paul," 135, 203

Palermo, Giuseppe "Uncle Salvatore": Black Hand rule-book, 25; role in counterfeiting, 46; arrest and incarceration, 48; release and death, 49; origin, 55, 69–70; farm sold to, 254n67; identity, 262n261
Palizzolo, Raffaele, 261n235
Palma, Joseph, 144, 303n195
Palmeri family, 145
Palmeri, Angelo, 145, 285n81, 289n191
Palmeri, Frank, 213
Palmeri, Paul, 214, 285n82
Panzarino, Joseph, 296n71
Paoli, Letizia, 2, 9, 229, 236
Paragallo, Vincent, 119
Parapalle, Vincenzo, 113, 119
Parisi, Giacchino "Jack," 158
Parlapiano, Giuseppe, 157
Parretti, Aniello, 116, 118, 120, 126, 129
Parretti, Tony "The Shoemaker": Nick Morello murder, 113; Generoso Nazzaro murder, 116; origin, 118; as the boss, 118; ritual, 119; police record, 120; enterprises, 121, 125; as member of gang, 126; convicted and executed, 128; death house visitors, 132,134; racial prejudice, 136
Parrino, Joseph, 177, 205, 296n76, 297n84
Parrino, Rosario, 176–178, 180, 205
Pascuzzo, Katrina, 48
Pasley, Fred D., 52, 142
Passananti, Antonino, 68–69
Pecoraro, Domenico, 42–43
Pecoraro, Giovanni: birth, 55; Joseph Petrosino murder, 66; origin and arrests, 67–68; Morello organization counterfeits, 68; murder of, 68; 12 condemned men, 288n165; mistaken for Carlo Costantino, 261n241
Pecoraro, Michele "Michael," 261n245
Pellegrino, Rocco, 24, 248n77
Pellegrino, Rosario, 288n173
Pennachio, Gaetano "Tommy the Bull," 206
Pepitone, Pietro, 59
Perri, Rocco, 145
Perrone, Gaspare, 295n44

Perrone, Santo, 295n44, 298n95
Perrone, Vincenza, 295n44
Peterson, Virgil W., 105, 141, 172, 174
Petillo, David "Little Davy," 155
Petrelli, Dominick "The Gap," 95, 176, 195, 205, 269n216, 306n246
Petrosino, Joseph: and New York Black Hand, 20, 22–23; head of Italian Squad, 22; Vito Cascioferro 1902 case, 39; Barrel case, 43; murder of, 64–66, 260n224; suspects in murder, 66–69, 71, 99, 261nn.246, 252; capture of Enrico Alfano, 106. *See also* Cascioferro, Vito; Morello, Giuseppe
Pettenelli, Gaetano, 26, 249n98
Petto, Tommaso "The Ox," 42–43, 45, 67, 254n59
Piazza, Angela, 37, 52, 256n122
Picataggi, Philip, 103
Pino, Carmela, 218
Pinzolo, Bonaventura "Joseph": as Black Hand extortionist, 29, 249n115; murdered, 94, 181; 1930 plot against life of, 175–176, 296nn 65–66, 300n130; age, 205; arrival in America, 249n121. *See also* Black Hand; Castellammare War; Riccobono, Joseph
Piraino, Anthony "Big Tony," 163
Piraino, Carmine, 300n128
Piraino, Giuseppe (died March 1930), 163, 228, 292n242
Piraino, Joseph "Clutching Hand" (died August 1930), 300n128
Piraino, Joseph S., 163
Pisciotta, Antonina, 144
Pistone, Joseph, 91
Pitkin, Thomas Monroe: Black Hand, 20; Black Hand and Prohibition, 34; Brooklyn Camorra, 105; Giosue Gallucci, 109, 120; Ignazio Lupo, 254n77
Pitts, Frederick, 140, 142–143
Plasterers' Information Bureau, 151, *See also* Gagliano, Tommaso; Mafia, New York City; Monforte, Antonio
Plescia, Frank, 308n57
Plumeri, James, 77
Polizzi, Alfred, 315n237
Polizzi, Angelo, 315n225

Pollaccia, Saverio "Sam," 205, 211–212
Pollaro, Gaspare, 181
Pomilla, Giuseppina "Josephine," 148–149
Pomilla, Nunzio, 89, 149, 151
Ponzo, Giuseppe, 225
Porrello family, 156, 160, 285n98
Porrello, Joseph, 189, 300n132
Porrello, Rosario, 300n134
Porrello, Vincente "James," 189
Powell, Hickman, 141, 193, 207
Prestigiacomo, Pasquale "Patsy Presto," 295n46
Prevete, Davide, 133–134
Prisco, Aniello, 102, 108–111
Profaci, Joseph: Joe Magliocco, 19; in Castellammare War, 95, 174, 296n58; emergence of in New York Mafia, 160–161; origin, 161, 203–204; link to Tampa, 161, 290n210; in Chicago, 161, 290n207; Brooklyn territory, 162–163; confusion over his crime Family's origins, 163–164; nepotism in Family of, 230; on conservative wing of Commission, 233; link to Joe Barbara, Sr., 291n213; enterprises, 291n214; member of Mafia "Grand Council," 315n237. *See also* "Americanization;" Cammarata, Emanuel; Cleveland 1928 gathering; Mama Mia Importing Company
Prohibition (Volstead Act): imagery, 12, 164, 196; Black Hand and, 34–35, 235; Volstead Act, 138; corruption, 138; historiography, 138–139; "High Seas" smuggling rings, 138–140; Americanization and, 139, 199, 202; organization of alcohol supply, 140–143, 164; hazards from domestic brewing, 143; racial divisions in supply field, 147; "Curb Exchange," 154–155; Jewish operations, 164; effect on Mafia, 235. *See also* "Americanization;" Atlantic City 1929 conference; Black Hand; *names of individuals*
Puma, Frank, 219, 222–223, 228, 313nn.155, 226

"Purge": Gentile on, 6; description of, 199, 207; no evidence for, 199–200, 207; identified victims of, 207–208. *See also* "Americanization;" Castellammare War; La Cosa Nostra; Unione Siciliana

Q

Quartararo, Amalia, 95

R

Racco, Rocco, 24
Raimo, Joseph, 33
Rannelli, Stefano "Steve," 181, 205, 299n122
Rao, Calogero "Charles," 89, 148, 151–152
Rao, Joseph, 205
Rao, Millie, 148, 286n105
Rao, Vincent John: link to Angelo Gagliano, 89; murder of Vincent Gulotta, 286n103; arrests, 148; licit businesses conducted by, 89, 147–148; residence of, 89, 300n122; and Stefano Rannelli murder, 300n122; "council of six," 310n95. *See also* Mafia, New York City; *names of individuals*
Rapi, Giovanni, 106
Rege, Andrew, 272n286
Reid, Ed, 36, 106, 260n233
Reina, Antonino "Tony," or "Nino," 84, 86
Reina, Bernarda, 52
Reina, Gaetano "Tommy": reputation, 19, 103; Joe Pinzolo successor to, 29; Reina as Family head, 80, 103; role in Barnet Baff case, 81–83, 85–86, 103; origin, 86; and Angelo Gagliano, 88–89; and Los Angeles Family, 103; territory (1930), 174; murder of, 174–176; as inheriting the Morello group, 273n300. *See also* Castellammare War; *names of individuals*
Reinfeld brothers, 164
Reuter, Peter: scarcity of good works on period, 5; exceptionality of Mafia, 9, 244n52; enterprise syndicates, 123; profits from organized crime, 236, 238; Joe Valachi, 293n13

Ricca, Paul "The Waiter," 212, 315n237
Ricci, Andrea: Navy Street boss, 108, 118; death, 108, 274n19; Giosue Gallucci murder, 111; Joe DeMarco murder, 112; Brooklyn ritual, 119; police record, 120; takeover of Harlem policy game, 122; "smoker" organized by, 123; relationship to group, 126; relationship to Morellos, 113, 130; Nick Morello and Eugene Ubriaco killings, 112–113; origin, 117
Ricci, Gaetano, 310n103
Riccobene, Enrico "Harry," 92, 179, 298n104
Riccobene, Mario, 92
Riccobono, Joseph, 296n65
Richter, Danny, 77
Rizzo, Charles, 286n123
Rizzotta, Ben "Tita," or Giovanni Batista De Sota, 84, 86, 267n168. *See also* Dragna, Jack
Rizzotta, Francesca, 87
Rockaway, Robert A., 20
Rofino, Michael E., 125
Roggers, Emmanuel, 33, 220, 312n148
Romano, Andrea, 39, 41
Romano, Giovanni, 143, 284n62
Romano, Giuseppe, 39–41
Romano, Salvatore, 32, 42, 250n144
Romano, Tony, 111
Romeo, Paul, 25, 248n89
Rosato, Joseph, 205, 210
Rosen, "Nig" (real name Harry Stromberg), 206
Rosenstein, Moses "Moe," 84–85
Rosenstein, Sidney, 79
Rothstein, Arnold, 1, 139
Roti, Bruno, 27
Rotundo, John, 26
Roughley, Harold, 33, 227
Ruffino brothers, 154, 173, 224, 311n132
Ruffino, Giuseppe, 173, 295n54
Ruffino, Salvatore, 173, 295n54
Ruggerio, Lefty, 91
Russo, Carmelo "Charlie Ross," 80, 82
Russo, Carmine, 132
Russo, Luigi, 207–208
Russo, Michael, 203
Russo, Sam, 226
Russomano, Giovanni, 108–111, 116

S

Sabatino, Vittoria, 292n238
Sabella, Dominick "Mimi," 205, 216, 298n103
Sabella, Salvatore, 27, 92, 179, 205, 216, 285n81
Sabio, Carmine, 142
Sacco, Anthony "Nino," 145–146, 285n82
Sacco, Stefano, 285n82
Saia, James, 149
Salemi, Lena, 52, 54, 87
Salemi, Vincenzo, 54
Salerno, Anthony "Fat Tony," 316n247
Salerno, Ralph, 91, 199
Salomone, Concetta, 66
Saltamaggio, Antonio, 54, 57, 257n131
Saltamaggio, Teresina, 54
Salvatore, Marty, 303n195
Santa Lucia restaurant, 108, 112, 118, 121, 130, 134, 277n133
Santino, Pasquale, 21
Santuccio, Girolamo "Bobby Doyle": Paul Kelly partner of, 20; murderer in Castellammare War, 94–95, 181, 191; birth, 95; feud with Lamoles, 95–96; and Maranzano, 191; year of immigration, 205; death, 270n228; and Mafia "Commission," 316n240
Santuccio, Joseph, 95
Santulli, Tony "Tony Cheese," 118, 120, 127
Sapio, Nicholas, 297n79
Sapio, Rosa, 297n79
Saracina, Salvatore. *See* Palermo, Joseph
Sardini, Peter, 300n128
Sausser, Harry, 140
Sberna, Charles, 256n124
Scaduto, Tony, 175, 193, 195
Scaglia, Pellegrino, 21, 247n49
Scaligi, Giovanni, 38
Scalise, Frank (real last name Scalisi): replaced as Family head, 157, 230; member of D'Aquila Family, 157; murderer of Joe Morello, 180; turncoat in Castellammare War, 183; head of former D'Aquila group, 187, 191; at Salvatore Maranzano's "coronation," 191; and planned assassination of Vincent

Mangano, 192; in Mangano group, 231; Joe Catania murder, 301n155
Schelling, Thomas C., 123
Schiavo, Giovanni, 34, 209, 309n86
Schiro Family: territory, 32, 137, 154, 174; Schiro as head of one of original Families in New York, 36; recruitment into, 93; and the Harlem Mafia, 131; operated victimless crimes, 137; Salvatore Maranzano a member of, 144, 178; Castellammare sourced component of, 173, 214, 216; Nicolo Schiro stance towards Joe Masseria, 178, 180; origin of Schiro, 214, 311n127; kinship within group, 214, 216; as conservative type of syndicate, 234. *See also* "Americanization;" Castellammare War; "Good Killers;" Masseria Family
Schultz, Dutch (real name Arthur Flegenheimer): at Atlantic City 1929, 141; on Salvatore Maranzano execution list, 191; murder of Maranzano, 195; and Joe Catania, 301n155; Daniel Iamascia and, 304n215; Harlem policy game, 305n242
Sciarra, Pietro, 262n270
Scibilia, Rosaria, 295n54
Scillitano, Michale, 95
Scimeca, Michael, 288n155
Sciortino, Pietro, 147, 285nn.94, 96
Sebastiano, Benny "The Ape," 297n86
Secret Service, U.S.: importance of Morellos, 29; fight against American Mafia, 36; investigation of Joe Morello, 39, 42–43, 46–48, 51; capture of Stella Frauto and affiliates, 39–41. *See also* Flynn, William J.; Morello, Giuseppe; Palma, Joseph; Wilkie, John
Selvaggi, Giuseppe, 14, 52, 101
Serio, Joseph, 57
Sgroia, Alfonso "Butch": gave evidence for state, 108, 126; Joe Verrazano murder, 115, 134; Frank Fevrola killing, 116; origin, 118; in Coney Island group, 118; police record, 120; history with

Coney Island organization, 126; sentenced, 128

Shapiro, Jacob "Gurrah," 193

Shillitani, Salvatore "Sally Shields," 94–95, 205, 270n222, 301n155

Siciliano, Paul, 213. See also Genovese, Vito; Russo, Carmine

Siegel, Ben, 193, 195, 305n236

Sifakis, Carl, 180

Simonelli, Carlo/Giuseppe, 121

Sindona, Giuseppe, 151

Siragusa, Joseph, 184, 208, 301n146

Sirocco, Jack "Big Jack," 76, 120

Smith, Dwight C., 123, 199, 209

Sorro, Joseph, 84–5, 267n158

Sospirato, Dominick, 156

Speciale, Salvatore, 89

Sperizza, Salvatore, 50, 255n107

Spero, Shorty, 91

Spilotro, Patsy, 271n255

Spilotro, Tony "The Ant," 271n255

Spinelli, Francesco, 29, 250n123

Spinelli, Pasquarella, 101, 109, 272n283

Spirito, Francois, 270n222

Stacher, Joseph "Doc," 164

Stoffenberg, Jacob, 175, 296n71

Stracci, Joseph, 302n160

Streva, Paolino, 38, 87, 252n12

Strollo, Anthony "Tony Bender," 231, 310n103

Struchfield, William, 33

Sullivan, Timothy "Big Tim," 246n21

Surace, Ferdinando, 24

Sylvester, Nicholas: role in counterfeiting, 46; sentenced, 48; paroled, 49; origin, 55; crimes before counterfeiting, 70, 101; as plasterer, 89, 268n180

T

Tagliogambe, Silvio, 155–156

Talese, Gay, 207

Taormina, Domenico, 289n177

Tartaglione, Giovanni, 113, 122–123

Tartamella, John, 77, 230

Tartamella, Sereno, 77

Terranova, Bernardo, 52, 54

Terranova, Ciro (also known as Ciro Morello): early life in America, 38, 54; associate of Morellos, 47, 51, 54, 130; Ignazio Lupo and, 50; arrival in America, 52; related to Catanias, 52,

257n129; Joe DeMarco murder, 105, 111–112, 127; death of, 127; Alessandro Vollero and, 134; as plasterer, 153, 268n180, 287n146; Joe Catania, 185; associate of Joe Masseria, 191; age, 204–205; Lomontes and, 271n262; Angelo Palmeri and, 285n81; one of 12 condemned Mafiosi, 288n165. See also Camorra (Brooklyn); Consiglio, Ruggerio; Lupo, Ignazio

Terranova, Lucia, 54, 56

Terranova, Salvatrice, 50, 52, 256n122

Terranova, Teresina "Tessie," 50

Terranova, Vincent: residence, 33; arrival, 52; member of Morello group, 54; as iceman, 70; Joe DeMarco murder, 112; murder, 155

Terranovas: horse rustling, 101

Terrillo, George, 158

Testa, Nicolo, 43

Thompson, Craig and Allan Raymond, 7, 20, 199

Tilocco, Sam, 189, 204

Tocco, Jack, 298n95

Tocco, William, 315n225

Todaro, Salvatore "Black Sam," 156, 189

Torres, Giovanni "Angel Face," 228–229, 315n218, 315n222

Torrio, John, 33, 140–142, 162, 202, 251n158, 283n49

Trafficante, Santo, 262n258

Train, Arthur, 29

Traina, Joseph: Empire Yeast Company, 151; in Salvatore D'Aquila group, 157; birth, 161, 204, 231; Ignazio Italiano, 162; Castellammare War, 183–4; on "Grand Council," 315n237

Troia, Joseph, 301n144

Troia, Vincenzo, 184, 301n144

Trombatore, Leoluca, 55–56, 60

Tropea, Orazio, 211

Troyia, Vincenzo, 42

Turkus, Burton B. and Sid Feder, 7, 193, 202, 207

Tyler, Gus, 91

U

Ubriaco, Eugene "Charles": shooting of, 106, 108, 112–114, 122,

124, 274n21; Joe DeMarco slaying, 112; Harlem policy game and, 123; Alessandro Vollero sentenced for murder of, 128; Tony Parretti convicted of murder of, 128, 132; birth, 130

"Uncle Vincent," 70

Unione Siciliana: Cleveland 1928 meeting and, 160, 163; Chicago lodge, 171; leadership as Sicilian, 209; myths over, 209; history, 209–210; Joe LaPorta and, 209–210; and Americanization, 210; sources on, 309n85. *See also* "Americanization;" Lupo, Ignazio; Yale, Frank

United Lathing Company, 148–149, 151–153, 286n118, 286n123, 287nn.141, 147. *See also* Gagliano, Tommaso; Monforte, Antonio

V

Vaccarelli, Paolo Antonio "Paul Kelly," 19–20, 34, 246nn.21, 23. *See also* Eastman, Monk

Vaccaro, Joe, 117–118, 129

Vachris, Antonio, 22, 260n224

Vaglica, Joseph, 204

Valachi, Joseph "Joe Cago": interpretation of public testimony, 3–4, 10; critics of, 7–8, 167–168, 293nn.12–13, 308n51; early life, 14, 95; Mafia initiation, 63; mode of entry into Mafia, 93–94; criminal record, 95; reasons entered Mafia, 95; on Vito Genovese, 133–135; Sing Sing prison companions, 134–135; Castellammare War and, 166–168, 172, 175–176, 179–182, 185–186; uses of testimony, 168, 196; limitations of evidence, 168, 196, 294n16; on La Cosa Nostra, 187–188; shown Maranzano's execution list, 191; Salvatore Maranzano murder, 195, 306n246; "Americanization," 200, 206–208; "Murder Stable," 272n283; "boss of bosses," 303n186; "Jew War," 305n239; on subject of Commission, 316n240. *See also* Castellammare War; La Cosa Nostra; *names of individuals*

Valenti, Rocco, 112, 127–128

Valenti, Salvatore, 268n180

Valenti, Umberto: and Fortunato Lomonte murder, 100; one of 12 condemned men, 155; rivalry with Joe Masseria and murder of Valenti, 155–156; member of D'Aquila Family, 157; murder of Rosario Pellegrino, 288n173

Vallone, Joseph, 27

Valva, Bruno, 28

Valvo, Amelia, 126

"Vassolona," 69

Vella, Giovanni, 37–38, 54

Verrazano, Giuseppe: murder of, 108, 114–115, 122, 124–127; role in Joe DeMarco killing, 112; conspiracy to kill, 134

Verro, Bernard, 52, 63

Vicchi, Marguerita, 158

Vieglo, Louie, 97–98, 271n249

Violi, Paolo, 262n270

Visco, Dominick, 237

Viserti, Joseph "Diamond Joe," 102, 272n291

Vitale, John, 225–226, 229, 315n218

Viviano, Joseph, 21

Viviano, Tommaso, 21

Vollero, Alessandro: arrest, 108; Joe DeMarco murder, 112; Nick Morello and Eugene Ubriaco murders, 112–113, 123; wounded, 117; place of birth, 118; as syndicate boss, 118; Brooklyn ritual, 119; police record in Italy, 120; enterprises, 121–122; official corruption, 124–125; relationship to other members, 126; conviction, 127–128; with Valachi in jail, 134–135; racial divisions in mob, 136. *See also* Camorra (Brooklyn); Mafia, America; *names of individuals*

Volpe, Gaetano "Guy," 28

Volpe, John, 134

Volpe, Santo, 231

Von Frantzius, Peter, 163

Vultaggio, Caterina, 285n97

Vultaggio, Santo, 147, 190, 216, 285nn.96–97

Vutera, Vincent, 56, 59

W

Weaver family, 297n87
Weinberg, Abe "Bo," 195, 305nn.242
Weiner, Joseph, 79, 264n51
Wertheimer, Mert, 135
Westchester Lathing Corporation, 148.
    See also Carfano, Anthony; Rao,
    Calogero
Wilkie, John, 29, 46
Williams, Jake, 76
Williamsbridge Investing Corporation,
    151. *See also* Gagliano, Tom-
    maso; Mafia, New York City;
    Monforte, Antonio
Wolf, George, 142
Woodiwiss, Michael, 166, 206
Woods, Arthur, 23, 73

Y

Yale, Angelo, 162
Yale, Frankie (real last name Ioele or
    Uale): and Black Hand, 34;
    friend of Anthony Carfano,
    125; liquor importation, 140;
    links to Chicago, 161–162;

Profaci took over territory
of, 162–163; early life, 162;
attacks on life, 162; murder,
162–163, 291n232; and Americanization, 202, 206; Unione
Siciliana, 209; as Masseria
member, 211; head of Brooklyn
bakers' association, 292n238.
See also Profaci, Joseph

Z

Zaffarano, Anthony, 16, 81–83
Zaffarano, Joseph, 16, 80–83, 85
Zaraca, Antonio, 109, 134, 274n27
Zarcone, Carlo, 254n55
Zarcone, Domenico, 254n55
Zarcone, Giovanni, 42–44, 55, 253n42,
    254nn.54–55
Zarcone, Pietro, 254n55
Zerilli, Joseph, 183, 229, 315n225
Zito, Frank, 27
Zito, Sam, 27
Zoccoli, Stefano, 28
Zurica, Salvatore, 125
Zwillman, Abner "Abe," 142, 164